£5.00

D1110020

*To all who have helped me, gamekeepers and poachers alike, in my thirty-five years of ferreting in Whitehall, and especially to Yolande Brook, my secretary and sole professional assistant, I dedicate this book, which is as much a record of her life as of mine.*

# Contents

# Foreword

FOR more than thirty years as an investigative journalist I specialized in secret matters which have brought me into close and regular touch with government ministers, defence chiefs, directors of Security and Intelligence, senior civil servants, ambassadors and others of influence. Because of my wartime background, when, as an Army scientific officer, I had been involved with secret weapons research, I achieved an intimacy with many of these contacts denied to most journalists. It was my good fortune that several of my wartime colleagues, both in the Forces and the Civil Service, went to the top in Whitehall and through them and others to whom they introduced me, I gained admittance to very restricted areas of information. I also had the advantage of being something of a protégé of Lord Beaverbrook which assisted greatly in securing and maintaining high-level contacts.

The result has been that most of my career has been spent close to the action, involving me in the receipt of much knowledge which was secret at the time, and in not a little professional danger, especially with respect to the Official Secrets Acts.

While ministers, defence chiefs and the rest came and went, I remained, for I never had any desire to be a newspaper executive. I therefore retained a perhaps unique continuity of knowledge and observation of the most intriguing parts of the Whitehall scene, using 'Whitehall' to include its secret out-stations and other departments which have been 'de-centralized'.

At the risk of appearing immodest, my position over a number of years may be illustrated by a true story which Christopher Soames (now Lord) recalled when we met recently. While attending a Cabinet meeting he noticed an adviser he had never seen before. Mischievously he passed a note to Duncan Sandys (now Lord) asking 'Who's that? Is it Chapman Pincher?'

It was Michael Foot (not yet Lord) who, while an opposition

back-bencher, was responsible for the gag that when the Defence
Ministry put out the sign 'CP to call', meaning Carter Paterson, the
removal firm, it was really intended for me to show up and receive
the next batch of leaks.

When the Defence Ministry issued identity cards to accredited
correspondents, the civil servants had humour enough to make mine
number 007. Shortly afterwards Major-General Gilbert Monckton
(now Lord) sent me the plastic strip he had glued to his telephone in
the Defence Ministry bearing the warning 'Pincher is listening'.

An oblique compliment was paid to me more recently by General
Sir John Hackett, formerly Commander of the Rhine Army and the
Northern Front in Europe in his tour de force, *The Third World War*.
Needing a journalist to break the news that the Chief of Staff had
warned the Prime Minister that Russian manoeuvres were really
mobilization in disguise, he invented Jardine Snatcher 'regarded by
some as the bane of Whitehall, by others as its only hope'. Jardine
was an England cricket captain. So was Chapman.

The circumstances which these anecdotes reflect provide me with
more than the means of presenting some interesting and occasionally
hilarious experiences which, in a few instances, might be of historical
value because otherwise they might go unrecorded. They also enable
me to offer some insight into the lesser known activities of Whitehall
and Westminster, particularly in connection with secret departments like MI5 and MI6, about which much more should be known
to the public.

One dominant thread connects the events which I have witnessed – the pursuit of power in its many manifestations, either
by politicians or by public servants operating on their behalf or in
their own interests, for considerable power is delegated to them and
they preserve it avidly.

My narrative will be intentionally discursive and I make no
apologies for intruding into the text because this is very much an 'I
was there' documentary, though as far as possible, I will let the facts
speak for themselves. Nor do I apologize for the name-dropping of
which I may be accused. Except in those cases where names cannot
be safely or fairly given, they help to establish the credibility of the
material.

To construe what follows as an attack on politicians would be an
error. Apart from the excess of vanity which leads most of them to
assume that they have some special capability to govern, they are

no worse and no better than any other professional group, though the proportions and privileges of the power which the more ambitious of them pursue, are so heady that they are, perhaps, subjected to stronger temptations. If I sometimes seem unkind it is only because my narrative, being restricted within the covers of a book, has to be selective. I am on good terms with most of my subjects, even with Sir Harold Wilson after ten years of bitter animosity.

Since so many of my friends and contacts have been knighted or elevated to the peerage since I first met them, I have been driven to give them their titles once and then refer to them by their surnames. No disrespect is intended.

Finally, since some readers may think that some of my disclosures indicate disloyalty on my part, I will risk appearing immodest again to tell what happened when I met Lord Maybray-King, the former Speaker and Labour MP, at an embassy party recently. After he had kindly expressed his pleasure at meeting me I said I was surprised because I had spent so much time attacking his party and its leader.

'Yes, but I noticed that whenever you did you always had your country's interest at heart,' he said.

I like to think that was true.

*Chapter One*

# An MI5 Mystery Resolved

IN 1977, a year after Sir Harold Wilson had resigned as Prime Minister, he was responsible for what became an unprecedented public attack on the efficiency and impartiality of the British Security Service, also known as MI5, which is the nation's main defence against espionage, sabotage and subversion.

As a result of interviews with journalists, Wilson was reported as having accused certain officers of MI5 of having tried to undermine him and his government. He was quoted as believing that some of this 'disaffected faction in MI5 with extreme right-wing views' had even suggested that there was a Communist cell in the Cabinet and that he and Lady Falkender, his·political secretary, formerly Mrs Marcia Williams, were part of it.

I have confirmed that these were indeed Sir Harold's views and that long before his feelings about MI5 became public knowledge he had been in the habit of sounding off about them in private and what might be described as semi-publicly. This had come to my notice when a most eminent Oxford Professor wrote to me to describe what had happened at a literary lunch he had attended in Leeds in January 1977. 'I happened to sit next to Sir Harold . . . He told me that MI5 had spied on him when he was Prime Minister, plotted against him, tried to secure his downfall. I was embarrassed by this conversation. Finally I said "But isn't MI5 under the Prime Minister?" He replied, "Oh yes, on paper, but that didn't make any difference." '

Some of Wilson's friends also told me that he had gone much further in his condemnation of MI5 in conversations with them.

These attacks were unprecedented because it had been an

unbroken tradition that ministers, and particularly Prime Ministers, avoided mentioning MI5 publicly, even in Parliament, as secrecy was the essence of its operations and, by virtue of its nature, MI5 cannot respond to criticisms.

The former Prime Minister's hostility, which caused consternation in Whitehall, was also uncharacteristic of Wilson in particular for, until then, he had been punctilious, to the point of enduring much damage to his political reputation, in avoiding criticism of the secret departments.

Early in his first term of office, after he had won the 1964 election, Wilson assured the public that his government would solve the Rhodesian problem 'in weeks rather than months'. Over the ensuing years while the Rhodesian problem worsened, political opponents reminded him of his boast yet he manfully resisted what must have been extreme temptation to explain why he had made it.

The truth was that he had based his statement, with justifiable confidence, on a brief provided by the Secret Intelligence Service, also called MI6, which is responsible for Intelligence, espionage and counter-espionage operations overseas. The officers who prepared this brief grossly overestimated the effect of trade sanctions against Rhodesia and equally underestimated the capacity of Ian Smith's government to secure assistance from South Africa, Portugal and elsewhere in circumventing them. They also misled Wilson badly on the extent to which Smith's colleagues in the Rhodesian government would stick with him. 'Weeks rather than months' was the considered view of MI6 and Wilson had every reason to rely on it.

Why, then, having taken it on the chin to preserve traditional secrecy on this issue – and on others – did Wilson 'go public' on his fears about MI5?

To most it has remained a mystery. The commonest supposition has been that Wilson knew MI5 had some damaging personal information about him connected with his sudden resignation and might release it through a leak to newspapers. His action in 1977 was therefore supposed to be calculated to shatter the credibility of MI5 so that whatever any of its officers might say they would not be believed.

This supposition is without foundation. The truth, which I have established by questioning witnesses and through personal involvement in certain secret episodes, is that the undermining activities which Wilson complained of were not only genuine but far more menacing than he revealed. Certain officers inside MI5, assisted by others who had retired from the service, were actually trying to bring the Labour Government down and, in my opinion, they could at one point have succeeded. The circumstances were so unprecedented in themselves that I can understand why Wilson eventually could hold his silence no longer.

The main function of MI5 since the Second World War has been to protect the realm from Communist penetration and subversion and, over the years, suspicion has been building up against certain Labour MPs, some of whom have become ministers.

One senior MI5 officer had become so incensed by the activities of two particular ministers that he decided it was urgently in the national interest for them to be exposed, irrespective of what his Director-General, then Sir Michael Hanley, or the Prime Minister might decree.

He was prepared to name the ministers and reveal details of their activities from his knowledge of the files containing evidence against them, some of it derived from undercover surveillance.

I should point out at this stage that the MI5 officer's projected disclosures were altogether different from the rumours circulating at the time of Wilson's public attack and which concerned Mrs Judith Hart and Dr David Owen, who became Foreign Secretary. It was alleged that MI5 had confused Judith Hart with another Mrs Hart, a former member of the Communist Party, and Dr Owen with Will Owen, the Labour MP who was arrested and acquitted on an Official Secrets charge in 1970. I find it hard to accept that an organization as generally efficient as I know MI5 to be could make ' such blunders but, in any case, the potential disclosures to which I am now referring were on a much more serious and damaging scale.

The dissident MI5 officer was also prepared to reveal details of a security scandal which had happened some years previously, during Wilson's first term as Prime Minister, and would have been highly damaging then had they not been kept secret for political reasons. A member of Wilson's government had been required to resign following representations by MI5 acting on information supplied by MI6 from foreign sources. Wilson was given evidence that the minister had placed himself in serious danger of being blackmailed by Soviet bloc Intelligence. The minister then resigned in a way which covered the truth. Efforts were even made to secure an official post for him to assist in explaining his departure and to provide a means of livelihood, but the Foreign Secretary of the day, who has confirmed the details to me, refused to oblige on MI6 advice. I did not hear the facts myself until recently and the laws of libel prevent my revealing all I know.

The MI5 officer, who had steeled himself to make the disclosures, knew that his action would cause such a sensation that it would certainly end his career as a public servant even if he escaped prosecution under the Official Secrets Acts. So he approached a very senior Whitehall personality, whose name I know but whom I will call 'Q' to preserve his anonymity.

Knowing that he would lose his pension, the officer needed some guarantee of future employment after he had made his sacrifice. He therefore asked Q, whom he knew to be sympathetic regarding the danger of left-wing activity by some ministers, if there was any way of obtaining a job in advance, perhaps in some security role, to ensure that he and his family would have some income.

Q did not attempt to dissuade him. Instead he contacted one of the best known figures in the City on his behalf. This City man, with whom I have discussed the issue and who is also averse to being identified, was keen to get rid of the Labour Government, so he took soundings in several large commercial firms. The responses were identical. Each firm regretfully pointed out that because the power of government was now so extensive it dare not risk employing the officer in any capacity. If the government survived it might take revenge on the firm for assisting in the exposure and this was a risk the firm could not entertain with the shareholders interests in mind.

On being told this by Q the MI5 officer completely lost heart and kept both his silence and his job. Had he been sufficiently encouraged to go through with his venture, the naming of three ministers in Labour governments as serious security risks might have been enough to bring the existing government down. Parliament could well have demanded an inquiry by the Security Commission or by a select committee and the MI5 officer was confident of the results.

Lest any reader should find it incredible that an officer in a secret department would be prepared to sacrifice his career and risk prosecution to do what he believed to be a public service, I should record that I have been sought out by several men who were determined to do exactly that. One instance involved an official from Government Communications Headquarters (GCHQ), the highly secret network of electronic eavesdropping and decoding stations based at Cheltenham, who wanted to expose an administrative scandal there. As he was near retirement and would have lost his pension and because the circumstances were not of major moment, I was able to talk him out of it. Another man, from the Foreign Office, who wanted the world to know of a situation he deplored, remained adamant, told all and suffered the consequences.

In 1975 Wilson had another reason to be angry about the activities of MI5. He has told me recently how one of his close friends, whose identity I know, told him that he had heard that certain officers of MI5 considered the Prime Minister himself to be a security risk.

'Naturally, I took steps to ask the Director-General, Sir Michael Hanley, personally if this was true,' Wilson told me. 'He replied that he believed it was true but that only a small number of right-wing officers were concerned.'

Wilson has stressed this 'right-wing' aspect of the MI5 affair. When it became clear that his attack might be made the start of a left-wing assault on the integrity of both MI5 and MI6, as had happened in the United States to the Central Intelligence Agency (CIA), he began to back-track on the accusations. The MI5 officers concerned became 'a small Mafia group of ex-members of the service'. This led to left-wing jibes that they were 'Fascists'. In fact, the MI5 officers and others from MI6 who agreed with them, simply felt that they were wasting their time trying to combat possible Communist subversion among civil servants if no action was to be taken against ministers.

I am certainly not a 'Fascist' having, like so many others now subjected to that slur, spent six years of my life in the war against Fascism, yet I too had drawn public attention to the doubts about certain ministers in sensitive positions.

From my own contacts with the secret services I was able to report in 1974 that a serious problem had arisen in Whitehall about allowing certain ministers to see top-secret information.

Intelligence about terrorist organizations was being supplied by MI6, derived from agents planted with the so-called 'freedom fighters'. Certain ministers were required to see summaries of this information but the Intelligence chiefs were worried because some of them were so left-wing and apparently so much in favour of the 'freedom fighters' that they might leak facts, if inadvertently, which could lead to the identification and probably to the liquidation of the sources. As a result certain information was withheld from these ministers.

During the last months of his premiership Wilson's suspicion that he and his ministers were being spied upon spread to include the CIA. He therefore asked his friend, Sir George Weidenfeld, the publisher since made a peer, to take a letter to Washington for onward transmission to the CIA without the knowledge of his own security chiefs. As the implications of this event have been exaggerated I will disclose the purpose and contents of the letter, which I have seen.

Early in 1976 Wilson became suspicious that surveillance by the CIA might have spread to Number 10. In particular he was worried about an American who claimed to be a doctor and was paying attention to Miss Peggy Field, Marcia's elder and attractive sister, who had long been linked with Number 10 and the Wilson family through her service as secretary to Mary Wilson.

Weidenfeld happened to be going to the USA so Wilson called him in late at night to ask him to deliver a personal letter to Senator Hubert Humphrey, another old friend. The letter contained five questions which Humphrey was requested to put to the CIA.

The first asked if the doctor, whose medical pretensions proved to be bogus, had ever belonged to the CIA. There was reference to two other men suspected of possible surveillance activities. The CIA answered that none of the three had ever worked for it. There was a request for enlightenment concerning the general extent of CIA activities in Britain over recent years and, as could be expected, the answer to that was non-committal.

Wilson wanted to know if any British politicians had been involved in the Lockheed bribes affair along with Prince Bernhard of the Netherlands. This was the scandal in which the Lockheed aircraft company had bribed officials and politicians in certain countries to secure foreign orders. The answer was that, while inquiries to date had suggested that no one was bribed, there was a possibility that 'something went on'.

Finally, Wilson asked if CIA money had been used to arm British mercenaries sent out to Angola, to which the answer was, 'Regrettably yes'.

The eventual outcome was a visit by George Bush, the Director of the CIA, who broke a journey to Germany to see Wilson. He said that the CIA was not trying to penetrate Number 10 and a former Director, William Colby, later insisted that Wilson had never been kept under any kind of CIA surveillance.

Of course, such denials count for little when sensitive aspects of secret Intelligence work are involved. There is no way, short of a Congressional inquiry, that the CIA would have been induced to admit such activities, especially after the furore over the Watergate affair. Wilson told me that he would not be surprised if the CIA had been watching him, so it seems that he was not entirely satisfied by the assurances from Washington.

Wilson's CIA suspicions may now seem of little consequence but the facts do rebut rumours, still current, that he was so perturbed about his own security chiefs that he asked the CIA to spy on them. There was never any question of this. He was, nevertheless, severely criticized in MI5 and MI6 for going behind their backs to the CIA and for making the fact public. His old political security expert, Lord Wigg, was particularly scathing about this when he telephoned me after reading about it.

Although Wilson's anxieties about MI5 and the CIA were brought to flash-point by specific events, they had long been simmering through his knowledge that deep Whitehall suspicion about the Communist connections of certain Labour MPs stretched back over many years. This is a situation which has engaged my continuing attention, at various intriguing levels, as I will now explain.

～◈◈◈～

*Chapter Two*

～◈◈◈～

# A Lunch with George Brown

MUCH of the information which has enabled me to observe at first hand how politicians, civil servants and service chiefs behave in their pursuit of power and authority has been secured during quiet – one might almost say conspiratorial – lunches. One which proved to be particularly productive I gave to George Brown, now Lord George-Brown, at the Écu de France Restaurant in Jermyn Street on

1 August 1961. This was some time before Wilson figured so prominently in his party but what Brown told me had consequences which profoundly affected Wilson's years as Premier and greatly influenced not only his behaviour but what people thought about him. There is no doubt about the exact truth of what I now relate because that same day I reported the facts, as was my practice, in a memorandum to Lord Beaverbrook. I possess a copy of that memorandum, and one result of the conversation has since been openly admitted, though it took me years to achieve its publication.

Normally George, who was shadow Defence Minister, picked my brains, because one of the oddities of British political life is that opposition leaders who could soon be Cabinet ministers entrusted with the nation's most secret affairs are denied Whitehall information which may be freely given to trusted journalists. This time, however, George had something to tell me. He needed my help.

He revealed that the Labour Party leaders, headed by the late Hugh Gaitskell, a true Social Democrat, had decided to rid themselves of the public criticism that some of their MPs were crypto-Communists – dedicated pro-Russian Communists posing as Socialists because they could exert more influence that way and might eventually achieve ministerial office. The leaders had convinced themselves that after what they called 'ten years of Tory misrule' a general election could not long be delayed (they had in fact to wait a further three years) and believed that the crypto-Communist charge, which they knew to be real, was a serious handicap.

Brown, who was not then the endearing figure of fun he became, but a thrusting and ambitious politician in line to become Prime Minister, told me that a small committee had been established secretly for the purpose of exposing the fraudulent Socialists and then expelling them from the party. The committee consisted of Gaitskell, Brown and Patrick Gordon Walker as he then was. Brown said they had a list of more than a dozen suspects and believed there were still more but there was nothing they could do without hard evidence of Communist Party or Soviet affiliation with which they could be confronted.

The committee had therefore decided to approach MI5, the Security Service, and MI6, the Secret Intelligence Service. They believed that MI5, which is responsible for countering Communist subversion in Britain, would have information on some or all of the suspects, including perhaps records of tapped telephone conversations and bank payments from Soviet bloc contacts. It was hoped that MI6, which is responsible for espionage abroad and for organizing defections from the KGB, the Soviet Intelligence Service, might have the names of subversive Iron Curtain contacts in touch with the British crypto-Communists. Regrettably, George explained, the committee knew neither the names nor the telephone numbers of the heads of MI5 and MI6 so it had been decided to ask me to provide them. In return, if and when MPs were to be expelled, I would be given the information in advance for publication exclusively in the *Daily Express*.

I knew that under Clement Attlee back in 1948 the Labour Party had expelled several MPs, including Konni Zilliacus, formerly a Finn, who had praised Soviet puppet governments and was regularly to be seen at the Russian embassy slobbering over the diplomats there.

Publication of the identities of the heads of MI5 and MI6 was banned under a D-notice, a defensive directive to newspapers to which the Press had previously agreed, but I could see no harm in supplying them to the leaders of Her Majesty's Opposition and did so. Naturally, until further notice from George nothing about the project was to be published, though he was happy for me to inform Beaverbrook about it.

In the following January Brown was called to the presence of the MI5 chief to be given the results. He was told that inquiries about MPs had proved negative but security men had discovered an agent of Soviet bloc Intelligence in a high position in the Labour Party machine in Transport House. He was Arthur Bax, who had been head of the Labour Party's Press department for sixteen years and was a close friend of the leaders. Brown was told that Bax had been receiving sums of up to £120 from the Czech embassy, a seat of subversion which intrudes repeatedly into the continuing history of Communist activity in Britain. There were records of telephone conversations, photographs, bank statements and other evidence.

The authorities had made no move because Bax had not breached the Official Secrets Acts. All he had passed on was confidential information about Labour Party plans and personalities. None of this was officially secret while Labour was in opposition, but, once the opportunity was offered, MI5 was anxious that he should be confronted and sacked because when Labour achieved office the situation could be different.

At our next lunch in the Jermyn Street restaurant Brown told me how he had carried out the unpleasant confrontation himself. Bax had denied the charges but confessed when shown the evidence that he had been passing on information for at least four years and was allowed to resign on the grounds of ill health.

Brown had also learned that, four years previously, the American FBI had warned Britain's Special Branch, the Scotland Yard detectives who are supposed to work with MI5 and carry out any necessary arrests, that Bax was a Communist. The FBI had got this information from a Soviet agent who had defected to the West. Special Branch had been unable to substantiate the FBI's advice and had not warned the Labour leaders. Neither had it passed the information to MI5 – a symptom of the notorious rivalry between security departments.

Though the uncovering of Bax was a matter of considerable public interest I was unable to disclose it then for two reasons. First, Brown insisted on confidentiality at least until after the general election because the news would be damaging to Labour. 'This looks like being one for your memoirs,' he said. Second, my newspaper could be subject to a libel action and Brown made it clear that in such an event he might be unable to confirm what he had told me and the security authorities would plead Crown privilege so that they could not be called as witnesses. Crown privilege is an iniquitous and outmoded legal arrangement which gives civil servants and other Crown employees virtual immunity from being required to give official evidence or produce documents which could substantiate a plaintiff's or defendant's case.

Brown did not treat confidentiality all that seriously. Lady Falkender told me she had passed Brown's Jaguar car parked at the Commons and she had noticed through the back window a letter with the name of the Director-General of MI5 on it! Years later Brown was to tell me how he regarded the whole cloak-and-dagger caper as something of a farce. When he became Foreign Secretary he insisted on visiting Century House, the twenty-storey monolith on the south side of Westminster Bridge, which is the headquarters of MI6, operating under the cover-name of 'Government Communications Bureau'. He argued on the reasonable grounds that if he was to be responsible for their operations, as any Foreign Secretary has to be, he wanted to be briefed by them in their lair.

No previous Foreign Secretary had made such a demand, which might even mean showing him the precious central card index (since computerized), with its busy team updating references to thousands of foreign agents and home-grown subversives, the 'Wendy houses', little, self-contained, combination-locked enclaves within the seven registries, and the 'file halls', where staff members making searches among the older dossiers are locked behind prison-like bars until they telephone to be released.

Everything was done to talk Brown out of the visit because of alleged security considerations. When he proved adamant, the MI6 chief insisted that he must be picked up from his home because a car leaving the Foreign Office might be tailed and so reveal the Foreign Secretary's connections with Century House. Further, he must not travel there in his own official limousine, which was recognizable.

Brown agreed to this pantomime and was appalled to find that the man who called for him at his house in the cover car was the most recognizable Whitehall 'spook' – Foreign Office parlance for an Intelligence man. He was the late Christopher Ewart-Biggs, sadly assassinated later by the IRA, who wore a black patch over one eye.

The purpose of this ludicrous exercise was to hide the fact that the Foreign Office runs MI6, the Secret Intelligence Service, though this was thoroughly well known. (Some years previously when Harold Macmillan had been Prime Minister he was forced to admit by clever left-wing questioning in Parliament that the Foreign Office controlled the Secret Intelligence Service and later said, privately, that this was the most damaging admission he had ever had to make!)

Such effort to conceal the obvious fact that Britain's embassies house MI6 agents under cover jobs is sheer self-delusion.

The Brown visit is still vividly remembered in Century House. He asked the chiefs there how they liked their spanking new block and when they replied that, while the rent was an improvement on that of the older buildings near Westminster Abbey, it was rather far from the centre of things, he snapped, 'The truth is that you don't like slumming it, do you? You don't like being so near to Peabody Buildings!'

These were the buildings of the Peabody Trust where Brown had been reared and, as a good Socialist, he was not one to miss a chance of striking a blow in the class war against men who, he suspected, were largely recruited from White's and the other exclusive clubs in St James's.

My own inquiries quickly showed that Brown had misinterpreted what the MI5 chief had told him about the unproductive search for crypto-Communists, or had been deliberately misled. Harold Macmillan was Prime Minister and as soon as he had been informed of the Labour leaders' request, as he had to be by the Home Secretary, he forbade any disclosure about any MPs. He realized that in the event of the publicity, which was inevitable, there would be an unroar in Parliament and wanted no part of any inquiry which might be interpreted as a breach of Parliamentary privilege.

There was the important factor that Parliament is basically a club and to be beastly to fellow members is just not done – at least not by Tories. Further, of course, Macmillan was astute enough to appreciate that it was better for the Tory Party if the public continued to believe that Labour was riddled with dangerous subversives.

MI5 had its own objections too. For the crypto-Communists to be expelled from the party, each would have to be confronted with the damning evidence. So far as MPs were concerned, MI5 felt it could not do that without dangerously prejudicing its sources, because the suspects and their friends would raise such a commotion within the privilege of Parliament, to which they would still belong.

I waited nearly seven years to relate the story, and even then without naming Bax. My guarded account in the *Daily Express* of 28 June 1968 stimulated great interest among Tory back-benchers who were keen to raise the issue in Parliament where the culprit could be named under privileged conditions, which then meant that the newspapers could report the facts. Again, the Tory opposition leadership under Edward Heath stifled any questions for the same old reasons and it took me until 1972 to subject Bax to the public censure he deserved. At my behest, Sir Frederic Bennett, Tory MP for Torbay, named him in Parliament and Bax publicly admitted his connection with the Czechs though claiming that his work for them was 'journalistic'.

Through my friendship with one of the girls who worked in the MI5 registry in Curzon Street, where dossiers on some two million people are kept on file, I learned that more Labour MPs than Brown believed were officially suspected of being crypto-Communists. Whether Harold Macmillan had been told this or not I do not know, but once, when we were shooting together after he had retired, he told me that he had not forbidden the Security Service to continue with its normal investigations into suspect MPs. They were to remain as subject to undercover scrutiny as any other suspect citizen. All he required was complete secrecy about any inquiries unless some case arose so blatant that it demanded prosecution, as it eventually did in the case of the Labour MP, Will Owen. The near immunity of MPs to security investigation did not come until Harold Wilson became Prime Minister and intervened in a manner which many MPs regarded as unwarranted, as I will describe in Chapter Seventeen.

My purpose in relating these events so long after their occurrence is to show that the Labour Party leadership has been fully aware for many years of the infiltration by dedicated Communists posing as Socialists and has done little that is effective to counter it, though the Gaitskell–Brown attempt deserved some credit. Indeed not only are some of Brown's original cryptos still in Parliament, where admittedly a few have mellowed, but some have achieved ministerial office and have been joined by more who feel they can safely flaunt their extremist objectives quite openly.

Who then were the suspect MPs? Regrettably libel again restricts disclosure but one who has since died can be named – Tom Driberg, who was elevated to the peerage as Lord Bradwell. He claimed to have been expelled from the Communist Party before he became an MP in 1942 but he remained a Kremlin agent of sympathy, sponsoring various Communist-front organizations, urging the withdrawal of troops from Northern Ireland, and there were deep suspicions inside MI5 that he was an active agent of the KGB.

The fact that this man, who was also widely known to be a homosexual pouncer of a bestial kind, haunting public lavatories to find quick conquests, as he described in his memoirs, could have become Chairman of the Labour Party, illustrates the extent to which blatant behaviour, political or private, is no bar to progress in that organization.

I asked Lady Falkender, whom I will henceforth call Marcia, for convenience not out of lack of respect, how it came about that Wilson who, according to Driberg himself, knew that the former Labour Chairman was a raging homosexual, awarded him a life peerage. The answer was that his old friend Michael Foot, who felt sorry for him – Driberg was going blind – asked for it on his behalf.

Another MP on the original list died recently but were I to name him I would inevitably be charged with defaming a man who cannot defend himself. Coupled with the laws of libel in life, that convention in death provides such people with almost permanent immunity from public censure.

As regards those crypto-Communists still sitting in Westminster, I can quote from a 1978 Intelligence report in my possession which states that 'at least fifty-nine serving Labour MPs – 19 per cent of the Parliamentary Labour Party – have current or recent connections with Communist, Trotskyist or other Marxist organizations. The incidence of such activities has increased enormously over the past five years.'

A list attached to this report names the MPs and gives details of their activities. It includes five ministers and four junior ministers.

This information substantiates allegations by an independent source, George Young, a former deputy director of MI6 with previous access to Intelligence evidence. In a private letter to David Yorck, a veteran of the American OSS (Office of Strategic Services), Young wrote in 1977, 'At one point under Wilson there were five ministers of the Crown whose membership of the Communist Party of Great Britain is not known to have been renounced and overlapping with them other ministers whose ultimate allegiance is outside Britain.' (It is only fair to add that Mr Young also alleged that the KGB was known to have concentrated some of its effort on Tory ministers while Heath was in office and may have secured a recruit among Tory politicians.)

It is my conviction that the security surveillance of certain Labour MPs goes back long before the Gaitskell–Brown attempt to make it official. The late George Caunt, once Wilson's election campaign manager, told me that as part of this process the Labour Party was penetrated by MI5 agents. Some of these were MPs and others were insinuated into Transport House. Caunt recalled that he was approached himself as a possible contact by an official of Transport House who was already working for MI5 in 1963. When he loyally reported this attempt to Wilson, with the warning that MI5 was operating inside the party, Wilson replied, 'I knew it!'

I know of two Labour back-benchers who were on the payroll of MI6, the Secret Intelligence Service, though there are probably more than that in the Parliamentary Tory Party. I have little doubt either that both major parties have been penetrated for many years by agents of the CIA. One of these, now dead, was a senior Cabinet minister in a Labour government. Peter Bessell has claimed he was a part-time agent for the CIA while serving as a Liberal MP.

What of Harold Wilson himself? Was his name on any list of suspect extremists? I am as sure as I can be that he did not figure in the Gaitskell–Brown project. There was no love lost between the Parliamentary Labour leaders and Wilson in 1961, when he was chairman of the party, but I saw no evidence to suggest that his name was put forward to the security authorities in an attempt to undermine his bid for the leadership of the Labour Left in succession to the ailing Nye Bevan. In 1967, when Wilson was Prime Minister, he was questioned in Parliament about the abortive Gaitskell–Brown inquiry, after I had passed relevant documents to Sir Tufton Beamish (now Lord). Wilson disclaimed all knowledge of it.

A document, of which I have a copy, suggesting that Wilson had Communist affiliations when he was a young don at Oxford was submitted to the 1977 Windscale atomic inquiry by a witness anxious to show that many of the objectors to the plutonium plant under discussion were politically motivated. But Sir Harold denied the charge absolutely to me when I drew it to his attention and, though he entered the contest for the Labour Party leadership as champion of the Left, the available evidence suggests he had always been a moderate at heart, appearing to be Left when it suited him because that was the way to power.

During his premiership he repeatedly acted against Russia's interests, often in secret. Several of these instances will figure in my narrative but it is opportune now to mention one which was typical.

Immediately after Rhodesia's declaration of independence, late in 1965, Wilson dispatched RAF Javelin jet-fighters to neighbouring Zambia's three airfields at Lusaka, Ndola and Livingstone. The RAF chiefs were worried that their pilots might be called upon to fight their white Rhodesian kinsmen but Wilson was able to assure them that there was no question of this. Officially the jets were being sent out to defend Zambia's airspace but in fact their purpose was simply to occupy the airfields and so prevent the Russians from doing so. Wilson feared that Russia would put pressure on Zambia's Kenneth Kuanda to accept Soviet MiG fighters for his protection and that once in it would be difficult to get them out. Kaunda appreciated the danger and agreed to having the Javelins, which enabled him to assure any Communist would-be 'helpers' that his air-defence needs were satisfied.

In spite of such information, which was fully available to the Intelligence authorities, alleged evidence that Wilson himself had been subjected to active surveillance by security men while he was in opposition early in 1974 came into my possession during inquiries about his resignation.

It consisted of details of a document said to be lodged in the registry of MI6 and the source had previously produced information so accurate as to cause great concern about its leakage. It was said to be a copy of a progress report on the surveillance of Wilson compiled by another department. Several pages long, it listed details of how he had been watched and followed, with the times in and times out of places he had visited and names of people he had contacted. Though the report was marked For Addressee Only it was seen by others, my informant told me. (Documents in MI6 are not given the usual Whitehall security classifications – Top Secret, Secret, Confidential or Restricted – because they are all regarded as being in an ultra-secret category.)

The timing of the surveillance, just before the general election when the miners forced the Heath government into a three-day week, may not have been coincidental. There was a general security fear that extremists might try to take advantage of the chaotic situation – it was clear that the prime objective of some trade unionists was to bring the government down and MI5 or CIA officers may have felt it to be their duty to find out the extent to which the Labour leaders might be involved.

The general impression of the details given to me suggested that the security officers were more interested in Wilson's possible contacts than in the Labour leader himself. But there were strong political overtones showing that the author of the report was opposed to Wilson's re-election as Prime Minister.

Statements expressed concern about his pro-Israeli stance during his previous premiership because of the danger that, if continued, it would sour relations with Arab states at a time of oil-supply crisis. There was anxiety that a new Wilson government might increase trade with Russia, leading to greater opportunities for KGB activity in Britain. There was mention of the fact that Wilson had previously refused to reduce the number of KGB agents posing as diplomats and trade officials in Britain and had criticized the Heath government for expelling 105 of them, arguing that the mass expulsion would do more harm than good through damage to Anglo-Soviet relations.

The informant said that the report recalled that against the advice of the security authorities, Wilson had previously agreed with the Russians to release the professional Soviet spies Peter and Helen Kroger, who had done great damage to Britain and might still be useful to the KGB, in exchange for Gerald Brooke, a lecturer harshly imprisoned by the Russians for doing no more than distribute anti-Communist literature in Moscow. They foresaw that on some future occasion when a valuable KGB spy was captured and imprisoned all Moscow might need to do to secure his release would be to make an excuse to arrest some hapless Briton. There were also fears that a new Labour administration would enforce reductions in the Secret Service as part of the general cuts in public and defence spending of which all government departments had been required to shoulder their share.

When I reported these details in the *Daily Express* there was no official denial of any kind. I have since learned that MI6 denied the report's existence to the Cabinet Office but, under the circumstances, any such embarrassing document would be a candidate for quick consignment to the shredding machine. When I discussed the alleged surveillance personally with Sir Harold, his only remark was, 'I am sure that Ted Heath did not sanction it.' The odds are that Heath would have known nothing about it. Any surveillance of Wilson would have been part of a continuing programme directed at Labour MPs and stretching back many years.

*Chapter Three*

⟨✣✣✣⟩

# Was Number 10 Bugged?

IN the summer of 1977 I reported that Wilson had been under
electronic surveillance during part of his time in Number 10 Downing Street and in his office in the House of Commons. Reaction all
round was extremely brisk – from Margaret Thatcher and many
other Tories, from Wilson himself and, after a long delay, from the
Prime Minister, James Callaghan.

During a wide-ranging talk with a regular contact who had access
to highly classified Intelligence he told me that, because of security
fears which had attached to Labour politicians for many years,
Wilson had been 'bugged' during his tenure of Number 10. Conversations were said to have been taped by surveillance techniques
introduced without the Prime Minister's knowledge, unlike those
foolishly installed by President Nixon, which were intended to provide a historic record of White House activities.

I had no intention of publishing the information, which I did not
regard as remarkable in view of my knowledge about the feelings of
certain officers in MI5, MI6 and the CIA towards any left-wing
government.

I did, however, check it out with two further reliable Intelligence
contacts, one of whom described a way in which bugs could have
been introduced and later removed.

A special government electronics unit called the Diplomatic Telecommunications Maintenance Service has the responsibility for the
routine debugging of Whitehall offices, outstations, British embassies and other places where enemy agents might plant listening
devices to eavesdrop on conversations about secret matters con-

ducted there. This unit is a specialist branch of Government Communication Headquarters (GCHQ), which is a cover name for the Foreign Office department mainly concerned with the monitoring and decoding of foreign diplomatic and military radio traffic. Fear that the KGB or other Intelligence agencies might plant bugs in secret offices from the First Sea Lord's to the Cabinet's is so real that the unit periodically checks them with sweeping devices rather like sophisticated mine-detectors. Even the cleaners of such offices are security checked to reduce the risk that they might be suborned into planting a bug on some agency's behalf.

It was suggested to me by a man with wide experience of this unit's activities that it would not be difficult for its operators to plant a bug on behalf of one of the secret services, in the Cabinet Room or anywhere else and later to remove it.

Like other sensitive offices the Cabinet Room is equipped with standard electronic equipment to detect intruders but this, of course, would almost certainly be switched off during a debugging operation. Such equipment is installed by a special Post Office security team in the offices and private homes of other senior ministers, defence chiefs and security chiefs. It can be switched off while the occupants are in residence and switched on when they go out so that any attempts at intrusion can be detected.

There is evidence that, in spite of such precautions, electronic and otherwise, which might be taken to safeguard Number 10, security there is not good. There was an instance in 1970 when a foreign interloper, a German tourist, was discovered inside Number 10, having entered through the back door. One of the witnesses to this event told me that the man got in 'while the policeman on duty was "having it off" with one of the girl secretaries'. This man was later suspected of having taken private documents belonging to Harold Wilson but, as I later discovered, someone else had removed them.

Another extraordinary incident, which would be funny were it not potentially serious, was described to me by a former Tory Cabinet minister who witnessed it. Two members of a Commonwealth conference being held in Number 10 were rather deaf and elaborate hearing-aids involving loudspeaker devices had been set up to assist them. A taxi-driver waiting outside was startled to find that he could hear all that was going on inside on his short-wave car radio. When he reported it at the front door he was disbelieved until someone came out and listened in horror.

What touched off my reports about the bugging of Harold Wilson was the sudden appearance in the *Observer* newspaper in July 1977 of his allegations that he had 'lost faith in MI5', a disaffected faction of which had been trying to undermine his government.

Tory MPs tried to induce Prime Minister Callaghan to deny this charge, as much in the interests of MI5's morale as for political purposes. All that Callaghan would do at that stage was to insist that, so far as his own experience was concerned, he was satisfied that the allegation did not constitute grounds for lack of confidence in the competence or impartiality of MI5 and repeatedly rejected any need for a special inquiry into the Wilson claim.

The day after the *Observer* allegations, Joe Haines, Wilson's former press secretary, published a report in the *Daily Mirror* headlined 'Why Wilson thought No. 10 was bugged'. It described how the former Prime Minister distrusted MI5 men so much that he suspected he was being bugged by them. Haines later reported that Wilson found what he thought might be a bug behind a picture of Gladstone in his study. 'Immediately suspecting that MI5 was listening in on private talks he called in an expert to probe the "bug",' Haines wrote. (The 'bug' later turned out to be a fitting for a picture light.)

If Haines's story is correct – and Wilson has not effectively denied it – the Prime Minister must have distrusted the official security staff because the debugging expert was said to have come from a private firm.

I still withheld my information but a few days later I dined with one of Wilson's closest confidants who volunteered the information that it was true that Wilson believed he was bugged in Number 10. I also learned that when he had been sounding off about his fears concerning MI5, Sir Maurice Oldfield, then head of MI6, wrote to the Cabinet Secretary complaining that his organization was becoming embroiled in the criticisms. He had duly received a letter from the Prime Minister's office assuring him that MI6 was not involved in the strictures. There was no doubt, therefore, that Wilson's fears and his strictures were real.

I therefore decided that it was my professional duty to my newspaper to report the information at my disposal and an article duly appeared under my name claiming that Wilson's fear that he had been under electronic surveillance was fully justified. Early copies of the newspaper were in the hands of Tory MPs, who were in late-night session, by 10.30 p.m. and they caused a furore with demands for the presence of Prime Minister Callaghan to respond to the report. Next day, the last of the session, the opposition refused to debate some important legislation unless Callaghan appeared, which he eventually did but with little to say.

The following day a colleague, who had been speaking to one of Wilson's close political friends who had been elevated to the Lords, called to see me. While standing in Parliament Square he had asked the Labour peer what he thought of my report that his former Prime Minister had indeed been bugged. The reply was that there was no doubt about it. 'But it's there that Harold was really worried about,' he added, pointing to the Prime Minister's room in the Commons. 'It was the bugging there that made him so furious with MI5.'

Recalling that my original informant had mentioned this room, a large high-ceilinged office overlooking New Palace Yard, and which I had visited in the past, I produced a report the following day saying that security men had bugged Wilson at the House of Commons as well as at Number 10. I also mentioned that Wilson suspected that he had been under electronic surveillance in his private homes.

In theory, any part of the Palace of Westminster could not be bugged without the Speaker's permission, which would not be given except under pressure from the Home Secretary or the Prime Minister himself. In fact security there is not good. The Prime Minister's office is equipped with a large table so that emergency Cabinet meetings can be held there but Wilson told me later that he had been warned officially that it was not secure enough for meetings of the Defence and Overseas Policy Committee.

There was good reason for such official doubt, as shown by the following event, which was described to me first hand by the MP concerned. Shortly before the arrest of Will Owen, the former Labour MP for Morpeth, Kenneth Warren, Tory MP for Hastings, found a wad of fifty pound notes in his Westminster locker to which he believed he had the only key. He reported the matter to the Commons police and handed in the money. It later transpired that Warren's locker was not the only one so patronized. Czech agents or others acting on their behalf had inserted the money in wrong lockers, presumably believing them to be Owen's. It was found that the key to Owen's locker fitted Warren's and several others.

It was assumed at the time that the Warren money was intended for Owen but there may have been other Labour MPs on the Czech payroll. In evidence to the US Senate Judiciary Committee, given on oath, a Czech defector called Josef Frolik claimed that several British MPs had been recruited by Czech Intelligence. This was confirmed to the committee by another Czech defector, Frantisek August, who gave evidence separately.

After a two-day delay Wilson issued a statement in which he stated that he found my allegations that he had been bugged 'incredible', claiming that had electronic surveillance been in force he would have known about it – a statement which made little sense to those who know the sophistication of modern listening devices and of those planting them.

Marcia went on record as saying that she thought bugging in Number 10 would be impossible because, when George Wigg had been security overlord, he had warned her that the whole place was an 'electronic minefield'. Wigg immediately denied this to me as 'absolute rot' and took legal advice because he felt that the mere suggestion that he had said such a thing held him to ridicule. After all, if the bugging of Number 10 is impossible why is it swept so regularly?

The limitations of sweeping techniques against some kinds of bugs were sensationally exposed recently by the American admission that an extensive eavesdropping system had been discovered inside its embassy in Moscow. The building had been regularly swept, particularly since the discovery of a listening device in a commemorative plaque presented by the Kremlin in 1958. Yet the system which the Americans revealed in June 1978 had clearly been there a long time. It included a powerful antenna leading to what was virtually a recording studio via a tunnel through which various devices had been regularly serviced. Yet sweeping had apparently given no indications, the system being discovered only following a serious fire which had damaged the top floor of the embassy.

It is, of course, almost certain that the bugs had been found some time before the Americans put out any statement about them, choosing a time of strained relations which suited them politically. It would also be standard practice to feed disinformation into the bugs for several weeks. But I am in no doubt, from what I have been told privately, that sweeping techniques had failed over a long period and there is general concern about this.

While calling for an investigation into the alleged bugging of Number 10 Wilson said that he had known me long enough to be sure that whatever my source, right or wrong, I would not have printed such a story unless I believed it. Later, in private, he told me that because of my record he felt it only right that he should say that.

Meanwhile the reports had generated noisy demands for Callaghan to set up a public inquiry not only into my allegations but into the criticisms levelled at MI5 by Wilson. I knew that no Prime Minister would sanction any public inquiry involving MI5, and all that the demands produced was a Downing Street statement about a month later which read:

> The Prime Minister has conducted detailed inquiries into the recent allegations about the Security Service and is satisfied that they do not constitute grounds for lack of confidence in the competence and impartiality of the Security Service or for instituting a special inquiry.
>
> In particular, the Prime Minister is satisfied that at no time has the Security Service or any other British intelligence or security agency, either of its own accord or at someone else's request, undertaken electronic surveillance in 10 Downing Street or in the Prime Minister's Room in the House of Commons.

The first paragraph was a rebuttal for Wilson and the second a rebuttal for me.

Wilson told me later that he had immediately agreed with the statement, which could only mean that he withdrew his allegations about the MI5 conspiracy against him. At this stage he was playing down his censure of MI5 and told me that while in office his relatively few dealings with the Security Service had been through the Cabinet Office.

'I saw so little of the heads of MI5 and MI6 that I used to confuse their names,' he said. This could well have been true but it made nonsense of his complaint that during his final period in office he had not known 'what was happening fully in security'. No Prime Minister ever does. He is, of course, told a great deal and the relevant reports from MI6 and important intercepts by GCHQ go to him daily in oblong yellow boxes. But he is treated on a 'need-to-know' basis by his security and Intelligence chiefs, being told only what they think he needs to know to fulfil his commitments. In any event he would not have time to know all that was in train even if the security authorities were prepared to tell him.

Because any Prime Minister is so busy I was naturally suspicious of Callaghan's claim that he had 'conducted detailed inquiries' into the allegations made by Wilson and by me. My inquiries into what had actually happened showed that the questioning had been

limited to the Cabinet Secretary and four other men and that much
of the actual interrogation had been carried out by officials.

The four were the Directors-General of MI5 and MI6, the Chief of
GCHQ and the Coordinator of Intelligence, a deputy secretary in
the Cabinet Office serving as go-between for the Prime Minister and
the secret services.

As head of all government departments the Prime Minister had
the right to demand information from even the most secret of them
but to what extent was he likely to get it if it happened to be highly
embarrassing? The weakness of any internal inquiry involving secret
services is that any denial they may make about clandestine operations such as bugging inspires little confidence because denial is part
of their stock-in-trade.

In 1976, for instance, I reported details of an attempt involving
three Palestinian terrorists and two Germans to shoot down an
Israeli airliner approaching Nairobi Airport. I stated that after
capture the five had been flown to Israel for interrogation. The entire
account was vigorously denied both by Israeli Intelligence and the
Kenyan government, yet not long afterwards, the five were put on
trial in Israel. When I reminded my Israeli Intelligence friends of
their categorical denial they shrugged and said, 'Well, you know
how things are in this game.'

Reluctance to brief a Prime Minister or anyone else fully on
Intelligence and security issues is also governed by something far
stronger than sheer secrecy – the paramount importance of Anglo-
American cooperation on Intelligence and security. The sad truth is
that the resources of MI5 and MI6 are so small and have been so
whittled down that they could not cope world-wide or even in Britain
without the help of two American organizations – the Central Intelligence Agency (CIA) and the National Security Agency (NSA).

Britain is totally dependent on the USA for intelligence from
orbiting satellites – now the major source. Most of the radio-
monitoring establishments in Britain have been built with American
money and are manned by NSA staff working jointly with GCHQ.
Dependence is so great and cooperation so close that I am convinced that the security and Intelligence chiefs would go to any
lengths to protect the link-up and that they would be right to do so.

So if the CIA or the NSA, which is responsible for planting the
listening devices it calls 'sneakies', overstepped the mark in Britain I
am sure that MI5 and MI6 would cover up for them. One prime

MI6 source, who admitted that representations had been made by Washington about some of the ministers appointed by Wilson, assured me that, 'Anything and everything would be possible if it was considered necessary to protect the Anglo-American joint Intelligence arrangements. They are priority number one.'

This dependence on the USA for Intelligence may seem unhealthy but short of financing a far bigger effort Britain's only alternative is to give the KGB a much easier run.

Shortly after Callaghan's statement I received an unsigned letter typed on House of Commons notepaper and posted there claiming that the use of the term 'electronic surveillance' in the Downing Street statement was a technical get-out and that non-electronic means might have been used to eavesdrop on Wilson. I knew that some listening devices do not use electronics. Best known of these was the brilliantly effective instrument inserted by the KGB into a plaque presented by the Kremlin to the American embassy in Moscow and erected in a room believed to be bug-proof.

The Americans were alerted by the British after a similar device had been found in the wall of the naval attaché's office in their embassy. The plaque had been hollowed out to contain a small metal drum with a needle attached. Microwave vibrations transmitted by the Russians from a short distance on one side of the building were picked up by a receiver the other side. The drum vibrated in sympathy but when anyone spoke in the office these vibrations were modified by the effect of the speech sound-waves on the drum. Soviet technicians were able to convert these modifications back into the original speech.

Such devices have been so greatly improved and are in such widespread use by the KGB that the level of microwaves beamed at Western embassies in Moscow has become so intense that there have been fears for the diplomats' health. To protect the staff, and also to prevent the bugging of telex messages and conversations, metal screens have been erected in some embassies.

Though not impressed by the anonymous suggestion about non-electronic bugging in Number 10, I went through the motions of asking the Downing Street spokesman if the statement had referred only to electronic surveillance. His immediate response was to say that obviously it referred to any kind of bugging. I was therefore rather surprised when he telephoned me some hours later to retract that remark and to state that the Prime Minister's announcement had referred to 'electronic surveillance' alone. He said that no further statement about any other form of surveillance would be forthcoming. Wilson was greatly interested in this development when I told him about it.

Early in 1978, Peter Blaker, Tory MP for Blackpool South, tried to resurrect the whole security issue concerning Wilson and his remarks about the secret services under Standing Order 9. I was alone with the former Prime Minister in an office in Parliament Street when the announcement that Blaker's attempt was being made in the House appeared on the closed-circuit television indicator installed there. Wilson was clearly concerned, though confident, because of his remarkable grasp of parliamentary procedure, that the Speaker would not agree to Blaker's request.

'Under the rules of Standing Order 9, Blaker would not be allowed to name me as an MP or to name Marcia,' he explained.

'Why not Marcia?' I asked.

'Because she is a member of the Upper House.'

'I had forgotten that,' I remarked.

'She does sometimes,' Wilson added drily.

*Chapter Four*

# The Truth about Wilson's Cohorts

WHILE Wilson's fears about the clandestine activities of MI5 against him probably reached their peak in 1975, he was already disturbed about them a year previously during the run-up to the second general election in 1974 – again with good reason.

It was at that time, in a pre-election speech at Portsmouth, that he made his intriguing declaration that 'Cohorts of distinguished journalists had been combing parts of the country with a mandate to find anything, true or fabricated, for use against the Labour Party.' Fleet Street in general has been puzzled by this declaration ever since for no newspaper was aware of any such activity and it was assumed that the Prime Minister, fearful of some new and dangerous disclosure, was taking pre-emptive measures to blacken the Press in advance so that whatever might be written would not be believed.

Once again this assumption was wrong. I was alone in knowing what had driven him to make the 'cohorts' allegation and it was nothing less than accurate Intelligence he had received of a campaign of denigration originally designed to be launched with the blessing of the Tory Party. He also had cause to suspect that his enemies in MI5 might be assisting.

I was also the person responsible, inadvertently – I could say stupidly – for letting him know all this and also for making him believe on the day that he made his speech that the opening shot of the campaign had just been fired.

In the early spring of 1974 I had learned that the Tory leadership, then headed by Edward Heath, was frightened that Wilson would launch a snap election in June. Labour had been returned with a minority position in Parliament after the joint disasters of the miners' strike and the three-day week and a second election that year seemed inevitable.

The immediate effect of settling the strike and getting industry back to normal had been to increase Labour's support prodigiously. Tory soundings indicated that the government might be returned with such a majority that some of the Tory leaders would lose their seats. The election therefore had to be delayed if possible, at least until the autumn and preferably beyond.

Before the previous election in February the Tory leadership had been given full information about the problems presented by the birth of two children to Marcia Williams following a love affair with a political journalist. Copies of the birth certificates had been sent to several MPs, including ministers. It was also widely believed that there had been problems, because of this love affair, over Marcia's positive vetting for access to secret documents, which might be exploited. And there were aspects of Wilson's reaction to the land deals row, when Parliament demanded details of land speculation by Marcia's brother, which were considered worthy of development.

I had discussed all these matters then with some of the Tory leaders because of their potential news value but Heath would have nothing to do with any of them and dissuaded several of his back-benchers from raising awkward questions in the House. He also rejected suggestions made to him by party workers that publicity might be given to the allegations about Jeremy Thorpe and the male model Norman Scott, which might have helped to upset some Liberal seats.

Heath's view as given to me then by Lord Aldington, one of his closest aides, was that the Conservatives were going to win the election anyway and wanted to be seen to have won it cleanly without recourse to distasteful denigration. In the event they lost.

By late April, however, some of the Tory leaders were taking a different view and I was put in touch with a Tory Party official, not now in Mrs Thatcher's entourage, who told me that the current thinking was that any means of discouraging Wilson from going to the country in June should be brought into play. While the leadership still disliked the whole idea of using personal denigration, these were desperate times and to use such means to prevent an election was not so reprehensible as using them to win one.

One or two back-benchers had already been alerted to ask pointed parliamentary questions and it was suggested that I might help there with advice and I did so. What was required of me in the main was that I should make use in the *Daily Express* of material in my possession so that other papers would be encouraged to do likewise.

In view of what I will shortly reveal, I must say that I have no certain evidence that Heath knew of this proposed campaign, though I have records of how I was assured by people close to him that he did and had approved of it with reluctance. I have been reassured on this point recently in some detail but it remains possible that others had taken the decision to act and had not told him about it.

I would almost certainly have taken part in the campaign because some of the material would have been very newsworthy – as the revelations of Joe Haines, Wilson's former Press officer eventually proved – but, as I explained to my Tory contacts, Sir Max Aitken, then my proprietor, had given firm instructions that there were to be no more attacks on Wilson and Marcia in the *Daily Express* unless there were new developments that could not be ignored. This ruling was partly due to the fact that Wilson had recently issued two libel writs against us over the land deals affair but mainly because Sir Max, who had some regard for Wilson, felt that the attacks on him and his entourage were going too far. However, I did promise my Tory friends that if some relevant news which just had to be printed should emerge I would do my best to secure it due prominence in the paper.

Nothing much happened until May, apart from a few damp-squib parliamentary questions. Then I was invited with my wife to lunch at a country house in Hampshire. It was a pleasant occasion because there were several people there I knew well, including a former senior figure from the Defence Ministry. Some of the lunch party whom I did not know were youngish or making an effort to look young by appearing in tight, faded jeans and other casual attire. I was introduced to them all but did not register the name of one of them, a balding gentleman, for it meant nothing to me.

After lunch some of us, including the balding man in jeans, retired to the music-room where one of the party set the ball of conversation rolling by asking me about Marcia's peerage which had recently been announced.

I have found that at almost any intimate gathering the conversation soon gets round to gossip about Wilson and Marcia and the rest of the party, with the exception of the gentleman in jeans, stimulated me with questions to tell all I knew. In the confidentiality of that household I did so, though much of the information was already well known to several of those present.

I discussed how the affair of the land deals had been handled in Parliament, pointing out how Tory back-benchers would be trying to accuse Wilson of misleading the House during his defence of Marcia's brother. I spoke of the allegations concerning Marcia's security clearance and how these might become public through a court action being brought by a certain Mrs Marjorie Halls, the widow of Michael Halls, Wilson's former principal private secretary in Number 10. In this connection I mentioned that Marcia's children would also be mentioned if the case came to court because Mrs Halls was claiming that the efforts involved in concealing them and other matters concerned with them had contributed to her husband's early death from a heart attack.

I mentioned that Mrs Halls was prepared to give evidence that on one occasion Marcia had telephoned her and threatened to cause Wilson's downfall if her husband did not get her telephone put right with greater speed.

I also told my audience – stupidly perhaps – that the Tories might be playing up some of these issues to prevent an early election and that I had been told that the fear of that was so great that Heath, who normally shunned such matters, had been talked into condoning them. I also pointed out that while other newspapers might make much of the situation, the *Daily Express* would not because the proprietor had forbidden it.

My dissertation was received with lively interest and prompted numerous questions, the only objector being the man in jeans who remarked that a smear campaign against anybody could never be justified. I made the point that, in my view, a smear campaign was based on falsehoods and inaccurate innuendo. What I had told them were facts and I had documents to prove them. I did not see how a person could be 'smeared' by the truth. Damaged yes, but not 'smeared'.

The party broke up very amicably and I thought no more about it until early June when I received a letter from Oxford signed by a Mr Martin Gilbert. He turned out to be a historian who had secured the right of being official biographer to Sir Winston Churchill after the death of the great man's son, Randolph. He was also the balding man in jeans.

The letter, which he had carefully marked Private and Confidential, was a memorized account of the whole of my conversation, some of it inaccurate and ending with a weird suggestion that Heath must be given the chance to disassociate himself from my private remarks.

I realized the probable purpose of the letter and replied to it pointing out the inaccuracies. My suspicion was confirmed a little later by a second letter from Gilbert. It told me that he had sent copies of his account of my private conversation to Heath and, as I suspected then and was to learn in detail later, to Wilson. The upshot of it was that Heath denied any knowledge of the campaign to discredit Wilson and his associates. Wilson's reaction as Prime Minister was to watch carefully for the first signs of any campaign and then to deal with it as best he could.

With June safely passed and Parliament soon into the summer recess, any activities by politicians were shelved or, as I now know, banned after Gilbert's letter to Heath. The only danger lay with the Press. On 20 September, two days after Wilson had called the general election for 10 October, he believed that I had made the opening move in a coming series of damaging Press reports when a short item about Mrs Halls appeared in the *Daily Express* under my name.

To appreciate the alarm which this caused in Number 10 it is necessary to know a little more about the Halls case.

In 1973 a friend alerted me to the fact that Mrs Halls, who worked in the Lord Chancellor's Office and whom I had never met, was about to sue the Civil Service Department for £50,000 damages for the premature death of her husband, Wilson's former aide in Number 10. My friend put me in touch with Mrs Halls and she told me that she would be lodging a claim alleging that the extra burden of coping with the tensions created by Marcia had contributed to her husband's fatal heart attack. She said she had already taken her case to the former Prime Minister, Heath, and showed me his reply in which he turned down any hope of payment. I agreed with his view and told her that she had no chance of winning the action because she would never be able to prove that Halls had not died from natural causes but she persisted and issued a writ against the Department, which I reported in the *Daily Express* early in 1974. This news, which was followed up by other papers, caused dismay inside Number 10 and this was greatly intensified when the Treasury Solicitor received fuller particulars of the claim.

These particulars, of which copies are in my possession, claimed that Halls had been instructed by Wilson to do all he could to keep secret the births of Marcia's children and that he had to spend so much time over her personal problems that he was having to work late every night and every weekend to get through his normal duties. They alleged that, as Marcia could not leave the country, she insisted that Wilson should not remain abroad for long when he had to visit the USA and other places on international business. So his programmes were unnecessarily tight, one trip to Canada in 1970 being so punishing that Halls, who accompanied the Prime Minister, was debilitated by it.

The second embarrassing facet of Mrs Halls's legal statements was the references to Marcia's fierce temper, her duchess-like demands and the blazing rows and slanging matches between herself and the Prime Minister. The third was an alleged account of how Halls and other civil servants had been required to issue some sort of waiver over Marcia's second positive vetting in 1969 when she was said to be scared of having to reveal the existence of the children to the security people, with the fact that the father was the diplomatic correspondent of the *Daily Mail*, specializing in writing about Whitehall and Westminster.

The Treasury decided to defend the action and Wilson must have been alerted to the details of Mrs Halls's claim.

Some Tory MPs made efforts to secure an airing of the alleged security aspects in Parliament alluding to the rumour that when papers were sent round to Marcia's flat in the later stages of her pregnancies they were sometimes taken in by her lover. Mrs Halls was in fact prepared to testify that her husband had told Sir William Armstrong (now Lord), the Treasury chief responsible for Downing Street security, that because of the babies situation Marcia should be asked to leave. He alleged that in such circumstances anybody else would be barred because it was just the kind of situation the KGB looked for in the hope of applying blackmail pressure. Mrs Halls claimed that this extra worry about security may also have contributed to her husband's death.

The parliamentary questions produced little change out of Wilson and the Halls case attracted little further interest though readers of the English edition of the German magazine *Stern* were intrigued to know why four pages of a July 1974 issue had been cut out by the distributors. The pages had carried an article headed, 'Mrs Marcia and the power in Downing Street', and included details of Mrs Halls's statement of claim.

Then in the following September I heard that Sir Douglas Allen, the head of the Civil Service, had promised to recommend an *ex gratia* payment for Mrs Halls which would mean that the court action could be dropped. She was told, however, that nothing could be done before the general election.

I told Mrs Halls that if I printed this she would almost certainly never receive the payment but she assured me that other journalists had the information. I therefore slipped the story into a column I produced each Friday and it appeared on the morning of the day that Wilson was due to make his Portsmouth speech.

I decided that the way to project the news in a personalized column was to pose the intriguing possibility that the minister who might be required to deal with the recommended payment might be Marcia herself. Wilson had made Marcia a peeress some months earlier and was therefore in a position to put her into the government. I had previously suggested that, following her criticisms of the Civil Service in her book, she might like the opportunity to put things right. I also managed to include the fact that she had produced two children in the context of their part in Mrs Halls's claim.

Nobody could blame Wilson and Marcia for believing that this article, at the very start of the election campaign, was the opening of the dreaded smearing. Gilbert had shown Wilson the letter he had received from Heath so the Prime Minister could be sure that the Tory leader would have no part in it. But journalists were another matter and once they started with their disclosures Tory back-benchers could take them up at the hustings.

Some idea of what could have happened had the campaign materialized as Wilson feared can be gathered from the sensation caused when Haines published his disclosures about life in Number 10 after Wilson had resigned. The bulk of those disclosures were available to me at the time of the election and had formed the basis of the conversation which Gilbert had reported. The Halls case was one of the major topics with which I had regaled Gilbert and had warned that the anti-Wilson campaign might be based, so the sudden revival of my interest in it immediately before the election must have seemed ominous in the extreme.

Haines records in his book, *The Politics of Power*, how it was my Halls item which triggered Wilson off to launch his 'cohorts' attack. As the Prime Minister's Press adviser, Haines was opposed to it, fearing it would alienate the Press further, which it did, but Wilson was determined to make his pre-emptive strike.

In fact the Halls item was no part of any Tory campaign and the timing was entirely fortuitous. The news had not been conditioned by the election but by the decision by Sir Douglas Allen to suggest the possibility of an *ex gratia* payment, over which I had no control whatever. It is easy to see, however, why Wilson misinterpreted it, especially when on the following Sunday the *News of the World* took up the story claiming that according to Mrs Halls (which she strenu-ously denied) she had been offered £40,000 to stop the case from going to court.

Marcia has since told me that she and Wilson believed that I had induced Mrs Halls to bring the action in the first place and was prompting her on every move when, in fact, I did not know her when she began it and then did all I could to persuade her against it because I knew she would lose.

My advice to Mrs Halls was proved sound when she received a letter from Sir Douglas Allen, a copy of which is in my files, with-drawing his offer to recommend any payment because of the public-ity it had received. Some of Halls's old colleagues like Lord Helsby, his former Civil Service chief, have told me that it is possible that the normal strain of the work in Number 10 was too much for him and that, foreseeing this, they had opposed his appointment there. They had, however, been overruled by Wilson who, like most Prime Ministers, wanted people around him whose loyalty seemed assured. Helsby told me he was prepared to give evidence for Mrs Halls to this effect.

At the time of writing the Halls case has never come to court though technically it is still alive.

I eventually received a letter from my host assuring me that Gilbert had apologized to him for breaking the confidentiality of his home. But some intriguing questions remain.

If my indiscretion at that lunch had not aborted the anti-Wilson campaign what effect might such a campaign have exerted on the ensuing election? Is it possible that Wilson decided to go to the country in October instead of the following spring to pre-empt a back-bench Tory denigration campaign against him before Parliament could reassemble? No doubt other considerations were far more important but his determined reaction through the 'cohorts' speech suggests that it could have been a factor.

As a further example of the desperation felt by Tory Party officials in the October 1974 election I will relate an episode involving me on the eve of polling day. I was telephoned at about 6 p.m. at my office by a Tory official, who is no longer there, to be told that on that very afternoon Sir Claus Moser, the government's chief statistician, had made a devastating statement during a lecture to postgraduate economists at Southampton University. This was to the effect that while Denis Healey, the Chancellor, was claiming that inflation was down to $8\frac{1}{2}$ per cent it was in fact much higher and would soon be up to 25 per cent. The informant, who said he was sure of his facts, suggested that this could make a good story for election eve. It would have been sensational had it been true but a call to Sir Claus's office, which was on the point of closing, showed that he had been in Geneva for the past three days and had given no lecture in Southampton.

I believe that the party official, whom I telephoned back to make sure I was not being hoaxed, had been hoaxed himself but it was a dangerous story to put out and I learned from Sir Claus's office that calls about it had been received from other newspapers. Had we printed the story, which Heath knew nothing about, and Labour had lost the election it would have gone down in history as another Zinoviev Letter.

Once back as Premier, Wilson was repeatedly urged to substantiate his claim about the 'cohorts' but always declined saying that he would be giving his evidence to the Royal Commission on the Press, which he had set up in May 1974 to inquire into the financial situation of the newspapers, their management practice, labour relations and other factors influencing their production and freedom.

A Fleet Street trade union leader who had come out in support of Wilson's 'cohorts' claim, saying he had details of big payments by newspapers seeking dirt on Wilson, also decided that he would submit his evidence to the royal commission. He was later sent to the Lords as Lord Briginshaw. I understand he submitted a tirade of about forty pages but nothing more has been heard of it.

Only when it was too late for the royal commission to consider any more evidence did Wilson submit his. The commission was headed by Professor Oliver McGregor (now Lord) who told me that he was therefore unable to investigate Wilson's allegations or call any witnesses such as Mrs Halls, me or Wilson himself.

As his reason for the delay Wilson claimed that he had several libel actions pending and, until these had been settled, could not submit the evidence, but nobody was much impressed by this argument.

He then issued his over-late statement to the newspapers and put a copy in the library of Parliament. This meant that his account was given publicity, but he avoided any questioning. Among his evidence was a statement that a 'prominent journalist known for his virulence of opposition to the Labour government spoke at length and had his words taken down by one of our most distinguished historians at a private house party about his determination to "expose" all manner of things.' It enabled him to castigate those newspapers like the *Express* and *Daily Mail* which he intensely disliked, while avoiding criticism of the *Daily Mirror* which supports Labour at general elections. By serializing Haines's recollections of life in Number 10 the *Mirror* had given sensational publicity to the 'all manner of things' which Wilson accused me of plotting to expose. But he ignored that.

Because of the unsatisfactory nature of this position the Press Council, under the chairmanship of Lord Shawcross, urged Wilson to appear before it and submit to questioning. At first Wilson took the view that as he had made no complaint to the Press Council there was no purpose in giving it any evidence, but in the early summer of 1978 he agreed to appear. His statement to the Council, and even the fact that he attended, are being held as confidential at the time of writing but I understand that his explanation of his 'cohorts' allegation was not regarded by the Council as disposing of it satisfactorily. It seems likely that he may be requested to appear again.

Harold Wilson is a forgiving man and has forgiven me. In his position I do not think I could ever have forgiven a journalist who had caused me so much trouble and distress.

*Chapter Five*

# The Great Hostile Machine

THE Soviet Intelligence service, which includes those similar but smaller services operated by the Kremlin's satellites, is the biggest machine for the garnering of secret information which the world has ever known – in peace or war. It has two main branches, the GRU, which directs military, naval and air espionage in all foreign countries, and the KGB – Russian initials for Committee of State Security – which covers all the other Intelligence and security needs of the Soviet government. As the KGB is the much better known, those initials will be used in this book to include the GRU as well.

According to a recent KGB defector in Britain, Captain Alexei Myagkov – and there are more defectors like him than is generally imagined – the KGB, which he calls the 'fighting wing of the Soviet Communist Party', has 110,000 full-time officers operating a huge army of agents and informers. He says that the number of agents listed in its register – willing or forcibly recruited – runs into millions, a figure bloated through the KGB's iron control over sister organizations in the satellite countries. Documents Myagkov brought with him underline the extent to which the KGB is required to use bribery and blackmail to penetrate Western governments and organizations.

Financial resources for these and other operations appear to be unlimited. Currently it is estimated that the Soviet Union spends more than £1,500 million on espionage, Intelligence and subversion – perhaps fifty times more than Britain spends. This disparity makes life extremely difficult both for MI5 and MI6, which together have the task of countering this massive effort while at the same time initiating Intelligence-gathering operations of their own. It is a reflection of the general disparity between the Soviet Union and the West in the field of defence. In spite of détente the KGB effort increases steadily in step with the Kremlin's relentless military build-up and is an essential part of it.

In foreign countries like Britain the KGB operates two kinds of espionage networks – one called 'legal', the other 'illegal'. A 'legal' apparatus is a network controlled by officers insinuated into a Soviet embassy or trade mission and who are therefore covered by diplomatic immunity if they are caught. Fuchs, Vassall and Philby, the Secret Service traitor, were controlled in this way.

An 'illegal' apparatus has no connection with any official Soviet organization in the country where it operates and any Communist bloc citizens who are caught can count on being disowned, at least initially, and are required to give nothing away when standing trial. Such a network was the Portland spy ring controlled by a KGB colonel who operated under the name of Gordon Lonsdale.

The whole machine is rigidly controlled by 'the centre', KGB headquarters in Moscow, and the field operators have limited autonomy. This is a fortunate weakness for it occasionally enables counter-Intelligence to pierce the KGB security screen. The methods used to do this are, understandably, secret but one example can be given.

The degree of KGB activity in Britain can be gauged by the density of the coded radio traffic between the Soviet embassy in London and Moscow. Though the meaning of some of the messages may never be broken, they are nevertheless recorded and stored for possible analysis. If the Soviet ambassador or some other senior embassy official has to visit the Foreign Office to lodge a diplomatic protest or deliver some other important message, he is given a firm briefing on what to say by Moscow and adheres to it so that there can be no misunderstanding. The statement he makes to the Foreign

Office can sometimes be matched with the coded instructions which Moscow sent him by radio, so the code for that day can be deduced. This may enable other more interesting messages sent in code that day to be deciphered.

The extent of Soviet espionage in Britain was sensationally exposed in 1971 when Heath and his Foreign Secretary, Douglas-Home, courageously decided that the time had come to expel most of those members of the Soviet embassy and trade missions known to be active Intelligence agents. Ninety Russian officials were ordered out of the country and fifteen others were told that they would not be allowed to continue in Britain when their tours of duty ended.

Normally when a Russian is expelled, the reasons are given in some detail to the Soviet ambassador if he is not too embarrassed to ask for them. It was expected that with a list of 105 he would certainly query some of them. Not so. Though it was never announced, the MI5 chief, then Sir Martin Furnival Jones, had detailed evidence of subversive activity ready against every one of them but he was not asked to produce it.

Some of these Intelligence agents had been posing as diplomats but most had been planted for cover in trading missions like Aeroflot, the Soviet airline, Intourist, TASS, the Soviet news agency, the Russian Wood Agency concerned with timber exports and the Soviet trade delegation itself. There had been an advantage to the KGB in concentrating its effort in the trade missions because the movements of their members are not restricted to thirty miles from London, as are the movements of Soviet embassy officials. Further, no records are kept of where they go or whom they see, except in the case of those under surveillance.

The government's move was received with dismay by the Labour Left and even by Wilson, who in a radio interview claimed that it was 'a bit of a phoney' introduced to help the Tories to win an important by-election. But when I discussed the matter briefly with Sir Alec Douglas-Home shortly after the expulsions, he remarked, 'The situation had reached such proportions that we had to go the whole way to expose it. Expelling a few as a gesture would have been meaningless.'

Wilson's attitude did not help to dispel Tory suspicions that in return for increases in Soviet trade he was prepared to allow the KGB some latitude, trusting in MI5 to curb their more dangerous activities.

The expulsion decision followed the defection of a KGB officer, who had posed as a member of the Soviet trade mission, called Oleg Lyalin, and it was commonly believed that he had put the finger on the whole 105 but this was far from the truth. With great skill and patience – and not a little forbearance considering the reluctance of successive governments to take action – MI5 had already built up a case against almost all of them. Lyalin's information, which revealed Soviet plans for sabotage and subversion on a really dangerous scale, finally convinced the government that tough action was necessary. More importantly it provided a reason which the public would understand and this was why the government was unusually forthcoming with information about Lyalin, who, of course, was quickly hidden away in a 'safe house'.

In Parliament, for example, the Attorney-General, Sir Peter Rawlinson (now Lord) revealed that Lyalin was a KGB officer belonging to 'that department whose duties and functions included the organization of sabotage within the United Kingdom and also included the elimination of individuals judged to be enemies of the USSR'. This was the assassination department formerly known by the initials SMERSH.

What Rawlinson did not reveal was that Lyalin's specific duty was to operate a network trained in subversion, sabotage and tactics to delay reinforcements to NATO passing through Britain in the event of war. He brought with him from Moscow detailed maps showing how to disrupt the ballistic-missile early-warning system at Fylingdales on the North Yorkshire Moors and other defensive installations. He also indicated that another network for the same purpose was being operated by the GRU, the Soviet military Intelligence branch, but security never managed to track any of its members down and they may still be operative.

Even after the expulsion of the 105 diplomats and trade officials there were still 450 left, a number of whom were suspect enough to warrant further expulsions, or, as a Foreign Office man put it, 'to give us a second-strike capability', if Moscow's retaliation against Britain's diplomats, including those who were Intelligence agents, proved over-severe.

The scale and nature of the KGB operations exposed by the government's action in 1971 should be sufficient answer to those who genuinely doubt that the Russians would bother to mount such an effort in the United Kingdom because, with defence being run down so much, there are no secrets worth penetrating. In the first place, there are important secrets, including those still generously provided by the USA, but the KGB's main effort is in building up a fifth column for subversion in the event of serious industrial strife that could be used to promote revolution and for sabotage in the event of war.

The importance of Britain to the military aspirations of the Soviet Union cannot be overestimated. Russia's main enemy would be the USA, the rest of NATO having no illusions that it could possibly withstand a major Soviet attack on its own. There seems to be little doubt now that the Kremlin would try to localize the fighting to Europe to prevent nuclear bombardment of the Soviet and American homelands. So its prime purpose would be to defeat the NATO forces in Europe quickly before they could be reinforced by air from the USA. Britain, the 'unsinkable aircraft-carrier', is the main American base for reinforcing Europe. The USA already has substantial air forces and large stockpiles of weapons in Britain and most of the rest would have to be flown into Britain first before transportation to the European battlefields. That is why the Americans are increasing their flying-tanker fleet in Britain – against local opposition round the airfields involved – to in-flight refuel the transport and combat planes which would come in over the Atlantic at a rate of one every four minutes.

It follows, then, that anything which disrupts American reinforcement through Britain is vital to the Soviets. Hence the KGB's concentration on setting up contingency arrangements for sabotage of installations, communications and other facilities crucial to the West in war.

The KGB and those who serve it mean business in Britain and those whose attempt to deride the menace of left-wing extremists as 'another Reds-under-the-beds' scare are assisting the Soviets, either unwittingly, or in too many cases for comfort, deliberately.

My inquiries showed that there had been intense opposition by Foreign Office officials to the mass expulsion of the KGB agents. Those on the Russian Desk complained that it would undo years of work of improving diplomatic relations and efforts to increase East–West trade. They also played on the fears that the Kremlin would retaliate with an equally savage dismissal of British diplomats and trade officials in Moscow, though the numbers there were much smaller. This argument had worked repeatedly in the past, with both

Tory and Labour governments, as the Russians built up the number of 'diplomats' in their London embassy to eighty-three compared with only forty in the British embassy in Moscow.

To their everlasting credit, Heath and Douglas-Home took the more realistic line that national security was being gravely prejudiced by a massive espionage and subversion operation and something had to be done about it.

It was also necessary to give their action the widest publicity. This began with deliberate leaks from Whitehall and it was agreed that MI5 should be permitted to draw further attention to the KGB threat by releasing a film it had taken four years previously of a Russian diplomat-spy collecting information left by a British atomic scientist in a 'dead letter box' – a secret hiding-place – in Surrey. For good measure the film included an interview with the scientist who had been working for MI5.

In hardening their resolve the Prime Minister and Foreign Secretary were strongly supported by a most able and determined authority on the KGB, Sir Dick White, the only man who has been head of both MI5 and MI6 and was at that time serving as Coordinator of Intelligence in the Cabinet. In the past he had repeatedly warned that the number of Soviet agents in Britain was so great that it was saturating the efforts of MI5 to shadow and control them. That is the in-built weakness of a small counter-espionage or counter-Intelligence agency. It can take up to eight agents to watch one suspect round the clock. So the opposition simply has to put in so many potential spies that it becomes impossible to watch them all. Before 1971, however, not even Churchill had been prepared to stage a public showdown with the Kremlin over the KGB, apparently on Foreign Office insistence that, unless the Russians are granted outrageous concessions, they will make life insupportable for the British diplomats in Moscow.

The Russian politicians whined and pretended to be extremely hurt by the resolute action, as they always do and as Brezhnev did to bully the Americans out of producing the neutron bomb, which could neutralize his advantage in battle-tanks. But they knew they were guilty and there was nothing they could do about it.

Indeed they were unusually relaxed about Lyalin once he was exposed. MI5 had been working on him for some time as a possible defector and he finally decided to transfer his allegiance after being arrested on a drunken-driving charge, which was never brought 'in the public interest' partly because of the threat of KGB revenge against him but also because he had proved so useful. Lyalin could not be brought into court because he had undergone immediate plastic surgery, organized by MI5, and it was essential that he should not show his new face in public.

The KGB's reaction was swift and predictable. As the number of agents it could house in Soviet missions was to be limited, at least for some time, it concentrated on increasing its efforts through the satellite agencies, the Czechs in particular.

By early 1974 such a large number of Czech 'diplomats' had been caught spying that they had to be expelled. But this time Heath forbade publicity, though it might have helped him to win the March election. With McGahey and other Communists hoping to use the miners' strike to bring the government down, news of yet another round-up of KGB operators could have been most useful to those, like myself, always prepared to publicize hard evidence of Soviet activity against Britain.

The Czech situation was drawn to Heath's attention by Julian Amery, who told him that MI5 had proof of blatant abuse of diplomatic privilege by thirteen 'diplomats', including the ambassador, but Heath decided against any public use of it, being so certain that he was going to win the election anyway and fearing that the Labour opposition would claim that the expulsions had been cooked up as a vote-catching gimmick. News of the Czech treachery and the thirteen expulsions did not leak out until after the Tory defeat.

With the return of a Labour government new opportunities for the KGB were opened up by the £950 million credit which Wilson provided for Russia to increase Soviet purchases from Britain early in 1975. Margaret Thatcher, the Tory opposition leader, was quick to point out that this soft loan freed roubles for the Kremlin to spend on weapons but the quickest result was an automatic increase in the size of the Soviet trade mission and the arrival of a new body of Russians available for KGB exploitation. These were inspectors, whom the Russians insisted on basing in all the factories and shipyards from which they were to buy. No limit has been imposed on the number of these inspectors who quickly exceeded 100 and are expected to increase, throwing a further strain on MI5. No comparable British inspectors are based in Soviet factories.

Expanding trade with Russia has also provided the KGB and other Soviet Intelligence agencies with new facilities for penetrating

Britain's naval defences and the Sea Lords are in no doubt that they are being fully utilized. Their concern is so great that I was specially briefed on the position by Admiral Sir Ray Lygo, then Vice Chief of the Naval Staff.

Instead of having to station obvious spyships outside the three-mile limit, the Russians can now send specially equipped merchant ships into ports to lie almost alongside their targets. This is made easy for them because the main naval ports, Portsmouth, Devonport in Plymouth and Rosyth in Scotland, all have commercial facilities close by them, Portsmouth's new container terminal being right in the middle of the naval complex. By putting in at Aberdeen and other Scottish ports, Soviet merchant ships can monitor the main radars of the UK air defence system.

The miniaturization of equipment which used to be so cumbersome that it could not be concealed, is now enabling the merchant ships to carry out short-range electronic surveillance of warships and shore installations with little fear of detection. It is difficult to know when a ship is listening in to communications and radar frequencies and almost impossible to jam it. All a visiting ship has to do is record what it hears and take the tapes back home for analysis. And the only thing a British warship or shore installation can do if it suspects its communications and radar operations are being bugged is to shut down. So a succession of Soviet ships can seriously interfere with naval activities.

Having no power to prevent any merchant ship using the commercial facilities, the Navy has to put up with seeing the Hammer and Sickle flying far too close for comfort. But nothing comparable can be done in Russia where the naval harbours are entirely separate from commercial ports and are barred to foreign shipping.

The KGB is also believed to be using visiting ships to plant and interchange its agents and to confer with subversive organizations in Britain. In Russia the movements of British merchant seamen visiting commercial ports are restricted but Soviet crews ashore in Britain can go anywhere and meet anyone. This also applies to the crews of Soviet ships 'on government service' – hydrographic survey, oceanographic and other research vessels which put in for 'rest and recreation'.

Because time limits any immigration and security checks on Russian seamen, who claim to speak no English, it is sometimes difficult to ensure that when Ivan, who may be a relief KGB agent, goes ashore, it is not Vladimir who reboards. There is nothing to stop Russian sailors already in Aberdeen from hiring cars and motoring anywhere they like. An American source alleges that Russian tank commanders brought in as seamen have been driving on routes from possible landing areas. This is unconfirmed but Navy chiefs do not discount it. As Admiral Lygo told me, they are seriously considering an even more sinister possibility – that merchant ships or research vessels visiting ports could plant delayed-action mines timed to explode weeks later as part of a surprise attack on NATO. This could be catastrophic because so much of the rapid reinforcement of NATO by the USA is scheduled to take place through Britain's ports.

The Navy is understandably silent about actual events but I have established that Soviet survey ships have repeatedly made excuses to get into Plymouth while nuclear submarines were being moved. They have tried to get into Leith for 'rest and recreation' to bug Rosyth during NATO exercises.

The Navy can refuse docking permission to a ship officially 'on government service' but it has no rights over Soviet merchantmen which are also really on government service. Even when the Navy tries to prevent a landing the ship sometimes turns up, claiming that the refusal message was never received. One ship which was refused entry for 'urgent supplies' went on cruising outside the three-mile limit for weeks.

Now that fishing by Russian trawlers off Britain is restricted, Soviet factory ships are standing offshore to buy fish and the Navy has little doubt that these too are equipped with Intelligence-gathering equipment. On top of all this there are undisguised Intelligence ships monitoring Polaris submarine movements in and out of the Clyde and rocket firings in Cardigan Bay.

The Navy would like to see far fewer Russian merchant ships in British ports but the Foreign Office and Trade Department are encouraging them, shrugging off the espionage danger as one of the penalties of living in a free society. As they put it, 'Trade with the Communists is a reality; war with them is only a possibility.'

Russia's Intelligence interests have also spread to the oil rigs and platforms in the North Sea. There is fair reason for this. For years the British and NATO defence authorities would have dearly liked to have set up underwater and aerial listening posts far out in the North Sea but the costs were prohibitive. Then, for commercial reasons, structures on which such devices could be mounted suddenly appeared. It would have been remiss of the defence chiefs had they not at least tried to secure permission to make use of the opportunity and the Russians are fully aware of this.

Certainly some of the rigs and platforms are not used in this way. One of my friends, who was head of European operations for the American Amoco oil company, decided that, as he had nothing to hide, the best way to stop the Russians from harassing his oil and gas platforms was to invite them aboard to carry out an inspection. This he did by a formal invitation to the Soviet embassy in London, even offering to provide a helicopter to ferry out the visitors. Taken unawares by such a bold reaction, all the Russians did was to disclaim any knowledge that any Soviet vessel had been trying to examine any platforms.

*Chapter Six*

# Civil Servants and the KGB

WHITEHALL'S top management, the senior civil servants and especially the 'permanent secretaries' club' – the heads of the departments of State – continue in office whatever governments may come and go. Far from being mere instruments of policy laid down by elected politicians, they exercise considerable power by virtue of their influence and they are extremely tenacious when their authority is threatened. Quite often what a minister would like to do in pursuit of government policy is whittled down or even reversed by the 'considered views' of his departmental officials. Senior civil servants can often frustrate the government's intentions by long delays intended to hold their position until a general election when, in the endless Whitehall game of snakes and ladders, 'everything may be back to square one'. I once heard a permanent secretary stoutly defend the inertia of the Whitehall machine because it curbs the politicians from making changes too rapidly.

Because they are part of that machine and stay in it so long, they have far greater access to secret information and deeper knowledge of what is really happening than ministers, who rarely last longer than two years in one post.

Such men therefore present tempting targets for KGB penetration and though it is hard to imagine a more difficult objective for a spy than the typical senior civil servant, the Russians occasionally try, as evidenced by an event which befell a Whitehall permanent secretary deeply concerned with defence and a member of several secret committees. He wishes to remain nameless so I will call him 'Sir A'.

He was driving down a country lane one Sunday afternoon, on his way to see one of his children at boarding-school, when a car overtook him very slowly and grazed the side of his vehicle. The erring driver apologized most profusely and offered to pay for the very minor damage. Having inspected it Sir A was pleasant about it and when they exchanged names and addresses he found that the man, who had literally thrust himself upon him, was a colonel in the Russian embassy. Sir A said he would have the damage repaired and would send him the bill.

A bill for £26 was duly sent off to the embassy but the colonel responded by saying that as he had no bank account in Britain he must pay in cash. Further, he insisted on handing it over personally to Sir A over lunch at a West End restaurant frequently used by Russians. Sir A demurred, but the colonel was adamant.

Sir A then consulted his ministry's security chief who said that he would much prefer it if he did not meet the Russian. There was no legal way in which the ministry could pay the £26 and Sir A was determined to get it so he turned up for the lunch, after being assured that the security authorities would give him cover.

The Russian was charming but instead of handing the money over discreetly he counted the pound notes out on to the table in a most obvious manner. Sir A was sure that somehow this process was being photographed to produce what could be a very compromising picture of a most senior and easily recognizable Whitehall defence official receiving money from a Soviet military attaché. He told me that he looked around carefully but could see no evidence of anyone taking an interest though he had not taken much notice of the staff.

Nor could he spot the MI5 man who was supposed to give him cover. Was he also, perhaps, a waiter?

Nothing more has come of this event to date. Sir A, having warned the security authorities, was not in an easily blackmailable position and has given the KGB no reason to make use of the episode. But I have little doubt that somewhere in the KGB archives in Moscow there is a photograph filed away waiting for possible use one day.

The persistent use of certain London restaurants by Russians has often made me wonder whether the KGB has an arrangement for surveillance at them. At others MI5 certainly has or can secure it at short notice.

A similar service is rightly available for armed bodyguards allotted to Cabinet ministers. Recently, when I lunched Roy Mason, the Secretary of State for Northern Ireland, at a famous restaurant near Piccadilly Circus I noticed a rather well-built man in his thirties lunching alone at a table about ten yards away from us with no obstruction in between. He meant nothing to me; but as we prepared to leave Mason nodded and he departed to wait unobtrusively on the pavement outside. He had reconnoitred the restaurant that morning, secured the right table to cover mine and sat quietly with his loaded pistol in his shoulder holster – just in case.

The fear that the KGB might have been rather more successful with an important figure in the Cabinet Office than they were with Sir A has led to special investigations by the security service since Callaghan took over as Prime Minister. This is what happened in this strange affair.

A certain Labour peer, who wishes to be unnamed though he gave me the information personally, received a complaint from a Foreign Office source that a high-level civil servant, whom we may call 'Sir X', was not only a Communist but a Soviet agent of sympathy. Believing this could be true, he sought the assistance of another peer who had been a Labour minister. This man had also heard of the fear from another source so he went to report the matter to the Cabinet Secretary, Sir John Hunt. Through another channel the head of the Foreign Office, Sir Michael Palliser, was also alerted.

Hunt assured the two peers that an inquiry would be made and later reported to them that the previous positive vetting of the suspect and the later inquiries had provided no grounds for considering him as a security risk.

Later, it was alleged that this same suspect had infiltrated ultra-left-wingers into other positions in Whitehall, so Sir John was approached again. Once more, after further inquiries, he assured my contacts that neither Sir X nor those he had recommended for Whitehall posts were security risks. There is no doubt, however, that Sir X, who refused to comment on the situation to me, holds Left-wing views and cultivates Left-wing friends. At the time of writing he is still in his appointment.

The way the KGB recruits civil servants, scientists and others who may prove useful was made plain to me early in my career as a result of an internal struggle for power in one of the trade unions, the Association of Scientific Workers, in which I was marginally involved.

The General Secretary, Ben Smith, had been a sufficiently dedicated Communist to have learned Russian and to have been to Moscow for training, but after observing fellow British Communists using methods against other Britons of which he profoundly disapproved, he had become alienated from the cause. One of his senior staff, however, who had been trained at the Lenin School in Moscow, remained devoted to securing revolution in Britain and Smith was sure that he was submitting long reports on Association members to the Russian embassy.

One lunch-hour he opened the man's desk and removed a sheaf of papers which turned out to be a very full account of a certain scientist's background, his personal weaknesses and other factors in his life which might lay him open to pressure or blackmail.

Smith hung on to the papers for a few days then confronted his colleague with the fact that he had them, declaring, 'Either you resign from the Association or I give the papers to Chapman Pincher who will blow the story in the *Daily Express*'. The man quit without an argument.

Smith gave me the facts on condition that I did not print them at the time but gave me permission to pass them on to MI5. It turned out that the official was one of many such talent-scouts submitting personality reports which had several purposes. Through them Moscow had already recruited a few sympathizers with special qualifications who left Britain to work in Russia. There were others so sympathetic that they might be persuaded to spy for ideological reasons, as the atomic scientist Klaus Fuchs did. Still more were thought to be open to bribery or sexual corruption. The KGB was also building up a dossier of people who might be specially valuable if Britain were invaded.

Such talent-scouts, who are still active, cannot be prosecuted because they are careful to do nothing which contravenes the Official Secrets Acts.

While great prominence is given to KGB victories culminating in the defection of people like Maclean, Blake and Philby, far more men defect from the KGB to the West, including deserters from the Red Army. A few volunteer their services simply by dropping in at the nearest convenient embassy, though before they can be accepted inquiries have to be made to eliminate the possibility that they are loyal KGB agents posing as defectors, a few of whom have managed to gain entry to both Britain and the USA for nefarious purposes.

Successful defections, however, are usually the result of a long 'courtship' in which a Western agent, posing as a diplomat or visiting businessman, has cleverly played on the weaknesses, fears and doubts of the subject.

Some Communists defect to escape victimization or arrest in their own countries. Others decide to switch allegiance to solve personal problems like family strife or the attraction of women living in the West, some of whom may be used as bait. Money or the prospect of a better financial life in the West may also be a major cause, but a few defect because they have genuinely come to hate the Communist system with its inbuilt rigours and brutality.

Occasionally the mechanics of the 'defector programme' reaches public notice because something goes wrong. This happened, for instance, in the case of Vsevolod Nadeinsky, a minor Soviet agent whose cover was the Intergovernmental Maritime Consultative Organization in London. Nadeinsky had fallen in love with an English secretary and efforts were made to induce him to defect, which he decided to do. Understandably, the KGB was determined to make him change his mind and put such pressures on him through his wife and mother in Moscow with damaging publicity claiming that MI5 had drugged and forcibly detained him, that he finally returned home where, no doubt, he had a hard time.

There have been diplomatically embarrassing scenes at London Airport and outside the Soviet embassy due to sudden changes of mind by would-be defectors. But the risk is always worth while because, beyond question, defectors are the richest source of Iron

Curtain Intelligence, second, I would say, only to surveillance satellites.

Once safely in the West, defectors are subjected to interrogation for many months because, while they may quickly provide all the information they consider to be important, other facts of significance to Western Intelligence may emerge during the prolonged questioning. Many are then given a change of name because of the real danger of revenge by the KGB assassination department and are never heard of publicly. A few, however, achieve some prominence by writing their memoirs.

I do not wish to discourage any potential defector but many of those defecting either way find the emotional adjustment extremely difficult after so many years in such a different society.

Victor Kravchenko, whose book *I Chose Freedom* became a bestseller, eventually shot himself in the USA.

When I was last in Australia I found that Vladimir Petrov, the rather small-time Soviet diplomat who defected there, lives a dull and friendless life. That is also true of several Iron Curtain defectors living in Britain, if only, perhaps, because they are never really trusted.

That the KGB looks after its own is beyond question, spies like Maclean, Blake and Philby being conducted to safe havens, while others are rescued through exchanges. That it eliminates its traitors, if given the chance, is also certain. General Walter Krivitsky, who defected to the USA, was found murdered in an hotel room in New York four years later. Konstantin Volkov, a KGB man who tried to contact British security in Turkey to trade secrets for money, was drugged, smuggled out of Istanbul and murdered in Russia after Philby had alerted the KGB to his imminent defection. Bogdan Stashinsky, a KGB agent who defected to the West in 1961, confessed to the murder of two Ukrainian exile leaders with a cyanide pistol. The fate of Leon Trotsky, who was pursued by Kremlin agents for eleven years before his skull was smashed in with an ice-pick, must always loom in the minds of defectors.

'I shall not need to see your departmental reports today . . . I had lunch with Chapman Pincher during the week.' Cartoon which appeared in the *UK Press Gazette* in January 1967 following complaints from the Defence Ministry and other departments to the author. (UK Press Gazette)

# GADF
## DAILY
## IDENTITY CARD

Nº 007

Name...... H. CHAPMAN PINCHER

Representing ...... DAILY EXPRESS

Date of
Expiry ...... 31 DEC 1964

Signature......

*Above* When the Defence Ministry first issued special identity cards to accredited defence correspondents in 1964, the top civil servants there paid Chapman Pincher the compliment of numbering his 007 — the identity number of James Bond.
*Right* Century House, the headquarters of the Secret Intelligence Service (MI6) near Westminster Bridge, London. (London Express)

*Above* Michael Foot, then a Labour backbencher, marching from the Aldermaston nuclear weapons station to Trafalgar Square with the Campaign for Nuclear Disarmament. Later he joined and remained in Labour Cabinets which, in spite of general defence cuts, continued to spend huge sums on Polaris missiles and other nuclear weapons. (London Express)

*Below left* Lord George-Brown, the former Foreign Secretary who nearly became Prime Minister but later resigned from the Labour Party on the grounds that it was being taken over by Left extremists. (London Express)

*Below right* The late Lord Bradwell, formerly Tom Driberg, the Labour MP who became Chairman of the Labour Party and was believed by many to be a Soviet 'agent of sympathy'. (ABC Television)

## Spy men kept a Premier taped

**Chapman Pincher Exclusive**

# WILSON WAS BUGGED AT No 10

Wilson: He complained

THE suspicion of Sir Harold Wilson that he was "bugged" by British security men when Prime Minister has turned out to be fully justified.

Inquiries have established that he was under electronic surveillance in No. 10 Downing Street on several occasions during his eight years there.

Sir Harold has revealed that he believes certain officials in M.I.5, the counter-espionage organisation, suspected the existence of a Communist "cell" in his Government.

He has even said that a small number of M.I.5 men suspected that he and his secretary, Lady Falkender, were part of it.

### Questions

Tory M.P.s want to know without delay why the security men went to such unprecedented lengths.

**WERE THEY** anxious about certain Ministers with whom Sir Harold had to deal?

**WERE THEY** aiming for high-level civil servants? (One senior Whitehall official is under investigation for suspected Communist affiliations).

**WERE THEY** possibly suspicious of one or more of the numerous personal friends who visited Sir Harold at Number 10?

Tory M.P.s are hoping to question Prime Minister Mr James Callaghan in Parliament.

One, Mr Peter Blaker, wants an independent inquiry into Sir Harold's reported allegations of "incompetence" in the security set-up.

Security chiefs themselves are curious to know how Sir Harold came to be aware that he was being bugged. The secret could have been known to very few people.

He learned about it when the surveillance was at its height a few months before he resigned in April 1976.

This activity by British security may have followed the unmasking of Guenter Guillaume, the close political aide of Willy Brandt, the former West German Chancellor. Guillaume was jailed in December 1975 as a Soviet bloc spy.

Leaks he revealed while under interrogation — which may have proved to be quite false — could have driven British security chiefs to check further on Number 10.

Surveillance operations are cloaked in such secrecy that it is not certain that they were carried out by M.I.5—properly known as the Security Service—though the

### Who was their target? Quiz faces Callaghan

results on tape would be passed to it.

My inquiries suggest that "bugs" were planted and removed when necessary by a special electronic unit linked with G.C.H.Q. — Government Communications Headquarters.

#### Cover

This is the cover-name for a Department dealing mainly with the interception and decoding of foreign diplomatic messages. A specialist unit carries out the routine cracking of secret Whitehall Departments to ensure their have not been bugged by Russia's K.G.B. or others.

These men must have periodic entry to every important office, including the Cabinet Office where Sir Harold worked and received visitors.

Security chiefs are extremely

bitter because Sir Harold has allowed his suspicions to be seen as the basis of a smear against M.I.5. They fear it may have started a campaign to denigrate both M.I.5 and M.I.6, the Secret Service, as has already happened with the C.I.A. in the United States.

"The K.G.B. must be delighted with what is happening," a former security official told me yesterday.

"When Sir Harold was Prime Minister he always claimed that the interests of national security were paramount."

My inquiries have confirmed that Sir Harold also believed he was in danger of being spied on by the C.I.A. He and his friend Lord Weidenfeld, the publisher to take letters to Washington complaining about it.

This was done over the heads of the British security authorities, who deny any C.I.A. involvement.

---

**Pocket Cartoon**
By Osbert Lancaster

"I hope, dear, you're beginning to regret all those unkind things you're always saying about MI5!"

---

Front cover story on the bugging of Harold Wilson at No. 10, *Daily Express* 29 July 1977. (London Express)

*Above* Wilson and his personal aides on board HMS *Fearless* during the 1968 talks with Ian Smith, Prime Minister of Rhodesia. The man between Wilson and Marcia is the late Michael Halls, then the Prime Minister's principal private secretary. The other men, from left to right, are Michael Palliser, now Head of the Foreign Office, Trevor Lloyd Hughes, the chief Press adviser, William Housden, the chauffeur-valet Wilson inherited from Harold Macmillan, and Joseph Stone, the Prime Minister's doctor.

*Left* Mrs Marjorie Halls, widow of Michael Halls, former principal private secretary to Sir Harold Wilson. She is holding the writ that she served on the civil service department, claiming that her husband's premature death had been hastened by the extra work imposed on him by the personal problems of Marcia Williams. (London Express)

*Above left* Oleg Lyalin, the KGB officer whose defection in 1971 gave the Heath government the final excuse to expel 105 other KGB men who had been posing as diplomats or trade delegates. (London Express) *Above right* Greville Wynne, the businessman jailed by the Russians for spying in collaboration with the Soviet traitor Oleg Penkovsky, pictured in 1973. (London Express)

The Anglo-Soviet exchange of the KGB spy 'Gordon Lonsdale', whose real name was Konon Molody, for the British businessman and MI6 agent, Greville Wynne. It took place at Checkpoint Heerstrasse in Berlin at dawn, 22 April 1964. For his world exclusive reports on this event, the author was named Reporter of the Year in the Granada 'What the Papers Say' awards. (London Express)

*Above* Donald Maclean and his wife Melinda, who joined him in Moscow after his runaway defection, photographed at the cremation service for Burgess who died of heart trouble in 1963. Later Melinda left Maclean for Philby. (Associated Press)

*Left* Guy Burgess, who defected with Maclean to Russia in 1951, pictured there ten years later. (London Express)

*Above* Harold 'Kim' Philby, the KGB spy inside the British Secret Service celebrates his 'clearance' by Harold Macmillan of being the Third Man in the Burgess and Maclean scandal. He gave a Press conference at which he could hardly have seemed more confident or relaxed. (London Express)

Philby in 1968, photographed in Moscow. (Paris-Match)

*Chapter Seven*

⌒◇§§§◇⌒

# The Spy inside the Admiralty

A CLASSIC example of a civil servant whose character weakness was detected by a talent-scout, reported to the KGB and then exploited, with grave damage to Britain's interests, is provided by the tragic story of John Vassall.

I will deal with the Vassall case in some detail because I was a major witness at the ensuing tribunal as a result of which two Fleet Street reporters from other newspapers ended up in prison for contempt for refusing to reveal their sources of information, while any serious attempt to make me reveal mine was studiously avoided. The case also assumed important political overtones because of inaccurate newspaper reports, some interesting aspects of which have not been revealed before.

John Vassall, who since his release from prison in 1972 has changed his name, was a twenty-nine-year-old junior clerk of established homosexual habits when he was sent to work in the British embassy in Moscow in 1954. There, through the attentions of Sigmund Mikhailski, a homosexual KGB agent employed in the British embassy as an interpreter, his weakness was quickly brought to the attention of KGB officers who used it to trap him into spying for them. As he describes in detail in his book, *Vassall, the Autobiography of a Spy,* he was 'surprised' by KGB officers during a homosexual encounter after incriminating pictures of previous adventures had been taken. By threat of exposure and other menaces he was frightened into becoming a Soviet agent, an assignment he carried out with success for seven years.

After returning to London in 1956 he was attached to Naval

Intelligence following positive vetting which failed to reveal any suggestions of homosexuality, though the Russians had detected this propensity soon after his arrival in Moscow. He abstracted secret documents, handing some over to KGB controllers for photograph-ing and later photographed others himself. He was arrested in September 1962 and sentenced to eighteen years' imprisonment.

The Labour opposition at that time always attacked the govern-ment on alleged failures in security and there were, inevitably, demands for an inquiry into how Vassall had been able to spy without detection for so long and why a homosexual had been recruited when this habit was supposed to be a bar to any post requring access to secrets. It seems unlikely, however, that such an inquiry would have been sanctioned but for the fact that two minis-ters, Lord Carrington, then First Lord of the Admiralty, and Thomas Galbraith, previously the Civil Lord, had been accused in the Press of negligence in terms which demanded an answer.

A three-man tribunal headed by Lord Radcliffe, a Lord of Appeal, was set up by Harold Macmillan to investigate the case, publicly as far as possible, and to report to Parliament. It had powers to require witnesses to attend and give evidence on oath and it opened its proceedings in London on 17 January 1963, a highly intriguing date from the security authorities' viewpoint, as I shall explain.

In the resulting report two of my ablest colleagues were censured for inaccurate reporting in circumstances which need never have happened had liaison inside the newspaper office been closer.

Months earlier, on the day after Vassall's conviction, I had explained in a long article how he had been caught. Security chiefs had failed to detect any leakages until a tip from a Russian Intelli-gence man defecting to the West put them on the trail – just as they had failed to detect Fuchs and Blake until alerted from foreign sources. I did not identify the defector for security reasons though I knew him to go by the name of Anatoli Dolnytsin.

If Lord Radcliffe had been as insistent on finding out the real source of my information as he might have been, I would have been obliged to accompany the other two journalists to prison for refusing to disclose it, but he had no intention of doing that because he had been advised by the security authorities not to question me too deeply. I have reason to believe that they would have preferred to ignore me altogether but the tribunal had to call me as a witness because my two colleagues, Percy Hoskins and the late Douglas

Clark, were deeply involved in the allegations against Lord Carrington.

Journalists tend to ignore articles written by their colleagues, usually because they are too busy with their next assignments, and neither Hoskins nor Clark had read mine. Pursuing the Vassall case with a senior police source, who should have been utterly reliable, Hoskins came up with a completely conflicting report, further developed by Clark, which he published in all good faith a fortnight after mine. He claimed that eighteen months previously, during investigations into Gordon Lonsdale's Portland naval spy ring, evidence was found pointing to the existence of another spy inside the Admiralty. If this were true, as Hoskins believed, then Carrington and the Navy security chiefs had known of the existence of a spy in their midst for eighteen months and done nothing about it.

Several newspapers had also published letters written by Galbraith to Vassall, who had worked for him, projecting them in such a way as to suggest an over-friendly relationship. These false allegations also required investigation by the tribunal.

As the published tribunal evidence shows, when I was asked by my counsel where I had secured my information that the clue to Vassall had been provided by a defector, I made the rather weak statement that it was a conclusion I had drawn from a conversation with Colonel Sammy Lohan, later of D notice fame (see Chapter Twenty-four), in the Defence Ministry. It was quite true that this conversation had taken place and that Lohan had warned me against falling into the trap of linking Vassall with the Lonsdale spy ring, but I had already been informed about the defector by a minister and told Lohan so without indicating the source.

It had been agreed in advance that I should mention Lohan's name to the tribunal, which should obviate the need for further questioning. Whether Lohan informed the security authorities about this or not I do not know but I was aware before I appeared before the tribunal that no serious attempt to discover my real source would be made. I am not suggesting there was any collusion between Radcliffe and myself. There certainly was not but he soft-pedalled on my evidence, as I had been assured he would.

He wanted to hear no more about the defector, who was still in Britain at the time assisting MI5. And all he did was to nod sagely when I lamely suggested that the reason I knew that Vassall had been positively vetted was because 'someone, somewhere along the line' had told me.

When Hoskins gave evidence, he was not asked, as might reasonably have been expected, why he had published his story when I had already given *Daily Express* readers a version which, if true, meant that his must be false. Further, any mention of the defector was studiously avoided in the published report which records only that the clue to Vassall had come from 'Intelligence sources'.

I was soon to discover why the tribunal had been so anxious to avoid any move which might reveal further information about Dolnytsin in public, especially as the security authorities were not sure how much I had been told about him. This same defector had given further leads during his debriefing by the CIA which, having been patiently and ably developed by MI5, had provided the final proof that Kim Philby had indeed been a Soviet agent and was also the Third Man in the Burgess and Maclean affair.

In between the conviction of Vassall in October and the tribunal, a senior MI6 official, whom I know, had been sent to Beirut to confront Philby with his guilt. In the safety of the Lebanese capital, where he could not be apprehended, Philby had blandly admitted the truth and while I was being interrogated by the tribunal on 14 January, the Intelligence and security authorities were biting their nails wondering what he was about to do as a result. So the last thing they wanted was any cross-examination which might lead to mention of his name at such a critical time. Philby in fact disappeared from Beirut to Moscow only eleven days later, while the tribunal was still taking evidence, but by that time any danger that Dolnytsin might be mentioned had passed.

As I had known the truth about Vassall's detection in greater detail than I had revealed in the newspaper, I greatly regret that I did not alert my colleagues to it individually. I suppose I thought that they would pick up the defector information from the article I had written. In any case I fancy that Percy Hoskins, who had the finest police sources of any journalist ever and is still the doyen of crime reporters, with a magnificent record for accuracy, would have felt driven to trust his own information.

Inquiries I made later led me to suspect that Hoskins was deliberately put on to a false trail by his police source who had probably been alerted by security to wean his Press contacts off the defector story – the reverse of the advice I had been given. The leads

THE SPY INSIDE THE ADMIRALTY

from Dolnytsin had come to MI5 via US Intelligence and because of the Philby implications the security authorities may have decided to encourage the spread of an alternative story. I was able to establish that the tribunal had been told *in camera* of the false trail and how it came to exist. One senior investigator indicated that he 'did not discourage' the story Hoskins used because it would serve to protect the real source.

Dolnytsin's name which, following the standard practice for defectors, would be a fake to help in concealing his identity, did not become public until July 1963. The way that this happened marks another extraordinary incident in MI5's strange machinations.

The *Daily Telegraph* had secured information that Dolnytsin was in Britain helping MI5, and efforts to induce the editor of that paper to suppress the information on the grounds that the defector's life might be at risk had failed. It was therefore agreed between the Director-General of MI5 and the chairman of the D notice committee that some revenge on the *Telegraph* was justified. The simplest way of wreaking this was by giving the story to every other newspaper, thereby depriving the *Telegraph* of its scoop. But how could MI5, which officially does not exist, do this?

The answer was ready to hand. The secretary of the D notice committee, Colonel Sammy Lohan, who was on leave, was hauled in to issue a statement over the Press Association wire service, which reaches all papers, that Dolnytsin's name should on no account be mentioned. The authorities calculated that this would ensure that every paper would print it on the legitimate grounds that the authorities themselves had been foolish enough to make it public.

That is what happened.

It later transpired that Dolnytsin was supposed to have defected in 1961 from the Soviet embassy in Helsinki, where he was working as a KGB officer under diplomatic cover, but the situation was further complicated by two other developments. First the Russians said that the only Anatoli Dolnytsin they knew about had formerly worked in Britain but was safely in the Ministry of Foreign Affairs in Moscow – which turned out to be true. Then the CIA leaked information in Washington to the effect that Dolnytsin had only visited Britain with its permission after an American debriefing lasting eighteen months. The CIA chiefs were said to be shocked by the publicity given to the defector.

None of this made much sense until action taken under the

American Freedom of Information Act in 1977 showed that the man who had defected to the CIA in 1961 with so much valuable information was really called Major Anatoli Golitsin. I suspect that the Dolnytsin announcement was partly a joint MI5/CIA ruse to confuse the issue, once the *Telegraph* had discovered that the defector was in Britain.

Creating this kind of confusion, which security men call 'muddying the waters', is common enough and is applied on what seem to be superficial pretexts. It is widely believed for example that, following a reorganization in the Defence Ministry, MI5 and MI6 are now officially known as DI5 and DI6 respectively. This is complete nonsense. Both departments were taken out of the Defence Ministry many years before the reorganization, MI5 being under the Home Office and MI6 under the Foreign Office. So no change in the nickname initials has ever been made. Once when I suggested to a senior MI6 official that I should make this clear in the newspaper he said, 'Why not leave it alone? It helps us to keep the issue confused.'

It was Golitsin, code-named 'Stone' in American documents, who gave information which led to the suspicion that Hugh Gaitskell, who died of an obscure disease aged fifty-six, had been assassinated by the KGB to get rid of a future Labour Prime Minister who was far too anti-Communist for the Kremlin's taste. After being turned over to James Angleton, the CIA's most knowledgeable man on KGB activities, Golitsin had claimed that before defecting he had heard from the chief of the Northern European section of the KGB that the organization was planning to murder a leader of an opposition party in his area. Gaitskell was the only leader who eventually fitted this prediction.

At this point I must record that Baroness Gaitskell, the leader's widow, does not believe that her husband died from anything but natural causes. Autopsy showed that he died of a rare virus disease called systemic lupus erythematosus. However, I have established from first-hand sources that the possibility that he was assassinated has never been entirely ruled out so far as MI6 is concerned. It seems that Gaitskell, who was planning a visit to Moscow, had dined at one of the Soviet bloc embassies shortly before he had been taken ill. Further, there is a division of the KGB which specializes in assassinations and has used not only poison sprays but has attempted to adapt the products of Soviet germ warfare for its purposes. Josef Josten, the Czech exile who lives in London, suffered from a mysterious disease for two years and is still under treatment from what he suspects were the tender activities of Czech Intelligence.

The Civil Service spy who did the greatest damage to Britain was the former German scientist Klaus Fuchs, who betrayed some of the most secret details of American and British nuclear weapons to the Russians at the time when the information was most valuable to their efforts to become an atomic power. The case of this ideological spy demonstrates the enormous value of a 'defector in place' – a man already inside a secret establishment whose services as a spy have been secured.

Fuchs's own daily work on the theoretical physics of nuclear explosives and the advanced mathematics involved was of immense interest to Russia and the only risk he ran was in being detected in the act of passing the results. He had no need to open safes or look at files he should not see. In addition, other secret information fell into his lap, as is well illustrated by the untold experience of my friend John Duckworth, later chief of the National Research Development Corporation. Soon after the war ended Duckworth, who had been working mainly on radar, returned to his first love, nuclear physics, specializing in the study of neutrons at the new atomic research establishment at Harwell. His immediate chief was Robert Cockburn (now Sir), and he was asked to consider the possibility that a beam of neutrons might be used as a ray weapon to detonate atomic bombs carried by enemy aircraft. The project was listed as 'atomic', which was a classification even higher than top secret.

After a certain amount of experimental work it was necessary to have some calculations which were beyond the mathematical competence of those in charge. So Duckworth was asked to refer his problems to the chief nuclear theoretician who was none other than Dr Fuchs. A little later the services of another member of the Harwell staff were recruited and this scientist was Dr Bruno Pontecorvo, who later defected to Russia and who, according to MI5, was undoubtedly a spy. So in this tiny team of ultra-secret investigators two were enemy agents reporting to Moscow.

It was just as well that the neutron-beam experiments came to nothing.

A copy of a detailed interview with Fuchs in Stafford Prison in 1953 is in my possession. It records that when the FBI interrogated him in prison he admitted giving the Russians information on the H-bomb from 1947 onwards, including some of the theoretical mechanics of triggering off the heavy-hydrogen charge, and, while claiming that they would still have to do most of the work for themselves, thought they would make one in three to five years.

It was generally believed that Fuchs did most of his spying in Britain and that MI5 was greatly at fault for failing to detect him. In fact most of his treachery was committed in the United States where he was run by a KGB officer who, though almost unknown in the West, must rank among the most successful spy-masters of all time. His name was Anatoli Yakovlev, who worked under the cover of being a vice-consul at the Soviet consulate in New York. It was his highly professional planning which allowed untrained spies like Fuchs and David Greenglass, an American soldier who worked at Los Alamos, to betray secrets of the atomic bomb's detailed structure. It was his control over the spy network, laboriously built up by colleagues, which enabled American couriers like Harry Gold and Julius Rosenberg to pick up not only nuclear secrets for dispatch to Moscow but many others, including radar developments.

Only the stupidity of some Russian delegates to United Nations discussions on the control of atomic energy in 1947 eventually led to the exposure of Yakovlev and his agents. They referred to secret American techniques and even used code-words which alerted the American delegation, led by the admirable Bernard Baruch, to the existence of serious leakages. It took the FBI a long time to track down all the traitors. By that time Yakovlev, who was called as defendant on a capital charge of espionage in New York's Southern District Court on 15 March 1951, had fled home to Russia.

The slender lead which finally enabled MI5's ace interrogator, Jim Skardon, to break Fuchs down and secure his confession, without which he could not have been tried, came from the FBI. The possibility that the KGB deliberately 'shopped' him because he had refused to supply further information, as he undoubtedly had, was rejected after serious consideration but it made sense because the benefit to Russia from Fuch's trial and conviction was probably greater than that accruing from his espionage activities. Russian scientists would have made the bomb from their own resources anyway but the damage to the Anglo-American interchange of nuclear information and to relations generally is still apparent.

For no reason connected with suspicion of espionage the USA had ended official exchange of nuclear weapons secrets with Britain immediately after the war and heroic attempts were made by the

Attlee government to restore it. All hopes of this faded after the Fuchs disaster. As a US senator put it at the time, 'Any proposal for pooling atomic secrets with Britain now would not have a chance in Congress and would not get ten votes in the Senate.'

When a Russian spying for the West is caught in Russia he is either summarily shot, or, if it suits the Soviet propagandists, put on show trial with minimal opportunity for defence and then shot. Any publicity in the Soviet media is angled at showing how villainous the British or Americans are in suborning Russian citizens and that is the end of it. In the West when a national is caught spying for the KGB the situation is different and the political results far more injurious.

In the first place it usually transpires that the spy has been operating successfully for years right under the noses of the security authorities, as happened not only with Fuchs but with Vassall, Philby and Maclean. MPs and the Press are then able to castigate the security services for failing to detect him and even for allowing him to be employed in the first place. In the process the KGB is seen to be highly efficient, which redounds to its credit, and the effect on relations with the allies of the nation involved can be quite severe.

I am in no doubt from talks I have had in Washington over the years that the worst effect of almost every trial of a British spy working for Russia has been the damage done to Anglo-American relations.

Harold Macmillan fully appreciated this, as he showed by his response when Carrington went to inform him, rather triumphantly, that the spy in the Admiralty, John Vassall, had been caught.

'Oh, that's bad news! Very bad news! You know, you should never catch a spy. Discover him and then control him but never catch him. A spy causes far more trouble once he's caught.'

American Intelligence has suffered its own problems and is sympathetic up to a point when British security falls short. But Congress and the Senate, which are ultimately responsible for keeping the Anglo-American alliance on defence and Intelligence in being, understandably take a more hostile attitude when American defence secrets are involved, as they usually are. So do senior officers of the Pentagon.

It has been largely to pacify American disquiet about British security that such extensive measures have been taken after each incident. When it was realized that Fuchs's disloyalty might be

rooted in his non-British birth a new rule demanded that civil
servants with access to secrets should be of British birth and preferably with both parents born in Britain. This led to very sad results
for some innocent people like Dr Boris Davison, who was forced to
quit the Harwell atomic station because he had relatives behind the
Iron Curtain. The security authorities feared that the Communists
might subject them to pressures which could prove intolerable for Dr
Davison and for others like him.

The fear of KGB blackmail in Whitehall and its outstations
reached such proportions that in 1969 the Institution of Professional
Civil Servants quietly informed me that the Home Office had issued
a directive to the police requiring them to report the names and
details of all civil servants charged with offences other than minor
motoring matters. The directive's purpose was to reveal possible
'defects of character' which might make them security risks. The
Institution, which is a union and had not been consulted, had
protested bitterly but the Home Office refused to withdraw its
directive.

There are two other aspects of the Fuchs case, which, though
insignificant, have remained firmly in my memory. On the day that
he was arrested I put my head round editor Arthur Christiansen's
door to tell him that night's big story was likely to be the discovery of
a spy inside Harwell.

'What's his name?' he asked.

'Fuchs.'

'Marvellous! I've always wanted to get that word into a headline.'

On the day after the Old Bailey trial my front-page report of it was
illustrated with photographs of actual documents which had been
secret when Fuchs had handed them over to his Russian friends.
They were greatly envied in Fleet Street and it was assumed that
some scientist friend had unfairly passed them to me. In fact I had
bought them the day before – over the counter at the Stationery
Office.

## Chapter Eight

⟡

# Spies in the Foreign Office

UNIVERSITIES offer productive hunting-grounds for talent-scouts seeking not only recruits to the Communist cause but agents for the KGB. This is true now and it was particularly true in the thirties during the rise of Hitler and appeasement of his behaviour by the British government. I was subjected to Communist attention myself at that time while a science student at London University, though with results suggesting that I was a rather unpromising target.

I had agreed to take part in a demonstration against Chamberlain or some other 'reactionary' politician, who was due to arrive at King's Cross Station. Along with a number of others in the then customary garb of grey flannel trousers and blazer, I had been equipped with a poster which I had folded up inside my blazer ready to be pulled out and held under the politician's nose accompanied by the usual chant of mindless slogans. Minutes before our quarry arrived plain-clothes police moved in, snatched the posters from their hiding-places and bundled us all out of the station. It was all done so professionally and so ruthlessly that I felt that a repeat performance was not for me.

Others, however, felt more deeply and committed themselves to Communism without reservation. Among them was a rather intense young son of a former Cabinet minister called Donald Maclean, who when head of the Foreign Office American desk in London in 1951, defected to Moscow along with Guy Burgess, another Cambridge recruit.

The disappearance of these two diplomats was first discovered by the *Daily Express* and I had some hand in the immediate inquiries, but my main journalistic interest centred around events which occurred several years after their flight.

While newspapers protest and sound alarms when government departments are detected putting out false or misleading information there are occasions when selected journalists deliberately help them to do so. I was involved in such a manoeuvre over Burgess and Maclean.

Early one morning in February 1956 I was summoned through an intermediary to see the head of the legal department of MI5, who urgently wanted help. A fortnight previously the KGB had suddenly produced Burgess and Maclean for interview in Moscow five years after their disappearance and that event, with everything they had said, had been subjected to minute analysis in the light of all relevant Intelligence available from British agents in the Soviet capital.

My MI5 friend, who being still alive remains nameless, told me that the analysis had produced one confident prediction – the Kremlin's rather sensational method of finally admitting that Burgess and Maclean were indeed in Moscow was only the prelude to further statements to be made by the defectors. These statements would be calculated to create the maximum distrust of Britain by America. And the Foreign Office would be discredited in the most scurrilous way by the naming of highly placed Foreign Office men who would be accused of being secretly anti-American and pro-Russian. In short, the former diplomats were to be given a new role as political provocateurs.

The timing of the Moscow statement was also seen to be linked with the forthcoming visit of the Russian leaders Bulganin and Kruschev to Britain two months later. During the Moscow interview Maclean had claimed to know former Foreign Office colleagues who found Britain's pro-American policy unacceptable, but had not identified them.

While the MI5 man was a brilliant briefer, I was not inexperienced in the type of operation in which he was engaged and I sensed that the real concern lay in the possible naming of Foreign Office men. Whether they were correctly or falsely accused, the damage could be considerable for it would undoubtedly lead to Labour demands for investigations into the charges. And some of those likely to be accused had by then reached high places.

I was therefore asked if I could induce the *Daily Express* to run a prominent article warning the public that whatever Burgess and Maclean might say in the future would be a KGB exercise and was not to be believed.

This was legitimate news and since it is not every day that a journalist is briefed by MI5 I agreed and a splash story, headlined 'Beware the diplomats', duly appeared on 27 February 1956.

During this discussion the MI5 officer confessed that though his organization was certain that Burgess had been a spy, it had no evidence that could be brought into court. There was no doubt whatever about Maclean's subversive and espionage activities over many years but, there again, the question of bringing the evidence into a court of law raised delicate problems.

The way Maclean had finally been identified as a Russian agent may not be generally known and illustrates how counter-espionage agencies function.

Throughout the war the US and British Intelligence services had monitored and recorded diplomatic signals sent out in code by foreign governments to their embassies and agents operating abroad. Naturally, prime attention had been paid to the German and Japanese traffic, with little attention to the Russian because the Soviet Union was an ally. Nevertheless, records of the Russian traffic had been stockpiled and eventually the Americans got around to decoding them.

This was more than a routine operation because the Cold War was in progress and there had been a marked increase in Soviet espionage against the USA, especially in the atomic field. There was a further reason why examination of these old records might yield some nuggets.

Normally Russian Intelligence used one-time pads for sending a message in code. In this system the person sending the message and the one receiving it each have an identical pad composed of pages each covered with lines of letters chosen at random. The encoder uses the letters from one page to encode a message and the decoder, knowing which page was used, can decipher it. The code is virtually unbreakable provided each page is only used once for each message. During the war, however, the Russians had run short of one-time pads and had been driven to use some pages twice.

This enabled the Americans to decipher the messages more easily and in 1951 the results had led to the conclusion that Donald

Maclean, then head of the American department in the Foreign Office in London but based in Washington during and after the war, was a dedicated agent of the Soviet Union.

This was the evidence with which Maclean was about to be confronted when he fled in June 1951.

News of Maclean's impending interrogation and possible arrest was known to very few people, but one of these, Harold 'Kim' Philby, happened to be a KGB spy. He was one of the most trusted officers of MI6, having even been head of its counter-Intelligence department and, at that time, was the chief MI6 representative in Washington for liaison with the CIA. He therefore heard about Maclean's predicament through information sent to him in secret, and in the KGB's interest decided that the diplomat had to be warned.

An easy way of doing this was at hand. Burgess had been sent to Washingtom to assist Philby and there was little difficulty in ensuring his quick return to London. While he could be charming, Burgess was an unstable homosexual and habitual drunkard with such a reputation for insulting remarks and riotous behaviour that he should never have been employed in any government department. The ambassador in Washington was already sick of him, as were various American authorities, so all that Burgess had to do to ensure his recall was to be caught speeding twice on the same day and in no fit state to drive.

Philby then instructed him to contact Maclean in London and warn him to escape from Britain by a route which was organized by the KGB. Burgess was not supposed to flee with Maclean but in the event he did.

Nothing was known for certain about Philby's part as the 'Third Man' in the Burgess and Maclean affair when MI5 sought my help in 1956, and such evidence as there was about the two defectors could not have carried much weight in a British court. There were no witnesses who could have been safely produced, even *in camera*, and Intelligence services the world over would rather let a spy escape than reveal their methods or sources.

In 1951, the authorities intended to interrogate Maclean and to produce a confession without which he could probably not have been charged. At that stage, they were confident that they could break Maclean down and secure information about his contacts.

In November 1956 my MI5 man contacted me again when

Burgess committed a technical breach of the Official Secrets Acts. After the diplomats had surfaced publicly in Moscow, Tom Driberg, the Labour MP and a fellow homosexual, visited Burgess in Moscow and, no doubt with KGB permission, secured enough information to write a book, *Guy Burgess, a Portrait with Background*. The publishers submitted this for clearance by the security authorities and once again I was called to the presence in the hope that I could help.

Burgess had given Driberg still-secret information about his war-time work in the Special Operations Executive. He had also given him the names of other men in secret departments. MI5 had gone through the motions of warning the publishers that they would risk prosecution unless they removed the censored parts, which was duly done. This cleared Driberg of any Official Secrets problems but Burgess had committed a breach by telling him the information. Neither Burgess nor Maclean had been granted Soviet citizenship so, even though they had defected, they were still subject to British law.

MI5 was most anxious that Burgess should know of this position and through the medium of the *Daily Express* they wanted me to make this clear. When I asked why they were clutching at such obvious straws I received an honest answer. Because the authorities still had no usable evidence against Burgess they had to do something to dissuade him from ever coming back to Britain. He had told Driberg that he wanted to return to see his mother and prove his innocence.

I was able to perform the service under the headline 'Burgess burns his boats', but this could not be done effectively without quoting some authority. Admiral Thomson, then the D notice secretary, was instructed to give me the necessary statements to be attributed to him, not to the officially non-existent MI5.

Driberg, who insisted that Burgess had been misunderstood, saw through the device but it seemed to work. Little more was heard about the two defectors until April 1962 when the worst appeared to be about to happen and my services were requested again.

A tip had been received from a Dutch Intelligence source that both Burgess and Maclean had been invited to a Communist conference in Cuba. What fussed MI5 was the further information that the airliner carrying them would be touching down at Prestwick Airport in Scotland on the way, no doubt with the KGB's blessing.

This put the security authorities and the police in an invidious position. In theory, following all the publicity highlighting the damage the defectors had done to Anglo-American relations, they should be arrested and charged under the Official Secrets Acts. In fact, as I already knew, there was little hope of doing this successfully and failure in court would make the government as well as MI5 look ridiculous. The last thing the government wanted was a trial, yet it would have to do something if the two men landed. The only answer was to prevent a landing. A deception plan had been devised and it was hoped that I would be part of it.

'What we would like you to do is to announce in tomorrow's newspaper that both men will be immediately arrested if they arrive,' I was told. An official Home Office statement – announcing that warrants for their arrest under section 1 of the Official Secrets Act had been issued – was to be made later that day, so all newspapers would be on the story but I knew it was largely a bluff.

I promised to consult my editor. As the *Daily Express* had been first with the news of the diplomats' disappearance he regarded any story about them as our special property. So, having satisfied himself that arrests would indeed be made, he agreed and the story was given front-page prominence the following morning. Whether this had any effect or not may never be known but Burgess and Maclean remained in Moscow.

Burgess died there, lonely and homesick, in 1963, seemingly unaware that he could have returned at least for a visit without encountering too much difficulty. I do not believe that the Director of Public Prosecutions would have sanctioned a charge on the feeble Driberg issue. The ignominy of an acquittal would have been too great.

Maclean still lives in Moscow and the security authorities hope he will remain there, remembering that even Fuchs could never have been arrested had he not confessed and pleaded guilty, there being insufficient evidence that could have been brought into court. There were even grave fears that having made a full confession, Maclean might retract it during the trial, claiming that it had been secured under duress, and the Attorney-General believed that in that case he would have been acquitted. Fuchs's confession had been obtained only by a very patient and resolute interrogator. Maclean after his sojourn in Russia might prove to be a tougher subject.

I suggest that the facts I present here show that the security 'establishment' did not want Maclean or Burgess back to face trial after they had escaped. It is also my view that they wanted Maclean to escape in the first place to avoid a trial then and encouraged him to do so.

The men who carried out the surveillance of Maclean before the expected interrogation were so clumsy that he quickly became aware that he was being followed on foot and by car. This is not the normal practice of MI5 or Special Branch who are polished professionals, and suggests that they deliberately made themselves obvious. Further, the official explanation that Maclean was not being watched when he escaped because he was spending the weekend at his country home, where surveillance would have been difficult, is unconvincing.

The trial of Maclean, had he not fled, could have been intensely embarrassing to the Foreign Office, which to many is the cream of the Whitehall establishment. The key figure in the operations at that time was Sir Stewart Menzies, the Director-General of the Secret Intelligence Service (MI6), which is responsible to the Foreign Secretary. He was so much an establishment figure that it was widely believed in Whitehall that he was a natural son of Edward VII. According to those who knew him it would have been almost automatic for him to take the view that the disgrace to Britain's name by allowing Maclean to escape would be far less than the damage resulting from a trial and the subsequent imprisonment of a high-level diplomat and son of a former Cabinet minister. If he simply vanished the government could claim that it had no evidence that he was a spy and leave the matter as a mystery – which is exactly what it did. Even the White Paper on 'The disappearance of two former Foreign Office officials' published four years later did little more than make excuses for the escape, claiming that had the security men seen Maclean and Burgess in the act of escaping, there was no admissible evidence they could have used to stop them. I give the security authorities the professional credit for knowing that the two traitors were escaping and possibly for observing their departure.

Whether the Labour government of the day took the same view or not may never be known. In those days MI6 was such a law unto itself that Menzies may well have felt he could do what he thought best without consulting ministers. The organization responsible for the shadowing – MI5 or the Special Branch – must have been told how their men should behave. But they could have been instructed to make the shadowing obvious to frighten Maclean as part of the softening-up process prior to interrogation.

IS—6**

I believe that the same procedure was adopted with Philby.

The suspicion that Maclean and Burgess were not the only traitors in the Foreign Office still persists though any diplomats of their vintage must now be retired or dead. There is still great interest in the identity of the Cambridge talent-scout who recruited them and several distinguished dons have been suspected. As MI5 puts it, 'Stones are turned over from time to time but nothing definite has been found.'

The procedure called positive vetting was introduced into the Foreign Office after the Maclean and Burgess scandal, when it had to be admitted, albeit reluctantly, that good family background, public-school education and the right club were no safeguards against treachery. As a result several officers were moved to posts of less importance to national security but, so far as is known, none of them was required to resign.

*Chapter Nine*

# Spies inside the Secret Service

OF all the defectors-in-place none can be more valuable than one who is working right inside the espionage or counter-espionage organization of an important target country. Of the very few of these who have been detected in Britain none was of such value to his Russian masters or did so much damage to the interests of his native country as Philby.

More has been written about Philby than about any other Briton spying for Russia and he is one of the few to have published an autobiography, though this is suspect because it must have been 'conditioned' by his KGB superiors. Nevertheless, there is still much that is not known about him, especially concerning the circumstances of his final physical defection to Moscow in 1963. Through contacts, who were close to what happened, I can contribute some facts and suggestions.

While Philby is usually projected as the cool, ever-careful professional spy – he reached the rank of brigadier in the KGB – he brought about his own downfall by a stupid error of judgement. This was his decision to have Guy Burgess to stay with him in his home in Washington when that notorious, if entertaining, personality was posted there by the Foreign Office in 1950. He continued to accommodate him even when his KGB controller in Washington warned him of the danger.

To Philby's dismay, when Burgess decided to accompany Maclean on his flight to Russia, thereby suggesting that he too had been a Soviet spy, suspicion naturally fell on the man who had befriended him in Washington.

So after the public and parliamentary row following the disclosure that Burgess and Maclean had disappeared, Philby was recalled to London for questioning by Sir Stewart Menzies, then Philby's chief as Director-General of MI6.

The circumstances of this recall are suspicious. As Philby himself has recorded, he was allowed to travel back unescorted, which the KGB in similar circumstances would never have permitted. Philby has disclosed that he was on the point of escaping from America to Moscow, a possibility which must have entered Menzies's mind. Yet no effort seems to have been made by the British authorities to stop him. The possibility that he was surreptitiously shadowed during the flight is remote in view of the facts Philby has told about his arrival in London, which seem too detailed to be fabricated.

I do not think it is generally known that during his interview with Menzies in the late summer of 1951 Philby virtually dismissed himself.

'Concerning your position, Kim, what would you do if you were in my place?' Menzies asked.

'I should tell me that I have to leave,' Philby replied.

'That is what I think,' Menzies said with some relief.

One of the most pressing reasons for Menzies's attitude was an urgent recommendation from the CIA chief that Philby should be fired because Washington officials concerned with the exchange of Intelligence and defence secrets with Britain were incensed that the man they had trusted had given shelter to such a villain as Burgess.

While suspicion that Philby was the Third Man who had warned Maclean was strong and inquiries to establish it were in train, there was no evidence against him so far as Menzies knew. The American intercepts of Russian messages which led to the suspicion about Maclean had also contained information concerning Philby's activities but MI6 had not been told of this.

Even if hard evidence had been available, I doubt that Menzies would have taken any other course, had it been avoidable. It was too easy for him and his senior colleagues to convince themselves that once Philby had been removed from access to further Intelligence he should be forgotten so far as the public was concerned. It would not be in the interests of 'The Firm' if it turned out that the man who was in line to become its Director-General and had already been head of counter-Intelligence was an officer of the KGB. Nor would it be in the national interest because of the enormous damage it was bound to inflict on the Anglo-American Intelligence alliance, coming so soon after the Fuchs case and the flight of Burgess and Maclean.

FBI documents, now available for inspection under the US Freedom of Information Act, show the extent to which the defections of Burgess and Maclean and later of Philby, damaged Anglo-American relations.

Had MI6 been left to its own devices, it would have preferred to regard the Philby case as closed except for 'turning over stones' to satisfy its own curiosity and to ensure that no other MI6 officers were involved. But MI5, then to some extent in rivalry and not unhappy to see its sister outfit in trouble, insisted that Philby should be subjected to a secret 'trial'. This was carried out with no success in the following year, 1952, by Helenus 'Buster' Milmo, a former MI5 man who is now a judge. Philby skilfully fenced his way through it, as he did a little later through a more sophisticated examination by MI5's ace interrogator William Skardon, who had secured the confession of Klaus Fuchs.

The 'trial' was successfully kept secret but the Press, and the *Daily Express* in particular, were determined to keep the Burgess–Maclean–Philby issue alive, scenting that there was much more to the story than had been revealed.

Immediately after the flight of the diplomats my own inquiries with Cyril Connolly, the author and critic, who knew Maclean well, produced Philby's name and the fact, then not generally known, that he had accommodated Burgess in Washington. I have a memorandum from a *Daily Express* investigator, Donald Seaman, dated 1953, stating that a former member of MI5 had assured him that Philby was the Third Man and had been a Communist from youth.

Not all the newspaper efforts were so productive. Against my advice, the *Express* hired the services of a man called Lieutenant-Colonel Oreste Pinto, who had written a wartime spy book and been hailed as the 'world's greatest spy-catcher'. He was in fact rather small-time but he was sent out into the blue with instructions to find Burgess and Maclean. When he had failed to report after several weeks, a rumour flashed round Fleet Street that the paper had received an urgent cable from behind the Iron Curtain reading, 'Have found Pinto', signed Burgess.

More professional reporters devilled away and few of them doubted Philby's guilt, but, such are the libel laws in Britain, the suspicions were unprintable, particularly as the Whitehall establishment was determined to protect both Philby and Maclean. The *Daily Express* was castigated for keeping watch on Maclean's wife when she was living in Switzerland because of its conviction that she was only waiting for the right moment to join her renegade husband, which she eventually did in 1953, only to leave him later to live with Philby and then to marry him!

I have little doubt that Philby would have been quickly unmasked in the USA where the libel laws are less restrictive on the Press. In the memoirs, *My Silent War*, which he eventually published in 1968, he gloats over the way he silenced Fleet Street investigators who remained convinced he was a traitor after Macmillan had cleared him in Parliament.

Though an official report on the Burgess and Maclean affair had been promised, nothing happened until the government was forced into producing something by the defection of a KGB Intelligence officer called Vladimir Petrov in Canberra in April 1954. It became known that he had told the Australian security authorities that both Maclean and Burgess had been recruited as KGB spies while still at university with the intention that they should work in the Foreign Office and that the KGB had organized their eventual escape. The Foreign Office therefore felt bound to produce a brief White Paper, which it again delayed until the autumn of 1955. It was an anodyne, doing little more than make excuses for British officials. There was, of course, no mention of Philby and this enabled Marcus Lipton, a Labour MP, to question Eden, then Prime Minister, in Parliament.

He asked him if he had 'made up his mind to cover up at all costs the dubious Third Man activities of Harold Philby'?

Lipton, apart from being an excellent constituency member, was one of those perennial back-benchers who delight in asking questions and latch on to any running story in the hope of getting their names in the newspapers or, better still, on television. It is most unlikely that he thought of the question himself but had been induced into asking it by someone else. This could have been a journalist or it may have been the Tory MP Henry Kerby, who was quite convinced that Philby was a spy. If this were so, Kerby's motive may have been merely to embarrass Eden but in the result he did a great service, unwittingly perhaps, to the Russian spy.

Eden was noncommittal but Lipton's question demanded an answer which was given in an ensuing debate by Harold Macmillan, the Foreign Secretary, who said that no evidence had been found to show that Philby was responsible for warning Burgess or Maclean. 'I have no reason to conclude that Mr Philby has at any time betrayed the interests of this country or to identify him with the so-called "Third Man", if indeed, there was one,' he said.

What Macmillan meant – as most politicians mean when they are driven to make this kind of statement – was that there was no admissible evidence that could be brought into a court. There was no other kind of statement he could make publicly and the upshot was that it amounted to an official clearance of Philby which, as the spy himself later revealed, relieved him of all anxiety. With the Foreign Secretary's statement behind him he knew that he could shelter more surely than ever behind libel laws, whatever the newspapers might discover. He was so relaxed that he held a Press conference in which he denied any Communist associations.

It is my belief that the security and Intelligence authorities were also relieved. They had been responsible, along with other Whitehall interests, for promoting the idea that Philby was not only innocent but being victimized by Press inquiries.

Whether Philby had formally left MI6 employment completely after his gentlemanly showdown with Menzies is academic because, in those days, MI6 officers had no formal contracts and did not even pay tax. (A former officer has described to me how Menzies had a slush fund of gold sovereigns in a desk drawer so that he could hand them out at will as bonuses or in payment for special jobs.) What is certain is that Philby's access to Intelligence information terminated completely in 1951 and was never restored.

Few people every leave MI6 completely, however. Even those who go into merchant banks and other genuine full-time commercial appointments which are not just cover jobs retain contact and provide services when they can. Indeed when they leave they are asked to sign an undertaking to this effect, if they are so inclined. So between 1951 and 1955 Philby, in return for departing with such tactful understanding, may have been employed in gathering Intelligence in Cyprus and elsewhere but he was never given anything he could pass on to Russian friends. I have checked this information at several points in the Intelligence network and am satisfied that it disposes of the belief that, even after his 'disgrace', Philby was employed as some kind of double agent.

From MI6's viewpoint, it has to be remembered that no action was possible against Philby at that stage and he was far better out of the country where he would be forgotten more quickly, and where prudent surveillance might lead to the detection of some of his Soviet contacts and even of British co-conspirators.

After Macmillan's clearance his position was much improved and he was sent out to Beirut under the cover of being a correspondent for the *Observer* to supply information to MI6 but remained barred from access to information *from* MI6. By this time, Sir Dick White, the former head of MI5, had been switched to direct MI6, following the rumpus over the political disaster after Russian sailors spotted a frogman, called Crabb, who had been spying on the hull of the cruiser which had brought the Soviet leaders, Bulganin and Kruschev, to Britain. A firm believer in Philby's guilt, he was horrified to find that he still had any connection with 'The Firm' but agreed, reluctantly, to the Beirut posting, after establishing to his own satisfaction that no Intelligence from headquarters ever went Philby's way.

Philby continued to send competent dispatches to the *Observer* and *The Economist* and could have continued his life as a rather drunken journalist with a rowdy domestic and social life, but, as happens so frequently with former spies, he was betrayed from the other side. A KGB defector, whom I have already named as Anatoli Dolnytsin, produced indubitable evidence during his debriefing by the CIA and later by MI5, that Philby was not only a spy but on the KGB's books as one of its officers. This put MI6 into a difficult position.

It had no wish to reopen public discussion of Philby but needed to satisfy its own curiosity and if possible induce the spy to reveal the full extent of his past activities. The fact that he was on foreign soil suddenly became a bonus, for it was argued that he was much more likely to confess there, where he would be harder to apprehend, than if recalled to Britain.

A senior MI6 officer who had been a close friend of Philby was therefore sent out to Beirut in the summer of 1962 to do some questioning. The only effect of this interrogation seems to have been to alert Philby to the fact that he had been betrayed and might need to take some action about it. The MI6 view was that Philby would not desert his wife and children, and so could hardly attempt to defect from Beirut without being seen.

By the end of 1962 further evidence against Philby was available through another defector, believed to be Colonel Michal Goleniewski, formerly of Polish Intelligence. A different MI6 officer, whom I know, was sent out for a further confrontation with Philby. This very able operator put the situation fully and bluntly to Philby who calmly confessed to having been a KGB agent for thirty years and denied none of the evidence built up against him. I have been assured that during several hours of interrogation he made a very full confession, which is believed to have been essentially true but, as a result, he could have been left in little doubt that if he returned to Britain he would be arrested and tried.

The officer who secured the confession and another MI6 official involved in the case at headquarters insist that they definitely wanted Philby back in Britain for more lengthy interrogation, mainly to discover any other contacts still, perhaps, operating in Whitehall and elsewhere. They claim that the Lebanese police had been alerted and had promised to cooperate in Philby's extradition.

I find all this hard to believe, even from friends. The MI6 chiefs must have known that with his KGB connections in Beirut and elsewhere Philby would be able to escape. Had he not been confident of doing so why should he have confessed? He had recently seen what happened to a spy who confessed – George Blake, another MI6 man who had been sentenced to forty-two years in prison.

If MI6 had really wanted Philby back they could at least have tried to induce the *Observer* to recall him for discussions about a different post or contrived some other device.

As the hard evidence which MI6 had acquired against Philby was then secret why shouldn't they have simply left him to drink himself away in Beirut? Once defectors to the West have parted with all their information they are free to sell their memoirs and many of them do. So there was no certainty, especially as two defectors, Dolnytsin and another man, had been involved, that the evidence about Philby would remain secret. Publication would have led to immediate demands in Parliament for his arrest and MI6 would have had to act.

To me the conclusion that the British authorities wanted to frighten Philby into defecting to the safety of the Soviet Union is inescapable. The trial of such a cool customer could have led to the naming of other Foreign Office and MI6 men and all kinds of horrors. The detailed leaks from the trial of George Blake, which I shall describe, had shown that an *in camera* hearing was no longer secure. If Philby defected, his story might remain wrapped in mystery for, as a KGB officer, it seemed unlikely then that he would be publishing any memoirs.

Philby duly obliged on the night of 23 January 1963, apparently leaving Beirut by Russian ship or by road via Syria and Turkey. According to MI6, the Lebanese police, who were supposed to be watching him, 'made a hash of it'.

First news that he was living in Moscow came six months later. Philby regarded himself as having reached 'home' though he had never been in Russia before. He remained reasonably silent and might have continued that way but for the fact that a team of investigators from the *Sunday Times* decided to write a book about him, with deep inquiries into all the available background. Heroic efforts, including the issue of an ingeniously worded D-notice, were made by the Foreign Office in 1968 to stop publication of the book (which was first serialized in the *Sunday Times*). This culminated in a public outburst by George Brown, then the Foreign Secretary, during a dinner at the Savoy, when he put the onus personally on to the late Lord Thomson, the owner of the newspaper.

There was little, if anything, in the book that was damaging to national security but it skilfully resurrected the whole Philby affair and focused fresh attention on the weaknesses of MI5 and MI6, and their rivalry. No doubt Brown was anxious about exacerbating American concern about the interchange of secrets but he was also trying to protect MI6, for which he was then politically responsible, in spite of its refusal to tell him the full facts of the Philby affair.

The book was published and induced Philby to issue his own account of his espionage activities, very much to the detriment of the British secret services. Its incompleteness has led MI6 to fear that when the time happens to suit the KGB he will publish a sequel.

It may be significant that in his memoirs Philby made no mention of the MI6 officer who made it clear to him that there was evidence enough to arrest him. A mark of gratitude?

It might reasonably be asked why Philby, who had done so much damage to his own country and might still do more, was not quietly assassinated. One of his drunken outrages could have served as a convenient cover, especially in a place like Beirut.

It is difficult to discover hard evidence that the British Secret Service has ever used assassination in peacetime to achieve its aims. I have, however, been told how the police chief who served Mosaddeq, the anti-British Iranian dictator, was killed by an agent acting on MI6's behalf.

I also know details of arrangements which were made to kill President Nasser during the Suez crisis of 1955. The MI6 man in charge of the operation described how the assistance of some young Egyptian officers, who were strongly opposed to Nasser, had been secured and how special weapons had been buried at a convenient spot near Cairo. They were never used because certain circumstances essential to the operation did not materialize. This failure, my informant said, was one of the reasons why the Suez gamble had to be abandoned, an event which proved disastrous for Britain. Strong American pressure against the invasion was expected and the quick elimination of Nasser had been essential before it became overwhelming, as it did.

Eden, then Prime Minister and the driving force behind the invasion, had vetoed an all-British effort to kill or capture Nasser using Special Air Service troops, but agreed, or turned a blind eye, to the MI6 operation in which the killing would have been accomplished by Egyptian officers, who were eventually dealt with by their President when he learned of their treachery.

I have little doubt that assassination – usually carried out by hired agents rather than by MI6 officers themselves – was occasionally used up to the time that Sir Dick White took over as MI6 chief in 1956, when it was ended. Evidence that this is still the situation – as witness the way General Amin has been allowed to rampage in Uganda – came my way following the Littlejohn affair in 1973.

This was the case in which two English brothers called Littlejohn were convicted of robbing a bank in Dublin and then claimed that they were agents of MI6, which had supplied them with their weapons and explosives. Following the considerable publicity generated by a government statement that, while the brothers had been put in touch with MI6 through a minister, they had never been recruited as agents, there was concern among staff members at Century House. Some of the women and junior staff did not relish working for an organization involving violence and assassination. Sir Maurice Oldfield, then the Director-General of MI6, therefore felt obliged to circulate a policy statement assuring the staff that no violence is involved in the espionage and Intelligence operations now conducted by the Secret Intelligence Service.

Further evidence that the hard-drinking, quick-shooting, womanizing James Bond image is hopelessly wide of the true mark is provided by the experience of a friend of mine – now, oddly enough, one of the world's foremost authorities on rhododendrons. As an Army officer in the Middle East during the Second World War, he had volunteered for a special MI6 mission which was not revealed to him during the tough and intensive training to which he was subjected. After he had almost completed the training, as he thought satisfactorily, he was asked to show Cairo at night to a senior naval officer who had just arrived there. My friend, who knew the night-spots well, responded magnificently and, believing it might be his last night out before the dangerous operation, decided to make a meal of it.

The captain seemed delighted as he was taken from one belly-dance bar to another ending up in a lusty night-club. The following morning my friend was called before the commanding officer to be told he was being returned to his unit as unsuitable for the mission. On the captain's evidence he was far too fond of liquor and women!

When the government reluctantly admitted that Philby had been a Russian spy following his defection to Moscow in 1963, a cynical jingle was sung in Whitehall:

Oh tell me Harold Philby, are there any more at home like you?
Oh yes indeed! There are a few.

This suspicion that other Communist agents who penetrated the British Secret Intelligence Service have gone undetected and may still be operating was strengthened, in my opinion, by Philby's memoirs, even taking account of the fact that they were doctored for propaganda purposes. There was far too much detail that rang true about the ineffectiveness of the security and Intelligence departments and about the destructive rivalry between them for the whole document to be dismissed.

The fact that Philby's Moscow masters permitted him to expose the flagrant weaknesses which enabled him and other Soviet agents to continue spying for so long suggests that these had been corrected, but I suspect that much of the self-delusion and it-couldn't-happen-here arrogance remain.

The introduction of positive vetting for all new recruits to MI6, which did not exist when Philby was recruited, might have weeded out Burgess. His homosexuality was well enough known at his old school, Eton, and as a result he was turned down when he applied for a mastership there. Positive vetting might even have barred Maclean, who had openly expressed extreme left-wing views at Cambridge. But it is very doubtful if Philby's traitorous character defect would have been spotted.

Quite recently it was discovered that an important officer in MI6 had previously been a Communist and had not declared the fact on his positive vetting form. Inquiries revealed that MI5 knew of his Communist associations but had failed to pass the information to its sister service, a defect in the Intelligence-security organization which has persisted for many years. The official left the service as a result and it was this case, I am told, which resulted in a former Foreign Office man being put in charge of MI5 when Sir Michael Hanley retired from the Director-Generalship in 1978.

At least one suspect spy was detected in MI5 itself during Wilson's premiership. He too was quietly removed by being induced to resign.

In 1961, shortly before the suspicion against Philby hardened into certainty, MI6 received its rudest shock to date with the discovery that one of its field agents had been working, with most alarming success, for the KGB. His name was George Blake, though he had been born in Behar of a Dutch mother and a father of part-Egyptian parentage. The government was restricting top secret Civil Service posts to British-born of British parents after the Fuchs experience, but this precaution was not applied to Blake when he rejoined MI6 in 1953.

Previously Blake had been working for MI6 from a base in Seoul, in South Korea, but had been captured by North Korean communists and held in an interrogation camp. It was felt that the birth limitation should not be applied to him on his repatriation because he had apparently worked well in the past, and had suffered in the prison camp as a result. It was also argued that applying the limitation to MI6 field agents in general would be counter-productive. Facility in languages, such as Blake possessed, was often an essential qualification and this often demanded the recruitment of foreign-born agents.

After rehabilitation Blake was posted as an MI6 officer to Berlin, where he remained for four years, supplying the Russians with material extremely damaging to the West.

My first connection with the Blake case was an urgent request from Admiral Thomson, then secretary of the D-notice committee, in 1958 almost three years before Blake was arrested. He told me that the Egyptians had exposed the entire British secret service network throughout the Middle East. Certain Britons – one named Swinburn, another named Zarb – had been arrested and many more British Intelligence officers working under diplomatic cover were having to be withdrawn. Thomson said that Nasser had let it be known that he was extremely angry with the extent of the British penetration and proposed to name all the agents on Cairo radio. This would mean that they could never be used again anywhere.

Thomson wanted a promise that if Nasser carried out his threat, the *Daily Express* would refrain from mentioning the names. If we could agree to that he then proposed to approach the other newspapers.

I told him that the request was crazy and could see no purpose that could be served apart from the obvious one of concealing an MI6 disaster from the British public. Privately he agreed with me and indicated that, against his advice and in some desperation, MI6 had asked him to see what he could do.

Nasser did not name the agents but the relief at MI6 would have been short-lived had it been known, as it was later, that the source of Nasser's information about the British network had originated from a KGB agent called George Blake. The Kremlin was supplying arms to Egypt and the last thing it wanted was British spies there.

Early in 1961, following a tip from an arrested German spy, an MI6 officer of my acquaintance was sent out to the Lebanon, where Blake was then based at the Foreign Office College of Arabic Studies. His mission was to fool the spy into returning to London for discussions about a new job involving promotion but really for

interrogation. The officer could not sleep all night worrying whether
Blake would take fright and defect, but he elected to return. Once he
was arrested the shock in Whitehall was so great that the Prime
Minister, Macmillan, did everything he could to blanket the fact
that he was an MI6 man. He ordered the issue of a D-notice
restricting the reporting of the trial on the confidential grounds that
agents placed in jeopardy by Blake were still being withdrawn from
behind the Iron Curtain. In fact that operation, so far as it was
possible, had been completed before he had been arrested. When the
D-notice was rightly ignored, Macmillan wanted to know why the
Admiral had been unable to 'stop the newspapers'.

Though MI6 had secured convincing evidence of Blake's
treachery from other agents they had none they could have brought
into court without prejudicing sources. At almost the last throw by
the interrogator trying to break him down Blake suddenly confessed,
providing a flood of information. There were fears that he might
retract in which event the case against him could collapse, but he
fully admitted the confession. As he pleaded guilty and the case was
held mostly *in camera* the public was given little information to
explain the stunning sentence of forty-two years. Parliament sensed
a scandal and the Labour opposition, which missed no chance to
claim that the Macmillan government was lax on security, kept on
demanding the facts.

At first Macmillan refused to give them on the grounds of national
security but as the Labour demands intensified he adopted the
'Privy Councillor's ploy'. He told the House that while it would
never be permissible for him to tell Parliament the facts he was
prepared to reveal them to Gaitskell, the opposition leader, and to
any other two Privy Councillors he might care to nominate. It was
understood that they would not pass on any of the information but
they could at least assure their own side that the government was not
withholding anything for party-political motives but only for
genuine security reasons.

Gaitskell nominated George Brown, his deputy, and Emanuel
Shinwell, a former Defence Minister. The three met Macmillan and
Sir Norman Brook, then the Cabinet Secretary, who did most of the
talking. The Privy Councillors were then given a list of Blake's
crimes, which shocked them deeply.

A few days later I was giving lunch to Brown in the Ecu de France
and no sooner were we seated than he began to tell me the whole

story. Blake had given the Russians the names of at least forty anti-Communist agents working for Britain abroad. Some of those operating behind the Iron Curtain had been rounded up and shot or imprisoned. That was the main reason for the severity of the sentence. It worked out at almost exactly a year for each agent the spy had betrayed.

The network in the Middle East which had taken years to establish was still in ruins. While working in West Berlin Blake had given the KGB photographs of every secret document passing through his office. Some of his information had enabled the KGB to kidnap prominent East Germans who had defected to the West. They were abducted back behind the Berlin Wall.

He had disclosed details of a 350-foot-long tunnel which the Americans had driven under the Russian sector of Berlin to plug into Soviet telephone cables. He had tried to warn the KGB that the professional Soviet spy, Gordon Lonsdale, and other agents in what became known as the Navy secrets ring were about to be arrested and it was the interception of this message which led to his recall from Beirut to London.

I listened to this recital with mounting interest but expecting the requirement that all was off the record. Instead Brown made it clear that he wanted the material used, though without mentioning him.

At first sight, this behaviour may sound disloyal but, as Brown pointed out, much of the information had already been printed as intelligent speculation and he genuinely believed that the rest was being withheld to save the government's face. He was also convinced that the elimination of the Tory government and the installation of Labour was much more in the national interest than the suppression of information about a revolting spy who was already in prison.

Admiral Thomson, whom I consulted without mentioning Brown, assured me that there was nothing to stop publication and volunteered that he had little doubt in his mind about who had given me the information.

My editor, then Robert Edwards, was particularly delighted with my news because it offered the opportunity to use a display gimmick he had kept in mind for years. When the splash story appeared in the *Daily Express* of 20 June 1961 there were forty little men in black coats over the headline '40 agents betrayed' to ram home the enormity of Blake's treachery.

The forty-two years, which seemed so savage to some, was actually meaningless, for in October 1967 Blake escaped not only from Wormwood Scrubs Prison but from Britain, quickly appearing in Moscow, where he lives in apparent comfort. Inquiries showed that a prison bar which had been removed during a previous break-out had only been weakly cemented in and Blake had been able to kick it out.

An extraordinary aspect of Blake's coolness was described to me by Sir Roger Falk, the businessman who had been a prison visitor at Wormwood Scrubs. Falk became friendly with Blake and, while not condoning his treachery, did what he could to help a cultured man who had been committed to prison for the rest of his life. Though an outstanding linguist, the spy was poor at figures and when he was running the prison canteen relied on Falk to add up the accounts. On the day that he escaped he had completed the accounts except for the addition. Falk was not due until a day later. So Blake left the accounts with a note to the Governor apologizing for failing to add them up.

Blake had escaped so easily that there were suspicions that MI6 had rigged the circumstances either to get rid of him or in some shady deal with the KGB. I am sure that this was not the case, nor is there any chance that Blake is really a double-agent working for Britain right at the heart of things in Russia.

Roy Jenkins, then the Home Secretary, was at pains to assure Parliament that the government had no knowledge of any plots or warnings of plots to rescue Blake but he was wrong. Patrick Meehan, a safe-blower, later to be wrongly accused of murder in a notorious miscarriage of justice, told me a different story when I visited him in Blundeston Prison near Lowestoft in December 1966.

Meehan said that he had been approached by a well-known British Communist in 1955 after he had organized the successful escape of a dangerous criminal from Peterhead Jail near Aberdeen. In August 1963, while serving eight years for attempted robbery, Meehan himself escaped from Nottingham Jail and ended up seeking refuge in East Germany, which he had managed to reach. He claimed that when he told the Communists there his background they told him they were interested in rescuing Blake and the Krogers, a man-and-wife spy team imprisoned for their part in the Navy secrets ring. He claimed he told them how they could do it.

Eventually the East Germans handed Meehan back to the British and when he was back in prison he gave a full account to MI5, warning that an attempt to rescue Blake would be made. I have little doubt that Meehan was telling me the truth.

It may well be wondered why Blake and Philby were never caught in the act of examining files they were not entitled to see or taking photographs or committing other breaches of security, for these must often have been necessary in view of the known extent of their espionage activities. In the days when people in MI6 were above suspicion, physical security was not so tight as it is now. Blake, for example, was able to capitalize on it. When the security man came round to lock his door during the lunch-hour when he was working in Berlin he hid behind his desk so that he was locked in. He then knew he could do what he liked for an hour or more without possibility of disturbance.

Century House now has its own security branch manned mainly by retired Intelligence officers – men brought in 'from the cold' – and some of the precautions they take are understandably secret but several can safely be mentioned.

The most secret parts of any Intelligence organization are its files and in MI6 the registries and file halls where these are kept are under combination-lock control. The danger lies in having a disaffected person among those with access to the locks and files. This could be an officer, as in Philby's case, but it could also be a quite junior clerk. Both MI6 and MI5 have to employ young people, mostly girls, to make searches in the files and there is constant fear that the Communists might plant a sympathizer, who could operate not only by reporting on the contents of files but by destroying them.

In all secure government offices there is, or should be, the closest check on copies of secret documents which have to be made for distribution to other outside departments. Access to the copying machine must be restricted, particularly in a place like MI6 where the number of outside officials receiving daily digests of Intelligence is quite high. Some idea of this number was provided not long ago by the volume of laughter heard in Whitehall following receipt of a Century House report with an unfortunate misprint. It is customary for such reports to refer to 'a source with good access' and one of them mentioned 'a source with god access', the comments made on it by various very senior gentlemen being extremely entertaining.

Just how real is the possibility that copies of secret documents can be smuggled out of buildings where security is lax was demonstrated by the case in which a girl typist in the Cabinet Office was convicted of selling them to a South African Intelligence agent.

Every office in such a sensitive building as Century House and even the canteens, have to be swept regularly for listening devices which might have been planted. As recently as 1977, however, I discovered that sweeping in secret departments can still be careless. The office of the Vice-Chief of the Naval Staff, in the Defence Ministry, had never been on the sweepers' list, though more secret matters were likely to be discussed there than in the office of the First Sea Lord!

Even computers loaded with secret information now have to be protected against bugging because it seems that when they are in operation they transmit waves which could be picked up. Some of the precautions which have been installed in Whitehall to forestall this are both extensive and expensive.

All buildings have to employ some outside staff for canteen catering, computer maintenance and other purposes and these offer a further source of possible infiltration. When the contract window-cleaners are due warning memoranda have to be circulated to all departments, giving the approximate times of arrival at each floor level, and all work is stopped so that documents can be covered. This is to counter the possibility that the KGB could have recruited one of the cleaners and equipped him with a camera.

Windows afford a further problem as science advances. It is now possible for a well-financed espionage organization to direct a laser beam on to a window from another building. As the glass oscillates slightly when people in the room are speaking the laser can pick up the vibrations and the speech causing them can be deciphered. It is difficult for the KGB to use this type of equipment in Britain, though it is utilized in Russia itself, but when I visited the office of a senior officer in the Defence Ministry he made a point of picking out a window in a private building across the road from which our conversation might at that moment be under surveillance. Laser listening is now so well established that I understand it to be in use occasionally by the police.

Precautions against all these espionage possibilities are in regular operation but they can still fail, if only through human error. At least one booby-trapped parcel has been successfully delivered to Century House though, happily, it did not explode when it was opened by the Middle East expert to whom it was addressed.

## Chapter Ten

Journalists and the KGB

IN one of his rare published utterances the Director-General of MI5, then Sir Martin Furnival Jones, told the Franks Committee on the Official Secrets Acts that the KGB and its satellite Intelligence services 'are very active in the press world in Fleet Street'. They are indeed, as I know from my own experience and that of several colleagues.

One defence correspondent on a newspaper which is now defunct, fell for the age-old trick where the husband accidentally appears during the act of the wife's seduction. He accepted several invitations to the Polish embassy and the wife of one of the attachés there made it increasingly clear that she fancied him. The husband invited him to his residence and when the journalist appeared the wife apologized for her husband's absence, explaining that he had been sent out of town. They were in an intimate situation on the sofa when the husband stormed in and made it clear that unless he received some recompense in the way of information he would make an unpleasant fuss.

The security authorities to whom the journalist reported his plight were in no doubt that the husband had been party to the set-up and that blackmail would undoubtedly have followed had not the man been wise enough to report what had happened. The journalist occasionally had confidential information imparted during briefings at the Defence Ministry and also had access to secret establishments during Press facility visits.

With a few journalists Soviet bloc Intelligence does not have to resort to such methods because they are only too keen to oblige, usually for ideological motives but sometimes for money too. Such a man achieved considerable success on a famous national newspaper until not long ago when he was exposed to his own employers by MI5, which had acquired a stack of evidence against him, including the extent of payments for his subversive services. This man, a dedicated Communist, had been required by his Soviet masters to appear to leave the party in order to secure an influential post in Fleet Street, which would give him access to government ministers and civil servants and to the customary off-the-record official briefings. Such was his success that there were suspicions that well-placed friends in Whitehall were helping him.

The security authorities got wind of his activities through the most usual channel – an East European Intelligence officer who defected to the West. As this man knew only the journalist's code-name, MI5 had some difficulty in tracking him down and when they succeeded no legal action could be taken because he had committed no offence actionable under British law. That he had given the KGB valuable service, including the names of potential recruits, was beyond question and when confronted with the evidence he left Fleet Street without argument.

It was perhaps inevitable that, during the years when my penetration of the defence departments was particularly deep, the KGB should have tried to recruit me. The way this happened was very much involved with the pursuit of power by a particular politician who was without doubt the most extraordinary MP I have ever encountered. He was Captain Henry Kerby, known to some of his friends as Bob, the Tory MP for Arundel, one of the safest of all parliamentary seats with an enormous right-wing majority. He was a huge man with a bald, cannon-ball head and rubbery features usually creased in a smile for he had a lively sense of humour. He also had the benefit of a beautiful wife, a rich mother, who eventually left him a considerable fortune, and an attractive family home in the country.

I knew he had been born in Russia, spoke the language so fluently that he was an official interpreter for the visit of Kruschev and Bulganin to Britain in 1956 and made many visits to Moscow where, as he put it, he was always given 'the red-carpet treatment'. No explanation of his interest in Russia was ever volunteered by him but it seemed that he was involved in promoting East–West trade, probably as a contact man. This was an interest he shared with

Harold Wilson, for both had special knowledge of the Russian timber import business, Wilson having served for nine years, while out of office, as consultant to Montague Meyer, a big timber importing firm.

In my early days with Kerby I had no knowledge of any relationship with Wilson. All his criticism seemed to be reserved for his own side and particularly for his Prime Minister, Harold Macmillan. On occasions when I sat in the Press gallery of the Commons above the Speaker's chair, Kerby, whose proper place was on the back-benches to the Speaker's right, would appear in the gallery on the left and peer down at his own side. When I asked him why he did it he replied, 'When you are down there you can't see your own side. When I'm up here I can watch them and say "What a bloody shower!" '

When the Tory Party was in trouble, as for example over Profumo, whom Kerby insisted on calling 'Perfumo', he would telephone me and cry, 'Frying tonight!'

Kerby's main interest in me was as a source of information and ideas for written questions he could ask in Parliment or for rumbustious motions that would never be debated. He rarely spoke in the House so when a general election came round he liked to tell his constituents that since the last one he had asked over a thousand questions and put down twenty motions. The arrangement suited me because I was able to plant questions which I had failed to answer by other means, or to produce an answer which I knew but could not use until it was covered by Parliamentary privilege. This gives MPs absolute protection in law about anything they might say in the Commons about anybody and extends to those who factually report their statements. But most of Kerby's questions were of no consequence to anybody except himself and the Whitehall effort in answering them must have cost the taxpayer enormous sums. They worked well for him, however. He said that all he needed to do to maintain his majority was to ask plenty of questions and secure the right number of OBE's for his local dignitaries and party officials.

Kerby's animosity to his own side reached back at least as far as the time when Anthony Eden was Foreign Secretary in the fifties. Kim Philby in the American edition of his own account of his work as a Soviet spy, *My Silent War*, published in 1968, recorded 'a curious episode which began with a letter from Captain Kerby MP who asked me to tea at the House of Commons. After explaining that he himself had been sacked from the Foreign Service, he told me candidly that he was gunning for the Foreign Office in general and Anthony Eden in particular. His own position, he said, was impregnable – he had one of the safest seats in the country and his local Conservative Association ate out of his hand. He had heard that I had also been sacked from the Foreign Service, and had surmised that I must suffer a sense of grievance. If I could give him any dirt to throw at the Foreign Office, he would be grateful.'

As there is some indication that Kerby was occasionally employed by the Intelligence services, because of his fluent Russian, it is possible that he may have been hoping to trap Philby into confessing that he was the Third Man in the Maclean and Burgess affair. That, however, would not link with the fact that he helped to induce Marcus Lipton, the Labour MP, to ask the Prime Minister, Eden, if that was the case. Such probing was the last thing that MI6 wanted. My information from inside MI6 suggests that Kerby's prime purpose really was to embarrass Eden, whom he frequently referred to as 'that pansy'.

At one of my lunches with Kerby I happened to mention that because of my anti-Soviet attitude over many years I was never invited to Soviet embassy functions as other journalists were. Beaverbrook had tried to get me a visa to visit Russia by writing personally to Mikoyan, whom he knew, in the rather ambitious hope that I might be granted some facility visit to a space launching site. The ambassador, Malik, was approached by my colleague Edward Pickering (now Sir) and he promised to support my application, but nothing ever came of it. In spite of all the apparent top-level support, my application remained at the bottom of some in-tray in Moscow.

Kerby immediately assured me he could arrange for an invitation to the embassy and though he disclaimed any connection with the event which ensued I was telephoned within two days by a man who introduced himself as Anatoli Strelnikov, the Press attaché. He said he had been waiting for an opportunity to contact me – though I later discovered he had already been in London two years – and asked me out to lunch. I joined him at a Greek restaurant.

Strelnikov was an impressive man, very tall for a Russian, perhaps six feet three, with a pleasant Slavic face and large protruding ears. He dressed well and had acquired the habit of carrying an umbrella. He wasted little time in pumping me about several stories I had written on defence matters in the recent past and was particularly interested in NATO.

After the lunch I was concerned that he might be under surveillance by MI5 and in that case the security authorities might suspect me. This would have been very counter-productive because at that time I was on close terms with the Defence Minister, Harold Watkinson (now Lord). I therefore approached MI5 for advice through Admiral Thomson, the then secretary of the D-notice committee. He came back with the news that MI5 were very interested in Strelnikov and would be putting me in touch with one of their agents Michael M——. They wanted me to continue to see Strelnikov but to report everything I could remember about the conversation. M——, a most pleasant and entertaining career Intelligence officer, told me that Strelnikov was an important KGB officer and that MI5, was looking for any evidence that would enable the Foreign Office to get him out of the country.

When I asked M—— about Kerby's position I was hurriedly assured that he was all right though no explanation of why he had put a senior KGB officer on my track was offered. I assumed at that time that Kerby might be some kind of double agent reporting to MI5 but it was possible that because he was an MP the security authorities were avoiding any action against him beyond keeping him under occasional observation.

I continued to see Strelnikov, who began to bring gifts of odd bottles of Russian champagne. I received several invitations to the Soviet embassy and to other embassies of the Communist bloc. The Russian embassy parties were big affairs, with the experienced guests arriving early to polish off the very limited supplies of caviare. Kerby and Strelnikov were always there, though never together so far as I ever saw.

After every meeting I would rendezvous with M—— and give him the gist of our conversation. It was clear that Strelnikov's immediate purpose was to discover the names of my contacts, either in the hope that they might be suborned or so that the KGB could assure themselves that what I was writing in the *Daily Express* was informed from inside sources, as indeed it was.

During the summer of 1960 I invited Strelnikov to a party I was giving at my country home near Ewhurst in Surrey. Among those present – and this was to have far-reaching repercussions including the D-notice affair in years ahead – were Henry Kerby and Colonel

Sammy Lohan, then deputy director of public relations in the Defence Ministry, who had never met before. Strelnikov behaved in an extraordinary manner. He insisted on locking his car though it was in view of the garden where we were staging a barbecue on a glorious June evening. Then when he decided to go he had lost his keys or thought he had, to the great amusement of Kerby who kept shouting at him in Russian, assuring him that nobody was going to bug his car.

While I was still in the process of seeing my Russian friend at intervals, I was approached by M—— in the spring of 1961 for assistance on another project. I agreed to help and as a result M—— and another MI5 officer came to a flat which I borrowed for the purpose. The other officer, who was never named, had a series of cards from an index which were case-records of men and women who had been suborned by Russian agents, some while in Britain, others while in Moscow.

The MI5 man explained that Britain was shortly to stage a large electronics exhibition in Moscow. Many young men would be going to represent their firms and some were already engaged on weapons work while the rest could move to that field one day. The Security Service had no doubt that they would be prime targets for KGB agents, some of whom might be women, and that compromising photographs of sexual indiscretions might be taken.

I asked what I could do. MI5 wanted me to print a series of case-records simply to show what the Russians did and how they did it. This would serve to warn the visitors to Moscow. Some of the case-records would show that by making a clean breast of any involvement at the earliest stage to the British authorities Russian blackmail threats could be circumvented.

I asked the MI5 man why the men visiting Moscow could not be warned individually or in groups. He replied that, as his organization was so secret that officially it did not exist, this was not practicable.

When I read the case-records they were so interesting that I immediately agreed to publish a selection of them and they appeared without any reference to the electronics exhibition on 5 April 1961.

A few days later I was asked to lunch by Strelnikov at Rules Restaurant in Maiden Lane. He wasted little time. 'That was a terrible article you wrote last week', he said, 'about the KGB.'

'How was it terrible?' I asked ingenuously.

'It was terrible for peace,' he said rather menacingly. 'What made you write it?'

'No special reason,' I countered. 'I had been collecting case-records for some time and found that I had enough to make an article.'

'But why write an article which is so terrible for peace?' he asked.

'Look, Tony,' I said impatiently, 'I am paid by Beaverbrook Newspapers to write articles and when I have collected my material it is my duty to produce it.'

Strelnikov gave a hint of a smile and seized on his opportunity. 'How much do they pay you?'

'Quite a lot.'

'Well, we will pay you more,' he declared.

'To do what?' I asked.

'Write for us! Work for us!'

I was not prepared to continue such a dangerous conversation and made some excuse to change the subject, but shortly after, when he came to pay the bill, he opened his wallet and as he took out a bundle of pound notes he showed them to me and flicked them saying 'Don't forget! Work for us!'

I made no comment but after leaving him immediately contacted M—— for an urgent conversation. He was delighted. 'Just what we've been waiting for! Report the offer to your editor. Tell him to make an official complaint to the Foreign Office and we will get him declared *persona non grata*. We can't wait to get rid of that dangerous bastard. You would have been a hell of a catch for him with all your contacts and your Right-wing reputation as a cover!'

I went straight to see the editor, the late Arthur Christiansen, on returning to the office. When I passed on M——'s suggestion that he should report my experience to the Foreign Office he looked at me scathingly and said, 'Are you mad? It's taken us months to get an office opened in Moscow and they'll kick us out.'

Later M—— told me, sadly, that there was nothing MI5 could do without the editor's letter, which would have had to be presented formally to the Soviet ambassador if a request for Strelnikov's removal was to be made.

So Strelnikov remained in London. Shortly afterwards he left for a tour of duty in the Foreign Office in Moscow and a photograph appeared of Sir Alec Douglas-Home and his Russian counterpart in

Moscow signing a test-ban treaty. There standing behind them, smiling as usual, was the bat-eared Strelnikov.

During the whole of our acquaintance Strelnikov had given me only one story – the news that Russian astronauts had been the first to enter space in a rocket flight. It was a world scoop and made a fine show in the newspaper but it turned out to be entirely untrue.

After my last meeting with M—— on this particular project he walked back with me to Fleet Street to continue our conversation, wearing a dark suit and a bowler hat. After saying farewell I entered the office lift and was followed by a colleague. 'Who was that chap in the bowler?' he asked. 'He looks like the typical man from MI5.'

Within days of Strelnikov's departure I was telephoned by a 'diplomat' from the Hungarian embassy who asked me out to lunch at a Hungarian restaurant in Soho. I realized that he was probably the take-over man since the Soviet embassy and those of the satellites in London operate as a single Intelligence organization under firm control from the centre in Moscow. I found the man a bore so I never returned the compliment and following a series of anti-Soviet articles by me, I was struck off the list.

I have never been invited to the Soviet embassy since, except when I specifically requested to attend the reception given to Valentina Tereshkova, the first woman to orbit the earth. Who should be there but Strelnikov, who had been allowed to return to London for a further tour of duty! Strange indeed are the mechanics of Whitehall when one part of the machine knows that a 'diplomat' is a dangerous Intelligence officer and another allows him back in the country.

Strelnikov avoided me in the crowded rooms of the embassy but there is no doubt that he was still busy on KGB business. Commander Anthony Courtney, the former Tory MP, later compromised by the KGB, was also at the reception and records in his book, *Sailor in a Russian Frame,* that the big Russian had given him a veiled warning that a campaign he had been waging in Parliament to point out how many Communist diplomats were KGB agents was most unwelcome.

It is sad that Courtney, whose fate I describe in Chapter Eleven, had not taken note of the MI5 case-records I had published. It was during the 1961 Moscow electronics exhibition that his Russian woman friend suggested she should accompany him to his bedroom at the National Hotel, where the KGB was waiting to photograph them.

The case-records which I had first published at MI5's request were later issued by that organization as the basis of a booklet called 'Their Trade is Treachery'. Written almost like a paperback thriller, it is a manual intended for perusal by officials with access to secret information and is not available to the public. Its contents, describing the often brutal methods used by the KGB to trap the unwary into serving as spies and saboteurs, would be a valuable warning to any citizen. However, such was the Whitehall objection to any publication of its contents – including those I had already printed – that after mention of the Official Secrets Act produced no result the *Daily Express* was threatened with an action for breach of Crown Copyright if we reproduced any of the contents verbatim.

Such are the extremes to which the secret departments will go to preserve their own peculiar brand of power. We did, however, call their bluff and printed two articles about the booklet with no prosecution.

To return to Henry Kerby, it has been reported that he was a member of MI6 but I can find nobody who remembers him there, though he may have been used occasionally. It is not impossible that he was an MI5 contact, some kind of double agent spying on the Russians but helping them occasionally in order to keep up the deception. I have a copy of a letter to Wilson in which Kerby claimed to have been a British secret agent during the war in enemy-occupied territory. So he might have put Strelnikov on to me with MI5's approval, knowing that I would report on him and possibly secure his expulsion, which so nearly happened. (The use of journalists in such a way, so that they are agents without realizing it, is common enough, particularly in the CIA, which terms such unwitting assistants 'Willies'.)

MI6 would not necessarily know if Kerby had been employed by MI5 because each service tends to be secretive about its contacts and sources. This even applies to different departments within the same service. An MI6 friend told me how he had wanted to contact a well-known industrial tycoon who was going to Russia. He thought he should ask him to look for certain things in factories he was to visit and then report back on his return. Not being sure of his man, he approached MI5 for an assurance that he was politically reliable. MI5's reaction was to urge him to avoid contacting him in any way. He was so mixed up with Anglo-Soviet friendship organizations and other Communist front activities that MI5 had him under some degree of surveillance.

My friend later discovered that the tycoon was already working patriotically for another branch of MI6 and had patiently been building up his contacts with the Russians on its instructions!

Kerby may also have been acting as an MI5 spy on the Labour Party. What undoubtedly happened was that Kerby regularly supplied Wilson with information about what was going on inside the Tory Party while Labour was in opposition. Letters, of which I have secured samples, some of them beginning 'Dear Guv', contained details of private Tory meetings, party plans and prospects and gossip about Tory leaders, most of it damaging. One private letter which Kerby enclosed had been sent to him by Sir Alec Douglas-Home, then Prime Minister, requesting his assistance in acquiring political contacts for the party to improve Tory relations in the Commonwealth. Kerby had scrawled in ink, 'So the boys are starting their own "secret service"! Pathetic! Henry.' Another marked Private and Personal from Roy Welensky in Rhodesia and including information about Wilson's stock there was also passed on.

Kerby made a private mission to Rhodesia with the assistance of the Duke of Montrose, who was living there, and put in a long report to Wilson highly critical of the Rhodesian leadership. He gave details of how sanctions were being broken and a breakdown of how the Rhodesian Cabinet had voted against the settlement proposals resulting from the Smith–Wilson talks on HMS *Tiger*.

Kerby attacked his own colleagues viciously in anonymous contributions to a private subscription digest called the *Weekly Review*, marking the parts which promoted Wilson's interests in red ink when sending them to him.

Letters to Wilson show that Kerby made untiring efforts over more than a year to induce the Prime Minister to secure his appointment as chairman of a committee on Soviet trade which was to be part of the British National Export Council. He claimed to be in close contact with a powerful delegation from the Presidium of the Supreme Soviet which visited Britain late in 1966. He was most anxious that Wilson should announce his appointment as full-time deputy chairman of the whole Export Council during the projected visit to London of Kosygin, the Soviet Premier, in the following February. He was prepared to resign his seat if given this appointment, pointing out that he would have to do so anyway because his constituency party would despise him as a 'traitor'.

The Export Council chiefs wanted nothing to do with him and he gave up his effort to join them in disgust in a long letter he addressed to Marcia in 1967. By and large the information was not of much value to Wilson and it seems he was suspicious of it because he handed much of it over to Wigg. But there was one item on which Wilson did act with results he came to regard as politically disastrous, as I explain in Chapter Twenty-four. It was information from Kerby which triggered off the D-notice affair which Wilson has described as his worst self-inflicted wound.

As his health deteriorated Kerby desperately wanted the dignity of a title. Joe Haines related in his book, *The Politics of Power*, that a go-between for Kerby, who happened to be the political correspondent of a Sunday newspaper, put forward 'the most bare-faced proposition in 1969'. Kerby, the journalist said, was prepared to pass on 'all the Conservative election secrets' in return for a life peerage.

When the June election of 1970 was announced the intermediary made a further approach saying that Kerby was now prepared to settle for a knighthood. Throughout the campaign information posted in Kerby's constituency poured through Haines's letter-box addressed to his wife in her maiden name.

One aspect of the mystery surrounding Kerby, who died in 1971, remains to be recorded. When Haines disclosed Kerby's apparent treachery it was obviously a painful experience for his widow and children. Wigg telephoned me to say that if I wrote to Mrs Kerby suggesting that she contact him he would be able to put her mind at ease. I did so and she certainly contacted Wigg. What he told her I do not know but I believe it was to the effect that whatever her late husband had done had been in the country's best interests. Knowing Wigg's poor view of the Tories that could also have meant the interests of the Labour Party.

*Chapter Eleven*

# MPs and the KGB

WHEN the Director-General of MI5 gave evidence to the Franks Committee in 1971, he made a point of stressing how MPs are in particular danger of attention from the KGB:

> The Soviet bloc Intelligence services are very active among political parties around the Palace of Westminster. Very many MPs are in contact with many Intelligence officers. If the Russian Intelligence service can recruit a back-bench MP and he climbs to a ministerial position, the spy is home and dry.

He had sound evidence to substantiate that remark, most of it secret and likely to remain so. As I have already mentioned in Chapter One, one Labour minister quietly resigned under pressure from the security authorities and from the Foreign Secretary acting on their behalf, and in 1970 the public was given some details of the activities of Soviet bloc Intelligence against MPs, the occasion being the arrest and trial of Will Owen, the sixty-eight-year-old MP for Morpeth, on Official Secrets charges.

Owen, who was head of a travel firm specializing in visits to East Germany, resigned his seat after being charged with giving Czech Intelligence information of a confidential nature which he had learned as a member of Parliament's Estimates Committee.

The original evidence laid against him had come from the Czech defector Josef Frolik, who claimed to have recruited and run several Britons as Soviet bloc Intelligence agents while serving at the Czech embassy in London.

At the trial, which lasted thirteen days, Owen admitted receiving

£2,300 from the Czechs which he had not declared for tax. He agreed that he had deliberately deceived the Special Branch officer who had questioned him and admitted that he knew that Robert Husak, the 'third secretary' at the Czech embassy with whom he dealt, was a spy. Husak was in fact the deputy chief of Czech Intelligence in London, and Owen claimed that he had been threatened by him.

His counsel admitted that Owen's conduct had been dishonourable but, after various disagreements among the jury, he was acquitted on the grounds that the information he had undoubtedly supplied was not within the terms of the Official Secrets Acts. He was, however, ordered to pay £2,000 towards his legal costs and was presumably taxed on his illicit earnings.

While security chiefs were extremely disappointed with this acquittal, NATO chiefs were even more so, being alarmed at the disclosure that a back-bench MP with commercial connections in East Germany should have access to information they considered as classified. A memorandum was sent out to security departments of several NATO countries suggesting that the British government would be taking steps to make any repetition of such a case extremely unlikely. However, I can find no evidence that any effective move was ever made. The main result of the Owen case was to make the Security Service very chary about recommending criminal action against any other MPs.

Perhaps if MPs had not been immunized against telephone tapping and positive vetting, Owen's behaviour would have been detected earlier. The positive-vetting form specifically asks, 'Are you or have you ever been a close associate of a Communist or Communist sympathizer?' If Owen had been required to reveal that he was associating with Husak, who was known to be an Intelligence agent, he would at least have been spared his Old Bailey experience, which was damaging to Britain, because the security authorities could have warned him of the dangers he faced, the threatening methods used by Husak being standard for the Soviet bloc.

A large number of MPs are in touch with Soviet bloc diplomats and officials for similar trade and social purposes and the attempt to suborn Owen was by no means an isolated instance.

In 1970 I was warned by an Intelligence contact that John Stonehouse, the former Minister for Aviation and then Minister of Posts and Telecommunications, who was known to be a friend of mine, had been in difficulty with his Prime Minister, Harold Wilson, over a security issue. No further information was forthcoming and for libel reasons I could not report it. The tip did help to explain, however, why Stonehouse had assured me more than once that he would never get any further in government under Wilson and for that reason was going into the business world.

The matter became public after Stonehouse's faked death by drowning off Miami Beach in 1974 when the Czech defector Josef Frolik revealed that he had also named Stonehouse as having been recruited by Czech Intelligence and that he had acted in that capacity while he was still a minister.

In a statement to Parliament while Stonehouse was still missing, Wilson disclosed that in 1969 he had called him to Downing Street and confronted him with Frolik's allegations in the presence of an officer from MI5. Stonehouse denied them and Wilson told Parliament that, in the result, it was concluded that there was no evidence to support Frolik's claims and that Stonehouse had not been a security risk in any way. Stonehouse had been allowed to continue at the Post Office until the general election of June 1970 when he retained his seat but was excluded from the new government.

When I questioned Wilson in 1978 he said he had simply taken the advice of MI5 that there was no evidence that Stonehouse was a spy. 'That's what they told me,' he said.

Once a person has been named by a defector, whether rightly or falsely, MI5 never loses complete interest. Following Stonehouse's appalling behaviour in securing false passports in the names of dead men to facilitate his disappearance, security authorities renewed their interest and visited Frolik in Washington to question him again. Frolik says that one of them apologized to him at Wilson's request, but Wilson denies this, and the MI5 officer responsible has since admitted that the apology was made on his own initiative to keep Frolik sweet.

One aspect of the continuing security interest appeared to show itself following Stonehouse's exposure in Australia, where he was living under a false name. It was revealed that police had been watching him for several days in the mistaken belief that he was Lord Lucan, the missing peer wanted on a murder charge. John Stonehouse bears little resemblance to Lord Lucan and I just do not believe that the Australian authorities ever confused them. I suspect that Stonehouse's exposure was delayed so that security men could watch him to see if he was meeting anyone of interest. There is no evidence whatever that he attempted to do so.

When I questioned Wilson about the Stonehouse affair he remarked, 'I never thought he was a spy but I always knew he was a crook!' During the years that I knew Stonehouse I never thought he was crooked and can relate one episode in support of this. While he was in charge of the Post Office, two American firms, Lockheed and Hughes, were in competition for a large electronics contract. A friend of mine who was involved with the Lockheed agency in Britain went over to see the parent company in the USA and was told that there was half a million dollars in it for Stonehouse if he could swing the deal their way. Stonehouse was told this but the contract went to Hughes.

Another example was the project to buy a huge computer set-up for Heathrow Airport to process the mounting mass of air-freight and Customs information. I was called in by Stonehouse to help him by campaigning in the newspaper for the contract to be awarded to the British company International Computers Limited, which was struggling to establish an international reputation. His chief, Wedgwood Benn, was supporting Treasury officials who wanted to buy American on the grounds that it would be cheaper. Even when foreign airlines operating at Heathrow were so determined to have the American equipment that they threatened to 'black' a British computer, Stonehouse held out and eventually won the battle. He had the grace to tell the *Express* editor that he would never have been able to push the deal through without the support we had provided.

I think that what happened to Stonehouse was partly the result of a close association with a mutual friend of ours, the late Geoffrey Edwards, who had made a sudden fortune out of arms sales. Edwards, for whom Stonehouse tried hard to secure a knighthood, was a most generous host and what Stonehouse saw as a guest at his splendid homes in Ascot and Barbados helped to drive him to try to make some quick money himself once he had decided that he had no future in politics. Clearly, while highly intelligent and personable, he did not have the business skill or temperament to do it by legitimate means.

The last time I saw Stonehouse was very shortly before his sensational mock disappearance. It was at a party given at the Savoy for Prince Philip following the showing of a wildlife film, and my wife and I were the guests of Lord Zuckerman. As we collected our buffet supper I noticed a tall man urging us to join his small table. It was Stonehouse and his wife Barbara. He was rather drunk, which in my experience was most unusual for him, and also stupidly out of place because the room was full of people who, conceivably, could have been useful to him in his business.

On the way home I remarked to my wife, 'Either John's business or his marriage is on the rocks.'

Both were.

At the time of writing, June 1978, moves are being made by Tory MPs to reopen the security aspects of Stonehouse's behaviour. The Prime Minister has received a letter from Cranley Onslow, MP for Woking, urging him to resolve the matter by an independent inquiry by the Security Commission, a small standing panel which can be called upon to investigate certain aspects of cases involving breaches of security.

In his letter, Onslow claims that Stonehouse's account of his connections with men who turned out to be Czech Intelligence officers contains inconsistencies which should be cleared up to satisfy Parliament and the public.

As a result, Callaghan saw Mrs Thatcher on Privy Council terms, showed her documents and convinced her that there were no good grounds for reopening the issue. The Prime Minister then tried to induce Wilson to agree that the matter should be referred to the Security Commission, knowing that it must produce a negative report embarrassing to the Tories, but Wilson declined.

In the summer of 1975 I was summoned to see a former MI5 officer to be given some most intriguing information about an MP. A defector called Frantisek August, formerly a major in Czech Intelligence in London, was about to return to Britain under a false name for a brief and secret visit. I remembered August as being the Czech spy-master named in the trial of Nicholas Prager, an ex-RAF sergeant jailed for twelve years in 1971 for betraying the secrets of Blue Diver, an advanced electronic countermeasure device fitted to Britain's V-bombers. I was given the name of a man in Wales he was to contact and told that if I could induce August to talk he could given me a most interesting story concerning the espionage activities of a well known Labour MP who, for libel reasons, must be nameless. It was said that this MP was not just an agent of Czech Intelligence but 'an officer of the KGB'.

I contacted the Welshman, who was highly embarrassed to learn that I knew of the impending visit, and made it clear that he would be of no assistance. I had him watched for a while in the hope that August might appear on his doorstep but without success. Eventually I decided that the only way to get more information was to ask a parliamentary friend to question the Home Secretary, then Roy Jenkins, as to why a man who had done such disservice to Britain was being allowed to set foot in the country.

Jenkins's reply revealed that August had already completed his visit and had returned to America.

A few months later in April 1976 August was to appear as a witness in US Senate hearings about the extent of Soviet bloc Intelligence activities against the USA and its allies and, under oath, stated that 'there were several members of the British Parliament recruited'.

August's purpose in visiting Britain remains a mystery I would dearly like to solve. MI5 clearly wanted me to know that he was coming. Why? Could this have been part of the MI5 faction trying to undermine Wilson by showing that one of his ministers had been a spy? I have a feeling that one day we may hear more of Mr August.

More recently Frolik has also named a Cabinet minister in the Callaghan government as one of the reasons why he is afraid to visit Britain. 'I do not fear the vengeance of the Czech service but of people who are highly placed and for whom I constitute a most unpleasant and dangerous witness,' he wrote to a Czech exile living in London. He then went on to name several of these people, including the Cabinet minister.

The Czech exile, Josef Josten, a former Prague journalist, reported the contents of the letter to the British security authorities who had presumably heard them when Frolik had been debriefed after he defected in 1969. To ensure that notice was taken of it Stephen Hastings, Tory MP for Mid-Bedfordshire, sent a copy of the letter to the Prime Minister in January 1978 suggesting an independent inquiry into all the defector's allegations. No such action is in prospect and none is likely while Labour remains in office.

For libel reasons it is not safe for me to name the Cabinet minister concerned. At the time of writing he is still in office.

Frolik is living under the protection of the CIA which vets every letter he sends out. So the CIA presumably had no objection to the naming of the British Cabinet minister.

The KGB may have aimed low with Owen but one of its branches, again Czech Intelligence, aimed high with Edward Heath. Simply because Heath was unmarried and seemingly not interested in women, Czech Intelligence headquarters in Prague conceived the idea that he might fall victim to a homosexual trap.

Looking for an apparently innocent means of making contact, Czech Intelligence sought out a virtuoso organist who was on its list of Czech homosexuals who could be induced to do its bidding. Arrangements were made by the Czech embassy for the organist to give two recitals in London in the early 1960s. Heath, not then leader of the Tory Party but obviously destined for high office, was invited to the concerts and apparently expressed interest in playing a famous organ in one of the great churches of Prague.

The plot was doomed to fail anyway because Czech assessment of Heath's character had been completely misinformed and in fact came to nothing because it was stifled by British counter-Intelligence. But the incident provided further evidence of the unremitting efforts of the Soviet bloc Intelligence system.

The Vassall case (see Chapter Seven) provided a typical example of how the KGB uses sex to recruit agents through the threat of blackmail in furtherance of the Kremlin's inexorable pursuit of power. The KGB also makes use of sex to destroy reputations if that suits the same purpose. The case of Commander Courtney was a classic instance.

Anthony Courtney is a former naval officer who entered Parliament as Tory MP for Harrow East in 1959 after a distinguished career, much of it in Naval Intelligence. He had learned to speak Russian and as a civilian was involved in promoting East–West trade, an activity which required visits to Moscow. During these trips he made several Russian friends, including an attractive woman called Zina Volkova. In the spring of 1961 when Courtney, recently widowed, was taking part in the British industrial exhibition in Moscow, this woman, on her initiative, accompanied him to his bedroom in the National Hotel.

Later, as a result of what he had learned about subversive KGB activities against British representatives in Iron Curtain embassies and trade missions, he made several speeches in Parliament urging that greater restrictions should be imposed on Soviet bloc officials working in London because the Foreign Office was making it too easy for spies to pose as members of missions.

He was warned both by the Russian ambassador's wife and by

Anatoli Strelnikov, the embassy KGB officer whom I described in the ' previous chapter, that his speeches were being very badly received by the Kremlin but he continued his campaign, hoping to introduce a bill to limit the diplomatic immunity granted to the Soviet bloc.

The KGB struck in August 1965 by sending a broadsheet to various ministers, MPs, newspapers and his new wife. It carried several compromising photographs taken surreptitiously when Zina Volkova had been with him in the bedroom, where the KGB had been waiting with microphones and hidden cameras as, no doubt, the woman knew.

The resulting scandal culminated in the selection of another candidate to represent East Harrow and Courtney's political and private lives were shattered.

There could be no doubt that this was a KGB exercise. Nobody else could have taken the photographs in the National Hotel in Moscow and the broadsheet proved to be almost certainly of Russian origin.

George Wigg, then in charge of security, had received a copy of the broadsheet posted by hand at his London flat. Since Courtney was just a back-bench MP Wigg suspected that the KGB had disgraced him for a more important purpose. As he told Courtney, and as he has since told me, he believed – and still does – that they were 'cracking the whip' at somebody else to warn them that a similar fate was in store if they ever stepped out of line.

Though I may have been small fry on the books of the KGB they have made several attempts to discredit me by statements in *Pravda*, *Izvestia* and other controlled publications that I am a British secret agent posing as a journalist, presumably with the purpose of making it difficult for me to obtain visas to foreign countries and perhaps even sowing doubt in the minds of my employers. On one occasion when Russia was friendly with Egypt, some interesting disinformation about me appeared in a Cairo newspaper revealing that not only was I a spy but was making a fortune out of mining arsenic in Sweden for use in German poison-gas weapons.

I have no evidence that the strange episode involving sexual scandal in the biggest possible way which I am about to relate was perpetrated by the KGB, but it occurred after I had done the KGB several disservices and the area concerned was very close to the Soviet embassy in Kensington Palace Gardens.

Some readers may remember how in 1965 six prostitutes were

found murdered at intervals, their bodies being found, usually naked, in the Shepherd's Bush area. They had all been killed by a sexual assault of a peculiar nature and the comparison with the notorious Jack the Ripper Murders was soon made.

Clues were so sparse that with the sixth murder the police finally appealed for information from anyone who had seen any prostitute picked up by a car in the West Kensington area on the night of 11 January.

Shortly after that date my wife and I went to Ireland for a week's salmon fishing and during that time an anonymous voice reported to Scotland Yard by telephone that he had seen a woman answering the murdered prostitute's description being picked up in Kensington Road by a man in a dark navy blue Jaguar of which he had noted the number, which in itself was an odd circumstance.

A check showed that the car was mine and the colour was correct. In my absence the police took possession of the car by a subterfuge and examined it meticulously for fingerprints of any of the victims. When they opened the boot there was a triumphant cry of 'Just look at this!' What they saw made them think that I was indeed the mass murderer. The plastic lining of the boot was heavily marked with recent blood-stains, which were just what they were looking for. The women had been killed elsewhere in a manner which produced blood and their bodies had then been transported by car to the places where they were dumped.

The blood-stains, which turned out to be the spoils of a big hare shoot in which I had taken part immediately before leaving for Ireland, were a temporary bonus for the anonymous informant, who could not have known anything about them.

By the time I returned home the car had been sent back surreptitiously and, apart from fingerprint powder still inside the glove compartment, I would have known nothing had I not discovered that it had been missing from my home and made inquiries.

John Du Rose, the Detective Chief Superintendent in charge of the case, which remained unsolved, was apologetic and eventually I joined the rest of those on the inquiry at dinner at the Dorchester. They agreed with me that the call had been a deliberate hoax. Anyone really seeing my car at night would have reported it as black because that is how dark navy blue looks in poor light.

There was, of course, little chance that I would be arrested for I could prove that my car had not been in London on the night in

·question but news that I was a suspect, however short-lived, might have leaked into the newspapers. With many of the much more elaborate disinformation efforts known to be perpetrated by the KGB, the consequences for the victim are often minor and seem based on the principle that so long as a little mud sticks, they are worth while.

*Chapter Twelve*

# The Sad Fall of a Good Man

UNTIL 1963 the sex lives of politicians were of little interest to the public, who took the civilized view that what men or women did in private was their affair so long as they did not break the law. It was widely known that Lloyd George had been such an active seducer that no chambermaid was safe but, so far as men were concerned, that was considered almost a plus. Men with drive are thought to be highly sexed and nobody demanded that politicians should be exceptions so long as they were reasonably discreet and did not end up in the divorce court.

My late employer, Lord Beaverbrook, made no secret to his friends about his succession of mistresses and remained interested in the casual conquest well into old age. Beaverbrook enjoyed telling a story which illustrates the prevailing attitude. In 1921 he was dining in a Piccadilly restaurant with two obliging American actresses called the Dolly Sisters when he was summoned to Downing Street to see the Prime Minister, Lloyd George. Knowing that Beaverbrook was an ardent Presbyterian the Prime Minister offered him the appointment of High Commissioner to the General Assembly of the Church of Scotland. Beaverbrook wanted it but thinking over his habits and of his immediate connection with the Dolly Sisters he˙ declined on the grounds that he was unsuited to the important office.

Lloyd George then turned to Bonar Law and said, 'Then Geordie gets it.' 'Geordie' being the Duke of Sutherland.

Beaverbrook raced back to the restaurant intending, as he said, 'to make the most of my freedom which I had retained by paying such a high price', and who should he see dancing with one of his Dolly Sisters but Geordie Sutherland!

This attitude changed, however, when the Labour leadership under Harold Wilson decided to exploit what was actually a minor sex scandal involving the Tory Minister for War, Jack Profumo. At the time the Labour leaders and George Wigg, then a back-bencher who initiated and coordinated the attack, convinced themselves that their entire thrust was on the grounds of security not morals, but many Tory MPs saw it as a thrust for political power and still do.

I regret having to rake over this sad affair in which I was involved, particularly as Profumo, a friend, has suffered so much and done so much to rehabilitate himself in society, but the case had profound and lasting effects on the behaviour of Wilson and some of his ministers during his premiership. This behaviour was occasioned partly by fears of Tory revenge but also, I suspect, by feelings of guilt. Profumo's own behaviour also illustrates the lengths to which a politician may be driven to retain power for himself and his colleagues, for what he did was alien to his normal code of conduct.

The whole affair is also instructive about how Whitehall departments operate and personalities react, especially as rare details of the activities of the Security Service, MI5, were revealed in the official report on the affair by Lord Denning. Further, it illustrates the constraints put upon newspapers by the libel laws and the devices which can be adopted to circumvent them.

Early in 1961 at Cliveden, the country home of Lord Astor, Profumo had met Christine Keeler, who had come to London to live as a call-girl. A friend of mine has since told me that he was one of the first to enjoy this girl's favour and that she was then 'young, fresh and very beautiful'. When I met her in 1963 she already showed the signs of her descent into her association with criminals. But when Profumo was attracted to her she was still pristine.

Also present at the Cliveden party was Captain Eugene Ivanov, a Russian Intelligence officer listed as assistant naval attaché at the Soviet embassy. He was a friend of a gifted osteopath called Stephen

Ward, who treated Lord Astor and had a cottage on the Cliveden estate. Christine was living with Ward.

Suspecting Ivanov, MI5 had been efficiently keeping watch on his activities for many months and had reported his chance meeting with the War Minister. As a result, the Cabinet Secretary alerted Profumo to the danger, passing on a suggestion from the MI5 chief that he might encourage Ivanov to defect. The War Minister wisely declined.

In the meantime Profumo had dated Christine and indulged in casual sexual relations – a not uncommon practice among modern politicians, I may add. Suspecting that MI5 had also discovered this affair, which they had not, he ended it, writing an off-putting letter which was later to prove most damaging to him.

It became widely believed that Profumo and Ivanov were both involved sexually with Keeler at the same time and Christine herself claimed that she took special pleasure in having them both in her bed within an hour of each other. However Lord Denning, who conducted an exemplary inquiry into the whole case, questioning every available witness, was convinced that Ivanov was never Keeler's lover.

Nothing more might have been heard of what was a private matter, for though MI5 eventually learned of Profumo's indiscretion it is not supposed to be part of its function to pry into morals so long as they do not impinge on security and there were no doubts about the loyalty of the War Minister, who had a fine individual war record.

But on 11 November 1962 George Wigg received a mysterious telephone call at the home of the Labour Party agent in his Dudley constituency where he was lunching. What appeared to be a deliberately muffled voice said, 'Forget about the Vassall case. You want to look at Profumo', and then hung up. The identity of the caller baffled Wigg and still does. It could have been an agent of the KGB intent on stimulating a damaging scandal, a journalist seeking a device to make public information held up by libel considerations, or somebody with a grudge against the War Minister or the Tory Party in general. The following month a former Labour MP, John Lewis, met Keeler at a party and she later told him of her involvement with Profumo and Ivanov. Lewis immediately reported the information to Wigg, who has always been deeply interested in security problems and must have seen its political potential. A former regular soldier with deep affection for the Army, he had recently crossed swords with Profumo in Parliament over a report concerning the heat exhaustion of men sent out to Kuwait without proper acclimatization. He had low regard for the War Minister, believing that he had been given misleading answers by him and had been treated shabbily. Lewis continued to keep him informed about Keeler's allegations, including a statement that Ivanov had asked Stephen Ward to use his connection with Profumo to discover the date when the Americans were to supply the German Luftwaffe with nuclear bombs.

In January 1963 Keeler, who was hard up, had supplied the letter from Profumo to the *Sunday Pictorial* and signed a conditional contract to sell her story to the newspaper. They did not publish it then but Fleet Street generally was soon aware of what she had to say and of its political implications. As Profumo was War Minister, I was immediately involved.

Major-General Gilbert Monckton, who was the Army's director of public relations, had organized an informal cocktail party in the War Office for Profumo to meet certain defence correspondents, of whom I was one, to discuss recruiting plans and other Army matters. I felt sure that Profumo would cancel it for fear that he might be questioned about the Keeler business, but he did not. He was completely composed, showing no signs of concern, and asked me to join him at lunch some time in the near future.

On 8 March a political news-letter called *Westminster Confidential* published some of the information Keeler was hawking, including the possible connection between the War Minister and a Soviet military attaché. At this stage Wigg convinced Wilson that the affair was moving to a climax but the Labour leader decided that Wigg should pursue the issue 'on his own responsibility'.

Christine's downhill career had involved her in becoming a witness in an assault case involving West Indians and when she disappeared she gave newspapers an opportunity to break some of their information. On 15 March the *Daily Express* had a front page with a banner headline 'War Minister shock', claiming that Profumo had offered his resignation to the Prime Minister and with a picture of him and his wife, the film star Valerie Hobson. On the other side of the same page was a picture of Keeler headed 'Vanished Old Bailey witness'.

Lord Denning's report states that the *Daily Express* witness told

him that the juxtaposition of the two pictures was entirely coincidental. In the interests of political history I can testify that was incorrect.
The juxtaposition of the two pictures was to give the *Express* a lead in
printing the story which all Fleet Street knew was bound to break.

As Denning reported, the *Daily Express* front page aroused great
alarm among the Tory Whips and among the other newspapers
which were wondering what they could safely do to get into the story.
On 17 March the *Sunday Pictorial* published a story linking Keeler
with Ivanov and the interest by MI5 but without mentioning Profumo. The *Sunday Pictorial* still withheld the dangerous letter from
Profumo to Keeler in which he called her 'Darling'. Most Fleet
Street newspapers knew of the existence of the letter, however, and it
was to play an interesting part in a conversation later between
Profumo and myself.

By 21 March Wigg decided that the time had come to act within
the privilege of Parliament. Late that night he rose to demand that
the House be told the truth about rumours circulating about a
member of the government front bench concerning Christine Keeler
and a shooting by a West Indian. He urged the setting up of a select
committee to investigate the rumours if they could not be categorically denied.

Crossman and Barbara Castle intervened, raising the suggestion
that Profumo might have been involved in the immediate mystery of
Keeler's disappearance, for which there was no evidence whatever.

Wigg assured me that he and his colleagues firmly decided against
going for Profumo on moral grounds because 'few in the House have
not been guilty of some sexual turpitude', and that national security
must be the issue. Whatever the original intention, the major thrust
was soon political. The greatest obstacle in Labour's restless drive to
oust the Tory government was Harold Macmillan – 'Super-
mac' – who had great popular appeal. The Profumo affair had suddenly offered an unexpected opportunity to undermine him.

Wigg's intervention convinced the Tory ministers that they
should act and it was decided that the Chief Whip should ask Profumo, 'Did you or didn't you?' When Profumo replied 'I didn't' he
may well at that stage have been assuring his colleagues that he had
nothing to do with Keeler's disappearance, which was the most
serious charge.

The Tory ministers, anxious to eradicate the danger to their
continuation in office as quickly as possible, recalled Profumo to

Westminster at 2.45 a.m. when he was half-drugged with sleeping pills. He waited while lawyers drafted a statement for him to read in the House next morning.

Macmillan had been made aware of all that transpired but took the view that he should not discuss the matter with Profumo at that stage since it would serve no purpose. When he learned that the War Minister was to make a statement refuting all allegations, even of sexual misconduct, he accepted the truth of it completely.

Profumo made his statement on 22 March. Truthfully, he said he had not seen Keeler since December 1961. Untruthfully, he said there had never been any impropriety with her and warned that if allegations were made outside Parliament he would sue.

Though Labour members said nothing audible during the statement, Wigg was soon to be sure that it was a lie because on 26 March he received full information of the relationship from Stephen Ward, the man who had been the means of introducing Keeler to Profumo and to many other people of note.

I already knew that Profumo had lied and must be doomed because *Daily Express* reporters had tracked down Christine hiding in Madrid. She had gone there with a man and they had so little money that she was desperate to sell her story, which she did for £800. On 25 March a copy of it arrived on my desk. It contained details of her relationship with Profumo which could not have been concocted.

Only that part of the Madrid dispatch concerned with the finding of Keeler was printed. Lord Beaverbrook ordered that her allegations about her friendship with Profumo should be withheld for two reasons. First, he did not want to smear the government with a statement by a woman of doubtful character who might not be telling the truth, though he told me he tended to believe her story. Secondly, the *Daily Express* was already involved in severe libel problems over the Vassall spy case. Lord Carrington, then First Lord of the Admiralty, was threatening to sue the *Daily Express* for libel damages, which, he had been advised, could be as high as £150,000. Beaverbrook feared that if the newspaper took the lead in showing that Profumo's statement was false, Carrington might be pushed into starting the action. Years later, Carrington told me that there had never been any real possibility of this because when he told Macmillan that he intended to sue, the Prime Minister forbade it, saying that there would be a general election soon and he wanted the support, not the enmity, of the Beaverbrook Press.

It so happened that one of my closest friends in Whitehall, Sir Richard Way, was permanent secretary at the War Office and therefore Profumo's chief civil servant. I therefore felt that I should warn him of Keeler's statement so that he could alert Profumo if he so wished.

We lunched together and he told me that Profumo was still protesting his innocence to him and that as he was also a close personal friend he had to believe him. When he read Keeler's allegations, however, he agreed that his political chief must have lied and would have to resign. Profumo had already discussed the practicability of resigning as minister in any case but decided that this could not be done without damaging the government and his future career as an MP. A reorganization of the defence ministries was to take place and it was considered regrettable that this was so far away that it could not be used as a means of covering up the resignation.

Profumo knew that some of his colleagues in Defence were turning against him over the issue.

The real danger, as Way saw it, was that to get money Keeler might make the facts sound much worse than they had ever been, especially as far as any security aspects were concerned. He had discovered that MI5 had been watching Ivanov's flat to see who had been visiting him and there was no evidence that Profumo had ever been there.

Though this meeting with Way had no impact on the case since he decided not to mention any part of it to Profumo, it was helpful to the *Daily Express* when the Press aspects of the affair became completely public with the setting up of the inquiry by Lord Denning and his subsequent report. I was able to assure Beaverbrook, as I did on 27 June, that our information had been made available to the proper authorities at the highest level almost immediately after we had received it. Apart from being a personal friend, Sir Richard was then chairman of the D-notice committee, so I assume that he warned MI5 of our information though he would not tell me about his relations with security.

I learned later that he had told the Chief of the Imperial General Staff, Sir Richard Hull, of my information and they had agreed that neither of them should say anything directly to Profumo. My relevant memo to Beaverbrook ends, 'I think these facts put us entirely in the clear as regards patriotic duty. We could not have moved faster in bringing the matter to the attention of the proper authority, who in this instance was undoubtedly Sir Richard Way.'

I mention this to show that newspapers in general are not unmindful of the national interest, as commonly alleged, and that friendship between journalists and senior civil servants can work both ways.

Sir Richard later wrote to Denning telling him I had shown him the *Daily Express* reports and admitting that, with hindsight, he might have made an error of judgement in failing to show them to Profumo. Denning replied that he agreed with his judgement that in these early circumstances he was right to have believed his minister. Sir Richard was not called as a witness by the Denning inquiry.

After Profumo's statement in Parliament I felt sure he would not wish to lunch with me as he had suggested but I was wrong. He invited me to join him and Major-General Monckton in the Savoy Grill where we were bound to be seen by many people. As we had aperitifs in the ante-room bar Profumo made a point of talking to everybody he knew, introducing me to those I had not met, and it was clear that he wanted the world to see that he could not possibly have anything to hide because otherwise he would not be lunching with a journalist specializing in Whitehall disclosures. This belief was fortified when we entered the grill room where he had reserved the table nearest the door where we were bound to be seen by everyone entering and leaving.

As always, Profumo was delightful company and he seemed relaxed enough for me to broach the Keeler affair. His response was, 'Look, I love my wife and she loves me and that's all that matters. Anyway, who is going to believe the word of this whore against the word of a man who has been in government office for ten years?'

'But what about the letters?' I asked, referring to what I understood were three letters from him to Keeler in the hands of newspapers.

'Letters?' he said. 'There are no letters.'

I believed him and was not unduly surprised when Monckton brought the lunch to a rather abrupt end explaining that the minister had an early meeting.

Events were brought to a conclusion by the activities of Stephen Ward, in whom the police began to take an interest on charges that he had been living on the immoral earnings of his call-girl friends. In attempts to have this called off, Ward provided information to the Prime Minister's office and to the Home Secretary and other MPs.

These indicated that Profumo had lied to the House, which Keeler confirmed in a statement she made to MI5, which continued to investigate possible security issues involving Ivanov and Ward. Questions were tabled in Parliament and Wilson wrote to Macmillan on the security issue. Macmillan assured Wilson that inquiries by MI5 had produced no evidence of any security breach, which was absolutely true.

Because of continuing pressure for a formal inquiry, Profumo was seen by the Chief Whip and told that if he had not been telling the full truth the results could be very damaging to the government. Profumo again denied that he had said anything that was untrue. Parliament went into recess on 31 May and the Profumos left for a short holiday in Venice, but by that time he could no longer live with his conscience and had decided to tell his wife the truth. He did so after their first dinner in Venice, when they decided that he must go back and face up to the situation. He resigned on 4 June, both from the government and from Parliament where he had served most ably for twenty-five years. He was held to have been guilty of contempt of the House and he was removed from the Privy Council.

On 9 August the *News of the World* started publishing Keeler's story, for which they had agreed to pay £23,000. This was the same story for which the *Express* had paid £800 but which it had forfeited by failing to print it. Once the *News of the World* started to run it Beaverbrook, who had banned its publication in the *Express*, berated the editor for not running it then.

After poor Jack's disgrace Monckton asked me to lunch. His purpose was to explain why he had brought our Savoy Grill meeting to a rather abrupt conclusion. He told me of his conversation with Profumo on the way back to the War Office in the taxi, for there had been no scheduled meeting to which the minister had needed to return.

'Wasn't that dangerous to tell Pincher there were no letters?' Monckton had asked. 'You told me yourself that the *Pictorial* have a letter.'

'But that's just it. He said letters and there is only one letter,' Profumo had answered.

I record this to show how certain Profumo must have been at that stage that the affair would blow over, and also to illustrate how, having been pushed by circumstances into a dreadful corner, his standards had become warped. Those who know Jack Profumo agree that normally it would be hard to find a more honourable man.

Harold Macmillan was such an honourable man himself that he has never really been able to understand Profumo's lapse. Some years later when spending the weekend with the former Prime Minister at a shooting party we discussed the matter. 'Why shouldn't I have believed him?' he asked. 'Not only was he a gentleman but he had won a libel action based on his denial and taken the money! He did, of course, give the money to charity,' he conceded.

Knowing as I do the illicit sexual affairs of many politicians, past and present, some of them grossly depraved, it is tragic that Profumo, who was regarded by most as an excellent War Minister, should have been ruined as he was. Normally membership of the club of Parliament is sufficient to ensure that fellow members close ranks when one is seriously attacked on personal grounds. Profumo was made an exception, I believe, because Labour politicians, desperate with being so long in the wilderness of opposition, saw him as a stepping-stone to power.

Happily he retains a sense of humour about the affair, no doubt because of the marvellous support of his wife. Not long ago I was a fellow guest at a partridge shoot and before he arrived our host suggested that we should all avoid any lunch-time subject which might embarrass him. We strove manfully and were succeeding when I happened to ask Jack about the prison work he had undertaken. He then proceeded to tell us about his first day as a visitor at Grendon when he had to 'welcome' a rather dangerous criminal with the usual advisory lecture.

'Who the bleedin' hell do you think you're talking to?' the prisoner asked angrily. 'You should be in 'ere your bleedin' self for what you done to the country.'

Profumo told the story with gusto.

When Parliament reassembled in June after the Whitsun recess Macmillan faced a debate on the Profumo affair, with Wilson and the other Labour leaders poised to abstract every ounce of political advantage from it. With Profumo gone their target was the Prime Minister himself. There was severe criticism of Macmillan's handling of the business from his side and when the House divided twenty-seven Tories abstained from supporting their leader.

Macmillan appointed Denning to undertake an inquiry into the whole circumstances leading to Profumo's resignation, including the part played by the Security Service (MI5), and to report on the possibility that national security might have been endangered. Knowing all the facts as he then did, if belatedly, he was confident that the findings would be negative on security damage and would show his own behaviour to have been statesmanlike, but his days as leader were clearly numbered.

During this time I went down to see Lord Beaverbrook at Cherkley. At one point in our conversation he stood up, and barked angrily, 'Why in God's name should a great political party tear itself to rags and tatters just because a minister's fucked a woman?'

It was a fair question but the steamroller was on the move and nothing could stop it.

When Macmillan's successor, Sir Alec Douglas-Home, went to the polls in October 1964 Wilson beat him by only four seats. Without the burden of the Profumo affair the Tories might have won, especially as Macmillan might well have been still at the helm.

Though the Denning report, a model of its kind, confirmed that no official secrets had been prejudiced over the Profumo affair I have since wondered, as he and the security chiefs did, whether that was really the purpose of Ivanov's exercise. Like any Soviet bloc Intelligence officer, Ivanov was under the daily personal control of the resident KGB chief in the Russian embassy in London, who in turn is always closely controlled by the centre in Moscow. To such professionals the sudden possibility of disgracing a War Minister and even of expediting the fall of a Tory government would surely seem more attractive than a few technical secrets and it would be surprising if Ivanov's brief had not been switched in that direction. Ivanov returned to Moscow in a hurry in January 1963, as usually happens with Soviet bloc diplomats about to be publicly exposed, but he had been in London when Wigg received the mysterious telephone call which first aroused his interest.

On his own admission, Stephen Ward, who eventually committed suicide, was a Communist agent of sympathy and may have been involved with his friend Ivanov in what turned out to be a character assassination of major political importance. So Denning may have been near the mark when he wrote that Ivanov's purpose may have been to divide Britain from the United States by weakening American confidence in the reliability of British ministers and the security service. 'If this were the object of Captain Ivanov with Stephen Ward as his tool, he succeeded only too well,' he wrote.

The denigration of public figures through rumours of KGB links is a continuing process. As both Sir Harold Wilson and Lady Falkender know, because I have discussed it with them, it has been suggested that, with the KGB so active, nobody can visit Moscow as many times as they did, on private as well as on government business, without being propositioned or compromised in some way, however innocently. Marcia's alleged hold over Wilson is believed by some to reside in some compromise connected with Moscow.

While inquiring into this possibility I have been assured personally by a former Director-General of the Secret Intelligence Service that no evidence whatever of any such compromise or unfortunate connection with Moscow exists and that, so far as the British Intelligence and security authorities are concerned, the rumour is baseless and the result of political malice.

I have checked that this is also the experience of Israeli Intelligence, which is extremely well served regarding the connections of foreign statesmen with the KGB, and it is hard to see how successive Israeli governments could have thought so highly of Wilson had there been the smallest shred of evidence of dangerous attachments with the Soviet Union, which is so hostile to them.

In his book, *A Prime Minister on Prime Ministers*, Wilson records his one and only association with the KGB when he was picked up and interrogated while visiting Moscow in 1954. He took a photograph of a woman carrying a child's bicycle. 'Unfortunately I photographed her outside the Lubyanka Prison and had to spend an unhappy hour under arrest by one of the less endearing members of the KGB,' he recalls.

# Chapter Thirteen

⊂⟋⟍⟋⟍⊃

# The KGB and the Forces

SERVICEMEN concerned with weapons, training and plans are obvious targets for the KGB but, to date, the British have not been particularly obliging. The Russians managed to recruit Chief Technician Douglas Britten and, through their Czech offshoot, Sergeant Nicholas Prager, both from the RAF. They were eventually detected, following information laid by defectors, and received jail sentences of twenty-one and twelve years respectively.

Britten, who was first approached in the Science Museum in London by a Russian claiming to be a fellow radio enthusiast, passed over useful information for six years for money. He was controlled by a KGB officer listed as a first secretary in the Soviet embassy's cultural department. Prager, of Czech origin, was recruited while on a visit to Prague and was controlled from the Czech embassy in London. He gave away the secrets of the Blue Diver, an electronics countermeasure device fitted to the V-bombers to help them penetrate Russia's radar screens.

Another Army NCO, Staff Sergeant Percy Allen, also sold defence information which cost him ten years in prison, but his customers were the Iraqis and Egyptians.

The only traitorous officers I can recall were Sub-Lieutenant David Bingham, jailed for twenty-one years, and former Flight Lieutenant Alistair Steadman, jailed for nine. They were not recruited but volunteered their services for money.

The Russian Intelligence men never stop trying and many instances where they tried and failed are on MI5's secret records. One case concerned an Army sergeant who worked as a clerk in

Whitehall. He played for the War Office football team and was approached in a pub by a KGB officer who claimed that he was interested in the game. He eventually accompanied the sergeant to matches, and through him was able to become friendly with other War Office clerks. Fortunately, Army security ended the promising relationship after the Russians had started offering money for innocuous information.

The KGB devotes quite a lot of time and money to talent-spotting among servicemen. They even hang about RAF and Army camps waiting to offer lifts in the hope of finding susceptible victims. The commonest gambit for hooking one is to offer money for unclassified documents and to proceed from there. Several have fallen for the trick of parting with books of notes made on courses. This has then offered the opportunity for the agent to threaten to report his victim to his commanding officer in the hope of securing something rather more productive.

Since the Second World War, no senior officer has been suspected of treachery but sadly this is not true of some of Britain's allies, the West Germans in particular. Several high-ranking German officers have committed suicide when about to be faced with security interrogation. Copies of detailed plans for NATO military exercises have been stolen from German offices. In 1968 three Russian spies even hauled away an American Sidewinder air-to-air missile from an Allied base in Germany, using a wheelbarrow, and sent it to Moscow.

There was one instance in which NATO documents of the highest possible secrecy were lost from the office of the NATO supremo, then General Norstad. The discovery was made by an RAF friend of mine who told me the story. He was horrified because the documents were nothing less than a copy of NATO's entire nuclear targeting plans. They gave the places in Russia and in the satellite countries which would be attacked with nuclear bombs in a retaliatory raid, together with details of the routes and the squadrons which would make the attack.

He expected an explosion when he broke the news to Norstad but the reaction, after the initial shock, was one of philosophical resignation. The Supreme Commander said he had little doubt that the copy was in Moscow by that time but, on reflection, he thought it was just as well that the Russians should know what to expect if they ever attacked the West. The only action to be taken was to switch the routes.

Had the public known about this grave security breach, the general concern would have been a great deal more intense than the NATO Commander's.

However, the worst NATO leaks were not perpetrated by servicemen but by a civilian, Guenter Guillaume, who was personal assistant to Willi Brandt, then West German Chancellor. He was shown to be a Soviet bloc agent who had been deliberately introduced into Brandt's entourage with such success that, when the full extent of his treachery was realized, one of the most senior British officials at NATO military headquarters exclaimed, 'My God, it's all gone!'

There have been American complaints that British copies of reports confidential to NATO have been turning up in Russia within weeks of their production. But if these suspicions are justified they are not only directed at servicemen in NATO. The Americans suspect that someone at a very high level in Whitehall is passing on the photocopies of documents.

The photocopying machine, now regarded as essential to most offices, has become a godsend to the 'defector-in-place' – the spy on the office staff. Before its advent he had to carry a miniature camera and risk being seen using it, as Blake did, or take documents out of the building to photograph them, as the Aviation Ministry spy Bossard did. Now, with further technological assistance kindly provided for him, he may not even have to risk smuggling out the photocopies. Many ministries are equipped with the telecopier, a desk machine which transmits facsimiles over the telephone system to any address where a similar apparatus is installed. Its purpose is to interchange documents and drawings between headquarters and out-stations, saving much time and money. If a defector-in-place can secure access to such a machine, all he has to do is to dial 9 to secure an outside line, dial the number of his 'spy-master', feed in the secret document and an exact copy appears at the other end in seconds, irrespective of the distance.

Whitehall security men are aware of the risks and claim they have taken all steps to ensure against misuse of the machine but, in the past, defectors-in-place like Philby, Fuchs and Vassall have built up such trust inside their departments that they were above suspicion.

A very obvious target for Communist subversion is the auxiliary force of 30,000 German civilians who serve Rhine Army. Many of them are essential to the rapid mobilization of the British forces in

Germany in an emergency. I have been assured that NATO counter-Intelligence is paying close attention to them but I would expect that they have been heavily penetrated by East German agents.

NATO has knowledge of about four hundred KGB teams trained to sabotage specific targets in West Germany. Hopefully, they would all be rounded up before they could do much damage but their existence serves one useful purpose. Action by them could be the first sure sign that what was alleged to be large-scale Russian man-oeuvres was really mobilization.

So far as is known, the KGB has concentrated its efforts on subverting a few individual servicemen, but subversion of the armed forces as a whole must be, at least, a long-term target. The recent attempted Communist takeover in Portugal has shown what can be achieved if a sufficient number of senior Army officers can be recruited. I would judge that British officers and men would be the most difficult target in this respect because of their long tradition of aloofness from politics, but that will continue to be true only so long as morale remains high. It has certainly been lowered over the past fourteen years by the uncertainty created by the defence cuts and the poor pay and conditions which have forced many young soldiers into doing odd jobs and their wives on to social security.

The recent march of loyal service wives to Number 10 to protest against poor pay and conditions is harmless in itself but is a symp-tom of circumstances which can be exploited if they are not quickly remedied. I already meet young officers who believe that having a trade union for the forces, while deplorable, may become necessary. I have no doubt that the penetration of such a union would immedi-ately become priority number one for the Communists.

In the general left-wing drive to weaken the nation's defences Soviet interests are being served by those Labour MPs and their supporters calling for further cuts of £1,000 million in defence spend-ing which would shatter forces' morale and recruitment.

As one of their contingency plans the Communists must have considered the possibility, however remote, that the Army or part of it might be used to assist them in imposing their rule on the rest of the community. Some credence for this was provided by Mick McGahey, the Communist miners' leader in Scotland, who claimed during the 1974 strike that, in certain circumstances, he would ask the troops to assist the miners. This utterance was taken seriously enough for government legal experts to consider whether it could be construed as incitement to mutiny.

There are, however, far more of the Left who profess to believe that the Army might one day be used to impose a coup by the Right, whatever that may mean. The fact is that apart from the National Front, which is currently of little consequence and unlikely to attract much serious support, the Right is poorly organized and there are no 'Colonels' in Britain comparable to those who have initiated coups in other countries.

The myth of the revolutionary power of the Right was exploded by the speed with which certain retired officers like General Sir Walter Walker, a former NATO commander, and Colonel David Stirling, founder of the SAS, were driven to shut down organizations which they set up to assist the police in dealing with mass civil disturbance. These organizations were smartly smeared as 'private armies' by the Left, though they had no access to weapons or any intention of securing any. Their sensible purpose was to help to support essential services like transport, communications and sewage disposal in the event of a Left-inspired general strike designed to bring the country to a halt.

Of these civil-assistance movements, only one remains – Unison, which has an emergency communications network operated by radio hams and an 'air wing' of pilots with privately owned light planes to carry messages in the event of a total disruption of the non-military broadcasting and telephone services.

Wilson himself was reported to be concerned about several right-wing movements like the Royal Society of St George and a Yorkshire organization called the White Rose. I asked him about this and he confirmed his interest though it was not difficult to convince him that, so far as the Royal Society of St George was concerned, it was nothing more than a band of well-meaning patriots keen to promote the image of Britain and preserve freedom and the monarchy.

The former Prime Minister told me that his fear had originally been stimulated in 1968 by news of a dinner organized by Cecil King, former chief of the *Daily Mirror*, who had turned against him. The main guests were Mountbatten and Zuckerman, then Wilson's chief scientific adviser, and they found themselves discussing the feasibility of replacing the Wilson government with an emergency 'business administration'. Zuckerman has told me of his reaction to this nonsense. He walked out and reported the conversation to Wilson.

I was also told from a Buckingham Palace source that, as something of a joke, Mountbatten mentioned it to the Queen Mother, who wagged her finger at him sternly saying, 'Have nothing to do with it, Dickie!'

As recently as the summer of 1978, I have been assured by a most senior British Intelligence official that the secret services, which are active in checking on all subversive movements, have no evidence whatever of any right-wing group aimed at disturbing the elected government in any way.

Wilson has denied to me that he had ever seriously considered that troops taking part in one of the major anti-terrorist exercises mounted in support of the police at London Airport might suddenly be switched to take over Downing Street. In fact, at the time of writing, at least, his fears seem to be centred more on the Left extremists and the activities of their friends in the KGB.

*Chapter Fourteen*

# The KGB and the Trade Unions

WHILE Britain's trade unions may be riddled with ardent Communists only too keen to follow the party line and to put the political interests of the Soviet Union before those of their own country, the Kremlin requires more. Through Soviet bloc Intelligence the party penetrates the unions wherever it can by recruiting active agents whom it hopes will be prepared to use their positions for subversion. These agents may operate at all levels from top executive to shop steward.

Their prime requirement is to promote industrial unrest and

disruption to create the conditions which favour the spread of Communism. The security authorities are in no doubt that some disruption in various key industries is orchestrated by Kremlin agents.

Their evidence for this is almost invariably kept secret, mainly to protect the sources, who are sometimes informers infiltrated into the unions and even posing as Communists, and ministers tend to be loath even to refer to it. However, an important exception was made – with every justification – by Wilson during the extremely damaging seamen's strike in 1966.

The National Union of Seamen began the strike as a protest against pay and conditions imposed by the employers but when the Labour government declined to back them it was quickly converted into a battle against the government. Wilson was provided with irrefutable evidence by MI5, including records of bugged conversations and photographs of intercepted documents, that the strike was being orchestrated by a few Communists imposing their will on the others and determined to bring in the dockers and other workers so that the country could be brought to a standstill.

He got nowhere until he frightened the Communists by a tough statement in Parliament in which he made it clear that the moderate members of the seamen's executive were being terrorized by a small professional group of Communists who planned their tactics 'with outside help'. To strengthen his case Wilson set up a meeting with Heath, then leader of the opposition, to convince him privately of the truth of his assertions. The full facts were given to Heath by MI5 men themselves, including one of the agents responsible for the bugging.

Within twenty-four hours the strike was called off. The moderates felt they had to exert some strength after Wilson's disclosure and the militants were scared that the full extent of their involvement with Soviet interests might be exposed if they did not back down.

While the final evidence against the militants had been collected as a result of a special operation, superbly performed, MI5 had been patiently gathering material against Communist agitators and their Soviet paymasters over the years. Some of it came from Communist Party headquarters itself, which has been penetrated by British security agents, who have even planted bugs there. In 1975 Communist Party officials were dismayed to find a listening device when redecorators stripped away some woodwork.

The extent to which attempts are made to suborn trade union

officials was indicated by the evidence of the two Czech defectors Josef Frolik and Frantisek August, already referred to in connection with their alleged recruitment of Labour MPs. The names of union leaders alleged to have been recruited were given to the CIA officers who interrogated the defectors and MI5 made further checks when the information was passed to them. The defectors also gave evidence on oath to a US Senate Judiciary Committee investigating Communist bloc Intelligence activities and as part of it Frolik said, 'I know that the Russians can work with the Communist Party of Great Britain because there are quite a few agents in high positions – not open Communists – working in the Labour Party and the union movement.'

Though the reports of these hearings were published by the US government, their full contents could not be mentioned in Britain because, unlike British government documents, they carried no privilege in law. However, I did manage to get the message to a patriotic organization called Aims for Freedom and Enterprise which took action by writing an open letter to the Home Secretary drawing his attention to the reports and to tape-recordings which take the allegations further. Even when Frolik produced a book, *The Frolik Defection*, which went into detail about his previous activities in London as a Soviet bloc Intelligence officer, the names of the trade union leaders he claimed to have attempted to recruit had to be omitted for libel reasons.

While the Labour government has since done all it can to suggest that Frolik was of little consequence, he was described in an official report by Senator James O. Eastland as 'a seventeen-year veteran of the Czechoslovakian Intelligence service and one of the most senior Eastern Intelligence agents to defect to the West since the Second World War'.

In 1976, I secured copies of tape-recordings of private interviews which Frolik had given in Washington. After hearing them I passed them to the Director-General of MI6 who had copies made, suggesting that his department had not previously had that information. Being concerned by the contents, I then passed them to Stephen Hastings, Tory MP for Mid-Bedfordshire and a former wartime Intelligence officer.

The response from some of his colleagues was such that at the end of December 1976 I predicted that early in the New Year much more would be heard about Communist infiltration of Parliament, the trade unions and other key institutions.

After long delays involving legal wrangles it was decided to ventilate the issue and in December 1977 Hastings under the privilege of Parliament revealed some of the names Frolik had given. This meant that he was immune to action for libel and so was anyone else who did not do more than repeat what had been said there and been published in *Hansard*.

According to *Hansard*, Hastings recalled that Frolik had named John Stonehouse as virtually a spy and suggested that Harold Wilson's defence of his former minister was not enough reassurance because Frolik was continuing with his allegation more strongly than ever. He then named four living trade union leaders who, according to Frolik, had been prime targets for Soviet bloc Intelligence. They were Jack Jones of the Transport and General Workers, Ernie Roberts, then of the Amalgamated Union of Engineering Workers, later a Labour candidate, Hugh Scanlon, leader of that union, Richard (then Lord) Briginshaw, formerly leader of one of the newspaper unions, and the late Ted Hill of the Boilermakers' Union, alleged by Frolik to be a secret Communist.

The mention of these names produced something of a furore in the Press and the reaction of the Labour MPs was predictably angry. The Prime Minister gave the impression that the allegations by Frolik had all been investigated and rejected and he rose to the defence of the trade union leaders. A Tory back-bench motion was tabled drawing attention to the fact that not only had the Home Secretary been informed about the existence of the tapes more than a year previously but that copies of them had also been handed in to MI6 at the same time. Mr Hastings's call for a select committee of inquiry was rejected but the stage had been set for such an inquiry in the event of the return of a Tory government.

There was no suggestion that Czech Intelligence or anybody else had achieved any success in their efforts to recruit trade union leaders but the names given by Frolik as targets indicate the levels at which Communist agents are prepared to try.

I learned later that the Intelligence authorities were not much impressed by Frolik's allegations against the trade union leaders whom he named. One of them commented, in the cryptic way they talk, 'The first pressings from a defector always have the most body', indicating that the naming of the trade union leaders came from the second pressings or even the third.

*Chapter Fifteen*

# The Eavesdroppers

OFFICIAL eavesdropping, now dignified by the name of 'monitoring', has gone on routinely in Britain since Henry VII established the secret services 470 years ago. Indeed the word 'eavesdrop' derived from small listening apertures built into the eaves of large houses frequented by important people so that their conversations in the courtyards could be overheard. Now, especially since the advent of the transistor and other miniaturized electronic devices, the surreptitious invasion of privacy has become all too easy.

The simplest of all instruments for this process and the readiest to hand is the telephone, and when I began to write about Intelligence and espionage in the *Daily Express*, the editor quickly received pleas on behalf of MI5 urging him to curb me from mentioning telephone-tapping. The argument was that while telephone-tapping was well known, any mention of it in the public prints reminded spies about it. A spy who had become rather careless, as occasionally they do, could suddenly be alerted about the danger he was courting.

These pleas were usually accompanied by the claim that MI5 had been doing very nicely with tape-recordings of some dangerous subversive – never identified – when he had suddenly dried up after one of my articles mentioning that telephone-tapping was an essential part of counter-espionage operations.

With telephone-tapping exploited in so many spy thrillers I argued that this was a ludicrous request in a so-called free society and, for the most part, the editor agreed with me. We both suspected – and I still do – that the requests were usually made on behalf of the government of the day, whatever its politics, because it could be embarrassed by parliamentary questions following publicity about any government-sponsored intrusion into personal privacy. MI5, which, unlike the Secret Intelligence Service, is an unconstitutional body never established in law, was also by its very nature anxious to latch on to any excuse which would help it to avoid publicity. As a former MI5 chief put it to me, 'What's the use of being a secret outfit if we can't stay secret?'

I was therefore pleasantly surprised when in 1957, following the setting up of a three-man Privy Councillors' group to inquire into telephone-tapping, the Prime Minister, then Harold Macmillan, published its report in full. The Security Service had tried hard with him, using its old card about the danger of alerting spies to telephone-tapping, but this was an occasion when the Prime Minister decided that security considerations would have to give way to the political advantages of giving the public an open statement which could not be criticized by his opponents on the grounds of censorship.

At the risk of incurring further displeasure from my MI5 friends I now propose to put on record more instances illustrating how governments, of all political shades, and the departments serving them are prepared to infringe privacy and personal liberty – sometimes with sound cause but more often in the pursuit of power in its various expressions.

All Whitehall ministries concerned with defence or other matters regarded as secret have their own internal tapping system to check that civil servants are not speaking too freely from their office telephones. This is done on a sampling basis – a few calls from the secret areas being monitored each day by security snoopers sitting at the switchboard. No permission is required for this to be done and the practice is made known to the staff as a deterrent. Occasionally it leads to a reprimand, as happened to a former Army colleague who telephoned me at my newspaper from Woolwich Arsenal with some information which was of no security value. My informant felt that certain people there were doing little work but drawing so much money that it was a scandal which should be exposed. Regrettably the call had been monitored and since it was a politically embarrassing situation which, as I have always maintained, is a higher security grade in Whitehall than top secret – my friend was hauled up before the local security chief and severely censured.

The monitoring system does occasionally lead to the detection of a dangerous culprit, however. A sergeant working in the Defence Ministry who decided he would like to sell some secrets telephoned a possible buyer from the public telephone box installed inside the building. This too was monitored and as a result the sergeant was followed, caught in the act and eventually sent to prison.

The tapping of private phones is organized by the Post Office, which has a full-time security division operating on instructions from MI5, Special Branch, the police and possibly other agencies. If the Post Office is required to tap your telephone this can be done quickly without entering your house. All conversations will be automatically recorded on tape at a special exchange. Sometimes one can hear clicks and flashing when a telephone is being monitored but modern equipment makes no background noise.

From letters I have received after writing articles about telephone-tapping, it is clear that many thousands of people suspect that they are being subjected to this indignity. In most cases the suspicions are unfounded but I have been able to *prove* that my telephone was tapped on several occasions.

Though I have been of some assistance to the Intelligence and security authorities from time to time they have never ceased to resent my ferreting efforts in Whitehall and have done all they could to limit them, concentrating on the discovery of my sources in the hope that they might then be silenced.

I discovered that my home telephone was undoubtedly tapped early in my career when I had consulted a group captain friend who had been appointed Inspector General of the RAF after retirement, giving up much of his leisure to the post. The subject was about the merging of RAF volunteer organizations and he gave me some advance information which, in fact, I did not use.

He could normally have expected a knighthood for his work but shortly before the relevant honours list was published he was asked to see the Chief of the Air Staff, then Sir John Slessor. He was told that Slessor had been called to see the Prime Minister, then Clement Attlee, who said that he had withheld the recommendation for a knighthood because the Inspector General had given confidential information to me.

This early experience taught me to use call-boxes for sensitive calls to contacts and to speak in riddles as far as possible. For example, years later during Easter 1957, when I needed to check a lead that Christmas Island was to be the base for Britain's H-bomb tests, I telephoned a most senior Defence Ministry friend at home to ask, 'If I were to wish you a Happy Christmas instead of a Happy Easter would it make sense to you?' His reply – 'It would indeed!' – was enough.

On further occasions very senior civil servants, two of them permanent secretaries of defence departments, have warned me after they had retired to take care on my telephone because it had been frequently tapped.

The question of who gives permission for tapping of private telephones is of considerable public interest but before dealing with that I must describe a situation which makes tapping a much more pernicious practice than is generally realized.

The professional eavesdropper's dream would be to have inside the home of every person who might become a security suspect a microphone which could be switched on to record all private conversations. As more and more people acquire a telephone that is just the situation which exists. The mouthpiece of an ordinary telephone is a highly sensitive microphone and the Post Office security service makes regular use of it to listen in to conversations inside private homes and offices.

This is what happens if the Post Office is required to fit your home with what has become known as a 'combined bug and tap'. First, they put your telephone out of order, then, when you report it, they say they will come and fix it and 'fix it' they do. The spring-loaded bar which goes down when you hang up the receiver is only a switch, so they insert a device in the base of the telephone which short-circuits it. The microphone then remains live when the telephone is hung up and an amplifying arrangement can make the sounds audible to anyone tapping the instrument and recording the conversations on tape. Any relevant parts of the conversations help to swell the police files or the two million dossiers in the registries at MI5 and MI6.

Bedside extensions are usually doctored at the same time so the secretaries who transcribe the tapes for examination by security analysts must hear some entertaining material.

While any private conversation by a highly suspect person can be of value to the security authorities, their main interest lies in what he says immediately after he has replaced the receiver after a telephone call. It is then he may reveal much that he took pains to hide during his guarded talk on an open line. Indeed, if he is a professional spy, he may say nothing at all on the telephone but simply hang up after a carefully timed interval which itself conveys his message or he may achieve this by coughing or panting in a prearranged way.

I discovered that my telephone had been bugged and tapped by a sheer coincidence. I had become friendly with a young scientist working at University College London, who had invented an ingenious television microscope. While preparing an account of it I learned that he had previously been employed in the Post Office security laboratory at Dollis Hill, the main research department in London. His task had been to 'refine' the domestic telephone so that a house occupant could not easily detect that his instrument had been 'fixed'. The original arrangement had required an extra cable leading from the telephone to the wall-connection and, as this was rather obvious to a discerning suspect, my friend's job had been to devise a way of eliminating it. I told him that I had reason to believe that my telephone had been fitted with the extra cable. I invited him home, he examined the installation and my suspicion was expertly confirmed.

Incidentally, the Privy Councillors' report on telephone-tapping made no mention of this extension of the intrusion facilities.

The extent to which bugging and tapping may be exploited is brought home to me every time I visit the London flat of a former member of MI5. If he wishes to speak about sensitive matters he either takes me into a room where there is no telephone or he pushes the biggest cushion in the room firmly over the instrument. Even he, it seems, cannot be sure that his conversations are not being monitored.

During the drive against Communists in secret departments some of the men who tap people's telephones had their own phones tapped and did not know it!

Nobody, in fact, is immune to tapping or bugging, not even the Prime Minister, as I have already suggested in Chapter One. Ministers and other MPs are supposed to be immune since Wilson prohibited the tapping of MPs' telephones in 1964, but this can be overruled by the Home Secretary, as it was in the case of Will Owen, and may be breached on occasion by MI5 or CIA 'cowboys' operating without political permission.

Beaverbrook told me that during his friendship with Maisky, the wartime Soviet ambassador to Britain, he suspected that his telephone was being tapped. He had been introduced to the Russian by

Aneurin Bevan, who was a revolutionary in MI5's eyes, and Beaver-brook was wrongly accused by Lord Halifax of giving Maisky details about Britain's weakness in the air. When he became Minister of Aircraft Production he gratified his curiosity by sending for the relevant file and found that his suspicions had been fully justified. This was later confirmed to me by his son, Sir Max Aitken.

The highest official figure ever given for the number of private telephones tapped in one year is 242. After working so many years in close proximity to security I suspect that the practice is much wider and is steadily increasing.

Statements in Parliament have given the firm impression that no private person's telephone can be tapped without the written author-ity of the Home Secretary in the form of a warrant. This is misleading in the extreme. In the first place, I have established, by questioning security officials who have obtained warrants, that the Home Sec-retary himself is rarely involved. He delegates the responsibility to one or more senior officials. Only when another minister, an MP or an important public figure is suspect does the Home Secretary himself have to sign the warrant.

Secondly, issue of the warrants is not restricted to the Home Office. It has been officially confirmed to me that legally any Sec-retary of State can approve a warrant for the tapping of a private telephone and there are fifteen of them in the Cabinet. This almost certainly means that any of those can delegate the responsibility to senior officials, though in practice only a few of them like the Secretaries of State for Defence, Foreign Affairs, Treasury, En-vironment and the Prime Minister himself are likely to be concerned.

I am quite certain that when my telephone was tapped it was usually on the authority of the Permanent Secretary of the Defence Ministry or, on rare occasions, of the Cabinet Secretary.

When a permanent secretary of a ministry – a civil ser-vant – orders the 'leak procedure' to be put into action following an apparent security breach, this automatically involves telephone-tapping if it is considered necessary.

Over the years I noticed that the inquiries following my disclos-ures tended to be more intense after the embarrassment of some minister than after what was alleged to be a straightforward security breach.

They were never more intense than in February 1966 when, through a high-level naval source, I was able to announce that the

First Sea Lord, Sir David Luce, and Christopher Mayhew, the Navy Minister, were going to resign over the government's decision to abandon aircraft-carriers without sufficiently reducing the defence commitments overseas. Wilson and Healey, his Defence Secretary, were still hoping to prevent the resignations, which were far more embarrassing than I knew at the time. All eight members of the Admiralty Board had submitted their resignations in writing to the Board's secretary, Anthony Griffin, now chairman of British Ship-builders. Had they gone ahead with them the government itself could have fallen.

Regrettably, Griffin had to tell the admirals that if they all resigned at once in such circumstances they risked losing their pensions. Most of them did follow Luce and Mayhew into resignation but piecemeal over several months.

The police can secure the tapping of a suspected criminal's telephone simply by applying to a senior Post Office official. The Post Office also now deploys what are called 'tiger machines' which can be linked with your telephone at the press of a button to monitor and record how many calls you make in a given period, which numbers you ring and for how long you speak. Their main purpose is to provide sampling statistics for improving the service but the machines do reveal the pattern of the activities and personal relationships of those subjected to them. Post Office officials admit that they utilize the machines on behalf of the police to assist criminal investigations and can do so on their own authority. I have no doubt at all that they are being used on behalf of MI5 and Special Branch too.

In these circumstances the Whitehall interpretation of the term 'suspected criminal' is of some importance. A breach of the Official Secrets Acts can be a criminal offence. So when my telephone was being tapped by the security authorities was I a 'suspected criminal', meaning that a Post Office official could sanction the tapping of my telephone without reference to any higher authority? I do not know the answer.

When a telephone is being tapped that event is somewhat derogatory to the person concerned. So how many officials know about it? I suspect that the number is not as small as it should be. I was warned on two occasions by middle-level Whitehall press officers to watch out as my telephone calls were being intercepted. It may be that the officers concerned had been questioned following tapped conversations they had had with me.

There are many people living in Britain who fall outside any restrictions governing telephone-tapping or any other form of eavesdropping. These are the diplomats and other staff in the foreign embassies and high commissions. Such places count as foreign territory and the security authorities need no permission from anybody to keep them under any kind of surveillance they choose.

This somewhat dilutes the immunity to telephone-tapping awarded to MPs and peers by Wilson in 1964. Any calls which any of them may make to Eastern bloc embassies or trading missions or to South Africa House, for instance, may be fully monitored and often are.

Of course the foreigners concerned are aware of what goes on and react accordingly, doing everything they can to avoid surveillance. Some idea of the precautions to which they are driven may be gleaned from those taken by the British embassy in Moscow. There is one basement room there believed to be absolutely bug-proof. It is a room within a room – a wire cage cantilevered from the walls and thoroughly sound-proofed. A visiting minister or official has to sit there to be briefed by the ambassador or to give him secret instructions.

Such sad precautions are essential in the modern diplomatic world. When British officials take part in any meeting in the Kremlin or elsewhere behind the Iron Curtain they are warned to avoid making notes for passing to each other or to keep them covered with the hand if they have to make them. Why? Because Soviet bloc Intelligence agents operate cameras through small holes in the ceilings of the meeting rooms. Photographs of any notes are analysed in the hope that they might yield information to assist the Communist negotiators later. Similar rooms exist in several foreign embassies in London.

These are extreme examples of how privacy at many levels is being eroded by stealth with the approval of ministers who find themselves unable to separate the public interest from their own.

Most of the telephones tapped in Britain belong to suspected spies, criminals, subversives, customs evaders, Communists, the New Left, Fascists, National Front leaders and journalists. There are a few journalists whose motives justify the procedure. The evidence which led to the deportation of the American writers Philip Agee and Mark Hosenball in 1977, for example, was partly based on telephone-taps. But the interest in my telephone was centred almost entirely on discovering my contacts, because I was obviously in receipt of information supposed to be known to very few.

I do not blame either the security authorities or the politicians for tapping my telephones. In their position I would have done the same. But as a result of their efforts they frequently confronted the wrong persons while never, so far as I know, discovering any of my high-level sources – apart from those who had no objection to letting it be known that they were assisting me.

One senior official who must have been very angry when he was suspected of leaking to me, because he has always carefully avoided telling me anything, is Sir Hermann Bondi, until recently Chief Scientist in the Defence Ministry. I encountered Bondi, whom I knew, at a space research conference in Venice in September 1970 when we exchanged pleasantries but nothing else. On my return to London a friend, who had been to a party given by Heath at Number 10, telephoned me to say that Bondi had been present and Lord Carrington had been introducing him around as his new Chief Scientist.

When I went to see Carrington a few days after my premature announcement of this important appointment had appeared he said rather huffily, 'I see you've still got your hot line into the ministry.' In fact my informant was not a Whitehall figure at all.

There is very little that the security authorities could have done had they discovered the identity of any high-level contacts and to illustrate why I will describe the circumstances of the only potentially damaging security breach I ever made, which was unwitting. The incident illustrates how insecure some senior civil servants can be and what damage others can cause by dishonest answers to Press inquiries.

In 1953 Sir Archibald Rowlands, one of the most respected permanent secretaries in Whitehall, completed his career at the Ministry of Supply and retired. At the invitation of Lord Beaverbrook, an old friend, he joined the board of Express Newspapers. Lunching with him one day at Kettner's, his favourite restaurant in Soho, I asked him if he could remember anything that I could safely investigate to produce a story for the newspaper.

'Ask the Ministry of Supply about the Nomination Committee,' he said.

He then told me that this was an informal group of British and American scientists which had been set up with the agreement of the

Pentagon to get round the American Atomic Energy Act, which forbade the exchange of nuclear weapons secrets with Britain or any other country. Nomination was its code-name.

'But that must be terribly hot,' I said. 'Congress would explode.'

'Try the Ministry,' Archie said mysteriously. 'See what they say.'

I could not wait to put my questions to the director of public relations at the Supply Ministry. His reply – after some days – was that he had made a thorough inquiry and found that no such committee or anything like it existed. In fact, as I learned much later, the inquiry had caused a tremendous upheaval and I was immediately subjected to intense surveillance with telephone-tapping, shadowing round London and everything else to discover the source.

Still fearing that any story about the committee might do damage, I telephoned a friend in the ministry who happened to be personal assistant to the minister himself. I urged him to put my questions direct to Sir James Helmore, Rowlands's successor, which he promised to do. After three days he had not responded and I later learned that he had been instructed to avoid doing so.

The result was that a small report of the existence of the committee and its function appeared in the *Daily Express*. It had no impact on the public but the telephone lines between London and Washington were soon humming about it, and with every justification.

As I discovered much later, the existence of the Nomination Committee was even more secret than I had been led to believe. It was an MI6–CIA group set up to exchange Intelligence about Russia's atomic activities and on the day after my report appeared it was about to hold its first meeting in Washington with Britain's leading nuclear experts, like Sir William Penney (now Lord) and Sir John Cockcroft in attendance. The American consternation and the British embarrassment can be imagined but, happily, in spite of its misgivings about British security, the CIA did not cancel the arrangement, partly perhaps because the British had some valuable atomic Intelligence to put into the pool.

So great was the Whitehall concern that Helmore took the unusual step of calling me in to see him and said, 'We have never before asked you to reveal your sources but this time I must tell you that whoever gave you that information is a traitor and it is your duty to give us his name.'

Knowing that Rowlands was certainly no traitor I refused and pointed out that if the ministry had taken a straightforward line and told me that there were good national reasons why the information should not be printed instead of burying its head in the sand I would not even have told the editor about it.

Years later, when I was lecturing to the War Course at Greenwich, I happened to be seated at lunch in the Painted Hall next to Professor R. V. Jones, the former Scientific Adviser to MI6, who has since recorded his crucial wartime activities in a superb book, *Most Secret War*.

'I have always wanted to ask you one thing,' he said. 'However did you find out about the Nomination Committee? It was more secret than the details of the bomb itself.'

'As the person has been dead a long time I can tell you – it was Archie Rowlands.'

Jones, who was at the Washington meeting in the capacity of Director of Scientific Intelligence, was dumbfounded and, clearly, Archie had never been suspected. But had they discovered that he was the culprit what could they have done without precipitating a major security scandal which really would have upset Anglo-American relations far more than the mere termination of the Intelligence interchange?

Over several years, Sir Frederick Brundrett, the Defence Ministry's chief scientist, was briefing me on secret matters quite openly, believing that it was helpful in promoting defence policy. But the Cabinet Secretary, Sir Norman Brook, could do nothing about it though he deplored it. He had to wait until Fred's retirement to take his petty revenge by withholding recommendation for the GBE, which for such a distinguished man should have been automatic.

I never discovered why Rowlands leaked such dangerous information but it is possible that he was not aware how super-sensitive it was. He had heard about it immediately prior to his retirement and, with a security system based on the need-to-know principle, may not have been told its full significance. Alternatively, it may have been just an expression of that human weakness – the vain delight of being in the know and making others aware of it. That is not an aspect of the pursuit of power but of the enjoyment of it. Few are immune to the brief satisfaction it provides and it is the main source of information for the investigative journalist operating in Whitehall.

So far as I am aware the fact that the Nomination Committee once existed has still not been officially revealed.

It was through Rowlands that I first learned that MI5 and the Whitehall defence departments sometimes manage to recruit or plant spies inside Fleet Street offices, a practice confirmed to me on several occasions since. One former director of public relations in the Defence Ministry assured me that he had been able to secure advance proofs of some of my articles, blandly claiming that his Intelligence about what was going on in Fleet Street was as good as mine in Whitehall. Similar information, I suspect, lay behind Wilson's statement that 'Fleet Street is a leaky place'.

Advance information about newspaper activities gives politicians and civil servants more time to plan counteraction and to react more effectively if presented with a disclosure in a first edition late at night. It also enables them to get off to an early start with their attempts to discover the source of the leak.

Such a situation arose in 1964 when the *Daily Express* announced that Greville Wynne, the British businessman imprisoned in Russia as a spy, was in the process of being exchanged for Gordon Lonsdale, the Soviet spy-master who had been jailed in Britain.

It was an occasion when I could not possibly disguise the fact that I had been given a monumental leak. Details of how the two men had been released and been flown to opposite sides of the Berlin Wall were in my report. The follow-up story the next day had an exclusive photograph of the exchange at an unlikely checkpoint when the other papers had mustered at Checkpoint Charlie.

The Foreign Office was quickly on to the fact that I knew of the impending exchange and through the good offices of Michael Hadow (now Sir), then head of the news division, I was able to arrange a deal. In return for exclusivity the editor agreed to hold the story out of the first edition so that the Russians, who wanted no advance publicity, would not have time to withdraw from the exchange.

There was, understandably, a major witch-hunt to discover my source with all devices, human and electronic, brought into play. Poor old Colonel Lohan was blamed, reference to this being made by Wilson three years later in the debate on the D-notice affair, but all Lohan had done was to assist in inducing me to have the story delayed for a few hours. My prime source was quite different and of far greater potential interest to the security authorities.

As can be imagined, the methods which the Whitehall authorities use to prevent their own telephones being tapped are every bit as ingenious as those they employ to tap other people's. The ordinary scrambler system which jumbled the signals as they passed through the wires and sorted them out at the other end has long been superseded by more intricate and expensive systems, linking sensitive offices in the different buildings, which account for the miniature 'sphagetti junctions' of pipes and wires running through the corridors of departments like the Defence Ministry. Closed-circuit television is also used to monitor people using corridors in particularly sensitive areas.

The potentialities of bugging devices for eavesdropping are now widely known through spy novels. They include the bleeper which can be fitted to a motor car to enable it to be followed, and smaller versions which can be carried by a person, camouflaged, if necessary, as buttons or brooches. These are used by the police in kidnapping cases to enable them to follow a person delivering ransom money. These days, however, criminals are only too aware of this danger and tend to search the courier before taking him to the place that matters, so even more ingenious devices have been produced to circumvent this. One of these, used successfully in a notorious kidnapping case in New York, was a complete suit in which the bleeping device had been woven into the material so that it could not possibly be seen. It was provided by the FBI to the father of a kidnapped son and led the police to the hide-out.

Similar ingenuity must be exercised when a bleeper has to be planted on a suspect to enable him to be followed. The first use of such a device to trap a spy was in the case of Frank Bossard, who worked for Russia inside the Aviation Ministry in the early sixties. He was already suspect. The security men wanted to catch him in the act of taking a secret file, to which he was not entitled, out of the ministry building so that they could follow him to the hotel room where he photographed his documents. Several interesting files were fitted with minute bleepers in the metal tags of the securing strings. The sound was picked up as Bossard passed through the office doors and he was followed.

Such devices have since been used to trap thieves at London Airport and in London stores so I am giving no secret away.

I have described in Chapter Three the brilliant Russian eaves-dropping device which for the first time enabled a room to be bugged without need for wires or batteries. The scurry in Whitehall when it was discovered in the British embassy in Moscow can be imagined. Every office was searched and though one of my closest friends was involved in the operation he would never tell me if any more had been found. There is, however, a story, which may be true or just part of Whitehall lore, that during the examination of Churchill's armchair in Number 10 great excitement was generated by the discovery of a carefully concealed microphone in one of the arms. This turned out to be part of a hearing-aid which Churchill, who was sensitive about his deafness, had caused to be inserted secretly into the chair by a private engineer.

While the great search was going on, top priority was given to finding an antidote which could be fitted in all secret offices to nullify the effects of the Soviet device should one be overlooked or be slipped in later. The answer proved to be extremely simple and was the brainchild of a scientist called G. M. Wright. It is still rightly covered by the Official Secrets Acts but I can safely reveal that the principle is not unconnected with the fact that a fluorescent strip light generates microwaves which can cause a crackle on a receiver.

British security treats the discovery of a KGB listening device as a matter of great secrecy on the sound principle that it never pays to let the Russians know how much it has found out about them. And, for a while; false information can be fed into the bug to mislead them and waste their time. The Americans, however, tend to make quick use of their counter-Intelligence successes for political purposes. Thus when they discovered the listening device in the plaque over the Moscow ambassador's desk they made great play of it on television, though it brought the KGB technical credit for a brilliant idea superbly applied. Earlier, when a similar device had been found in the British embassy in Moscow no mention was made of it. More recently the discovery of KGB equipment installed in a chimney in the American embassy in Moscow was used to help the US government to discredit the Russians in the war of words over Communist incursions into Africa.

Another indignity to which those suspected by Whitehall may be subjected is the surreptitious tape-recording of their conversations. This can be achieved by directional microphones which can be pointed at a certain table at a restaurant and record all that is said there from a considerable distance. Such a device was used by MI5 against Harry Houghton and Ethel Gee, the Soviet spies operating

inside the secret anti-submarine warfare establishment at Portland.
It was also used against me during the inquiries into my relationship
with Colonel Sammy Lohan of the Defence Ministry, which culminated in the D-notice affair.

During a recent and nostalgic lunch with Lord George-Brown he
recalled how Wilson had called him in more than once when he was
in the Cabinet to complain of our friendship and assured him that
full details of our various lunches and meetings were available.

There have been odd occasions, however, when I have been only
too delighted to have my conversation recorded because those doing
it made such fools of themselves. One afternoon I was asked to pay
an urgent visit to a senior official in the Defence Ministry to discuss
an item I had written that day about the possible British purchase of
an American atomic bazooka missile with the wonderful code-name
of Davy Crockett. When I entered his office, with which I was
familiar, I saw a stranger sitting at another desk. He was introduced
as a new assistant but in fact was an MI5 man set up there to
interrogate me and, as I learned later, to record the conversation.

'We don't want to talk about Davy Crockett,' the official said
grimly. 'It's about another article you did two days ago in which you
said – and he then began to read from it – "Western Intelligence
authorities are convinced that the four Thor missile sites on Britain's
east coast are immune from attack by Russian rockets and will
remain so for another year. Bomber Command's airfields are also
safely out of range of them." '

He folded his arms, sat back and declared, 'That is straight out of
a top secret Intelligence report from an agent behind the Iron
Curtain. It has put his life in danger and it's your duty to tell us who
leaked it to you. The Americans are going to create a hell of a row
about it and . . .'

By that time, with an irrepressible smile, I was reaching into my
pocket for a page I had torn from an American magazine called
*Missiles and Rockets,* which specialized in leaks from the Pentagon. I
had brought it because it carried the Davy Crockett material I
had used. Also, on the back, was all the information which I had
used to write the item about the Thor Intelligence report. I have
never seen a Whitehall official or an MI5 man so embarrassed and
confused.

Over the years I have been repeatedly accused of leaking secret
information which was genuinely derived from open American

sources. One instance caused such a commotion on both sides of the Atlantic that I take this opportunity to explain, for the first time, how it occurred.

Towards the end of 1946, when the Cold War was already declared, two of the most important military secrets in the West were the all-up weight of the American atomic bombs – then the only ones in the world – and the rate of production of these weapons. The all-up weight, meaning the weight of the complete weapon when loaded into an aircraft, determined what type of plane could be used to deliver it and how many one plane could carry. It also determined whether, as might be possible in view of Germany's development of the V2 rocket, the atomic bomb could be fitted into a missile.

There had been wild guesses in newspapers about the weight – from the size of a golf ball to a ton – but nobody had published the true weight and only a small number of British officials covered by the Official Secrets Acts were supposed to know it. Yet on 2 November of that year I was able to publish a report in the *Daily Express* correctly giving the all-up weight as four tons and the production rate as six bombs a month with eight in store.

The way I secured this 'scoop', which greatly enhanced my Fleet Street reputation, borders on the ludicrous.

One evening after leaving Fleet Street I went to the Players' Theatre Club, where I had been a member for several years, and while ordering some drinks saw Sefton Delmer, then chief foreign correspondent of the *Daily Express*, standing there. He introduced me to his companion, Wilfred, also known as Peter, Burchett. I was delighted to meet Burchett who had given the *Express* a great exclusive by filing the first dispatch out of Hiroshima after its devastation by the atomic bomb. He had been hired blind by the paper while serving abroad and the editor knew so little about him that he had to invent his Christian name, choosing Peter, which turned out to be wrong.

Burchett, a wiry Australian, told me he had been with the American forces on the Pacific island of Tinian, from which the bombers operated in their two nuclear raids on Japan. Quite casually, he told me that he had seen one of the weapons. General Kenny, the US Air Force commander on the island, had taken several correspondents to see the bomb personally, no doubt assuming that as the war was coming to an end secrecy was not that important, though they were instructed not to write about what they had seen. During the few

moments they gazed on the weapon, hidden behind a sheet, he told
them the weight of the bomb and the production rate.

After questioning Burchett further and then making some
inquiries in Whitehall, I talked with the editor and we decided that,
provided Admiral Thomson, the D-notice secretary, could assure us
that we would not be prosecuted or he didn't want to suppress the
information on some other reasonable grounds, we would print it. I
therefore wrote my report and submitted it in writing, fully expecting a peremptory turn-down.

The following day, after discussion with defence and security
authorities, the Admiral ruled that the report could not be suppressed because neither the Official Secrets Act nor the D-notice system
could be applied to American weapons. Further, he explained why
the authorities believed that the information, though accurate,
would not help the Russians much. According to MI6, Burchett,
who had given me permission to use his name as the source, was
dedicated to the Communist cause, which became evident when he
covered both the Korean and the Vietnam wars from the Communist side. So great was his zeal in promoting the Communist viewpoint
that the Australian government refused to renew his passport and he
was exiled from his own country for nineteen years, though he denied
being a Communist agent.

I also discovered later that the bomb which Burchett and the
others had seen was a 'gun-bomb' – a weapon containing a short
cannon to impel the lumps of nuclear explosive towards each other at
high speed. The gun-bomb had been quickly abandoned in favour of
a more refined device based on a different principle.

Nevertheless, revealing the all-up weight and the production rate,
which both still applied to the new improved bomb, was a bad
security breach and, in spite of the obsolescence of the weapon which
Burchett had been shown, I cannot believe that General Kenny
knew of his Communist leanings. Eventually it became apparent
that the Russians had almost certainly known the facts before the
bombs were even dropped when the treachery of Klaus Fuchs, the
former German atomic scientist, was revealed in 1950. Fuchs had
worked in the Los Alamos laboratories where the bombs had been
designed.

At the time of my report none of this was known to Parliament or
to Congress and the reactions there were fierce.

*Chapter Sixteen*

# American Intelligence Operations in Britain

WITH the full agreement of successive British governments, the USA mounts extensive and expensive Intelligence-gathering operations in the United Kingdom.

There are three main reasons for this. First, the USA has a huge military investment in Britain in the form of air bases, nuclear weapons dumps and the missile-submarine base which it operates at Holy Loch in Scotland. It has to protect this investment and it has suited Britain to allow the Americans to be responsible for their own security and Intelligence. Their installations are an obvious target for KGB penetration and subversion and for sabotage in the event of an emergency, and the government could not afford the additional expense of responsibility for their protection.

Second, Britain's geographical position offers excellent sites for long-range electronic eavesdropping on activity behind the Iron Curtain. Britain's coasts are also ideally sited for underwater surveillance of Soviet submarines operating in the Atlantic approaches and the Channel.

The installations and facilities for this work are so expensive to build and operate as to be beyond Britain's means. The US government has paid the bulk of the costs and shares the findings with the British secret services.

Thirdly, Britain is well placed for receiving messages from Intelligence-gathering satellites launched and wholly paid for by the USA. Because of the failure of Britain's space research efforts – due to financial decisions not technical limitations – there is total dependence on the USA for this type of information and again this is generously shared.

The USA deploys branches of four of its most important secret services in Britain – the Central Intelligence Agency (CIA), the National Security Agency (NSA), the National Reconnaissance Office (NRO) and the Defence Intelligence Agency (DIA). There is also a very small Federal Bureau of Investigation (FBI) unit, usually only about two men, for liaison with Scotland Yard's Special Branch.

Security about all these departments is extremely tight but over the years I have learned enough about them to give a fair idea of the extent of their activities.

As a result I am convinced that the Anglo-American alliance on Intelligence and security is every bit as vital to Britain's survival as a free country as the partnership in nuclear weapons. Up-to-the-minute Intelligence of the potential enemy's intentions has never been so important and without US assistance Britain's modest efforts could not provide it. I also doubt that the KGB operations in Britain could be effectively countered without American support.

The CIA, which is the best known US Intelligence agency, and the most vilified by Russia's left-wing supporters, directs a substantial operation from the US embassy in London. Unlike the British situation where espionage and counter-espionage are the responsibilities of separate organizations, the CIA covers both. It therefore liaises closely with MI6 and MI5 so that, as far as possible, there is no wasteful overlapping on targets.

As the CIA operates a much bigger defector programme than MI6 can afford, inducing Iron Curtain Intelligence officers, diplomats and scientists to join the Western side, it is often in a position to provide leads on spies operating in Britain. Such leads are passed to MI5 for action and have led to the arrest of such spies as Fuchs and Vassall, but sometimes the CIA conducts its own undercover inquiries on British soil. Privately it claims to have provided much of the evidence against the 105 KGB men expelled from Britain in 1971.

It has a strong case for operating in Britain because the US government provides far more defence and Intelligence secrets to Britain than it receives in return and seems to be constantly concerned about the way certain people, whom the Americans consider to be security risks, are allowed access to them.

I have established that the CIA has repeatedly complained to MI6 about certain Labour ministers, past and present. These complaints certainly go back to 1970 and possibly before.

At the time of my allegations about the bugging of Wilson in Downing Street I was asked to see a former high-level MI5 officer who had been instructed to assure me that MI5 had never bugged the former Prime Minister. 'If anybody bugged him it must have been the CIA,' he commented.

Under such circumstances the CIA would be unlikely to reveal its activities to the British authorities, in spite of their close cooperation. There are areas of mutual reservation where certain material is restricted on the grounds that the other side does not need to know, or because the Intelligence interests of Britain and the USA happen to conflict. For this reason some British security and Intelligence files are stamped 'for British eyes only'. I have heard of one embarrassing situation when a CIA man visiting Century House travelled in the lift with a secretary carrying such a file.

In all NATO exercises it is now assumed that fifth columnists in all Western European countries will attempt widespread disruption of military movements by sabotage to communications and other installations. Because of particular American concern about the viability of Britain as a reinforcing base in the event of war, the CIA has paid its own attentions to potential subversives and saboteurs who could delay or disrupt the airlift. These have included trade union leaders and officials inside TUC headquarters, militant shop stewards and students.

Privately the CIA claims that it established definite Soviet involvement during the miners' strike of 1973 and one source suggested that Heath was warned early in 1973 that some of the miners' leaders, like McGahey, were planning industrial action with the object of bringing his government down. A former Tory minister present during the eventual negotiations between Heath and the miners told me that McGahey took pains to tell Heath that, so far as he was concerned, the object of the exercise was to 'get him out of that chair'.

The links between some left-wing Labour MPs and foreign revolutionaries like Chilean·Marxists, not only allowed to settle in Britain but encouraged to do so, have been investigated by the CIA.

Labour MPs have from time to time raised objections in Parliament to this American activity.

It is not only American secrets which the CIA chiefs worry about but the sources behind the Iron Curtain providing them. A leakage of a series of secrets can so easily direct the KGB to the person providing them.

Over the years the CIA has found it difficult to understand why ministers known to have Communist affiliations or background are not barred from access to secrets. They remain perplexed when civil servants and servicemen have to be positively vetted while ministers are immune to this precaution. Such fears may be exaggerated but the US government agencies have to answer to Congress, sometimes in the full glare of a public hearing, so they demand that either the British authorities investigate their suspicions or they do it themselves.

They do this whenever they can by recruiting informers within the government. As I have already stated, I know the identity of one former Labour Cabinet minister who was in regular touch with the CIA. An American source has recently written to me insisting that the CIA still has an agent inside the Labour Cabinet but I have not been able to confirm this.

CIA activities in Britain have probably been curtailed, at least temporarily, as a result of the public censure to which the agency has been subjected in the USA, particularly since the Watergate affair. This self-inflicted damage to the capability of the USA to defend itself and its allies has been joyously welcomed by the Kremlin. There were grave fears that MI6 and MI5 might suffer similar castigation affecting their efficiency, especially after the publicity given to verbal attacks on MI5 by Wilson, but happily this has come to nothing though various Communist front organizations keep trying.

The effort mounted by the CIA in Britain is modest compared with that of the much bigger and more secret National Security Agency, which operates so discreetly that the initials are said to stand for 'Never Say Anything'. This is so closely interlocked with its British counterpart, Government Communications Headquarters, that the two are best considered together. The NSA has a headquarters in the US embassy in London, while GCHQ has its headquarters in Cheltenham, but the two agencies tend to run joint establishments, which is an excellent arrangement for Britain since the USA bears the main burden of the very large costs.

The prime joint purpose is long-range electronic surveillance of

Russia's clandestine activities wherever this can be achieved.

The simplest installations monitor the coded radio messages by which the Kremlin communicates with its embassies and the KGB links up with its agents. Intercepted material is decoded where possible by cryptographers using computers and other electronic means based both in Britain and at the NSA's enormous headquarters at Fort Meade in Maryland.

It has to be admitted that, because of the scale of the research and production effort required, American electronics expertise is way ahead of Britain's in certain fields. The NSA claims to know the call-sign of every Soviet aircraft. The links which the Americans have devised and established for intercommunication between the various branches of its Intelligence-gathering services, some of which I have seen in action, border on the incredible. Vital intercepts can be in the hands of the Defence Department in Washington literally in seconds. A submerged American missile submarine which is being harassed by a Soviet hunter-killer can record and transmit the 'signature' of its pursuer – details of the particular sound of its wake and the beat of its pumps – to a computer in the USA and receive the type and name of the Russian vessel by quick return.

Most of the NSA installations in Britain tend to be rather pointlessly camouflaged as military and naval establishments or radio research stations. The main ones are near Harrogate, Chicksands in Bedfordshire, Bude in Cornwall, Edzell in Scotland and Haverfordwest in Wales. There was a very large station at Orfordness in Essex but this was closed down after only short service because the results could be obtained more cheaply by satellites.

Some of the methods used, such as over-the-horizon radar, are both complex and highly ingenious, giving, in some cases, the capacity 'to look right down Russia's throat'. What this means is that even the radio conversations of Russian tank commanders on manoeuvres deep in the Soviet Union can be monitored.

In the USA the NSA uses the latest computer storage and retrieval technology to collect millions of international telegrams, telex messages and many international telephone calls for possible Intelligence purposes. This 'dragnet' operation is also conducted to some extent in Britain.

Both the NSA and GCHQ are able to use their facilities for 'disinformation' purposes – to feed false information to the Russians in the hope that it will mislead them not only about Allied developments but about their own. The Russians cannot afford to ignore what they believe might be genuine information, so disseminating electronic disinformation is useful if only because it takes up the time of Soviet counter-Intelligence experts who might be more usefully employed.

One sophisticated way in which this is achieved is to feed out false telemetry signals so that they appear to be coming from a rocket which the Russians have launched and give a misleading impression of its performance. The NSA uses satellites for this purpose which, I suppose, could qualify as a 'dirty trick'.

A Special Projects Division of the NSA is also responsible for the production and planting of what it calls 'sneakies' – eavesdropping bugs introduced inside 'hostile' targets, which may be homes and offices of suspected persons.

The extent to which this is practised in Britain is difficult to discover. I have established to my satisfaction that such devices were used in the past during the surveillance of trade union officials and student groups and I have been given unconfirmed information that they have been used in the surveillance of Labour ministers.

Efforts appear to have been made by Communists to infiltrate local labour employed at some of the NSA eavesdropping establishments and since the USA is responsible for internal security at its stations it is reasonable to suppose that all means would be employed in the investigation of possible suspects.

The National Reconnaissance Office is responsible for control of the large numbers of surveillance satellites launched by the USA. These are now of extreme importance because they do carry not only cameras but listening devices, heat sensors to detect rocket firings, radiation sensors to detect nuclear tests and other still-secret developments of almost incredible effectiveness.

The NRO has stations across the world and Britain plays only a small role, but the satellite information supplied by the USA is of incalculable value. However, this is not to say that the agent on the ground has become obsolete. According to Jim Skardon, MI5's brilliant interrogator, now retired, the most productive source of Intelligence – and of leaks – is still the wagging tongue.

The Defence Intelligence Agency, which is the most straightforward of all, coordinates the Intelligence efforts of the Navy, Army and Air Force to assess the armed strength of potential opponents and the state of their weapons research and production. It works closely with Britain's Directorate of Defence Intelligence in Whitehall, which is just as well because the strength and effectiveness of that most important department has been halved by Labour's defence economies.

## Chapter Seventeen

# MPs, Ministers and Security Checks

IT might be thought with fair reason that if certain candidates for ministerial appointments gave cause for doubt on security grounds they would be passed over, but such is not the case. The causes of this relative immunity and its consequences are of considerable public interest.

After the Canadian spy trial in 1946 which revealed that a British nuclear scientist called Alan Nunn May had been a Communist spy, the British Labour government under Clement Attlee decided that it must take some action to prevent further security disasters. Britain's American partners in the wartime atomic bomb effort were already restricting nuclear information and this resolve to preserve nuclear secrecy had been hardened by the Nunn May exposure. The government was determined to equip the RAF with nuclear bombs and a complete stoppage of the flow of information from the USA would prove very costly to Britain and delay the day when its government could attend international conferences as an independent nuclear power.

While the Labour leadership was much more resolutely opposed to Communists than it is now, it was reluctant to publicize its move against the Left and the first inquiries into the political background of scientists and other civil servants in government employment were made surreptitiously. People who were obvious risks were switched to non-secret work – by promotion if necessary – or made redundant.

The scientists and civil servants involved soon realized what was going on and there were internal allegations about witch-hunts, but the first major publicity resulted from a report of mine in January 1948 that two scientists, who had been former Communists but disclaimed current attachment to the party, had been dismissed from the secret rocket research station at Westcott, Bucks. The two men had complained about their treatment in a little magazine published by the rocket station and as I happened to be a subscriber to that journal the story was handed to me on a plate.

This publicity led to parliamentary questions and open complaints from civil service unions. The Labour government's 'purge' of Communists became officially accepted policy in March 1948 when Attlee gave details of a 'purge procedure', whereby those who felt wrongly accused could take their cases before a three-man purge tribunal.

In the advice given to candidates for the Civil Service a clause was inserted in December 1948 stating 'the government have decided that no one may be employed in the Civil Service in connection with work, the nature of which is vital to the security of the state who is believed to be either:

1 A member of the Communist Party or the Fascist Organization.

2 Or associated with either the Communist Party or the Fascist Organization in such a way as to raise legitimate doubts about his reliability.'

The inclusion of Fascists was a ruse to suggest that not only Communists were being barred. In fact at that time the 'Fascist Organization' was virtually non-existent. My informant in the MI5 registry told me that the number of Fascists then on file was 'minute'. Presumably it is bigger now with the emergence of the National Front though this is essentially an anti-immigration organization with no parent country comparable to Russia ready to receive pilfered information.

The Attlee government steam-rollered all opposition and the purge was intensified after the conviction two years later of Klaus Fuchs. The first stage of this intensification was the restriction of certain posts, including some in the defence industries, to those who were British-born of British parents, though the defection of the diplomats Burgess and Maclean in 1951 showed this precaution to be of limited value.

The effects of these KGB penetrations of most sensitive areas in Whitehall and its outstations greatly exacerbated American concern for the safety of those secrets it shared with its chief ally to a degree which has influenced the behaviour of every British government since.

The next stage in the struggle to keep Communist sympathizers out of sensitive posts was the introduction in 1952 of positive vetting, a procedure in which the individual under consideration is first required to fill in and sign a questionnaire giving personal details and asking about Communist affiliations past and present. The names of three referees must be given and inquiries into the person's veracity and background, including peculiar sexual habits and especially homosexuality which is a special bar because of its blackmail potential, can then begin. These are conducted by a team of investigators recruited mainly from retired police and servicemen.

Any blatant lie is likely to disqualify as was succinctly stated by a former Deputy Director of MI6 when explaining to me the procedure for vetting applicants to that service. 'The sort of questions you are asked are, "Have you ever been a member of the Communist Party?" "When you were at public school did you ever bugger your fag?" The applicant says "No" to both, then when they make inquiries they find that though he never was a Communist he did bugger his fag. So he's out!'

The weakness of the system, to which even the most distinguished civil servants must submit, is that it can easily fail to detect any person who is determined to conceal his connection with the Communist Party. I discovered such a case during the reign of Duncan Sandys (now Lord) as Aviation Minister, and the incident not only illustrates the continuing concern about causing offence to the Americans but shows how a determined ministry will try to manipulate the Press.

While lunching with Ben Smith, then general secretary of the Association of Scientific Workers, who had been an active Communist but had fallen out with the party, I learned that the Aviation Ministry had belatedly discovered that one of its senior civil servants had long been a member of the Communist Party without disclosing it. Because of this he had been quietly transferred to non-secret work. When Sandys heard that I was making inquiries about this case he immediately telephoned Lord Beaverbrook to assure him that if the truth was printed it would do great harm to the interchange of defence secrets with the USA. His argument was rather potent because the official concerned had only recently ended a two-year stint as the government's guided weapons representative in Washington. So Lord Beaverbrook agreed to spike the story. Sandys went a little too far, however. He was due to make a speech at Farnborough air show and wanted to create a stir by announcing the first successful flights with a device which became known as the Flying Bedstead, later to develop into the jump-jet combat plane.

The *Daily Sketch* got wind of the Bedstead, and even secured pictures of it, but publication was stopped by the Aviation Ministry by threat of prosecution under the Official Secrets Acts. The *Sketch* withheld its excellent scoop, and a fortnight later Mr Sandys got the full publicity from his speech when pictures of the machine were issued to all newspapers.

Beaverbrook's reaction was typical even though the offended newspaper was a rival. 'Sandys is taking too much for granted,' he barked. 'Print the story about the missile man.' Print it we did and there was no worsening of relations with the USA, so far as we ever knew.

The introduction of positive vetting, which applied to those already in secret posts, was immediately successful. Officials in several ministries were quietly moved and in a few cases were dismissed. Even in a department of the Post Office handling secret communications, several suspected Communists were transferred to non-secret work. They included some of the telephone-tappers!

This anti-Communist drive still continues officially, though little is heard of it now, and presumably applies to the 'New Left', the rash of more openly revolutionary groups like the International Socialists.

Neither the purge nor the positive vetting procedure has ever been applied to government ministers though appointment to several posts gives immediate access to extremely sensitive information. The double standards of political leaders in this respect were well illustrated by the behaviour of Premier Attlee at a private meeting not put on public record before. On receipt of a note from Washington that the USA would discontinue providing any secret defence information if any of his ministers had ever been involved with Communism, he called in the ministers who needed to be informed of it. They included John Strachey, the War Minister, who had previously been publicly associated with the Communist Party, speaking regularly at Communist rallies, George Strauss, the Supply Minister, and Lord Pakenham (now Lord Longford), both of whom had once been associated with moves to improve cooperation between the Labour and Communist Parties.

Attlee read the American note, then snapped 'That doesn't apply to any of you does it?'

Realizing that the question was rhetorical none of them replied.

'Right. Then that settles it,' the Prime Minister said and dismissed them from the room.

Remote as he was, Attlee must at least have known of Strachey's Communist connections and any senior civil servant with such a record would have received less superficial treatment. More recently Denis Healey, while Secretary of State for Defence, made light of the fact that he was a card-carrying member of the Communist Party when at Oxford University in the 1930s and it may be considered unreasonable that such political activity so long ago should be held to have any significance. Nevertheless, under the Labour government's own rules it would probably have barred him from any senior Civil Service post involving access to secrets and he would almost certainly have disqualified himself by his statement to the Labour Party conference after the war when he was twenty-eight that, 'The Socialist Revolution is already firmly established in many countries in Eastern and Southern Europe. The crucial principle of our foreign policy should be to protect, assist, encourage and aid in every way the Socialist Revolution wherever it appears. If the Labour movement in Europe finds it necessary to introduce a greater degree of police supervision and more immediate and drastic punishment for their opponents than we in this country would be prepared to tolerate, we must be prepared to understand their point of view.'

Since 1964, as the result of a Conservative decision, every minister on first appointment is briefed by a senior MI5 officer about the ever-present threat of espionage and the Whitehall system of protective security opposing it. The Foreign Secretary, the Home Secretary and the Defence Secretary are briefed by the Director-General of MI5 himself, but officially no inquiries, overt or covert, are made, though it is my belief that security officers find ways round this ban in certain cases, using a little private enterprise.

The main reason given for the immunity of ministers to positive vetting is that the process takes so much time. After winning a general election a Prime Minister is expected to announce his new government quickly because otherwise departments of State would be without political leadership. It would be highly embarrassing if a person appointed to an important position had to be moved from it six weeks later because the vetting procedure had revealed that he might be a security risk.

In practice, however, when there is a change of government most of the senior posts tend to be filled by members of the previous shadow Cabinet and such people could be vetted leisurely while in opposition.

It is also claimed that most senior Cabinet ministers have become Privy Councillors before they achieve high office through service in junior appointments and that the oath they take when achieving that honour is sufficient security cover. The oath includes the words, 'I will keep secret all matters committed and revealed unto me.'

With respect to Privy Council matters the oath is rarely broken, if ever, but the cavalier manner in which Privy Councillors of all political persuasions have leaked confidential information, including Cabinet secrets, when it has suited them demonstrates the limited value of this oath in general security terms.

Wilson appeared to believe that the MPs oath of allegiance was enough: 'I do swear by Almighty God that I will be faithful and bear true allegiance to Her Majesty Queen Elizabeth II, her heirs and successors according to law. So Help Me God.' But servicemen swear such an oath on joining the Forces and positive vetting is compulsory for those whose duty requires access to secrets. Indeed, the former Prime Minister told me with some pride that his security overlord, George Wigg, had discovered about 3,000 airmen who had not been positively vetted when they should have been.

In any event such an oath or affirmation may have negligible significance for dedicated Communists who tend to be atheists and are enjoined by Lenin, the founder of their peculiar creed, to cheat or lie if it will advance the movement.

It is also argued, naïvely I think, that Parliament being such a gossip-shop, the chief whips soon hear about any scandalous or subversive behaviour by their MPs. They were unaware of the sexual habits of Lord Lambton, the junior minister for the RAF, who eventually resigned when others discovered them. Positive vetting might have prevented a damaging scandal in his case.

Even when the whips are aware of scandalous behaviour they do not necessarily take any action. As already mentioned, the homosexual activities of Tom Driberg in public lavatories were widely known. Woodrow Wyatt, a former Labour MP, recalls how he waited outside the lavatory in the Palace of Westminster while Driberg was inside 'having one of the chefs', as the former Chairman of the Labour Party, later elevated to the Lords, put it himself. I am assured that Winston Churchill's remark on the occasion of Driberg's marriage, 'Well buggers can't be choosers!' was not apocryphal and Driberg claimed that it was only because Wilson knew he was a practising homosexual that he had never been given ministerial office. Driberg also boasted openly about the ways he used to avoid prosecution when caught by the police at a time when his habits were criminal. One is left suspecting that he must have been granted some sort of immunity.

If the head of MI6 took so many years to discover that one of his senior officers, Kim Philby, was a KGB agent, what chance has a chief whip of hearing about a minister or MP who may be similarly engaged? The possibility that MI5 might warn him has been considerably diminished by a so far unexplained action by Harold Wilson which came to light in 1966. He then told Parliament that though a Privy Councillors' report on security had recommended that MPs should not be treated differently from members of the public, he had reviewed the position and issued a directive to MI5 and Special Branch forbidding the tapping of telephones belonging to MPs. I have established that this ban is interpreted as also applying to the surreptitious opening of mail and examination of bank accounts. It also applies to the Lords, which means that elevation to the pecrage provides a Soviet agent of sympathy with considerable protection.

Significantly, the only objections to this gratuitous grant of near immunity to security surveillance came from Tory opposition MPs.

I am by no means alone in believing that ministers with access to secrets should be subject to positive vetting. In May 1976 Lord Shawcross, a former Labour Attorney-General, called for an end to the system which gives ministers immunity from security checks, claiming that some British ministers, past and present, would fail them. Prime Minister Callaghan has since declined a Tory MP's suggestion that British MPs with special interest in defence should be able to volunteer to undergo positive vetting to enable them to participate in secret NATO briefings, though this is established practice in several NATO countries.

What would a Labour or Tory government do if the security authorities produced undeniable proof that a minister, and particularly a senior Cabinet minister, was a Soviet agent? This question has been suggested to me as a subject for an interesting novel by a former officer of MI6, who was not prepared to say whether such an eventuality had ever arisen but did hint that considerable thought had been given to the possibility.

After considering all eventualities I suspect that the matter would be completely suppressed 'in the national interest'. First, the Prime Minister would insist that any trial would be too damaging to Britain's image abroad, particularly in the USA. Second, even if the opposition leaders learned the facts, there would be a closure of ranks, not only in the national interest but because of the damage to the image of Parliament. Third, if the Director of Public Prosecutions were approached he would be likely to decide that the chances of securing a conviction would be too small because essential witnesses, such as defectors, could not be produced in court and because it is extremely difficult to catch a minister under the Official Secrets Acts.

*Chapter Eighteen*

# The Self-authorization Game

TO date no minister or ex-minister has ever been prosecuted under the Official Secrets Acts though many of them have leaked official secrets. There is a simple reason for this – any minister, by virtue of his office, has the power to indulge in what is called 'self-authorization'. He can decide at any moment to downgrade secret information and bring it outside the scope of the Acts.

This means that, in theory, a minister who wanted to publish some secret information of use to a potential enemy could do it in absolute safety simply by releasing it, either in a speech or to a journalist.

James Callaghan made the legal situation quite clear when discussing this possibility with the Franks Committee on the Official Secrets Acts: 'I suppose in the case of a minister in charge of a department it would be difficult to find a circumstance in which he could not authorize himself to release the information and therefore under the Act it would be very difficult to catch a minister.'

In practice most ministers use their self-authorization powers for perfectly honourable purposes, such as to provide some exclusive information for a speech, which will guarantee headlines or, as happened in the instance I shall now describe, for sound national or departmental reasons.

In March 1962 Julian Amery, then Air Minister, asked me if I could possibly write a series to show how powerful Britain's nuclear deterrent really was. He was concerned by the continuing Labour jibe that the deterrent was useless, partly because of its effects on Britain's allies but mainly because it was affecting the morale of the RAF bomber crews, who were spending very long hours by their loaded bombers on quick alert to counter any surprise Soviet attack.

I knew the true strength of the RAF's nuclear capability – 175 bombers, most of them at that time fairly sure of reaching their targets in the Soviet Union – so I said I would be delighted to oblige provided he could offer some exciting new information, particularly in the way of photographs. I suggested that one certain way of getting the articles printed would be for me to be photographed alongside a British H-bomb, pictures of which had never been released before. Amery thought that would be out of the question on security grounds but within twenty-four hours he telephoned me to say he had fixed it.

I went to an RAF Vulcan station in Suffolk and there I was photographed leaning against the tail of an enormous H-bomb. Its appearance in the *Daily Express* triggered off the inevitable questions in Parliament but Amery deftly warded them off without revealing our deal.

Any paper which had printed the picture without permission would have been prosecuted under the Official Secrets Acts and I have little doubt that the Crown prosecutor would have insisted that serious damage had been done to the nation's security. As it was, a

Minister had decided for worthwhile political motives to trade off security for publicity.

During a meeting of the Parliamentary Labour Party, the proceedings of which were supposed to be private but were inevitably leaked in full, Wilson provided information which would have led to angry ministerial accusations, had a journalist been responsible.

After the revolution in Libya, Gadhafi banned all flights of British military planes over his country, which had been the regular route for ferrying troop reinforcements to Aden and the Persian Gulf and beyond. Turkey and Iran solved the problem by granting overflying rights on condition that they were kept secret. No security was involved, since the Russians knew all about it. The secrecy was to save embarrassing the Turks and Iranians who, being Muslims, did not want to be accused of aiding the British to fight other Muslims. A letter had been sent to all editors by the D-notice secretary asking them to refrain from revealing the routes, and this had been generally observed. For some reason, it suited Wilson to refer to the routes at his party meeting, to the annoyance of the editors who then felt free to use the information themselves.

On many occasions ministers have self-authorized themselves to release secret information to me for less obvious reasons. Sometimes when in danger of losing an argument with the Foreign Secretary, a Defence Minister would impart some classified item, publication of which would weaken his opponent's position in Cabinet. Occasionally a minister would have been forbidden for diplomatic reasons to release some information involving the USA. As such a release would redound to his personal credit I would be given the means of publishing it. There were odd occasions where sensitive information was whispered in the obvious hope that somebody else, disliked by the informant, would be suspected of providing it. The information might be given to me directly by the minister in a private discussion over lunch – a 'decent interval' of a few days being allowed to elapse before it appeared in print – or it might be imparted through an official.

Occasionally a minister would provide information out of friendship over a convivial meal or simply because he was one of those politicians, happily for journalists reasonably common, who just cannot keep their mouths shut and derive satisfaction from demonstrating that they are 'in the know'.

There were sometimes official inquiries into how the information had leaked but when a minister was involved they quickly subsided.

Had Richard Crossman been alive when his diaries were published he could almost certainly have pleaded 'self-authorization', though to what extent this power continues to reside in an ex-minister is unknown. Following Wilson's strictures on MI5, which had been made to BBC investigators, Tory back-benchers suggested that he should be indicted for breaching the Official Secrets Acts. The attempt proved abortive and for the reasons I have stated it is extremely unlikely that charges could have been substantiated in court.

Ministers also seem to be immune from legal action or even censure for leaks occasioned through negligence. This was demonstrated on the occasion in May 1965 when Cabinet papers left in Prunier's Restaurant in St James's Street by Crossman fell into my hands.

Crossman, then Housing Minister, had been reading the documents while having a late supper alone. Major Geoffrey Blundell-Brown, a company director and staunch Tory supporter who was an acquaintance of mine, happened to be dining with friends at a nearby table. After Crossman had left the restaurant Blundell-Brown noticed a wad of papers under the vacated table and retrieved them. There were eighteen pages concerned with Cabinet discussions about housing aspects of the government's Race Relations Bill and including a summary of a Cabinet meeting.

As I then had a flat within fifty yards of Prunier's, the Major brought them to me, being incensed by Crossman's scant concern for security especially when the Labour government had made such capital out of the alleged security aspects of the Profumo case. Further, Wilson had returned to the security charge from the Dispatch-Box only a few days earlier. When I read the documents I could see that politically they were highly embarrassing for the government as they contained details of a disagreement between Crossman and the Home Secretary, then Sir Frank Soskice, over the housing of coloured immigrants.

I was delighted to receive them because during the last major debate of the dying Macmillan government on the Ferranti over-payment for missiles, great play had been made, falsely, of security leaks to me by Julian Amery, then the Aviation Minister. Wilson accused the whole Tory administration of leaking so much that it was 'incontinent'. So the following morning I took the papers in to the editor to decide on action.

My first move was to telephone Wigg, Wilson's security overlord, to alert him. He telephoned Crossman, who had not missed the papers, and then rang me back to warn me that we would be prosecuted under the Official Secrets Acts if we published any of the papers' contents. He then urged me not to print anything about the incident on the grounds of 'charity'. I remembered the charity he and Wilson had meted out to my friend Jack Profumo so I did not commit myself but told him that the papers had been handed back to the finder who would be turning them over to the police.

The following morning the *Daily Express* described how the papers had been found and referred to their contents in general terms, making a row in Parliament inevitable. During it Labour turned all its anger on Blundell-Brown for failing to return the papers quietly to Crossman, something I do not think would have happened had a Tory government been in office and the papers had been found by a Labour supporter.

I could find no evidence that Crossman had received even a mild rebuke from Wilson. A service officer or senior civil servant might not have received such generous treatment.

Crossman's own reaction as recorded in his diary was most interesting. He wrote that he thought that I had done everything to reduce the embarrassment for him when the reverse was true. He also called Blundell-Brown Blundell-Smith, which suggests that the diary entry was written after the event and had not been checked against *Hansard*. I pointed out this error to *The Sunday Times* before it serialized the diaries, and it was then removed from the subsequent book.

*Chapter Nineteen*

# Deception by Whitehall

FOR many years the Foreign Office operated what was really a psychological warfare branch under the cover name of the Information Research Department (IRD). Its main purpose was to counter Soviet bloc propaganda and to disseminate information and disinformation to undermine Communism in Britain and elsewhere and particularly to expose Communist front organizations for what they are.

Various journalists were recruited to work for the IRD, which was largely financed by the CIA. They used information supplied by IRD or produced their own. I was approached as a possible operator, after recommendation by a Defence Ministry official, but declined. I did, however, allow myself to be dissuaded from writing about the IRD. Most journalists who worked freelance for the IRD were paid – as was the staff of a well-known magazine.

In May 1977 the Labour government, for reasons of its own, not unconnected with the Watergate scandal, succeeded in winding up the IRD, which presumably pleased the Kremlin.

Other departments of state, the Defence Ministry in particular, have small, but usually highly effective units specializing in deception operations and I have been associated with some of those, though never for payment.

The most important of these operations, in which I had the distinction of playing a leading role, concerned the first test of a British H-bomb in 1957. The success of this test was crucial to the government's defence policy on two counts. Without it the government could not begin production of megaton bombs for the RAF, which were to form the nation's independent strategic deterrent for the next few years. Secondly, the information derived from the test would also permit the nuclear scientists to press forward with the development of a megaton warhead for the big missile, code-named Blue Streak, which would eventually replace the bombs. Because the accuracy of this missile would be somewhat limited, it could be reasonably certain of knocking out its target only if the explosion was big enough to devastate a wide area. In short, without an H-bomb warhead the giant missile made no sense.

Through my close friendship with the late Sir Frederick Brundrett, then the government's chief defence scientist, who was opposed to unnecessary secrecy in Whitehall, I was able to discover that the test would be carried out near Christmas Island, an isolated British possession in the Pacific, and announced this as early as April 1956. The Prime Minister, Sir Anthony Eden, confirmed it in the Commons two months later.

During the following year there was a steady build-up of political opposition to the test. By March not only left-wing politicians but churchmen and scientists were clamouring for its abandonment because of the danger to the rest of the world from radioactive fall-out.

This danger was negligible because, at considerable risk of failure, the government had decided to test the bomb by dropping it from a Valiant bomber so that it could explode high in the air. A ground-burst would have been cheaper and more certain to succeed but that type of test caused the most fall-out.

This precaution, though well publicized, did not stop the Communists from making the most of the possibilities. This was in Russia's interests because, as the bulk of the US bombers would be operating from the American mainland, the RAF had undertaken to provide 80 per cent of the first retaliatory strike against Soviet cities, being much nearer to these targets.

The Socialists, led by Gaitskell, decided to join in to the extent of demanding a postponement until more was known about the dangers of fall-out but they and the rest were greatly embarrassed when, on the very day Gaitskell made his demand, the Russians staged a ground-burst test of a huge and dirty megaton bomb.

The Foreign Office, which always hates upsetting any foreign country, had been warning the government that unless it completed the Christmas Island exercise by the summer it might become impossible to stave off demands for the international banning of. anything but underground tests, for which Britain had no facilities. What disturbed the government even more was a Foreign Office report that a Japanese threat to prevent the explosion by sailing a thousand small ships into the danger area, from which all shipping had been barred, had to be taken seriously. Intelligence reports confirmed that the Japanese meant business and might be joined by some Australians opposed to the test.

Code-named 'Operation Grapple', the test had therefore become a race against time and it was essential to foil the 'suicide ships'. In this connection I was telephoned by Brundrett, who asked if I could motor down to his home near Portsmouth for an urgent talk. He took me into the garden and explained what was happening.

The government had decided that a deception plan had become essential. Sir William Penney, the atomic weapons chief, who had not been scheduled to go to Christmas Island at all, had booked a BOAC flight to Sydney on what would seem to be the first leg of a journey to Christmas Island. That flight had been selected so that he could not possibly get to the test site before the middle of June. So would I please publish this information and raise two questions about it? First, did this mean that the test had been delayed for a further six weeks because the scientists had run into technical trouble? Second, was the trouble so serious that Penney was going to sort it out and supervise the first explosion in person?

Brundrett told me that the whole thing was a fake. There were no troubles and the test remained scheduled for mid-May. The object was to fool the Japanese and anyone else into delaying the departure of suicide ships for the testing ground.

Appreciating the immense political consequences and British embarrassment if the test had to be abandoned, as was becoming increasingly likely according to the Foreign Office, I agreed, providing I could carry my editor, then Arthur Christiansen, with me. I did so. Provided I could confirm that Penney had indeed made the booking, which I did, he was willing to collaborate as a patriotic gesture. There was one provision – I was forbidden to tell Beaverbrook about the deception until after the test when, as I anticipated, he gleefully approved of what we had done.

My article duly appeared as the lead story in the *Daily Express* of 29 April under the headline 'Penney – surprise flight. He goes to H-Island in June'.

The first bomb was duly exploded on schedule on 15 May. There had been no sign of suicide ships apart from one small boat flying the Japanese flag, which turned out to be manned by RAF officers pulling the Navy's leg. Whether the deception plan had played any part I never knew, but on my arrival on Christmas Island later the task-force commander of Operation Grapple, Air Vice-Marshal Wilfrid Oulton, greeted me with, 'We owe you an enormous debt.'

I visited Christmas Island along with several other journalists to witness the second explosion and conspired there in a further deception which may not sound so creditable but offers me an opportunity to pay overdue honour to a great journalist, the late Sir William Connor, who wrote under the name Cassandra in the *Daily Mirror*.

We had flown out to Honolulu under a pledge of secrecy, expecting to be taken out quickly to Christmas Island, but were told there that the test had been held up for a few days by unfavourable winds. Shortly before we joined the sloop from which we were to witness the explosion, we were addressed by an RAF officer who gave us some disconcerting news. The test would have to be held on a Friday and, because of time differences and poor communications from the sloop, it would not be possible for our eye-witness accounts to reach Fleet Street until Saturday. That meant that the news would break in the Sunday papers which had no representative there, apart from the Reuter agency man. So the *Daily Express* and other weekday papers, which had spent large sums getting us out there, would be scooped.

The RAF officer suggested that there was only one solution – the Brigadier in charge of the Press visit, who would join us on the sloop, would tell us in advance exactly what the explosion would be like. He could do this with absolute accuracy because this second test would be almost identical with the first, from which the Press had been excluded in case it should fail. We journalists would then be able to write our reports in advance and they could be held on Christmas Island. Then, once the bomb had been exploded, a fast plane would fly them to Honolulu where they would be transmitted at least in time for the late editions of Saturday's papers.

After a brief discussion it was agreed that, though we all deplored this situation, we should have to take part in the deception – save for Bill Connor, who alone insisted on being totally honest.

'We shall be fakes – frauds!' he cried angrily. 'I'll have no part of it!'

Nor did he. The *Mirror* was the only paper which failed to receive a 'first-hand' account of the historic blast.

The *Daily Express* received my copy in plenty of time for its first edition. In return for my help with Operation Grapple, the RAF officer had warned me several hours in advance of the others of the problem we should all face. I therefore took quick action.

Having witnessed several nuclear bursts and after gleaning some local details from the RAF officer I wrote my account there and then, depositing it with one of the cable companies with which I had previously established contact. The company agreed to hold it until the first official news flash announcing the bomb had been detonated reached Honolulu. If we were going to pre-write the story, as we obviously were, I was not going to leave mine to the mercy of my friends on Christmas Island.

The early arrival of my copy did nothing to help Connor, who received only harsh words on his return for failing to provide a dispatch until the Monday when, though the only honest eye-witness account, it was similar in detail to those published by the *Mirror*'s rivals forty-eight hours earlier.

To his eternal credit, Connor never let the truth be known in Fleet Street, where the trade papers would have printed it with glee. I do not think I could have resisted leaking it in the circumstances.

Connor's integrity was as high as the standard of his prose and I salute him.

I must record one further Whitehall deception about Operation Grapple. The official statements put out by the government claimed that the three test explosions – a third bomb was detonated in June – had been highly successful. In fact, as I was told secretly after returning to London, they had all been something of a flop. They were big blasts, as I had seen for myself, but the yield had proved very disappointing. This had to be kept secret because there would have to be a repeat of the operation after improvements had been made to the weapon and the government believed that the Socialists would make political capital out of the partial failure.

In the result, William Cook (now Sir), the ingenious scientist in charge of the tests, performed a near miracle on his return to the nuclear weapons research station at Aldermaston. A highly success-ful bomb was tested in the spring of 1958, in defiance of Labour claims that a further test might ruin prospective summit talks, on which it had no effect at all.

The deliberate issue of false statements by government departments to deceive an enemy in wartime is regarded not just as permissible but essential. Occasionally, what Whitehall regards as the justifiable use of lies spills over into peacetime operations and there is no better example of this than the case of Commander Crabb, the naval frogman, whose fate has remained a mystery to many.

I was involved in the journalistic inquiries into the Crabb affair, some of which resulted in much misleading speculation about this courageous man after he was reported 'missing presumed dead' in 1956. Since then, however, first-hand information which should resolve the mystery has come my way and I now put it on record.

By the early 1950s, with the development of sophisticated skin-diving equipment, it had become routine practice for navies to indulge in underwater Intelligence operations against warships of potential enemies. Nowhere was this more resolutely or more blatantly practised than in the harbour of Leningrad. Commanders of British warships on goodwill missions there knew that their hulls were being minutely inspected by frogmen seeking details of new Asdic devices, screw dimensions and other features betraying the ship's fighting capability.

No British complaints were ever lodged about these activities. The Admiralty knew that they would be denied, the Soviet Press would make no mention of them, and as the Foreign Office puts it, they would be 'counter-productive' to Anglo-Soviet relations.

In 1953, when the Russian cruiser *Sverdlov* visited Portsmouth to take part in the coronation celebrations, the Intelligence authorities wanted to make maximum use of the opportunity for a little frogman action themselves but even aerial photographs were forbidden by ministerial authority on the grounds that the coronation 'was not a proper occasion for such activities'. The CIA did manage to secure revealing photographs during that visit but little was known about the vessel below the water-line. So, when *Sverdlov* returned to Portsmouth in October 1955 with other warships on a naval goodwill visit, MI6 decided that this further opportunity should be exploited.

The man selected for the task was Commander Lionel 'Buster' Crabb, who had won the George Medal for wartime underwater operations in the Mediterranean, particularly in Gibraltar, where he had removed limpet mines from British ships as fast as Italian frogmen attached them. Apart from being the outstanding expert he had the additional advantage of being a freelance, having recently retired from the Navy. If anything went wrong, the Admiralty, which was officially responsible for protecting the Russian ships in a British harbour, could deny all knowledge of his activities.

Nothing did go wrong, however, and whether Naval Intelligence knew what Crabb was going to do or not they were delighted when his findings were passed to them by MI6.

Eight months later the Soviet Union's two most important politicians Bulganin and Kruschev were due to pay a goodwill mission to Britain at the invitation of the Prime Minister, Sir Anthony Eden, arriving at Portsmouth in the cruiser *Ordzonikidze* with destroyer escort.

Whether the initiative for a repeat performance came from Crabb or from MI6 I do not know but it was decided that surreptitious underwater inspection, with photography if possible, should be made and Crabb begged to be allowed to perform the task. No precise payment was arranged in advance but it was understood that it would be generous. Admiralty Intelligence officers were informed and, while making it clear that officially they could know nothing about the operation, they were keen on it and keener still to see the results.

With hindsight and in view of the political potentialities, the decision looks crazy, but such activities had become so routine that nobody believed the Russians would make much fuss, even in the unlikely circumstances that they found out about it.

As is customary, the operation was kept as secret as possible and only Crabb, a few of his intimates and a small faction in MI6 knew anything about it whatever. It would not have been normal practice to tell even the Minister of Defence, who would have felt duty bound to inform the Prime Minister, who would then have forbidden the operation.

On 17 April, Crabb and an MI6 officer booked into the small Sallyport Hotel in Portsmouth High Street, the Intelligence man giving the fictitious name of Bernard Smith and – incredibly – stating his address as 'Attached Foreign Office', the standard cover for MI6 operatives.

The next day the MI6 man suffered a slight heart attack but insisted on carrying on and very early on the morning of the 19th, the two went unobserved to the selected point of entry. The frogman put on his suit and an oxygen closed-circuit breathing apparatus designed to enable him to remain submerged for up to an hour without releasing tell-tale bubbles, and flippered his way towards the *Ordzonikidze*, which had berthed the previous day.

It has been suggested that his equipment was poor but I have been assured by someone who saw it on that day that, while it was not Navy issue it was first-class, though the closed-circuit method had inherent dangers.

At 7.30 a.m. Crabb was seen by Russian sailors momentarily swimming at the surface near one of the destroyers. He was having difficulty in getting down deep enough and had decided to return for an extra pound of ballast weight. He did so, not realizing that he had been seen.

After a discussion with the MI6 officer, Crabb decided to take a break and return for the final inspection in the afternoon. That is why his colleagues in London received a telephone call from him at 9.30 a.m. and why he was seen in a pub at 2 p.m.

Crabb never returned from the afternoon dive and MI6 is totally convinced that he died accidentally through oxygen-poisoning, damage to his oxygen supply-line, or through diving too deeply under the cruiser's keel. He had, in fact, been a bad choice for the task in spite of his courage and experience. He was forty-six, drinking and smoking heavily and not really fit.

Perhaps it was the unfortunate necessity to return for that extra pound weight which sealed his fate. Had he been able to complete the surveillance at the first endeavour he might have been alive today.

Soon after it became clear that the mission was likely to become public, a senior detective visited the Sallyport Hotel and removed relevant pages from the register.

Contrary to expectation, Bulganin and Kruschev decided to make political capital out of the affair but only, it seems, to take revenge for an insult which had been inflicted on them not by the government but by the Labour opposition. On the night of 23 April, before anything about Crabb's fate had become public, the two leaders were guests at a special dinner given by the Labour Party Executive Committee at Claridges. Gaitskell and Brown in particular made angry comments across the table about the brutal oppression of human rights in Russia.

The fact that Crabb was missing, presumed dead, was announced by the Admiralty on 29 April, accompanied by the false claim that he had not returned 'from a test dive in connection with trials of certain underwater apparatus in Stokes Bay' – three miles from Portsmouth. During a private interchange of notes between the Kremlin and the Foreign Office, the British authorities then admitted that the frogman, whom the Russian sailors claimed they had seen, must have been Crabb.

The Kremlin decided to publish the notes and on 10 May, by which time the Soviet leaders were back in Moscow, Eden was required to answer questions in Parliament. Horrified at what had happened, he assured Parliament in all honesty that what had been done was 'without the authority or knowledge of ministers'.

Intent on making party-political capital out of the situation, the Labour leaders forced a debate but before that was staged the Russian leaders attacked them in *Pravda* and *Izvestia*, claiming that their purpose was to distract the British public's attention from their anti-Soviet actions during the Russian leaders' visit, meaning the row at the Claridges' dinner.

Eden, who wanted to minimize the impact of the Crabb débâcle on East–West relations, deplored the debate and refused to give any further information. By this time, however, it was clear that the Admiralty claim that Crabb was testing new equipment was fraudulent and this had to be admitted. Eden also said that 'disciplinary action' had been taken against those responsible for the 'misconceived and inept operation'.

The MI6 officer who had accompanied Crabb was not affected but, following a secret inquiry headed by Lord Bridges, other MI6 men were interviewed and received a few mild reprimands. The affair was, however, a watershed for MI6 as a whole. The Director-General, Sir John Sinclair, known as 'Sinbad', who died early in 1978, retired slightly earlier than expected and Sir Dick White, then head of MI5 was put in charge. For MI6 to be subjected to a man from the rival organization was just about the most serious censure that could have been imposed.

Since the Crabb disaster, Foreign Secretaries, who carry the responsibility for MI6, have not felt it prudent to remain aloof from its activities as in the past.

The headless body of a frogman was washed up near Chichester Harbour in June 1957, ten miles from where Crabb had disappeared fourteen months previously. Examination showed that what was left of the suit on the body was identical with that worn by Crabb. From this and other evidence the coroner concluded that the remains were indeed those of the gallant commander, who had died in the service of his country.

The absence of the head gave rise to a theory that Crabb had really been captured by the Russians in Portsmouth Harbour and a headless body dressed in his suit had been dumped from a Soviet submarine as a cover. It transpired, however, that the body with the head attached had almost certainly been dredged up by a lone fishermen a few months previously. He had grabbed the head to haul it in and it had come away in his hands. Having dropped the whole thing in horror the fisherman had reported the incident to the police, who recorded it but took no action, presumably disbelieving it.

Even after the inquest the Admiralty repeated its fatuous claim that Crabb had been testing underwater apparatus in Stokes Bay.

In 1964, when Wilson was Prime Minister, an attempt to reopen the case was made by a back-bencher who purported to have evidence that the Russians knew about Crabb's mission in advance. Wilson declined to oblige. Like Eden before him, he thought that the Russians had secured more than enough political advantage from the episode.

Government departments are not only prepared to lie and mislead to cover up mistakes and stupidities but use other methods of deceiving the public. One of these was employed against me by a civil servant of great distinction, the late Sir Archibald Rowlands, then Permanent Secretary of the Ministry of Supply.

Early in 1950 I discovered through a disgruntled trade union official that a blunder, which could rightly be described as monumental, had been made in the construction of the first of the two giant uranium reactors then being built at Windscale in Cumberland. When the seven-feet-thick concrete shell of the furnace was finished, scientists from the Harwell research station carried out routine crack-detection tests and found that the wall through which the uranium rods would be loaded was porous to atomic radiation, and therefore highly dangerous.

At first Sir Charles Mole, then buildings chief at the Ministry of Works, feared that the furnace might have to be scrapped and the second one alongside it was also suspect. Workmen were ordered to drill out the faulty areas and to force in concrete under pressure. The repair, if possible at all, would be very costly and production of the atomic explosive, for which the reactors were being built, would be delayed.

It was at this point that my informant alerted me to the situation. I confirmed his claims that the error was due to bad workmanship and inadequate inspection and was keen to expose what I considered to be a public scandal, but during my inquiries Sir Archibald, whose department was responsible for Windscale, decided to stop me. He telephoned the editor and warned him that if the *Daily Express* printed the information we should be prosecuted under the Official Secrets Acts.

This was sufficient to hold up the story for a year while the repairs were fortunately effected. Again Sir Archibald tried to prevent any mention of the event, but when the editor insisted he gave way. He then confessed that he could not understand why we had not printed the story in the first place because the government would never have prosecuted us. The bludgeoning use of the Official Secrets Acts to take revenge on a newspaper which had exposed a scandal would have been too obvious.

There are occasions when government officials deceive themselves, sometimes with consequences which waste their time and public money and occasionally with results which are hilarious.

One of the latter variety concerned a Secret Intelligence Service training exercise, which illustrates what strange things may go on beneath the public's nose without their knowledge.

Before trainee spies can be safely sent out 'into the field', where they are in constant danger of detection, they are required to undergo tough experiences both in the techniques of interrogation and of resisting interrogation. On a bleak Saturday in January 1956 two such trainees had been told that a man, who was roughly described, would emerge from a government office near the Thames Embankment carrying a briefcase and walking a few paces behind the easily recognizable Home Secretary who, incidentally, had no idea he was being used in this way.

The trainees, who knew that their quarry was another trainee agent from a different course, were told only that the man had certain information of great value and it was up to them to get it. That was all.

Sure enough, the Home Secretary was followed out by a rather small individual with greying, crinkly hair and one of them tailed him while the other followed him along the Embankment in his car.

At a convenient point the man was stopped and told, 'The chief wants to see you.' Believing he was returning to his office he got into the car and eventually found he was being driven to a flat in the Old Brompton Road, one of several leased by MI6.

The trainees had picked up the wrong man, who was in fact a clerk from a branch of the Stationery Office.

Once inside the flat he was taken before a third trainee and interrogated in a way which terrified him. His trousers were removed and searched and the papers in his briefcase were tested for invisible ink.

After an hour or two it was realized that something must be wrong and this was confirmed by a telephone call to headquarters, which advised the immediate release of the suspect but with no explanation that would infringe secrecy.

The clerk was bundled into the street after being told that he must never tell anybody what had happened. After turning the events over in his mind he decided he had been kidnapped by lunatics and went to the Chelsea Police Station to report it. The police were doubtful about his tale but asked him to accompany a constable to the flat. The clerk found the block all right and pointed to the door behind which he had been so roughly handled. The constable asked the clerk to remain below while he knocked on the door, which was opened by a gentleman who had not the faintest idea what the policeman wanted. It was the wrong flat.

On the way to the block the constable had noticed a Volkswagen, which was then not so common, standing outside. He asked the owner of the flat if it belonged to him. When told it did he became much more interested.

'That's a foreign car isn't it?' he asked.

'So what,' said the owner irritably.

'So what are you doing using it to kidnap innocent people off the streets?'

Eventually the man who had been kidnapped was brought up to identify his captor and to the policeman's chagrin announced that the real flat must be one floor higher up. It was. The policeman knocked, was admitted and emerged twenty minutes later with a satisfied smile but no explanation for the unfortunate victim who was simply assured that everything was all right. It was all top secret and he must never tell a soul about what had happened, especially as he was a government servant. 'Understood?'

The civil servant understood and there we leave him, but the farce had barely begun. The irate owner of the flat below had meanwhile telephoned the *Daily Express* who sent two reporters round to get his story. They were in his sitting-room when the owner of the flat above, an MI6 instructor, called to explain to his neighbour what had happened. He was shown into another room and there explained under the strictest secrecy the reason for all the trouble. Meanwhile the *Daily Express* reporters were listening to all he said through an open door.

Shortly afterwards I was telephoned at my home by Admiral Thomson on behalf of security. He had heard that the *Express* were going to print the whole story and begged me to stop it.

'It will make MI6 look so stupid that it is bound to have a bad effect on their relations with America,' he pleaded.

It was an old ploy but for his sake I agreed to ring my editor and get his view. As the Admiral was also one of the editor's old friends he agreed to spike the story. So I telephoned the Admiral with the glad news.

An hour later he rang me again. 'I thought you said you'd stopped it.'

'I have.'

'Well let me tell you that at this very moment you have two reporters watching the flat which contains three men from MI6 and your reporters are being watched by two men from MI5!'

The story had been stopped but the news editor nevertheless wanted to secure the maximum information in case the editor decided to change his mind next day.

After further pleas on behalf of security the story was finally suppressed but one question remained unanswered. Why hadn't the real man been behind the Home Secretary as planned? The Admiral gave me the reason when we met some days later. He had missed his train!

In such exercises in London some of the stores like Simpson's in Piccadilly, which have two or more entrances on different streets, are often used for shaking off pursuers. There is a story, perhaps apocryphal, that the Simpson's manager buttonholed one of the MI6 men one day and said, 'For God's sake, couldn't you sometimes use Harrods for a change?'

I have no wish to give the impression that MI6, which normally works effectively under extremely difficult conditions, has any monopoly of the syndrome which used to be called SNAFU – Situation Normal All Fouled Up. The Defence Ministry has more than its share as evidenced by an Army security operation worthy of Laurel and Hardy. Devious, undercover arrangements had been made to secure regular supplies of two militant and scurrilous left-wing magazines, which occasionally leaked military secrets. They could be bought on the bookstands but Army security wanted to avoid all possibility that the Defence Ministry might have to admit in Parliament that it was paying for them. It had therefore been arranged for a civilian to buy them and each time they arrived he telephoned a confidential number in the Ministry to tell a woman civil servant there that 'they' were ready for collection, without, of course, mentioning the dreaded names on the open line. Regrettably a letter from the Army accounts department to the civilian paying him the money and thanking him for his cooperation, was sent to the wrong address, ending up with an irate Covent Garden businessman, who passed it on to me.

Self-deception frequently enters into the authorities' reaction to a leak or what they suspect is a leak and there have been several occasions when the wrong people have been accused of giving me information and have been subjected to unpleasant interrogation as a result. When a minister, senior civil servant or security official decides that there must have been a security breach a standard 'leak procedure' is brought into play. In a case involving me, for example, all possible suspects in the Defence Ministry, however senior, would be asked when they had last seen or communicated with me. Those who had to admit this misfortune would then be grilled and be required to sign their denials. They always were denials for I know of no single instance where the leak procedure revealed the correct source. This was confirmed to me recently by Lord Carrington, the former Defence Secretary, who confessed, 'I often put the dogs on to you but they never came back with the bone.'

The extent to which the leak procedure can produce a wrong and damaging result is illustrated by a conversation I had with a former Director-General of MI6 while he was still in office. I had published a novel called *The Penthouse Conspirators* in which the head of MI6 and the head of the KGB were each located in a penthouse atop a skyscraper building – Century House in London and a new building in Moscow. This was purely a fictional device to present a position where these two powerful gentleman sat wondering what the other was planning. After the novel appeared the MI6 chief – 'M' of the Bond novels but 'C' in real life – said to me, 'Oh, we found out who told you about the plan for the penthouse on top of Century House. It was quite an exercise because not many people knew that we once intended to have the Director-General living on the top.'

'But I never did know it,' I said truthfully. 'I made the whole thing up.'

One wonders what rocket the innocent suspect received and how his chance of promotion might have been affected.

While criticisms of MI6 and MI5 over their failures are somewhat unfair because their secret triumphs cannot be trumpeted, Sir Martin Furnival Jones, a former Director-General of MI5, admitted, when questioned by the Franks Committee, that they were justified. There have been cases, however, where criticism was not only unjustified but fabricated, the most entertaining of these being the Case of the Little Dutch Watch-repairer.

Shortly after the last war no spy book or newspaper attack on MI5 was complete without mention of a Dutchman who set up as a watch-repairer and jeweller near Scapa Flow in the Orkneys long before hostilities began. A quiet little man with gold-rimmed glasses, he ingratiated himself with the community, managing on occasion to return to Rotterdam to see his relatives.

In October 1939, very shortly after the declaration of war against Germany, the battleship *Royal Oak* was sunk at anchor in the impregnable harbour of Scapa Flow with the loss of more than eight hundred men. A German U-boat had hit the ship with three torpedoes and the man who had supplied the detailed information of the harbour defences to the U-boat commander, Lieutenant Prien, was the little Dutch watch-repairer, who was really Captain Von Muller, a German naval officer.

This story was recorded in newspaper cuttings in such detail that when writing a series on MI5 in the 1950s I included it.

I submitted the series to MI5 for security clearance and, while normally they would not comment on matters of fact, in this case they decided to be more helpful. It was explained to me, convincingly, that the little Dutch watch-repairer was a myth. He had never existed. Prien had sunk the *Royal Oak* by brilliant and daring seamanship.

I told the librarian at the newspaper that the cuttings on the watch-repairer, which gave his name and all sort of personal and family details, should be destroyed but, apart from putting a warning note in the envelope, they were retained. He argued that every other newspaper would be keeping them so we should retain them too. No doubt they are still there in most newspaper libraries recording the exploits of a spy who never was.

*Chapter Twenty*

# Disinformation and Defamation

ONE of the tasks, both of MI6 and the KGB, is to discredit each other in the hope of diminishing confidence in the eyes of the parent government and of allies and to lower morale within the opposing service. It is a battle which has been going on for fifty years using the well-established weapon of the forged document and the false rumour.

So far as the KGB is concerned these activities are directed from a *dezinformatsiya* department in Moscow which produces ideas and material for use throughout the world.

Photographs of faked secret documents alleged to have been taken inside government establishments have been sent to me anonymously on several occasions in the hope that my newspaper would print a story showing how bad British security was and demanding a Parliamentary inquiry.

Over the years I have received more than a score of forgeries aimed at discrediting the Admiralty, Defence Ministry, MI5, MI6, the CIA and the French security system. I have always suspected that the forged document purporting to be a Swiss bank account held illegally by Edward Short was a KGB-inspired device to discredit the British government through one of its senior ministers.

In July 1974 I was among several journalists who received a photocopy of a statement of an account with the Swiss Bank Corporation in the name of Edward W. Short, MP (now Lord) giving his correct home address. The account was in credit by 163,000 Swiss francs – about £23,000. I was immediately suspicious because I imagined that any such account, which would be highly illegal, would be numbered not named. I therefore tried to contact Short at the Commons. He kept me waiting on various pretexts and so I handed in a note to him explaining my doubts but received no response. Other newspapers, however, reported the fact that they had received copies of the bank statement which, after police inquiries, was shown to be a forgery.

Commander John Morrison of Scotland Yard came to see me to secure a statement and take away the documents including the envelope for fingerprint examination, my prints being taken in the process to eliminate them from any others. So far as is known their inquiries came to nothing.

There were suspicions that some Tory or other anti-Labour source was responsible for this deception but in my view it had been done professionally, a genuine account secured in Zurich having been doctored.

Short could have been selected as a KGB target for discrediting because a little while previously he had admitted being marginally involved with a corrupt businessman in Newcastle, T. Dan Smith, who was eventually jailed and had admitted taking £250 from him in expenses. Happily the forgery fell flat and this was one instance where the libel laws prevented what could have been an unpleasant, if temporary, smear of a leading politician.

While Soviet disinformation is often subtle it is sometimes crude, apparently being based on the Goebbels axiom that the bigger the lie the more it is likely to be believed. This was so in the KGB's crackpot announcement in 1965 that the Great Train Robbery was really engineered by the British secret service to secure extra funds for its spying activities.

This fantasy was promoted on the KGB's behalf in English over Moscow radio by a highly intelligent radio journalist called Boris Belitsky, who used to send me New Year cards, possibly in the hope of raising doubts about me with MI5.

Stories to be put around by rumour are also fabricated by Intelligence experts who look for what they call 'fertile areas' which have already been given wide publicity, like the train robbers.

In the summer of 1977 I received two long letters from Tenerife from a man claiming to be an officer of an American Intelligence agency on retirement leave there. They were full of the most intriguing information, mainly about Labour ministers and their links with the Communists. There were details of American and KGB operations against British politicians and trade union leaders and allegations of tax evasions by ministers and overseas accounts. There was also accurate information about secret establishments.

I showed the letters, which had an indecipherable signature, to several senior men who had been involved with Intelligence and it was their view that whoever wrote them was no amateur.

I retained them because a third letter had been promised, but when this did not materialize I handed them over to MI6, fearing that they might be subtle disinformation put my way on behalf of the KGB. At the time of writing they are still being processed.

Of course, MI6 does its share of blackening the opposition with fabricated evidence against both institutions and individuals, though it tends to be more restrained than either the KGB or the CIA, which has suffered severe damage following publicity about the activities of its 'dirty tricks' department.

The Russians claim that the extension of this mutual defamation battle to include 'memoirs' was begun by the British with the publication of Greville Wynne's account of his experiences in Soviet prisons in a series of articles in 1964. Wynne's account was considered by the Russians to be a breach of the gentlemen's agreement between governments under which he had been exchanged for Gordon Lonsdale, the KGB officer whose real name was Konon Molody.

MI6 did not approve of the Wynne memoirs (which it had no power to suppress) because it feared that Russia would retaliate, perhaps by revealing the names of British Intelligence agents together with such details of their careers as they knew. (There are, of course, those on the MI6 payroll whose cover is known to have been blown and they cannot just be dismissed. Their documentation bears the warning signal Sovbloc Red, while those whose cover is believed to be still secure are Sovbloc Green, Sovbloc Amber being the designation of those where there is some doubt.)

The British suspicions were well founded. The KGB immediately directed Lonsdale to write his memoirs for British and American consumption.

While spying has always been a dirty profession untrammelled by ethics or honour, there was one rule to which all sides had normally adhered until the memoirs battle – they had refrained from identifying each other's agents by name whenever possible. The reason was self-preservation. Once a spy is publicly identified it becomes impossible to use him anywhere else in the world. So the secret services of all nations had shunned tit-for-tat disclosures which could only make life difficult for all.

I was alerted to the KGB's reaction by an Intelligence contact as soon as it was learned that publication arrangements were being made through a Polish agency in Warsaw where Lonsdale was living, with the request that I should warn the public in advance that the memoirs would be a KGB propaganda exercise. I duly did that and when they finally appeared as a book called *Spy* they made little sense except as a product of a falsification service. They were, in fact, less damaging than had been anticipated.

The British security authorities hoped that this would be the end of the mutual defamation exercise but Lonsdale had named a few Americans with whom he had become friendly and the CIA was determined on revenge.

It responded by publishing the papers of Oleg Penkovsky, a colonel in the GRU who spied for the West as a defector-in-place in Russia and was far more valuable than Philby ever was to Moscow. Penkovsky volunteered his services in 1960 for ideological reasons when he became convinced that the Kremlin leadership under Krushev was likely to plunge the world into nuclear war.

Run jointly by MI6 and the CIA for sixteen months, Penkovsky had handed over 5,000 photographs of secret documents and during visits to London and Paris on official business missions revealed a great deal more verbally. With an extraordinary range of knowledge due to his military and social position, he provided technical details of Soviet weapons, combat units and military preparedness, plus that rarest of all espionage prizes – accurate information about the political intentions of the Kremlin leadership.

The last included facts about Soviet plans to use Cuba as a nuclear rocket base and Russia's real capacity to withstand determined American pressure to insist on the rockets' removal, which quickly proved to be of the greatest value to President Kennedy during the Cuban missile crisis.

Penkovsky was regarded as being so important that everything possible was done to encourage him, including deferring to his strange whim during one visit to London to walk round the City in a British officer's uniform. He also demanded to meet some of the Chiefs of Staff and this was done. It was even said that in order to enable him to see the Queen at close quarters, which he had greatly desired, he was invited to a garden party at Buckingham Palace, after which his enthusiasm to serve Britain knew no bounds.

Whether it was this odd behaviour which alerted KGB counter-espionage may never be known, but he was arrested along with Greville Wynne, the British businessman who had bravely acted as an MI6 courier and in other patriotic ways on visits to Moscow. In 1963 Wynne was sentenced to eight years' imprisonment, eight British and five American 'diplomats' were declared *persona non grata* and Penkovsky was shot. No objection to his execution was audible in the West. Had Fuchs or Blake been hanged, howls about British brutality would have been deafening.

The extent of the value of Penkovsky's information, though played down publicly by the KGB, was indicated by the scale of the shake-up in the Soviet military Intelligence services after his execution.

The CIA and MI6 have an arrangement as part of the Joint Intelligence Agreement that the defectors to one agency are eventually made available for interrogation by the other so both services had full tape-recorded accounts of long statements made by Penkovsky and copies of the documents he provided.

By one of those flukes which all journalists need and of which, perhaps, I have had more than my fair share, I was the first British newspaperman to hear about these 'diaries', said to have been taken from a secret drawer in Penkovsky's desk in his Moscow flat and smuggled to the USA by the CIA. The diaries were said to give Penkovsky's version of his association with Greville Wynne and described his undercover work in exposing the build-up of Soviet missiles in Cuba. They explained how the Americans were misled into believing that they were lagging far behind Russia in the production of H-bomb missiles, and other fascinating matters.

I had happened to be in New York on my way to Washington and called in to meet the American publisher of my first novel, *Not with a Bang*. Over dinner the publisher asked me if the *Daily Express* would be interested in serializing a book about the Penkovsky diaries and then explained, without reservation, what they were. The book was a concoction put together by the CIA but it was all said to be based on genuine material. During Penkovsky's visits to London and Paris hours of conversation with interrogators had been recorded. The 'diaries' were built up from those recordings and from a mass of typed and written documents Penkovsky had provided in addition to his photographed documents.

It had never really seemed likely that Penkovsky would keep an incriminating diary or other documents in his desk, even in a secret compartment for his own satisfaction or as a posthumous gift to the West. In fact the *Daily Express* eventually secured evidence that he almost certainly had not done so by interviewing his widow in Moscow and examining the desk.

The publisher gave me permission to report the existence of the 'diaries', though not to reveal that they had been put together by the CIA, and this I did by sending a short dispatch under a Washington date-line and this was published in April 1965. I sensed that the British security authorities, who must have provided much of the taped material, would be opposed to the book.

This was confirmed when I was approached again by a Defence Ministry contact acting on behalf of MI6 with the request that when the book eventually appeared I should make it clear to the Russians that the British authorities had nothing to do with it and had in fact vigorously opposed its publication.

*The Penkovsky Papers* shattered the no-names convention by identifying seven hundred Soviet officers and civilians involved in security work. The book even committed the unpardonable foul of declaring that many Soviet ambassadors were members of the KGB or GRU.

When the British edition appeared the Soviet ambassador protested to the Foreign Office on the grounds that it was a forgery. Forgery was too strong a word – but the book was certainly an exercise in psychological warfare, as the CIA has since been forced to admit.

Such was the simmering anger of the KGB over the CIA's Penkovsky exercise that retaliation was inevitable. What MI6 feared most was that Philby, then safely in Moscow, would be required to produce his memoirs and that these would be designed to make British Intelligence, the CIA and the FBI look as incompetent as possible. Philby duly obliged in 1968 with his memoirs *My Silent War*. Ten years later there are fears that a second volume from Philby may be on the way. As an MI6 officer put it, 'His first book did finish rather abruptly, didn't it? There must be more to come.'

It may well be asked to what extent MI6 should use businessmen like Greville Wynne or journalists to collect information which in Russia could put them in the category of spies and subject them to a trial where justice is a farce. There is, of course, no onus upon ordinary citizens to indulge in amateur espionage if they are approached. The responsibility is theirs and the risks are made plain to them, yet it is refreshing how many consider that reporting back is their patriotic duty.

The plight of any Briton jailed for spying in Russia has been alleviated by the postwar habit of exchanging captured spies, as happened in 1964 with Greville Wynne and Lonsdale. It is a system which invariably gives an advantage to the Russians because they always demand a more important spy in return. Lonsdale, for instance, was a professional espionage officer while Wynne was mainly a courier. In 1962 the KGB had secured the return of Rudolf Abel, another senior officer who had operated with great success in the USA, for Francis Gary Powers, the US pilot shot down over Russia. Gerald Brooke, who was exchanged for Peter and Helen Kroger, professional KGB members of the Portland spy ring, was not a spy at all.

The Russians have no compunction in making life harsh for a British captive whom they want to exchange. The man's condition is reported to the British embassy in Moscow, which applies pressure for the exchange to be effected on urgent humanitarian grounds.

As a further refinement the Russians are not above faking up a case against a visiting Briton in order to secure a body to exchange for a valuable spy who has been captured or even to keep one in reserve.

It is standard practice to feed disinformation to all spies who are under control, meaning that they have been detected but have deliberately not been apprehended. This gives counter-Intelligence an opportunity to repair some of the damage by feeding in misleading material, a process which may be continued for several months, though it has to be done with extreme care and ingenuity.

The same process can be used with a Russian Intelligence officer who believes he has recruited a spy, who in fact has immediately reported his situation to the security authorities and is working for them. This happened with a computer expert employed by the National Research Development Corporation, which was set up to finance promising inventions and scientific discoveries. The Russian was stuffed with misleading technical information for months before the KGB analysts rumbled it, when he was quickly declared *persona non grata* and sent back to Moscow.

In the psychological warfare against the IRA, the Army ran an 'Information Policy' operation in which false stories were foisted on newspapers to such an extent that an official was forced to leave for overdoing it. Shortly before 'Information Policy' was abruptly scrapped, I was visited by a colonel representing Army Intelligence who brought details of an Ulster situation which he felt I could reveal with consequent damage to the IRA, provided I did not disclose the source. I was delighted to oblige but on analysing the material found that it was so full of clumsy inconsistencies that it was obviously a fake. I complained to a very senior officer and some unnamed disinformation 'expert' duly received a severe rocket.

Soon after the start of the publicity about the Watergate affair in May 1973 I received a tip from a trusted British Intelligence source which has since made me suspect that I was fed some disinformation on President Nixon's behalf, possibly at the request of the CIA. I was told that Nixon aides had initiated the bugging and the burglary of Democratic Party headquarters in the Watergate complex in Washington for genuine security reasons. Information was alleged to have reached the White House that the Cuban government had secretly paid five million dollars into Democratic Party funds by a roundabout route to help defeat Nixon in the presidential election. As this would have been a wholly illegal interference by a foreign country, the White House was determined to find out if it was true, my source claimed.

The White House was supposed to have hired a freelance team to photograph Democratic Party fund documents. Meanwhile, after the break-in became public, Nixon and his aides were alleged to be 'taking it on the chin' to avoid creating a diplomatic incident which could sabotage the new relationship between the USA and Russia.

The reason for the Cuban action was supposed to stem from the rapidly improving Soviet–American relations initiated by Nixon's previous visit to the Kremlin. As part of the deal under which Brezhnev, the Soviet leader, secured huge quantities of American wheat to prevent a near famine, Nixon was known to have suggested that Russia should cut its support for the Communist regime on America's doorstep in Cuba.

Brezhnev was said to have agreed but the information was leaked by a Kremlin hard-liner to Castro, whose immediate reaction, my information alleged, was to do all he could to get Nixon out of office.

Nixon was said to be determined not to expose this real reason for the Watergate affair, at whatever risk to his reputation, because it would create a most difficult position for Brezhnev who was due to visit Washington.

Quite an ingenious story, which the *Daily Express* printed as no more than a theory and with the rider that it could be a Nixon cover put about by the CIA!

Now, in his memoirs, Nixon has confessed he conspired with his aides to put the blame on a Cuban plot.

If the CIA did try to foist that one on me it was only a modest dirty trick for them. There have been recent occasions when CIA 'dirty tricks' have been so dirty that some individuals in the agency refused to take part in them or, having done so, deeply regretted it to the point of resigning. Refusal to participate has also occurred in MI6. The occasion best remembered in that organization was in 1947, when the British Government was responsible for the mandate for governing Palestine. In deference to Arab objections, Britain tried to restrict Jewish immigration from Germany and other parts of Europe where many Jews had lost their homes. Shiploads of Jewish immigrants regarded as illegal, many from displaced persons' camps, were intercepted at sea or refused permission to land in Palestine. To assist with this difficult and unpleasant problem the Foreign Office instructed MI6 to sabotage some of the transport ships. The damage to the machinery was to be inflicted in ports and not while the ships were at sea. Nevertheless, some members of MI6, who were not themselves Jewish, rejected the instruction, to their abiding credit. There were, however, others who obeyed.

The dirtiest of all dirty tricks which I have ever heard of was generated by MI6 during the early part of the last war, but happily was discarded. Its purpose was to discredit Japan, which was not then at war but was clearly supporting Germany.

Some bright operator had discovered that the bulk of the sanitary towels used by American women were imported from Japan and his idea was to infiltrate thousands of them into the USA, all boldly labelled 'Made in Japan' and loaded with itching powder or some other dreadful irritant.

The feminine outrage against the Japanese could have assisted the Allied cause but few would disagree that this would have been carrying disinformation a little too far.

～✦✦✦～

*Chapter Twenty-one*

～✦✦✦～

# Deception in Westminster

REGINALD MAUDLING tells a story about a minister being driven across Dartmoor on a dirty night by a senior civil servant after holding an inquiry in the area. At a crossroads they were stopped by a man who was wet through and wheeling a punctured bicycle. 'I'm lost,' the man cried hoarsely. 'Can you tell me where I am?'

'You're on Dartmoor,' the civil servant replied and drove on.

When the minister remonstrated with the civil servant for failing to be more helpful he replied: 'Minister, I gave the perfect answer. It was truthful yet revealed the minimum of information.'

That seems to be the general guide for the answers to parliamentary questions written by civil servants when MPs try to secure information for the public. Indeed, there is a special expertise attached to drafting these answers and unless the question has been deliberately planted so that the minister can gain some credit by producing an informative reply, it is usually applied. The resulting cost in time and labour to the taxpayer is enormous, especially in the case of questions which have to be answered orally because all the supplementary questions have to be foreseen and ways of forestalling informative answers to them devised.

The purpose of this parliamentary game is to prevent the opposition from scoring points but its effect is to deprive the public of information. The newspapers do their best to counteract it by

securing information through the back doors of the Whitehall
departments and when this happens nobody pretends to be more
annoyed than the MPs themselves. Ministers have been repeatedly
asked by back-benchers why I and other journalists have been
informed before they were. The standard misleading answer by the
minister concerned is that he is not responsible for what appears in
the newspapers, and is delivered in such a tone as to suggest that the
Press reports are incorrect even when they are not. Yet, with the
exception of the reports of their own select committees, which are
covered by parliamentary privilege, MPs have no right to be given
information in advance of the public in general.

There are occasions when a misleading answer to a question in
Parliament is no more than the automatic reaction to a situation
from which a quick escape is needed. James Prior told me of such an
instance which, by chance, had happy repercussions, when he was
Tory Leader of the House. Wilson suddenly asked him if he would
give the date of the autumn budget, a barbed question to suggest that
the government was in financial difficulties. Immediately Prior
responded by declaring, 'There is not going to be an autumn
budget.'

Next day about £1,000 million was added to share prices because
uncertainty in the City had been removed. Prior told me that the
Cabinet had not considered the question of an autumn budget but he
had to give an answer and had taken a chance.

There are various subterfuges which governments employ to
avoid revealing embarrassing information. The commonest used to
be that disclosure 'would not be in the national interest' but this
seems to be giving place to 'this information could only be obtained
at disproportionate cost'.

The straightforward lie in the House.is regarded, in theory, as an
unpardonable crime and Profumo was disgraced as a result, but
some exceptions are accepted, as when Stafford Cripps denied that
the pound would be devalued when the decision to do just that had
already been taken. It is my belief, however, that misleading information bordering on lies has become much more prevalent in recent
years and that this is a symptom of the increasing arrogance of
ministerial office. The sad gibe that you can't believe what you read
in the newspapers is now paralleled by a growing suspicion that you
can't believe what you are told in Parliament. Time and again when
ministers are exposed after giving false information they are able to

laugh it off with little difficulty. The most blatant case in recent times was Healey's assurance to the public during the second 1974 election that the rate of inflation was running at 8¼ per cent when it was much higher.

Another item of misleading information perpetrated by Healey had serious consequences for Western defence, as was explained to me only recently by the Turkish ambassador. After Healey scrapped the building of further aircraft-carriers it became necessary, while he was still Defence Secretary, to backtrack on that decision to some extent and build some mini-carriers equipped with jump-jet aircraft for anti-submarine defence. As this laid Healey and his government open to ridicule, the word 'carrier' was forbidden for the new ships, which were called 'through-deck cruisers'. Some years later the Russians, who had built their first aircraft-carrier, the *Kiev*, in the Black Sea, wanted to send it through the Dardanelles, which should have been forbidden by the Turks as a breach of the Montreux Treaty. By citing the British precedent the Russians insisted that the ship was a 'through-deck Cruiser' and there is no ban on cruisers under the Treaty. The Turks were therefore unable even to protest and the *Kiev* passed through to the open sea, as will her sister ships.

There is no doubt whatever that during parliamentary debates opposition leaders of any party are prepared to make false assertions in the hope of scoring political points. This practice tends to be most blatant during the run-up to a general election and a perfect example of it is provided by the debate on the Ferranti Bloodhound missile affair in 1964 – the last debate of the session and of the Tory government.

The debate was about the excessive profit which the Ferranti electronics firm had made by producing an excellent missile on time and well below the anticipated costs agreed to by the government. Julian Amery, the Tory Aviation Minister, should have been congratulated for inducing the firm to repay more than £4 million excess profit. Instead, because I had printed a series of exclusive reports about the case, the Labour opposition used the debate to accuse Amery of leaking information to me to such an extent that Wilson said he was 'incontinent'. In fact neither Amery nor his department had told me anything. All my information had come from the industrial side.

The Labour leaders should have known this from the nature of the facts I had printed, but they were determined to have a field day at Amery's expense.

There were those in Whitehall who believed that the Ferranti affair and the debate about it did more to help Labour win the election than the Profumo affair.

Of all the deceptions perpetrated on the British public by Westminster, whether deliberately or unwittingly, few have been more patent than the joint effort by Tories, Socialists and Liberals at the time of the expulsion of the Ugandan Asians by Amin in late 1972. I am in no way criticizing the fact that these unfortunate people, who were at the mercy of a primitively cruel dictator, were allowed into Britain. It was the political manner in which it was accomplished that was deplorable because it involved repeated statements and assurances which were false.

Some 30,000 Asians, originating mainly from the Indian subcontinent, had lived most of their lives in Uganda, many being born there after their ancestors had emigrated there to find employment in the days when it was a British colony. Because of their success in competition with Africans, especially in trading and business, Amin decided to expel them, mainly to provide jobs for Africans but also to divert attention from the sad state of the Ugandan economy under his misrule. Africanization was being steadily pursued by Kenya and Tanzania as well but because it was being done gradually, and still is, nobody has accused the political leadership there of being racialist.

When some place had to be found for the expelled Ugandans the story that they and other East Africans had been promised homes in Britain by Duncan Sandys, Iain Macleod or some other Tory leader at the time of Ugandan independence was resurrected. There never had been any truth in this. In 1968 even the then Labour government assured the House of Lords that no firm pledge had been given to East African Asians.

What had really happened was that those Asians who declined to accept Ugandan citizenship were issued with UK passports to enable them to travel on business or on holiday. These passports were not the same as those issued to ordinary citizens of the United Kingdom under the authority of the Foreign Office in London. They were special passports issued by the local British passport office in Kampala and they specifically did not carry the right of abode in Britain.

This was first drawn to my attention by Enoch Powell and, after the Foreign Office had checked with its legal advisers, I was told officially by a Foreign Office spokesman that the Asians had no right to a home in Britain and that this had never been promised to them. I made this clear in a newspaper article but the politicians continued to insist that such a legal right existed. In an emotional speech at the Tory Party conference a few weeks later the Home Secretary, Robert Carr (now Lord), said that he would not remain a member of a government which 'went back on its word'. There was, in fact, no 'word' to go back on.

By the time the Asians were irrevocably on their way the real truth was put on record by the Foreign and Commonwealth Secretary himself, then Sir Alec Douglas-Home, in a written Parliamentary answer which I spotted tucked away in the back of *Hansard*. It stated – and it is there for anyone to check – 'At the time of independence of the former British East African territories no specific undertakings were made either about the entry of East African Asians as such to the United Kingdom or about retention of citizenship.'

Every word of that answer would have been carefully vetted by senior Foreign Office officials before it was placed on the historical record of Parliament and there can be no doubt about its accuracy.

The admission was underlined shortly afterwards by another written answer stating, 'All sovereign states have the absolute right to decide for themselves to whom they will grant or deny admission to their territory.'

This was in complete conflict with the repeated Home Office assertion that it had no choice but to let in the Ugandan Asians, who were being referred to as 'our citizens' and 'our nationals', because it was bound to do so by international law.

When the argument that the Asians had a right of entry to Britain under British law was shown to be incorrect, politicians had claimed that the government was required to let them in under international law. Even the Lord Chancellor, Lord Hailsham, lent his authority to this. But the definition of a British 'national' had been clearly laid down by the government a short while previously in the treaty of accession to the Common Market. It stated that to qualify as 'nationals', citizens of the United Kingdom and Colonies must have a right of abode in Britain and be exempt from UK immigration controls. The Ugandan Asians failed to fulfil this requirement, as the Foreign Office eventually admitted as a result of my persistent inquiries.

At a joint meeting of the Conservative Home and Foreign Affairs

Committees, Sir John Foster, the distinguished lawyer, challenged the government's decision that Britain had a legal obligation to admit the Ugandan Asians under international law. Sir Peter Rawlinson, then the Attorney-General, agreed that there was no precedent in international law. The issue was a matter of opinion, on which he admitted that 'even an Attorney-General can be fallible'.

The Asians, or a proportion of them, could have been admitted on compassionate grounds as refugees, as happened with Jews persecuted by Hitler. Instead, Westminster continued with the pretence that they had full rights of citizenship until they were on the way, when the truth was quietly placed on the historic record.

What were the reasons for this?

I believe that the dominant reason was the government's fear of world censure if, as a result of British unwillingness or delay, Amin started liquidating the Asians after he had claimed that they were Britain's responsibility. Ministers were convinced that there was no time for delay and feared that, unless they could insist that there was no way out of accepting all the Asians, many Britons, especially those in cities with an already large coloured population, would raise objections to accepting 30,000 more.

I also suspect that some ministers were kept in ignorance of the true legal situation by their officials while others were so anxious to welcome the Asians on humanitarian grounds that the legal facts were considered to be of little consequence.

I was told by Bruce McKenzie, a white Kenyan friend who knew Amin well – too well as it turned out later – that the President had told him that he was astonished at the weakness of the British government in so quickly giving way to his demands.

He also provided some interesting insight into another aspect of the affair – the abortive attempt by exiled Ugandans to overthrow Amin by an invasion from neighbouring Tanzania.

This is what happened. Two nights before the projected invasion a Douglas DC9 airliner of East African Airways, of which McKenzie was a director, was parked on the airfield at Dar es Salaam in Tanzania where the crew were night-stopping for an early take-off next morning. In the middle of the night the plane was hijacked by Africans, one of whom was an East African Airways trainee pilot. He flew the plane to Kilimanjaro Airport, where a force of about eighty commandos was waiting with guns and demolition explosives. Their purpose was to make a surprise flight to Entebbe about 350 miles away and destroy Amin's planes parked on the airfield there, so depriving the Ugandan dictator of the bulk of his air power.

The trainee pilot forgot to unlock the wheels of the DC9 as it came in to land and the four tyres burst, rendering the plane unserviceable. As there were no spares at Kilimanjaro the operation had to be abandoned. Meanwhile a ground force of exiles set out for Uganda but the main weight of Tanzanian troops expected to join them desisted when Amin's planes started to bomb Tanzanian towns.

Amin and his whole revolting regime may well have been saved by four burst tyres!

In 1969 when the Labour government became obsessed with 'getting the books straight' in time for the next general election I was responsible for a savage row in Parliament during which the Tories accused Labour of 'cooking the books'. The government, which had never stopped talking about the balance-of-trade deficit it had inherited from the Tories, was determined to go to the polls with a surplus and it was my belief – and still is – that some of their trade figures had been presented in a most misleading way.

Roy Jenkins, then the Chancellor, had appeared on television saying that the first signs of a real trade recovery would be good figures for two months running because a single month's statistics could be misleading. Spectacular figures were issued for August and September in a way which, so far as the public was concerned, made them look 50 per cent higher than they really were.

What happened was that inaccurate figures were issued to the media with a footnote in small type explaining what the real figures should be because of some discrepancy which had come to light. The result of this was that the television and radio splashed the inaccurate figures in their evening news programmes watched by millions, presumably because those responsible did not read the footnote. As a result the government secured a political advantage.

It just so happened that this cheerful news immediately preceded the Labour Party conference and five by-elections. It also happened that the opinion polls showed a big swing to Labour after the trade figures were issued and a big swing away from Labour in the by-elections after my allegations had been published in the *Daily Express*.

I did not believe that any minister, least of all Jenkins, had been responsible for the way the trade figures had been presented. That was Whitehall work. But I did criticize the fact that the government had done nothing to correct the false impression. As I pointed out in the newspaper, the position of a board of directors in a similar situation would have been highly suspect. In trying to explain why their accounts declared a profit falsely inflated by 50 per cent it would have done them little good to claim that the correct figure was given in the small print at the end. Nor could they expect much sympathy for their failure to correct the false impression they had created.

I exposed a further objection to the Whitehall presentation of the trade figures. The government was buying a large number of American aeroplanes, having cancelled the British counterparts, allegedly to save money. However, it insisted on excluding these substantial imports from the monthly trade figures on the grounds that they were being paid for on long-term loans. This, of course, improved the monthly trade balance and I argued that, if this was permissible, then exports being paid for on long-term credit should also be excluded. Whitehall would have none of this, however, and these exports continued to brighten the trade figures.

My modest campaign for a fairer presentation of the true facts resulted in a major debate in which the chief contestants were Jenkins, who had the benefit of Treasury and Board of Trade advisers to help him, and Anthony Barber (now Lord) who had not been properly briefed. As Wilson records in his memoirs, Jenkins easily won the verbal battle but, for anyone who understood all the facts, his explanations were not impressive.

I believed, as did the Labour leaders, that Jenkins's verbal victory was the end of the matter, but towards the close of the election campaign in the following June the Tories suddenly took up the trade figures again. Wilson, who had looked like taking the battle in his stride, tried to show that the import figures, which had risen, were artificially inflated by the purchase of two American jumbo jets for BOAC. He was immediately reminded of the fact that the far greater imports of American military aircraft had not been shown. The trade figures row rumbled on until polling day and, as it gave the Tory leaders an issue to latch on to during an otherwise rather spiritless election, it may have helped to swing the votes which gave the Heath government a working majority of thirty seats.

Shortly after the 'cooking the books' row had subsided in the Commons, but before the ensuing election, Roy Mason, then President of the Board of Trade, was asked at a private meeting of exporters if he could present the trade figures in a less misleading way. Mason replied that his department had worked out a more realistic method of showing the trade figures before I had made my disclosures but the government had since decided against going ahead with the changes because 'It would appear to be supporting the *Daily Express* charges and giving in to them.'

*Chapter Twenty-two*

# News Management

MY long experience of prising information out of Whitehall has convinced me that senior civil servants are afflicted with a pathological preoccupation with secrecy which might be called 'suppressomania' and seems to be incurable. Part of the joy of being at the top is being in the charmed circle of the few 'in the know' and civil servants say that this is what they miss most when they retire. Releasing any information reduces the extent to which they are exclusively in the know.

It is also my belief that the mandarins do not want public debates on major issues such as spending and tend to regard Parliament as a rubber-stamp to be used when the issues have been decided. Whatever contempt may be poured on an administration that produced Watergate, the American voters and their representatives are not treated so cavalierly. When a Congressional or Senate committee wants information, senior civil servants and Service chiefs are required to attend and provide it, genuine security being catered for by deletions in the published report. In Britain 'security' is pleaded to the extent that a select committee of Parliament can be denied information essential to forming a considered judgement.

The most glaring example in my experience was provided by a report of a select committee on expenditure which considered the proposal to replace the Polaris deterrent with a more advanced American missile called Poseidon. The Defence Ministry officials refused to supply cost estimates on security grounds though full details of the dollar costs had been published in the USA. In this the mandarins were abetted by Lord Carrington, then Defence Secretary, who also declined to give the committee the information.

I suspect, however, that in this case, things never being what they seem in the Whitehall–Westminster complex, Carrington was protecting his staff as well as his secrets. The Navy planners had made a monumental mistake when preparing their estimates for securing Poseidon, on which they were immensely keen. They had given an estimate of £250 million, but discussions with the Pentagon, which had already deployed the weapon, showed that the true cost would prove to be almost double that figure.

Had this emerged during questioning by the select committee, the Navy could well have been accused of trying the old trick of deliberately underestimating costs to secure a weapon and then blaming inflation and other factors for the eventual price.

This capacity to suppress information to which the public is entitled, backed as it is by the Official Secrets Acts, is an important aspect of the way news is 'managed', which is a polite way of saying 'manipulated', in Whitehall.

Nobody doubts that in the Communist world news is managed in the sense that it is withheld, manipulated or even sometimes manufactured to suit political objectives. This is a prime purpose of State control of the Press and broadcasting media along with the equally important objective of stifling criticism of the politicians in power. Despite the common belief that Britain is free from censorship, from state control of newspapers and from political tyranny over journalists, attempts are repeatedly made by politicians and civil servants acting on their behalf to suppress news or to present it in a warped manner favourable to them. News management is regularly exercised through the large public relations and press departments operated by Whitehall.

No patriot could quarrel with the original purpose of the Official Secrets Acts, which was to deter espionage and sabotage. It *is* necessary to safeguard details of new defence equipment and the really secret workings of the nation's espionage and counter-espionage departments, especially when publicity might seriously interfere with a specific operation in progress against a spy. But 'official secret' has come to mean, in the Whitehall mind, anything which has not yet been *officially released*. Indeed, this was the definition laid down by Sir Norman Brook in a directive which is still in force – any information arising in a government department is officially secret until it is officially released. In short the Whitehall attitude is, 'It's secret because we say so.' To accept this, of course, would be the absolute negation of the journalist's purpose. Newspapers and the public would become totally dependent on the carefully vetted and sometimes doctored hand-out.

The Official Secrets Acts are rarely *used* against journalists but the ever-present *threat* of their use makes them an effective instrument of censorship. The casual mention of the Official Secrets Acts is occasionally used by Whitehall public relations men trying to put the reporter off a particular story, but this technique is more used in the context of another instrument of censorship – the D-notice system which I shall discuss separately.

Ever since the Vassall Tribunal when some reporters were made to reveal their private sources of information and others went to prison after refusing to do so, the threat of further tribunals in cases of leakages has also hung over the Press. The government's standing Security Commission can be converted into a tribunal by Parliament at any time. There are also other persuasion techniques. Both politicians and senior civil servants commonly use loaded arguments in efforts to achieve suppression of news to which they object.

It is no coincidence that the growth of news management in Whitehall has been accompanied by an increase in the number of public relations officials and by moves to put them more firmly under political control. Thus the very large PR set-up in the Defence Ministry has been reorganized to put the Forces information officers under the control of the PR men directly responsible to the Defence Minister. They are not permitted to give to reporters any information which could remotely carry political implications. They must report the inquiries to the Defence Secretary's man who then answers in what he considers to be the correct manner. When I was discussing these changes, which were pushed through by Healey, Sir Patrick Nairn. then a senior Defence Ministry official explained: 'If you want to take possession of a city you first capture the wireless station and put one of your own men in charge of it. That's what Healey has done.' I could not have put it more succinctly myself. The extent to which the politicians now lord it over the Chiefs of Staff.

regarding publicity for the Forces was demonstrated in the spring of 1978 by Callaghan's anger because they had dared to release information which showed how dangerously Service morale had fallen because of the government's pay restrictions.

One of the more cunning ways in which Whitehall officials suppress legitimate news is to leak it under the bond of confidence to those journalists most likely to discover it. Experienced newspapermen soon learn to avoid this because it makes publication very difficult, even if the information is secured later from another source, but occasionally one is trapped by a sudden statement smartly followed by, 'Of course I am telling you this in absolute confidence.'

The motives of a politician who approaches the Press for assistance are usually clear but occasionally they beggar understanding. One such occasion centred on a visit to my flat near St James's by John Stonehouse, then in the Ministry of Technology under Anthony Wedgwood Benn, who prefers to be called Tony Benn.

Stonehouse, who had telephoned me to make the appointment, told me that he had Benn's authority to tell me that Cuthbert Wrangham, the chairman of Short Brothers, the semi-nationalized Belfast aviation and missile firm, was being fired. It was suggested that I should write a report that night announcing the fact.

As I knew Wrangham, who prefers to be called Denis, I did nothing of the kind but telephoned him instead. He was not available so I left a message with his secretary who assured me that her boss had heard nothing about being fired.

Next morning Wrangham went to town to see Benn and was bluntly told that my information was correct though he had no idea how I had heard about it.

On 21 June 1967 I published a front-page report announcing that Benn was trying to oust Wrangham so that he could make changes at Short's which the chairman was resisting. Three weeks later Wrangham resigned after Benn had made it clear that he would sack him if he did not. It emerged that Benn's move had arisen out of the possibility that Short's might be involved in an inquiry which could reveal that the firm had made too much profit out of a government contract, though the sum was comparatively small. Benn, being the arch-champion of nationalization, wanted to be in a position to tell Parliament that he had taken resolute action before the news of the inquiry became public.

The explanation Benn gave to Parliament when questions were

raised following my Benn-inspired disclosure was that he wanted to reorganize the company and thought this could be done more easily under a new chairman. He also denied that there had been any leak to me.

I never did discover why Benn had adopted this strange way of getting rid of Wrangham unless he thought it might help to discredit the chairman, who in fact had an excellent record of service to the company and was greatly respected in Northern Ireland. His leak to me happened during the height of the D-notice affair and it may have been Benn's purpose to let me know that not all Labour ministers were taking sides against the *Daily Express* and its defence correspondent. Whatever his purpose it was a strange way to run government business.

With considerable justification, politicians accuse the Press of being equally adept at 'managing' the news or even more so, if only because they are more professional at it. The so-called 'Press barons' receive most of the criticism on this score on the grounds that, while having no official responsibility, they are ardent in the pursuit of influence and power.

I am in a position to provide some facts about the particular Press baron most often accused of bending the news to his own purposes – Lord Beaverbrook.

He was always ready to admit that he used his newspapers to promote his political aims and told the 1948 Royal Commission on the Press that he 'ran his papers purely for propaganda and with no other purpose'. He stressed that great efforts were made to keep the propaganda out of the news columns as otherwise the papers would not sell and that these efforts sometimes failed.

It has to be admitted that they often failed, mainly, I believe, because many senior members of the staff were afraid to disagree with Beaverbrook, wanted to please him or, having been so long in his service, thought the way he did. For example when Beaverbrook, known in the office as 'the Chief Reader', realized, correctly, that Lord Boyd-Orr, the former agriculturalist, was grossly exaggerating when he ranted on about imminent famines in the East, the foreign staff filed reports about the 'world rice glut' and the 'world wheat glut'.

It is a common misbelief that journalists distort and even fake their reports to make them more sensational. I have found little truth in this. Certainly in the *Daily Express* there has never been any enduring kudos to be gained by inaccuracy. Almost invariably someone complains and though editors 'stand by' their reporters there is usually an internal row and the offending writer quickly becomes branded as dangerous.

It cannot be denied, however, that many newspaper reports are inaccurate when judged by those who know something about the issue being discussed. Some degree of inaccuracy is inevitable by the very nature of daily journalism, and this is particularly true about reports involving anything technical. The requirement to give the information in potted form, understandable to every reader, involves over-simplification. The story has to told in limited space, which rules out the kind of qualification and development any expert on the subject would expect. So he tends to damn the whole report though it may have communicated the essential truth of the story to millions. A complete report is sometimes condemned as inaccurate and may even be the subject of a libel action simply because the critic has concentrated on the headline. The public should have some sympathy for headline writers, for they have to give the nub of a report in very few words and these have to be of such a length that they fit the page. The fact that so many excellent headlines are conjured up sometimes within a few minutes has always been a source of wonder to me and to others who have tried writing them.

Another source of inaccuracy is the reporter's difficulty in discovering what the truth really is. Any journalist is only as good as his sources and these, however eminent, are sometimes misleading, occasionally deliberately so. Even the most 'unimpeachable' source may mislead himself. I can remember lunching with the permanent secretary of one major Whitehall ministry and dining with the permanent secretary of another on the same day. Both had been called to a ministerial meeting at Downing Street presided over by Winston Churchill and each gave me an entirely different account of the resulting decision. In consequence the story I wrote proved to be wrong though it eventually turned out to be correct when the decision was reversed about a year later.

Occasionally one can perpetrate an inaccuracy simply because one's contacts are so good. This happened in connection with a decision by the Conservative government shortly before the first election in 1974 to go ahead with a naval version of the Harrier jump-jet at a cost of £60 million. I was given a leak by a Cabinet source and printed it but on the morning after it appeared the miners' strike was on and the government rightly felt it could not be seen to be refusing to increase their pay and spending so much on new armaments.

The most dangerous high-level tips to act upon are those concerning personal appointments as these can be the subject of change at the last minute. A colleague of mine was told that Lord Mountbatten was to be called in by the Attlee government to tour the coal mines giving pep-talks to the miners to induce them to increase their output, as they had done in the war. When the story leaked Mountbatten was so furious that he refused to do the job and the whole story was then denied.

While lunching at the home of a former Chief of the Air Staff he gave me some interesting news about V-bombers which I printed. The next day the Air Marshal in charge of the RAF's press relations, who had been present at the lunch, telephoned me to say that the story was incorrect. 'But you heard the CAS tell me it was true,' I protested. 'Why didn't you stop him?'

'Who am I to correct the CAS?' was the answer.

Newspaper proprietors are not the only ones who suppress news. Editors frequently have to resort to self-censorship and so do reporters, usually in the interests of their contacts. I knew some days in advance in 1971 that the old Rolls-Royce company was to be made bankrupt, but the editor, then Derek Marks, agreed with me that a premature announcement could have disastrous consequences.

I was also given advance knowledge that British Eagle, the airline, was about to go bankrupt. My source was someone who had been approached as a last resort for a large loan and had refused it. When I consulted one of the directors he urged me to keep quiet because the company was trying to recover some of its airliners, which were in transit abroad and would be seized by foreign creditors. I felt that there was no alternative but to suppress the news until it was officially announced.

There have been some occasions when I have not run a story through self-censorship only to see it appear in a rival paper. The late Lord Sieff gave me the news, which was then very confidential, that the Russians were allowing Jews to emigrate to Israel at a rate of several hundred a month. This was really startling because the Russians were backing the Arabs against Israel and the last thing the Arabs wanted was another major influx of Jewish immigrants. Why the Russians permitted this I have never understood because it was before 'human rights' became an issue of much political significance to the Kremlin. Sieff enjoined me to keep the news secret because if there was an outcry from the Arabs the Kremlin might have to stop the flow. I obliged but within a few weeks the story leaked in Washington and into all the British papers – with no particular outcry from the Arabs.

The libel risk is the commonest cause of suppression by newspapers and a personal experience may serve to illustrate how dangerous the libel law can be. In 1970 I published a novel about the Intelligence game under the title, *The Penthouse Conspirators*. Needing a good-looking young politician as a central character. I decided to model him on Dr David Owen, then Minister for the Navy, whom I knew. I also needed him to have a close link with the NATO Supreme Allied Commander, who was essential to the story, so I married him off to the commander's daughter, which gave him an American wife. And because I had recently been staying in Cowes and had some local colour I gave the young minister and his wife the hobby of sailing. I had called the commander General Schreiber because I wanted him German-born, like a former American general I had met called Schreiver.

As the novel progressed I realized that my copy of Owen was getting a bit too close because I knew he happened to have married an American girl. So I hurriedly made his profession before entering politics that of a barrister instead of a doctor and introduced a few other minor changes.

After the novel had gone to print I happened to look up Owen in *Who's Who* for another reason. Not only was his hobby sailing but his wife's maiden name had been Schabert. Had he felt he had cause to bring a libel action no court would have been likely to believe my assertion that the name was entirely a coincidence.

Beaverbrook was accused of running a campaign of denigration against Lord Mountbatten and, though this was denied, I can testify that there was some truth in it. One day I was summoned to lunch at Cherkley where the other guest was a Canadian who had been involved in a fantastic wartime project called Habbakuk, which Mountbatten had promoted while Commander-in-Chief of Combined Operations. Habbakuk was to be a colossal unsinkable aircraft-carrier made of ice and sawdust to operate in the Atlantic. As fast as bombs blew bits out of it, refrigeration machinery installed in it would freeze more sea-water to fill the crater.

The Canadian told me that he had been present at a demonstration where Mountbatten was determined to show how strong his ice-sawdust mixture was. A block of it had been set up and Mountbatten was alleged to have whipped his pistol from his pocket and fired several shots at it.

'You can see what an irresponsible thing that was,' Beaverbrook said as we sat on the verandah. 'He could have killed somebody. You should write about it.'

As Mountbatten, the First Sea Lord, was of greater value to me as a friend than an enemy I did no such thing and heard nothing more about it from the Chief Reader. Later, when Mountbatten became Chief of the Defence Staff, enmity became even more counter-productive and I conspired with the editor, then Edward Pickering, to put an end even to the belief that there was a feud. This proved remarkably simple, suggesting perhaps that nobody had tried very hard before.

In A. J. P Taylor's diligently researched biography, *Beaverbrook,* the author states that it was Macmillan who brought about the reconciliation with Mountbatten by arranging a meeting in 1963. He may have brought them together but Pickering and I had resolved the problem long before that and, as a result, my relations with the former Chief of the Defence Staff, First Sea Lord and Viceroy of India have been most cordial.

I was curious to discover the origin of the feud because I knew that Beaverbrook and Mountbatten had been close friends, especially during the years when Beaverbrook's mistress was the delightful Jean Norton, a close friend of Lady Mountbatten. Beaverbrook's daughter, Janet, believes it stems from the Dieppe raid, in which many Canadian lives were sacrificed to no purpose. Beaverbrook believed Mountbatten to be responsible to such a degree that, according to Janet, when he met Mountbatten after it he held out his hand and said, 'Shake hands with one of the few Canadians you haven't murdered.'

Mountbatten himself assured me he has no idea why it started. According to his recollection it began suddenly at a convivial dinner when Beaverbrook leaned across the table and cried, 'Between you and me, Dickie, from now on it's war! It's war!'

There is also a belief that the dislike had its roots in Mountbatten's close friendship with Pandit Nehru and their joint part in securing Indian independence.

It could have originated at some other point of conflict because Mountbatten was a power-seeker himself and far more successful in this respect than Beaverbrook. He was able to wield overt power through his high offices because, though partly royal, he was not so royal that real power had to be denied. The fact that his relationship with the Queen and Prince Philip was known to be so intimate added to his great influence in Whitehall, where his office, dominated by a painting of his bearded father, Prince Louis of Battenberg, was known as 'Earl's Court'. Civil servants were overawed by him, as were foreign visitors, for he knew how to deploy his flair for showmanship. Once when he entertained foreign officers from the Central Treaty Organization at an officers' mess in the Tower of London, one of them remarked, as they passed through the massive gateway lined with Yeoman Warders, 'Does Lord Mountbatten own many residences like this?'

I too was awed by him until a shooting lunch when the redoubtable Lady Sopwith, who had known him for many years, commanded, 'Now, Dickie, sit next to Harry and *don't* mumble.' From that moment our relationship was more relaxed.

My success with ending the Mountbatten feud and other incidents convinced me that one did not have to be a yes-man to get on with Beaverbrook.

Some of those around him fell into the yes-man category because they found it easier to agree than to argue with him and face the consequences of possibly being proved wrong. There is a story that when one such man was seen horse-riding with Beaverbrook at Cherkley some observer remarked, 'There goes Napoleon and his Marshal Ney.'

'Surely you mean Marshal Yea,' was the rejoinder.

The danger with being a yes-man to Beaverbrook was that he was so often wrong on matters of fact. If the facts were uncheckable and he indicated that the information came from a very high-level source, which he would never name, it was all too easy to become the author of a false report. This happened in connection with information he gave me when the Russians shot down an American U2 spy plane, capturing the pilot and withdrawing from important summit talks as a result. Beaverbrook told me there had been two U2s, one of which returned to base with the information that the other had suffered a flame-out of the engine. In trying to relight it the pilot had dived so far that he came within the range of Soviet anti-aircraft missiles and was hit. Much later I was able to establish that this was incorrect. The Soviet missiles had been powerful enough to shoot the U2 down at high altitude.

I cannot remember a story ever passed down to me from him either directly or indirectly that turned out to be as he described it. More often than not there was no truth in it at all though he believed it himself at the time.

He would sometimes pick on the most trivial story in the paper and try to prove it was wrong. On one occasion a two-line filler at the bottom of a page stated that someone had caught an angler fish weighing 80 pounds. He sent me a caustic note saying that angler fish never grew more than a foot long, though I had not written the report or had anything to do with it. He just knew I had written a book about fishes. I responded by sending him a rather nice book from my library showing that he was wrong. I heard nothing more and he kept the book.

The most persistent of Beaverbrook's dislikes, which certainly coloured the content of the *Daily Express*, was his dislike of the Germans. During the war the word 'Nazi' was banned from his newspapers. 'Call them Germans' was the instruction on the office notice-boards. He was not having the Germans putting the blame on the Nazis when they were defeated, as he believed they had got away with blaming the Kaiser after the previous war.

This dislike revealed itself when our former Rome correspondent, Corrado Pallenberg, a full-blooded Italian, was called to the presence. Beaverbrook was convinced that with a name like Pallenberg, his employee must be a German and made it clear that he had no time for him.

This animosity, born of his government experiences in the two world wars, made him sympathetic to the Soviet fear of the Germans and when in 1954 the Western powers decided that it was in their interests to induce West Germany to join NATO, for which purpose it would have to be rearmed, he vehemently opposed them. In this campaign he tried to use the power of his newspapers but without much success. Reporters were sent to West Germany to discover signs of Nazi resurgence but, apart from the obvious fact that the senior officers of the regenerated German forces would have to be former servants of Hitler because there were no others, they filed back little usable copy. In desperation Beaverbrook conducted a 'Don't rearm the Germans' campaign with hoarding posters produced at his own personal cost. At the same time he prodded his editors relentlessly to produce some supporting news. Little was forthcoming in spite of their efforts until what looked like the answer fell into my lap.

One of my country neighbours in Surrey with whom I had become friendly was Lord Russell of Liverpool. He was a barrister and, after a distinguished Army career winning three Military Crosses and reaching the rank of brigadier, was serving as Assistant Judge Advocate-General to the Army and RAF. He had been senior legal adviser to the Commander-in-Chief Rhine Army during the trials of German war criminals and had often told me that, human memory being what it is, the terrible crimes committed by the Nazis in their concentration camps would soon be forgotten. They had been fully reported in the newspapers when Buchenwald, Belsen, Auschwitz and the rest were overrun by the Allies and again during the trials of Goering and the Nazi gangsters but there was no easily available permanent record. He therefore consulted me about the wisdom of writing a book for which he had thought up a title, *The Scourge of the Swastika*.

I told him that, because of the horrific nature of the text and the photographs he proposed to include, sales would be slight but libraries would buy it so his main objective would be achieved. I confirmed this professional view by consulting the editor, Arthur Christiansen, and others.

Russell pressed on and sent pre-publication copies of the book to the Lord Chancellor, his political chief who had previously given him permission to produce an historical work on the subject, and to friends including me. I offered serialization rights to Christiansen but one look at the book convinced him that his first opinion had been right.

Then early in August 1954 Russell telephoned me to see him about 'a sinister development'. The book was due to appear just when the government was about to support the arming of the Germans and what it did was to show the dreadful things they were capable of once they were armed. The Chancellor, Lord Symonds, had therefore been ordered to tell Russell that the book would have to be withdrawn, because no servant of the Crown could be permitted to inflame resentment against the new ally, particularly in France and Italy, where there was even wider opposition to the rearmament than in Britain. The Russians too would make maximum propaganda out of the book, Russell was told.

I realized right away that here was a potential political row which fitted Beaverbrook's requirements perfectly. It was about to be exacerbated by Russell's determination to stand firm and resign rather than suppress what he rightly claimed to be history.

The following morning I drew Christiansen's attention to the developments and arrangements were made to splash the story in the following day's paper. To give us absolute exclusivity I hid Russell and his wife in a suite at the Savoy, taking him to the newspaper at 11 p.m. to see his story coming off the presses.

Christiansen was still opposed to serialization of the contents of the book and advised me to tell Russell to try to sell them elsewhere, a Sunday newspaper being the likeliest market. I ignored this advice, however.

As expected, the banning of the book caused uproar in Whitehall with the Foreign Office making itself look rather foolish in the process, and Russell wrote a campaigning front-page article on 'Why I chose freedom'.

Such was the response both from the public and from Beaverbrook that the editor asked me if I could possibly secure the serial rights from Russell though he had twice rejected them. I replied that it would be difficult but I would try when in fact I had already quietly secured first refusal.

*The Scourge of the Swastika* became a best seller in a score of languages and the controversy rumbled on for weeks. But it made no difference whatever to the rearming of West Germany.

Though I remained very friendly with Russell, who thereafter called me 'the architect of his success', my only further connection with the book was as a witness in a libel suit brought by Russell against the satirical magazine *Private Eye* in 1966. It had alleged, among other things, that Russell had exploited human suffering to make money and I could testify that, on some of the best professional advice, he had been told that it would not sell but nevertheless had gone ahead with it in what he believed to be a service to society.

He was awarded damages of £5,000 and heavy costs which, in those days, nearly broke *Private Eye*.

Elsewhere I give examples of how, for personal reasons, Beaverbrook suppressed the illnesses of Churchill and President Kennedy. Another suppression on his instructions occurred during the long illness of Field-Marshal Montgomery and I attributed it to Beaverbrook's objection to denigrating a great general when he was too ill to reply. It transpired that I was quite wrong about his reason, which deprived me of a most fascinating world scoop about the best-kept secret in military history, though I was unaware of it at the time.

In 1959, after lunching with a retired air vice-marshal of considerable eminence during the war, the late Kingston McCloughry, I dictated the following memorandum to Beaverbrook.

A highly placed friend who was deeply involved in Intelligence during the war told me that there is a terrific story about Monty which has never been told. Monty was always right about where and how Rommel would attack because he just could not be wrong. Shortly before Monty took over command – and increasingly so while he held command – the British Intelligence service gained complete knowledge of the codes in which Rommel signalled to Berlin and to his subordinates. The entire battle plan for the Battle of Alam Halfa was known to Monty beforehand. That is why he knew he could safely dig in his tanks to meet the enemy on the Alam Halfa Ridge.

Rommel's plans for all the future battles in the desert and in Normandy were known beforehand. A message from him to Berlin giving his opinion that Britain and America would land in Normandy was picked up and so was Berlin's reply to the effect that the Allies were certain to land near Calais. News of Rommel's death was also picked up from the signals.

My friend, who is very cagey on details of how this was done, made it clear that it was no simple code-breaking. I gathered – perhaps wrongly – that there was some spy who revealed the codes every time they were changed.

If this story can be checked and used it could be sensational, especially in the context of Monty's cockiness in repeatedly saying in his TV shows how he figured out what Rommel was going to do and was always right.

I have had some confirmatory evidence of this from a naval source but would not regard the facts as anything like hard enough yet to use.

When I have enough I will sound out MI5 on the security aspects.

Having received a message from the Chief Reader to leave Monty in peace I did not pursue it further.

Not until 1974 was the real story behind my information disclosed when a retired group captain, Fred Winterbotham, who had been involved in the Intelligence aspects of it, published a book called *The Ultra Secret*. Briefly, what had happened was that the Germans, with characteristic meticulousness, had developed an encoding machine, which the British called 'Enigma', and put their trust in it right through the war. The machine, an electro-mechanical device which predated the computers now used for such work, produced a coded version of any message fed into it. As the code was random and therefore different every time, the Germans were confident that it must be absolutely safe. They also had machines which quickly decoded the message at the German receiving end.

Hundreds of these machines were manufactured and distributed to the German Forces and ancillary services. By great good fortune one of them fell into British hands before the war and with remarkable brilliance a team of British mathematicians, chess-players and Intelligence experts succeeded in building a machine called 'Ultra' which automatically decoded Enigma messages. As a result almost every important move by the German Forces was known in advance to the British, who passed their information to the Americans.

From Goering's grandiose orders to his Luftwaffe pilots in 1940 to Hitler's last despairing commands from his Berlin bunker, five years later, the information was in the hands of Churchill, Roosevelt and the British and American commanders sometimes within minutes. This advantage must have helped to sustain Churchill's faith in victory when Britain reeled under the overwhelming German armaments.

It was advance information from Ultra which enabled Fighter Command to organize its tiny force so that there were always a few to engage the Luftwaffe bombers. It produced the vital Intelligence which led to the sinking of the *Bismarck*. When the German battleship had escaped, after blowing up the British battle-cruiser *Hood*, its admiral sent a long Enigma signal to Germany. This revealed his position.

Winterbotham's disclosure, followed by many more since, showed that Monty's was not the only reputation in need of historical reassessment.

I am convinced that Beaverbrook's reason for forbidding me to pursue the story in 1959 was based mainly on his knowledge of it while serving in the wartime government. He was always extremely secure on such matters. I doubt, however, that he knew why the whole Enigma story had been kept so secret so long, even in the USA. The true reason, which is not generally known, is almost laughable.

Though the British Intelligence triumph had made the Enigma machine obsolete the Germans and other nations, apart from the USA, did not know this. So after the war the West Germans and the Swiss continued to manufacture them and sold them widely to developing countries in Africa, the Middle East, South America and elsewhere. The leaders of those countries, with whom the possession of sophisticated defence equipment is often a matter of prestige, were using them for sending secret diplomatic and military messages by radio in the belief that the codes were unbreakable, and the British and Americans were decoding them all.

This was why Whitehall was reluctant to allow Winterbotham to tell his story, almost thirty years after the end of the war.

While some men drive themselves to achieve power openly, the appurtenances of office being part of the satisfaction, others prefer to influence events through intermediaries. Beaverbrook was an excellent example of the latter category. Though he achieved office during two world wars he was never comfortable in government for long, deriving more satisfaction through imposing his views directly on politicians, as he did in the case of the Prime Minister Bonar Law, or attempting to do so indirectly in private or through his newspapers.

He took the view that the leader columns in his papers should reflect his views and either wrote them himself or carefully vetted the efforts of those working under his directions.

He claimed that he did not influence the presentation of the news but, of course, it was inevitable that he did so. His editors tended to give prominence to what would please him and, for the most part, they thought the way he did anyway. They, in turn, influenced the journalists they hired and trained.

I always found Beaverbrook's methods of influencing those individual writers whom he liked and cultivated quite fascinating. He never, in my experience, gave direct orders about any story of any importance. He would telephone and say, 'Don't you think it would be a good idea if you did so-and-so. But, of course, don't do it if you don't want to. It's only a suggestion.'

Or he might say, 'I heard so-and-so. I think that would make a good story for the *Daily Express*. But I leave it all to you.'

When he was away he would rattle off a cascade of ideas and suggestions, each directed to individuals, on to a Dictaphone which would then be typed by a secretary on to a long roll of paper. This would then be cut across with a razor-blade and the various paragraphs would appear on the desks of those concerned. I soon discovered that it was possible to ignore them, though occasionally a reminder would come by telephone or by a further dispatch from the depths of Cherkley or Canada announcing, 'I didn't get far with my idea on so-and-so did I?' Then some explanation had to be forthcoming.

Early in my career I learned that it was possible to tell the Chief Reader he was wrong – provided my facts, which he would make strenuous efforts to check, were correct – and the way this happened opened my eyes to the oddness of his character.

One day, soon after I had joined the paper, I went to see the features editor with an idea.

'Great, great,' he responded. 'But do it when you come back from Dusseldorf.'

'But I'm not going to Dusseldorf.'

'Oh, haven't you heard, you're flying there after lunch.'

The features editor then explained what Christiansen, the editor, had told him. Beaverbrook had telephoned with a story that some young German scientist had invented a way of making cement out of rubble. Having made his first fortune out of financial deals in cement, Beaverbrook was immensely impressed.

'I always said some young feller would find a cheaper way of making cement. This is terrific. The Germans have millions of tons of rubble. All those bombed-out buildings! Get the story.'

I immediately told the features editor that the story must be wrong. Cement had to be carefully compounded of specific substances with adhesive properties. Rubble contained brick-dust, wood, plaster, metal . . .

'Take my advice and go,' he said solemnly. 'Don't argue with the Old Man. You may be a scientist but he had made a fortune out of cement by the time he was thirty!'

I was not impressed with this argument and had no intention of failing on such a mission so I rang an expert at Portland Cement who confirmed that the idea was crazy. I then went in to the editor, who also urged me to fly to Dusseldorf to make sure.

'It's a waste of money,' I insisted. 'Now if Lord Beaverbrook

meant concrete, there might be something in it. But you would still
have to add the cement.'

Suddenly the editor thought I might possibly be right. 'OK, I'll
ring him and tell him what you say,' he said wearily. 'But God help
us all!'

He sent me out of the room, which was the standard practice when
any executive had to speak to the Lord. When he called me back in
he was smiling broadly. 'You don't have to go,' he announced.

'What did he say?' I inquired.

'He said, "I knew it was bloody nonsense all the time" and
slammed the phone down.'

It could be dangerous to make a joke against Beaverbrook but
there were times when he would take it. Because of his unique
manner of speaking – a peremptory Canadian drawl – it became the
custom of those of us in the office who knew him to imitate his voice
when speaking to each other. The best imitator was the late Percy
Elland, editor of the *Evening Standard*. One day Trevor Evans (now
Sir), the industrial correspondent, who was no slouch at copying
Beaverbrook's voice himself, picked up the telephone in his office
and hearing the inevitable, 'Ah well now, wat's the noos?' answered
in a similar accent being sure it was Elland calling. In fact it was
Beaverbrook who, fortunately, was amused.

Having his favourites, he was prepared to take argument and
opposition from some and not others. He certainly took it in full
measure from an effeminate valet he employed. Once when I was
called to Arlington House the valet had locked himself in Beaverbrook's bedroom and refused to come out or let his Lordship in
unless he apologized which, in front of me and with a twinkling smile,
his Lordship duly did.

While Beaverbrook liked meaty conversation and disliked wind-
bags, whom he would interrupt during a drawn-out story by asking,
'What time does the train get in?' he retained the politician's essential
ability to speak eloquently yet say nothing of consequence. I saw him
display this with consummate skill at the great international exhibition in Brussels in 1958.

Beaverbrook had decided to visit it and had several important
Canadian guests including prime ministers from various maritime
states. When the Russians heard that he was there they invited
him to make a specially conducted tour of the Soviet pavilion, to
which he agreed. As the exhibits were fairly technical, including

*Left* Captain Henry Kerby, the former Tory MP for Arundel and Shoreham, who served as a spy inside the Conservative Party for Harold Wilson, reporting to him regularly in writing, both while the Labour leader was in Downing Street and in opposition. (Jack Stockdale)

*Below* On one of the few occasions when the author has been invited to the Soviet Embassy, he is seen here shaking hands with Valentina Tereschova, the first woman to orbit the earth. Between them is the Russian ambassador, Alexander Soldatov. (London Express)

# 40 AGENTS BETRAYE[D]

*AND ALL*
*BY THIS*
*MAN* ☞

## New shock over spy Blake

### By CHAPMAN PINCHER

**G**EORGE BLAKE, the Secret Service agent who spied for Russia, betrayed the names of at least 40 other British agents to the Communists, I understand. My investigations over the last 12 weeks also reveal that many of these agents have disappeared and several are believed to have been executed.

The unprecedented sentence of 42 years' jail on Blake was confirmed by the Appeal Court yesterday. By coincidence, it works out at about one year for each agent he betrayed.

Blake also revealed the methods used by agents to acquire information and get it back to Britain.

As a result, some of the most important sections of the Secret Service behind the Iron Curtain and in the Middle East have been ruined at a time when intelligence about Russian missiles and troop movements matters so much.

Blake had access to the names of British agents in several overseas networks because he worked in various departments of the Secret Service.

This enabled him to learn the names of James Swinburn, James Zarb, and other Britons

### A SON

GEORGE BLAKE'S wife, Gillian, 28, gave birth to a son—their third child — 10 days ago. If Blake gets full one-third remission he will be 65 years old and his son 28 before they meet in freedom.

alleged to be agents operating in China. He passed these to the Russians who later gave them to Nasser.

The result, almost the entire British Intelligence network in the Middle East, built up over years, had to be withdrawn.

Yet it is believed that part of Blake's work when he was posted to the Foreign Office college of Arabic studies in the Lebanon in September 1960 was to help re-establish this network which he had helped destroy.

I can also reveal that when Blake was freed from imprisonment in Korea in 1953 he was not screened by MI5. The experts in this procedure but he has own colleagues in MI6.

### In Berlin

They decided that after six months you Blake should go back to Secret Service duty.

Later he went to Berlin—and gave the Russians photographs of every secret document passing through his office.

The effects were indeed on a security scale during subsequent Blake gave to pass on that he was leaked to and could then get his camera freely, filming documents much them for an hour.

Blake was the most difficult type of spy to detect. He spied for political motives, not for money. He lived quietly and was completely secretive.

He may have been shot. I record has not easy for the British investigators to prove him to establish just what he had done for the Korean communists, is correct with Communism.

### 15 space eyes will watch Russia 7

#### By CHAPMAN PINCHER

A RING of 15 American spy satellites keeping constant watch on Russia to detect rocket launchings is to be tied in with the big radar warning system being built at Fylingdales Moor, East Yorkshire.

A station to track the position of the satellites and receive information from them to feed to the U.S. is to be set up at Kirkbride, near the Cumberland coast.

The spy satellite network called Midas (Missile Defence Alarm System) will give the U.S. 30 minutes' warning of an incoming Russian rocket and Britain six minutes. Details of the Anglo-U.S. agreement for sharing it are to be announced next week.

Midas satellites will orbit continuously over Russia 300 miles up. Their electronic eyes are highly sensitive to the infrared rays given off by rocket exhausts.

Alarm signals radioed from the satellites will alert the giant radar stations in Fylingdales, Thule, Greenland, and Clear, Alaska.

#### SIRENS

These will then track the missiles, predict their point of impact, and feed the information to a huge screen called the Iconorama at North American Air Defence H.Q. in Colorado Springs.

If instruments there rule out a false alarm, warning sirens will automatically wail in British, U.S. and Canadian towns and bomber bases.

As the Russians consider the Midas satellites to be replacements for the now-banned U2 spy planes, it is expected they will try to shoot them down over Soviet territory.

The 300-mile-high satellites, each weighing more than two tons will revolve round the Pole instead of the Equator. An experimental Midas is to be launched in California this month.

*Left* The author's report on Geor[ge] Blake in the *Daily Express*, 20 Ju[ne] 1961. (London Express)

*Above left* Christine Keeler, the girl in the Profumo scandal, photographed in 1963 while appearing in the court case at the Old Bailey. (London Express)
*Above right* Lionel 'Buster' Crabb, the brave frogman who lost his life while investigating the underwater structure of a Russian cruiser in 1956. (Keystone Pictures)
*Below* In this official RAF photograph Chapman Pincher stands by the tail of an enormous H-bomb capable of destroying an entire city. The picture — the first ever of a British H-bomb — was authorized by the Air Minister, then Julian Amery, to secure publicity for the British nuclear deterrent.

When Harold Wilson undertook to present the Granada journalistic awards for 1966, it did not please him when he had to hand the accolade of 'Reporter of the Decade' to Chapman Pincher. Smiling for the cameras, he whispered, 'You wouldn't have got it for your story this morning' — referring to yet another report Pincher had written in criticism of Labour's defence policy. (Press Association)

" The trouble about life is that the people you would like kidnapped, never are!"

Cummings' cartoon of Harold Wilson's feelings about the author, amongst others. (London Express)

Cummings

WALL of WHITEHALL

ACHTUNG!
IT IS VERBOTEN
TO FIND OUT WHAT
THE GOVERNMENT
IS DOING !!

10

WILSON
PROBES
AVIATION
'LEAKS'
TO PRESS

MINES

'. . . yes, Colonel Wigg, the new security arrangements are splendid — but don't forget to shoot Chapman Pincher on sight!' Cummings' cartoon for 18 June 1966. (London Express)

[Colo]nel Leslie 'Sammy' Lohan, for[merl]y Secretary of the D-notice [Com]mittee, and the central figure [along] with the author in the celebrated [D-no]tice Affair, as a result of which he [resig]ned in 1967. (Press Association)

*Above* The firing tubes of the huge submarine **HMS** *Resolution*, which house the Polaris missiles on which Britain mainly depends for deterring a Soviet nuclear attack if ever she has to stand alone. In spite of left-wing insistence that the missiles should be scrapped, successive Labour governments have continued to spend large sums on refurbishing them. (Central Press)

*Below* Blue Streak, the British ballistic rocket on which £100 million was spent before it was scrapped, finds a prophetic location for a night-stop on a journey from a Cumberland test-site to the launching pad at Woomera, Australia. (D. R. Woodbridge)

## Aid to gunmen as hostages await showdown

# AMIN'S DEADLY HIJACK GAME

**Chapman Pincher** and **Michael Brown**
IN LONDON                    IN PARIS

**FREED** hostages flown home from the Entebbe Airport hijacking have told security chiefs that Uganda's President Amin has been giving full support to the terrorists.

During interrogation they said that he:—

GAVE the six terrorists extra weapons, including sub-machine guns.

LET two more Arabs join them at Entebbe.

TOLD Ugandan troops to help guard the hostages so the hijackers could sleep.

### Why I did it

As the remaining hostages—98 passengers, mostly Israelis, and 12 French crew—waited under threat of death in a hot, cramped airport room for the terrorist deadline of 11 a.m. tomorrow, Western observers believed Idi Amin's priorities were twofold.

His first is to save the lives of the hostages, his second to secure the release of as many Palestinian prisoners as he can from Israel and so gain prestige in most of black Africa.

That could be why he is playing the hijack his way—providing an entirely new challenge to both the Kremin and the Israelis who are concerned mainly with outwitting the terrorists.

In the middle of the drama yesterday the President, with his wife Sarah and son Mwanga, flew off to the Indian Ocean island of Mauritius.

Presiding over the 48-nation Organisation of African Unity, he explained his position.

If he had refused to act as negotiator, he said, the hijackers were prepared to kill all 275 hostages then aboard an Air France plane. The 110 people now left were "very comfortable" but "divided into groups and surrounded by explosives."

President Amin indicated he would go back to Entebbe to see if Israel meets the deadline to free 50-odd prisoners by tomorrow.

### How they did it

Released hostages returning to Europe were reluctant to speak publicly for fear of harming the Israelis still held at Entebbe after five days.

However, they disclosed that they were sometimes guarded only by Ugandan troops while the hijackers slept or ate—and the soldiers warned that they had orders to shoot escapers.

This situation has made it impossible for the Israelis to adopt the standard tactic of prolonging negotiations to exhaust the hijackers.

The hostages reported that from the moment of touchdown the terrorists — members of the Palestine "Popular Front" led by a German—and Ugandan troops were "very friendly," while Idi Amin is said to have been seen embracing them.

Some of the critics have gone so far as to suggest it was the President's idea to concentrate the death threat on the Israelis and free the others. At any rate, the separation of the Israelis, including women and children, is said to have been carried out by Ugandans.

President Amin could be facing serious risks in his deadly game.

HE IS a fanatical Moslem and bitterly opposed to Israel. But there is growing concern in the West that if Israelis die at Entebbe the result could be a new war in the Middle East, for Israeli tempers are at trigger-point at what is seen as a national humiliation imposed by the Palestinians.

HE IS, as a recent target for assassination, chancing treachery at home while he is in Mauritius. But he is relying on the airport crisis to keep his troops occupied.

## Exclusive: Why the door was opened for the Israeli freedom raiders

# AMIN'S FATAL TREACHERY

### By Chapman Pincher

AS ISRAEL celebrates the spectacular rescue of the hijack hostages from Entebbe Airport, I can reveal today that a monstrous act of treachery by Uganda's President Idi Amin opened the door to freedom.

For the key to the success of the operation was Kenya's agreement to co-operate with the Israelis in yesterday's raid.

Kenya acted in this way because of an interest for months ago when Amin seethed freely and aircraft supplies to Kenya Palestinian terrorists who almost succeeded in using them to shoot down an Israeli El Al airliner packed with passengers leaving on Nairobi Airport.

### Release demand

It was three terrorists who were detained plus two more who live at least who were with the Palestinian fighters when Israeli authorities to justice compliance to the Israelis without which the terror airliner could not have been detained.

This is what happened.—

On Sunday January 27 three Palestinian Arabs equipped with SAM-7 heat-seeking anti-aircraft missiles took up hidden positions

shortly before the arrival of a packed Boeing of El Al from Johannesburg due to fly later to Tel Aviv.

Their purpose was to shoot the SAM missiles as it came in to land creating maximum casualties. It could well have crashed into the airport terminal or on to houses used by visiting mem Kenyans.

Before they could fire the target Kenyan security men on the South General Service Unit—a Unit of G.A.S.—who had observed the terrorists carrying out a reconnaissance the previous evening, pounced and arrested them.

### Smuggled arms

Inquiries established that they had flown to Nairobi in December with violent than supplied by the British Embassy in Beirut which operates for Kenya there.

The missiles machine guns, grenades and pistol they were carrying had been smuggled across the border from Uganda with Amin's permission the terrorists prisoner was frightened by the fact that the El Al pilot which have been African as well as Israeli aboard.

### Bazooka attack

It was also quickly established that two of the Arabs had staged the abortive bazooka-rocket attack on an El Al Boeing 707 without taking off from Orly airport, Paris, in January this year.

At the following Tuesday two Palestinians—a man and a woman—arriving in Nairobi to find out what had happened.

They flew in on South Arabia air

## If Amin caused McKenzie's death Kenyatta's anger will be intense and the consequences serious

# ENTEBBE'S LAST VICTIM?

### By Chapman Pincher

**B**RUCE McKENZIE, the British-based white Kenyan killed mysteriously after visiting General Amin, was the most remarkable man I have met.

He was a high-level politician, ambassador extraordinary, Intelligence agent, agricultural expert, successful business man, authority on big game, military adviser with close links with Britain's SAS, arms dealer and outstanding pilot.

He has flown me many times over the Ngong hills where his light aircraft crashed, possibly as the result of a time-bomb planted while it was parked at Entebbe Airport in Uganda.

I had been planning to fly with him, because he was making arrangements for me to visit Amin.

A big man of great physical strength and courage he was also a rip-roaring, rumbustious, fun-loving human being who seemed to know everyone of importance in any field in a score of countries.

At his splendid homes in Cranleigh, Surrey and in Kenya, I have met leading figures from M.I.6, the C.I.A. Israeli and Iranian Intelligence, statesmen of several nations and Royalty.

### Trusted

For many years McKenzie, who was born in South Africa, was the adviser whom President Kenyatta trusted most.

When Kenyatta needed to send an embassy to the British Prime Minister, the German Chancellor, French President, Shah of Iran, Israeli Prime Minister or any other statesman he usually sent McKenzie.

Over the years he secured great benefits for Kenya in the form of military aid and soft loans.

If it is proved that the aircraft in which he died was blown up by a bomb, Kenyatta's anger will be intense and the consequences could be serious.

The purpose of his last mission was to repair political and economic relations with Uganda.

These had been greatly harmed by Kenya's complicity in the Israeli raid to release 110 Jewish hostages, held by Palestinian terrorists at Entebbe Airport in July 1976.

McKenzie, who was 58, had an outstanding war record in the R.A.F., winning the D.S.O. and D.F.C.

He was known for daredevil experiments, like fitting an aircraft with a huge army gun which nearly capsized the plane when he fired it.

He decided to farm in Kenya after the war, clearing a leopard-infested crater to do so.

Realising that black rule in Kenya was inevitable, he decided to give the Kenyatta Government all support he could.

He stood for the Kenya Parliament, becoming Minister of Agriculture and the only white man in the Government.

Later he became financial adviser to Kenyatta and helped run the main national airline, a shipping line, a motor company, a bank, a cattle ranching project and flower-growing concern which is the biggest single employer of labour in Kenya.

He also rendered important Intelligence services to Britain.

To achieve all this he spent three months solid of every year travelling in aircraft.

### Network

Through close friendship with Colonel David Stirling, who founded Britain's SAS, he set up an SAS type of security force which has played an essential role in Kenya's stability.

He was instrumental in retaining close defence and Intelligence relations with Britain.

He also built up a joint Intelligence network with Israel which had sensational consequences.

In February 1978, when I was staying with him in Nairobi, I learned about an attempt made a few days earlier by two Palestinians to shoot down a packed El Al airliner due to land at Nairobi airport.

Following an Israeli Intelligence tip, the security unit McKenzie had organised caught the terrorists, who were preparing to assemble a Sam 7 guided missile.

The Palestinians also had other weapons which had almost certainly been smuggled across the border to them from Uganda where Amin, a Moslem, supported the Palestinian cause.

After the mission failed, black burglar by shooting him with a revolver.

In 1976, not long before the Israeli raid, McKenzie piloted me and our wives from Nairobi to Entebbe and then on to a four-day conference far out in the Uganda bush on the banks of the Nile.

I did not feel safe until at

**Kenyatta with trusted adviser McKenzie.**

The author's article in the *Daily Express*, 26 May 1978, on the assassination of Bruce McKenzie, in a bomb explosion in a light aircraft travelling from Entebbe to Nairobi. McKenzie, a White Kenyan, had been an influential adviser to President Kenyatta for many years, especially on international affairs. He played a vital role in securing Kenyan cooperation for the Israeli rescue of hi-jacked Jewish travellers from Entebbe airport in Uganda in 1976. (London Express) nuclear matters, I was bidden to fly over and join him as guide.

'I don't want these Russians pulling any wool over my eyes,' he said when I joined him at the Hotel Metropole.

They would have had to get up very early in the morning to do that.

As he anticipated, following his former admiration for Stalin, the Russians were all set to make political capital out of the visit if they could. When we adjourned to a private room for caviare and vodka after the tour, there waiting for us was my old friend Boris Belitsky, from Moscow radio. With his political astuteness and wonderful command of English, he pushed his microphone in front of the Old Man every time there was a possibility of an answer to the Communist credit. He answered everything but they got nothing whatever of political value.

Seeing him sitting there with his trilby pushed back on his head and a mischievous smile, as he cleared trip-wire after trip-wire with brilliant use of words, is one of my most vivid recollections of him.

He was equally entertaining that evening when Sophia Loren arrived in the hotel restaurant with a considerable entourage. He had never met her but he was over at her table in a trice and brought her back to sit at ours, while her entourage ate on their own.

A somewhat less serious occasion on which Beaverbrook intruded his personal requirements into the paper arose while I was staying with him at Capponcina, his beautiful villa at Cap d'Ail, near Monte Carlo.

We were sitting by the swimming-pool talking politics and Beaverbrook was wearing a straw hat with an enormous brim. Suddenly the peace was shattered by an explosion. A high-rise block of flats was being built behind the villa, to Beaverbrook's extreme annoyance, and the constructors were blasting into the rock.

The little man rose in anger and called for his servant. 'Send for the mayor,' he commanded and the Mayor of Cap d'Ail duly appeared. He was shown the stones in the swimming-pool and the particular pebble which had struck his Lordship's hat and humbly promised that he would see to it that it never happened again. He had not been gone ten minutes when another explosion sent a fresh shower of debris over us.

'Goddamn it!' my host shouted. 'Get the mayor back here again!'

This time the mayor was told that if there was one more blast Lord

Beaverbrook would leave Cap d'Ail never to return and he would see to it that a lot of other residents would fail to return too.

The mayor explained that it had been impossible to prevent the second blast because the workers had already tamped the explosive into the hole and could not get it out. Beaverbrook nodded but repeated his warning.

All was peaceful for about an hour when a bigger explosion than ever rocked the ground and not only deposited another bucketful of gravel into the pool but sent a boulder through one of the windows.

'Right,' Beaverbrook said, 'That's it. I want you to go back to London this afternoon and write an item for the William Hickey column. Say that the British have endured the blockbuster aircraft bomb, the flying bomb and the rocket-bomb but that's nothing to what they will have to endure if they come for a holiday at Cap d'Ail. Of course, don't mention me.'

This was duly done.

In retrospect this sense of mischief was Beaverbrook's most endearing character and he never ceased to express it.

One afternoon when he wanted the editor of the *Daily Express* to write a powerful leader castigating the government for its over-dependence on the United States he told him, 'Telephone me in half an hour and I'll give you the line to take.'

During that time Beaverbrook made his butler, Albert, search out an old gramophone record and an equally ancient instrument on which it could be played. When the editor rang back Beaverbrook told him to wait a moment and then listen for the line for the leader. For a few minutes all he could hear was, 'Come on Albert. What the hell are you doing Albert? Wind the bloody thing up!' Then over the telephone to the *Daily Express* office came the reedy strains of an old song, 'Working for the Yankee Dollar'. The editor got the message and that was the headline on the leader next day.

However, the fun he created did not compensate for the damage he caused in the eyes of many politicians. I once asked Enoch Powell, who was then Health Minister, if he would like to meet Beaverbrook.

'No, thank you,' Enoch replied. 'I like to recognize evil but I have no wish to embrace it.'

I do not think that Beaverbrook was evil but there were many who did.

⌒∾𝄞∾⌒

## Chapter Twenty-three

# The D-Notice Affair

UNLIKE most of his predecessors as Prime Minister, Harold
Wilson had always been extremely Press-conscious and concerned
about what was written and said about him. While leader of the
opposition he had gone out of his way to make himself friendly to the
lobby correspondents – those journalists accredited to Parliament
who agree to operate on the understanding that when given briefings
'in the lobby' they will not reveal their sources. Once installed in
Number 10 he encouraged journalists to see him there and invited
them to drinks and cocktail parties on a scale which convinced many
of them that here at last was a Prime Minister who really appreciated
the value and influence of the media in political life, as has been the
situation in the USA for many years. Though I had been a savage
critic of the Labour Party, because of its destructive attitude to the
nation's defences and especially to the nuclear deterrent, I was
welcomed by Wilson when, through the good offices of my friend
George Wigg, he gave me an hour alone with him in the Cabinet
Room late in 1964.

Our conversation ranged over many items, one remark being
especially memorable in view of what was soon to happen: 'Of
course, I've always been an East of Suez man.'

For secrecy's sake I had been required to enter Number 10 by a
side door connecting with the Paymaster-General's office in
Whitehall. For the same reason I expected to be ushered out the
same way but was directed to the front door. As I emerged from
the Cabinet Room, who should have been kept waiting for his
appointment with the Prime Minister but my old friend Sir Solly

Zuckerman (now Lord). the 'court scientist'. Knowing how rough I had been with Wilson in the past he was astonished that I had been admitted to the sanctum.

As the Labour government intensified its assault on the Forces, with the cancellation of the TSR2 bomber and vicious destruction of its jigs and tools so that no subsequent Tory government could resurrect it, I increased my attacks, larding them with as many embarrassing leaks from angry service chiefs as possible – a development which was to lead Wilson to describe me in his statement to the Royal Commission on the Press as 'a prominent journalist known for his virulence of opposition to the Labour government'.

By and large, however, Wilson's honeymoon with the Press in general continued until 21 February 1967 when a front-page report of mine in the *Daily Express* put an end to it through what became known as the D-notice affair.

In his book, *The Labour Government 1964–1970*, which Wilson wrote after his election defeat, he described the D-notice affair as 'self-inflicted, in personal terms one of my costliest mistakes in our near six years of office'. It did him very serious political injury, not only with the Press, which united against him, but with the public and with Parliament. This is how Marcia describes it in her book *Inside No. 10*:

> Now began the time when Number 10 was dominated by the D-notice affair. This was a story which was to be played out throughout the first six months of that year . . . We all became obsessed with the matter. The whole lamentable affair had hung like a heavy cloud over us for many months. It had sapped the energies of the Prime Minister and his morale.

Apart from the fact that Wilson's obsession with the D-notice affair eroded the time he should have spent on proper affairs of state, the details are of public interest because they illustrate the devices which a Prime Minister and his political supporters are prepared to use in a democracy to get their way. They show how the truth can be manipulated by conspiracy between the offices of Whitehall and what can befall those who fail to do the bidding of the mandarins operating the Whitehall machine. And they provide revealing insight into what can go on behind the seemingly dull façade of those stolid government buildings.

In order to appreciate the incidents which constituted the D-notice affair, some effects of which are permanent, it is essential to understand what the D-notice system is.

When, after the Second World War, it was realized that the Cold War with Russia and its satellites had arrived, the Attlee government decided that the 'voluntary' censorship which had existed during the war should continue in some form. Because the government felt that it could not impose censorship in peacetime, a typically British scheme for securing the same result was hatched by Whitehall in conjunction with the BBC, which was already under government control, and with the newspapers, most of which were still in the hands of a few Press barons who were approached privately.

The government's case was greatly strengthened by the recent emergence of atomic weapons which, through the mystery surrounding them, commanded a special degree of secrecy because it was deemed essential that the Russians should learn nothing that would help them to make their own.

The result of these talks was the setting up of a Services, Press and Broadcasting Committee consisting of representatives of those government departments involved with defence, security and Intelligence and others representing the newspapers and BBC. This body, of which a counterpart had existed before the war, was empowered to issue 'Defence notices', abbreviated to D-notices, to the national newspapers and BBC requesting their collaboration in suppressing publication of information about matters mentioned in the notices.

What happened in practice was that Whitehall representatives would say to the Press members of the committee, 'Look, a new tank which we have developed may be seen going through its paces around the Salisbury Plain area. We don't want the enemy to know about this tank yet. Will you agree to the issue of a D-notice requesting suppression of any information about it?' In such a case, the Pressmen, who had plenipotentiary powers on behalf of all the newspapers, would invariably agree and the D-notice, marked Secret, would eventually make its way to all the newspapers except the *Daily Worker* (now the *Morning Star*) which was not trusted to withhold the information from Moscow.

There was a common misbelief that the government could 'slap a D-notice' on to any subject it liked and that the media would then be muzzled. That was not the case. The Press and broadcasting representatives always had to be consulted. But in practice there was some truth in the suspicion. The Whitehall departments almost always got their way because their representatives were top men with titles who could overbear the Press representatives with the argument that, 'I'm afraid this matter is too secret even to tell you but we can assure you . . .' Further, the Press representatives in those days tended to be elderly men who could be spared and for whom some job was needed.

The committee agreed that if Whitehall wanted to issue a D-notice in a hurry, the secretary could do this if he secured the agreement of any three of the Press members. He rarely failed for he knew which ones to telephone. The whole of the Press was then saddled with yet another restriction. Even this arrangement, which would never be tolerated in the USA, did not satisfy the 'Permanent Secretaries' Club', the top civil servants who ran Whitehall. They objected to any Press representation on the committee and wanted to keep any decisions about the release of official secrets completely in their grasp. In this connection the then editor of the *Daily Express*, Edward Pickering (now Sir) and I were approached by senior officials of the Defence Ministry for collaboration in destroying the D-notice system, which we refused.

While there was nothing binding about a D-notice once issued, a breach by any newspaper would be regarded as a breach of the whole system to which the Press had in principle agreed. So, in fact, the system was an extension of the Official Secrets Acts, inordinate fear of which was the legal instrument which kept the Press and BBC under a considerable degree of censorship. Only the British could have pretended that the D-notice system was really voluntary and it was hypocritical for British politicians and newspapers to take such a critical view of countries which openly censored the Press. The late Arthur Christiansen, the editor when I joined the *Express*, would never allow me to mention the D-notice system in the paper. At first I thought that this was because the mere existence of the system was secret. In fact Chris told me later that it was because he was ashamed to let his readers know that he was a willing party to any form of censorship.

As officially organized by Whitehall, the D-notice system was useless. The notices arriving in Fleet Street were marked Secret and inside two envelopes, the inner one being marked For the Editor's

Eyes Only. This meant that some secretary delegated by the editor was under standing instructions to put the notices in a safe immediately. If the editor read them he rarely understood them for the longer ones were often technical. If a story which might infringe a D-notice came in late at night there was nobody to open the safe. In practice, it worked effectively because of a Whitehall subterfuge, which by its nature could not be made official. The committee was run by a most able and charming ex-rear-admiral, George Thomson (later Sir) who had been chief Press censor during the war. His reputation for fairness and assistance to the Press wherever possible was legendary and his advice to those like me, who really had to cope with the D-notice restrictions day by day, was as follows: 'Look, forget about D-notices. Whenever you are writing a story which could have defence, Intelligence or security implications telephone me. I am always available day or night. Read it over to me and I will tell you whether all or any of it offends a D-notice. If I am in doubt I will take advice and ring you back. You have my word that I will do all I can to enable you to print anything which is genuinely not against the national interest. If I make a mistake and you offend the Official Secrets Acts as a result I will take the blame – in court if necessary.'

Few if any Fleet Street men had more recourse to Thomson than I had. In fact I developed the habit of reading over every relevant story I wrote whether I thought it offended a D-notice or not. This helped him if he was telephoned by rival newspapers who had read the first editions of the *Daily Express* round about midnight and wanted to follow them up. If they telephoned him to find out if my story offended a D-notice he knew the answer and could get back to sleep without making further calls.

As one who has always considered Press freedom as the freedom of the public to be told the truth through the medium of the printed word, I should, in theory, have been opposed to any infringement of it through D-notices or anything else but I knew enough about the activities of Soviet agents to believe that it is essential to safeguard details of new defence equipment and the secret workings of the nation's espionage and counter-espionage departments. In this regard the D-notice system as operated by Admiral Thomson and later by Colonel 'Sammy' Lohan worked perfectly, and it enabled me not only to get much apparently sensitive information into my paper but also assisted the government to such an extent that I was able to tell the tribunal on the Vassall spy case (see Chapter Seven) that I had letters sent on behalf of the chiefs of MI5 and MI6 thanking me for my cooperation.

That then was my reputation for attention to the national interest concerning security and defence problems until the afternoon of 16 February 1967 when a Mr Robert Lawson came to my office in the *Daily Express* to see me by appointment. He told me that he had worked in two cable offices, Commercial Cables and Western Union, as a telegraphist and had a story to tell of great public interest.

He then told me that all the cables and overseas telegrams sent from and received by those offices were collected daily and sent to a government building for examination by the security authorities. He said they were held there for forty-eight hours, during which they could be examined or photographed, and were then returned to the cable companies. He said that his inquiries showed that this had been routine practice for at least two years and possibly longer. He believed that all overseas cables and telegrams handled by all other cable offices and by the Post Office were treated in the same way.

I told Lawson that if a person were under suspicion as a spy, it would be normal practice in any country for the security authorities to intercept his cables but that I was not aware that *all* cables, however personal, were being made available for vetting as a continuing process. He assured me that this was the case and I told him that I would make further inquiries.

I then asked him what motivated his determination to get the information published. He said that after reading recent reports about the way letters belonging to a certain organization were being opened and vetted, he felt the public should know about the far wider intrusion into the privacy of cables. He said he was particularly concerned that commercial information sent out in private by firms such as ICI could become available to the government.

At no time did Mr Lawson ask for money and I made it clear to him that the *Daily Express* would not be willing to pay for such information. When Lawson had left I telephoned my friend Turlough O'Brien, director of public relations at the Post Office, to ask if what Lawson had told me was true. He told me in confidence that substantially it was. All cables were available but only those specially selected went for thorough scrutiny by the security authorities.

I then telephoned Colonel L. G. 'Sammy' Lohan, secretary of the D-notice committee, and told him the information which Mr Lawson had given me. Lohan, a thickset man with a large moustache brushed in the military style, twinkling eyes and an enormous enjoyment of life, had become a close personal friend from the days when he had been the deputy chief of public relations with the Defence Ministry, which he did so well that he was eventually given the D-notice job on retirement. I asked him if there was any D-notice to prevent its publication, if it proved to be true. Lohan assured me categorically that there was no D-notice to interfere with the publication of such a story.

I had always understood that once the secretary of the D-notice committee had given his decision, no further ruling was required, but I did not write the cable story on 16 February because I was heavily involved with the Defence White Paper, which had been published on that day, and also decided to make further inquiries.

The next day Lohan rang me to say that he would have to ask me not to print the cable story after all because it would cause a diplomatic furore as every embassy would immediately think that its cables were being read. I thought this was a feeble reason and said so, pointing out that I understood that embassies were allowed to send messages in code.

Lohan nevertheless insisted that concern about the embassies' reaction was so great that, if necessary, George Brown, the Foreign Secretary, would intervene.

On the Saturday evening I happened to be dining with Abba Eban, the Israeli Foreign Minister who was visiting Britain. I asked him whether he would be concerned if cables from his London embassy were read by the British security authorities. He laughed and said that he would expect them to be read. That, he explained, was why all embassies sent cables of any consequence in code. On Monday 20 February I agreed to lunch with Lohan so that he could make a final effort to prevent the Express from running the story. After we had sat down at my regular table in the Écu de France, Lohan produced two D-notices, saying that they were the only two that could possibly be applicable and that in his view neither was. Nevertheless, he was under the greatest possible pressure and asked me to pass on his direct request to my editor to suppress the cable story.

In this context he explained that cables were vetted by the security authorities in the hope of establishing a 'pattern' of messages which might lead to information of security interest. He said that since a foreign agent or person inimical to the State would not use the same cable office but would keep moving about, it was essential for all the cables to be available.

I told him that I had no doubt that examination of all cables would provide some very useful information but that to me it seemed an excessive infringement of privacy in a free society. I further said that I was sure that everybody in the restaurant would think the same if they knew about it, and he agreed. I pointed out that the same arguments could be advanced in favour of opening all letters – if this were practicable.

At no further time were D-notices mentioned. When we left the restaurant together I told him that I would write the story according to the facts, as I understood them, and give it to the editor with Lohan's urgent request that it should not be printed. I told him that if I were the editor I should certainly print it and I promised to let him know the editor's decision.

After deep deliberation with myself and the office lawyer the editor, Derek Marks, a fearless journalist if ever there was one, decided to print the story I had written. It appeared the next day but not before Lohan's warning that the Foreign Secretary himself would intervene duly materialized in farcical circumstances of the kind which dogged George Brown's career.

While dining with a friend that evening Brown received a call from the Foreign Office alerting him that my story had been printed in the Glasgow edition of the paper which had just come off the presses. Hoping to prevent its appearance in the later English editions he telephoned Sir Max Aitken, the Beaverbrook proprietor, believing he would be at the *Daily Express*. He was in fact at a convivial dinner himself at the Garrick Club. The *Express* switchboard put Brown through to the Garrick and Sir Max spoke to him from the porter's box there. As it was an open line Brown spoke somewhat in riddles believing that Sir Max was in the newspaper office and must therefore know what he meant. In fact he knew nothing whatever about the story since proprietors are not necessarily told the contents of the next day's paper. When the conversation ended Brown was confident he had killed the story and gave the glad tidings to the Foreign Office, so his anger on discovering later that this was not the case was understandable.

As Lohan had predicted, the news that government officials had secret arrangements enabling them to examine personal and poss-ibly intimate telegrams caused a furore, although it transpired that the system had been in operation for many years.

By a fluke, a routine parliamentary question about D-notices was down for answer by the Prime Minister the day the cable-vetting report appeared. Sir Burke Trend, then Cabinet Secretary, and Wigg did all they could to stop Wilson from using it as a peg to accuse the *Daily Express* of a security breach, because they realized it was bound to undermine the D-notice system. Wigg has told me that he advised Wilson that if any minister should risk having his fingers burned it should be the one responsible departmentally, the Foreign Secretary, George Brown. Wilson's action in branding the *Express* was certainly not a spur-of-the-moment decision for he has admitted that he first asked Edward Heath, then Tory leader, to discuss it with him.

Wilson claimed in Parliament that the motivation behind his determination to attack the *Daily Express* was that my disclosure had put men's lives at risk. I was assured by friends in the Defence Ministry involved in the inquiry that this was not true and no evidence to that effect was ever given to Heath, who was taken into Wilson's confidence on the issue as leader of the opposition, or to the Privy Councillors who investigated the whole affair.

I have discovered since that there was, by chance, a specific and highly secret Intelligence operation in progress at the time. Lohan had known this but had been instructed by the Foreign Office to deny it to me if I should ask whether any such operation was the reason behind the official concern. I did ask that very question and, if the answer had been in the affirmative, nothing would have been published but Lohan carried out his instructions and assured me that nothing special was in train.

While Wilson lambasted my action I received some unsolicited public support from Harold Macmillan, who said that while there were times when my activities used to annoy him he always found me 'absolutely straight and fair'. He added, 'I remember once having to ask him not to publish something on the grounds of national interest and there was no question. I believe he is telling the truth on this.'

Inside the office we suspected that Wilson's attack was not uncon-nected with various articles about Marcia which had appeared in the *Evening Standard*, the *Express* sister evening paper. Events were to show, however, that the real reason was much more interesting and had originated from the extraordinary Tory MP for Arundel, Captain Henry Kerby.

Wilson himself told me recently that what really underlay the whole D-notice affair was a tip in writing from Kerby that Lohan, who was strongly anti-Labour, was giving Tory MPs, including himself, ammunition for embarrassing parliamentary questions and still more embarrassing supplementary questions mainly on issues affecting defence matters. From that moment, Wilson told me, he was determined to sack Lohan but some legitimate excuse had first to be found. I have secured supporting evidence for Wilson's admission in the form of a copy of a letter Kerby wrote to Lohan on 8 February 1967 thanking him for help with framing Parliamentary questions intended to embarrass Wilson.

A further disclosure by Kerby about Lohan's activities seemed to provide the very thing. Lohan had met Kerby for the first time at a party at my country house and following that encounter, in which they seemed to take to each other since both were jovial extroverts, they met again at a party given by another journalist. As Lohan entered the room Kerby called him over and asked, 'Come on Sammy, what's the latest Whitehall scandal?'

Lohan then regaled them with a story I had already heard concerning the alleged sexual exploits of a certain Labour minister who, according to reports which had originally emanated from a Fleet Street source, was having an affair with a lady with Communist leanings.

The minister concerned has since convinced me that the story was untrue but after absorbing the details and asking for more, Kerby wrote next day to Wigg reporting Lohan's allegations and promising to send more if he could get them. Kerby's line was that it was wrong for any civil servant to spread rumours about a minister of any party. Lohan had also criticized the government's handling of defence, questioning Wilson's motives, and this too was reported. At Wigg's suggestion Kerby took Lohan out to lunch and encouraged further criticism of the government.

Fearing revenge for the Profumo affair, Wigg sought out the minister. He flatly denied the allegation but this development fortified Wilson's determination to rid himself of Lohan. So Sir James Dunnett, the permanent secretary at the Defence Ministry responsible for Lohan, was ordered to fire him. No easy method of doing this without revealing Kerby's part in the affair existed and an under-secretary, who had been instructed to find a way failed to do so. The department considered offering Lohan £2,000 out of the security slush-fund to go quietly but this was considered inappropriate and no action was taken in spite of repeated reminders from Number 10 that Lohan should be on his way.

Suddenly the publication of the cable-vetting story with Lohan's failure to induce my editor to suppress it presented a ready-made excuse for the hatchet-job. At the same time it could be used to settle some old scores with the *Daily Express* and with me.

Wilson's first plan was to have the D-notice committee itself pass judgement on the *Daily Express*. Being loaded with mandarins the result would have been inevitable but he unintentionally put this out of court by an undiplomatic remark at a political party given by the *Daily Mirror* group. One of the Mirror group editors, Lee Howard, was on the D-notice committee and in front of others Wilson remarked, 'And I hope you'll take this opportunity to get that fellow Pincher.'

Howard was so embarrassed that he resigned from the committee next day and the whole idea that it should sit in judgement of another newspaper had to be dropped.

The Prime Minister therefore appointed a committee of Privy Councillors under the chairmanship of Lord Radcliffe, a distinguished judge with previous experience of dealing with security problems. Selwyn Lloyd was to represent the Tory interest while Emanuel Shinwell (now Lord) was selected by Wilson because he believed he would be hostile to the *Daily Express* in Labour's interest.

The Radcliffe committee's terms of reference were:

> To examine the circumstances surrounding the publication of an article in the *Daily Express* of 21 February entitled 'Cable vetting sensation' in relation to the D-notice system and to consider what improvements, if any, are required in that system in order to maintain it as a voluntary system based on mutual trust and confidence between the government and Press in the interests alike of the freedom of the Press and of the security of the state.

During the eleven days I and other witnesses gave evidence to the tribunal, my own experience showed me how dangerous such a situation can be and how an answer given incompletely or misunderstood by the judges might cause a miscarriage of justice.

Much was made by Labour MPs of the fact that the *Daily Mail* had agreed to spike the cable-vetting story, which Lawson had also told them about, while the *Daily Express* printed it, the inference being that the *Mail* was a more patriotic paper. The reason the *Mail* failed to print was rather different – it had been unable to get official confirmation of the story and had accepted a denial of it. I had secured confirmation and it made all the difference but, because I knew that the Post Office official who had done me this service could be in serious trouble for doing so, I did not reveal his name in my written submission to the Radcliffe committee. I was therefore surprised to see this man, Turlough O'Brien, director of public relations in the Post Office and an old angling friend, appear as a witness.

When he was questioned concerning my telephone call to him asking if the cables went down to a government security establishment for examination he replied, 'I told him they *don't* all go.' That sounded like a denial of my statement and would, I believe, have been so interpreted by the committee but I was able to whisper to my counsel, Sir Peter (now Lord) Rawlinson that O'Brien had really said, 'They don't all go, only some go.'

When tackled by Rawlinson, O'Brien admitted that this was so and Lord Radcliffe immediately appreciated that I had in fact received official confirmation so there was no doubt that my account of the cable-vetting procedure was accurate. I am convinced that had I not been present to induce my counsel to jog the witness's memory, the committee could have concluded that I was not a truthful witness.

I know this was likely because at a dinner given in my honour later by Sir Max Aitken, Selwyn Lloyd, who was one of the guests, told me, 'It was when we started examining witnesses that we all realized you were telling the truth.'

By that time the published report of the Radcliffe committee had also revealed that the Post Office authorities had submitted an untruthful memorandum saying that O'Brien had told me that the cable-vetting story was untrue.

Colonel Lohan's rather desperate attempts during the secret hearings to discredit my standing in the journalistic profession, in the hope of improving his position with the mandarins, did him great harm. Lord Wigg later told me that it was because the government wanted to expose what they called 'Lohan's character defects' that they insisted on publishing almost all the evidence, including his allegations concerning the *Daily Express* and myself which were inaccurate.

Certain evidence which Whitehall had secured about Colonel Lohan was not published, however. George Caunt, who assisted Wigg as a researcher after leaving Wilson's service, told me that among his papers he saw records of tapped telephone conversations of Lohan speaking to friends taken by the security authorities. I also believe that Lohan was followed about London at the behest of those seeking information with which to damn him. Details of a visit he paid to my London flat were certainly known to his Whitehall enemies.

It would seem that this surveillance of a distinguished Whitehall official – his predecessor had been knighted for his work as D-notice secretary – had lasted many months. On one occasion weeks before the cable-vetting episode, when Lohan joined me for lunch at a restaurant, he insisted on moving away from my regular table to another, claiming that a conversation we had held there some weeks previously had been retailed back to him in detail by one of his friends in MI5. In case this should seem too far-fetched I can testify that conversations in restaurants are bugged from time to time, usually by someone sitting near by with a directional microphone. I am not suggesting that the Prime Minister ordered this action. His continued insistence that a way must be found to get rid of Lohan would be enough for the 'machine' to have organized it.

I might say here that Lohan remained a friend of mine for I fully understood that he was fighting for his professional life and had believed that what he had said to my discredit in this endeavour would not be made public. The only reason it was made public was to strengthen the government's case for getting rid of him.

Poor Lohan knew, during those few hours that he was giving evidence, that everything was at stake for him – his prestigious post, which could have continued until he was seventy, his reputation, his pension and the knighthood he could have expected for the public service he had given unstintingly. His efforts to undermine my credibility during the secret hearings had no other motive save self-preservation.

To Wilson's astonishment and fury the Radcliffe committee's report exonerated me and the *Daily Express* completely. It ruled that my account of the cable-vetting had not been inaccurate, had not breached any D-notice and that there was no evidence of any intent to defy D-notice conventions.

Further, it rejected the view of the Foreign Office and much of the evidence given to the committee by the Foreign Secretary. It also showed that under instructions from the Foreign Office a Defence Ministry spokesman had given false information to the Press. The Foreign Office man mainly responsible was Christopher Ewart-Biggs, who had close connections with MI6. On the day that he was assassinated in a Dublin bomb-explosion Wigg telephoned to say cryptically, 'You needn't mourn. He was no friend of yours.'

Most Prime Ministers, however critical they may have been in opposition, are captured by the Whitehall machine and feel compelled to protect it and those who run it but Wilson went too far in this understandable process and in doing so inflicted the wound on himself which ruined his relationship with the Press for ever more. Unable to admit that he had been wrong, he rejected the findings of the impartial committee he had set up himself and with Wigg and other officials cobbled up a White Paper designed to uphold the Foreign Office and Defence Ministry views, which had been fully considered by the Radcliffe committee and rejected, and to show that Lohan and I were both villains.

The White Paper was designed to throw the maximum blame on the *Daily Express* in spite of the Radcliffe exonerations and the utmost was to be made of alleged damage to national security without indicating what that might be. Foreign Office security officials were excused for failing to take Colonel Lohan into their confidence when briefing him on how to deal with me on the grounds that he had not been 'positively vetted' for access to top secrets. Lohan insisted that he had been fully cleared for access to top secrets for many years and was positively vetted again two years ago after he took on the D-notice job. If he had not been vetted the security authorities were at grave fault because many secret documents passed through his hands while he was in the Defence Ministry and he continued in close association with MI5 in his D-notice job.

There was a unanimous outcry from the Press, epitomized by a Cummings cartoon which showed batsman Wilson given out by the umpire after all three stumps and bails had been sent flying but still insisting that he was 'Not out'. Never before in the history of Fleet Street had all newspapers closed ranks against a politician as they did in this case, with even the pro-Labour *Daily Mirror* lambasting Wilson for his 'Whitewash Paper'.

The level of smear and innuendo resorted to by Labour politicians to blacken Lohan, me and the *Daily Express* was probably unprecedented. One MP, who later publicly stated his regrets about it, tried to suggest that Lohan and I were both drunk when we were discussing the issue in a public restaurant. This was certainly ludicrous in my case for I have a reputation in Fleet Street for being rather abstemious, shunning the haunts of the great 'champagning' journalists, and, though Lohan enjoyed a drink, on that occasion he could hardly have been more sober.

Great play was made of the fact that Lohan had discussed secret matters with a journalist over lunch in a public restaurant. In fact many Labour ministers had discussed far more secret affairs with me over restaurant tables. Once when I was lunching with Wigg, in the Hunting Lodge near Piccadilly, he received an urgent call from Number 10 and took it at the next table, which was empty. Allegations that Lohan and I were too intimate even had overtones of homosexuality, which also gave a belly-laugh to those who knew us.

Wilson's penultimate move was a debate and in this he and his side behaved even more reprehensibly than they had by publishing the 'Whitewash Paper'. Before the debate, Hugh Fraser, Tory MP for Stafford and Stone, told me he had met Wigg in the Commons and had concluded that the government, 'had a googly', which they would produce during the debate, which again had the intention of blackening Lohan to the maximum and me with him. The 'googly' turned out to be a statement by a Labour back-bencher, Raymond Fletcher, who had newspaper connections, saying he had just returned from Fleet Street which was buzzing with rumours that Lohan had been a major source of leaks to me. Neither I nor my colleagues had heard of any such rumours and I do not believe they existed, but this action by Fletcher gave Wilson the chance to develop this damaging theme after he had taken the unusual step of speaking last in the debate which was to end at 10 p.m. – a device which ensured that nobody in the House could challenge his assertions. These were to the effect that the relationship between Lohan and myself had been a matter of security concern to the previous Tory government, an allegation which *The Times* called 'a pitiless innuendo' and which was condemned by Lord Radcliffe and Selwyn Lloyd as a smear.

Condemnation of the Prime Minister thundered on to such an extent that in his memoirs he confessed that, 'The rejection of the Radcliffe Committee's findings compounded my original offence in the eyes of the Press, and comment upon the government and particularly on me, became even more bitter. What was of more concern was the danger that the affair might destroy relations between the Press and the defence and security authorities. It was a very long time before my relations with the Press were repaired.'

In my view they never were repaired. Instead the bad blood generated then repeatedly showed itself, in particular as the exaggerated criticism of his relationship with Lady Falkender and of his resignation honours.

No previous Prime Minister has been vilified by the media as Harold Wilson has. The origin of this in my opinion lies in his failure to accept defeat over the D-notice affair with grace. His apparent inability to admit that he might have been wrong ruined his credibility. Of course, had the truth been known that the whole sorry business was essentially a device to enable him to get rid of Lohan and which had run away out of control, public and Press reaction would have been even greater.

Under pressure from Lohan's union the Civil Service then set up its own inquiry, carried out by a small group of senior civil servants headed by Sir Lawrence (now Lord) Helsby – which Lohan, with some justification, called a 'kangaroo court'. It was really a disciplinary board set up to examine 'his attitude and behaviour during the Radcliffe hearings and to examine discrepancies in his evidence' and was the final stage in the Prime Minister's long battle to get him out of Whitehall. At the start of the inquiry one of the civil servants present told him, 'In fairness, such an inquiry is normally followed by resignation or dismissal.'

In a grilling which lasted a day and a half Lohan was specifically asked to withdraw a statement he had made to the Radcliffe committee that whoever briefed the Prime Minister to make his charge that the *Daily Express* had breached D-notices was wrong and had done 'a wicked thing'. He refused and reiterated it.

Two of the inquisitors, including Helsby, visited Henry Kerby, who was seriously ill following an arterial graft operation, and took evidence from him about his part in the affair but eventually decided to ignore it.

In 1977 Colonel Lohan, then sixty-five and ailing, confirmed that he had been 'shopped' by Kerby. 'I was shown proof of this by the Civil Service tribunal which investigated my case,' he told me. 'I have kept copies of letters I sent to Kerby little knowing what he was

doing with them. Later the security authorities told me of the awful
extent to which Kerby had been the eyes and ears of the Labour
government.'

The inquiry decided that there was no truth in Wilson's smear
that Lohan had been a source of classified leaks to me or any other
journalist but his fate was already determined, as Helsby recently
confirmed to me. He was allowed to resign but went on the record as
saying that he had been sacked. He was right. Around that time I
gave a lecture to the Joint Services Staff College at Latimer, the
commandant then being Air Vice-Marshal Stewart Menaul. At the
preceding dinner I was told that a few days previously the lecturer
had been Sir James Dunnett, permanent secretary at the Defence
Ministry, who had been unable to stay for lunch because in his own
words he had to get back to Whitehall to sack Lohan. 'You'd think
that with Rhodesia, the Middle East and the economy the Prime
Minister would have other things on his mind,' he had said. 'But all
he's interested in is sacking Colonel Lohan.'

The appalling treatment of Lohan incensed the media still further
against the Prime Minister. For many months whenever Wilson was
cartooned in the *Daily Mail*, for instance, he was given a dunce's hat
with a big D for D-notices on it.

Lohan in fact was one of the shrewdest Whitehall men I ever met
and had followed the tradition set by his D-notice predecessor with
great skill. He was also the most entertaining and it was through his
friendship with journalists that he had been able to win almost all his
battles for suppression of genuinely dangerous information.

I can say now that when Lohan had previously been deputy
director of public relations in the Defence Ministry he had indeed
leaked information to me. But it had always been on the instruction
of a minister or a senior civil servant and in the ensuing Whitehall
rows created by civil servants, who were unaware of the real sources,
he manfully took the blame. On several occasions when I had asked
him why he did this he had shrugged and said, 'It's part of the job.'

Only once did Lohan leak to me inadvertently and he immediately
asked me not to use the information, which I was sorely tempted to
do for there was no security involved. This was the news that King
Hussein of Jordan was to marry the daughter of an English colonel,
the eventual Princess Muna, which he had heard from the Foreign
Office. I withheld the information, which did not break for a further
three weeks.

Of course Wilson was right in saying that Lohan was anti-Labour but then so are almost all the civil servants who really care about defence and the Forces. A Labour government with a powerful left wing clamouring for cuts in Forces' spending for pacifist reasons or to provide more money for more vote-worthy objectives is bad news for those who believe, as Lohan did, that a real capability for self-defence is a necessary foundation for continuing freedom.

The affair effectively destroyed the D-notice system which had served both Britain and the Press so well for more than twenty years. The Prime Minister had shown that the D-notice secretary was not to be impartial as he had been in the past and that an editor who rejected a request for news suppression was to be reviled. Lohan's successor, a former professional naval Intelligence officer, was housed inside the Defence Ministry to function under close control by the senior civil servants.

Under new rules it was made clear that if the secretary made an error of judgement which resulted in a breach of the Official Secrets Acts by a newspaper, that would no longer be a defence in the event of a prosecution.

For the next ten years I virtually ignored the D-notice system and my attitude has since been fully supported in the courts in an Official Secrets case involving the *Sunday Telegraph*. Mr Justice Caulfield ruled that, 'There is no duty in law for any editor of any newspaper to go running to Whitehall to get permission to print an article. It is not the law that once a document emanating from an official source is stamped Confidential that anyone handling it is breaking the law.'

In those few words the judge exposed the confidence trick on which Whitehall's near censorship of the news had been maintained. This had been based on an edict by Sir Norman (later Lord) Brook defining an official secret as any government information that has not been officially released. The judge made it clear that this had been a gratuitous and unjustifiable extension of the law.

Even more reprehensible than Lohan's experience was the treatment eventually meted out to Turlough O'Brien, the Post Office public relations chief who had admitted the truth to the Radcliffe committee that he had in fact confirmed that cable-vetting by the security authorities did take place. As this ran counter to the untrue document submitted to the Radcliffe committee by the senior Post Office officials and to what the Foreign Office wanted him to say, the last dagger was reserved for him. He was prematurely retired. Lohan had undoubtedly caused problems for the government and its Whitehall mandarins but all that O'Brien had done was to tell the truth when pressed, as I was sure he would.

Those officials who had lied and encouraged others to lie were duly promoted in spite of their exposure by the Radcliffe report.

After the disreputable issue of what Lord Radcliffe himself called, 'the government's poor little White Paper' I did not speak to Wigg for two years. Then one day my home telephone rang and a voice said, 'This no-speak has gone on long enough, Harry. I don't mind inflicting wounds in battle but I don't like to see them fester.'

It is hard to resist a man who can bring himself to do that.

I did not speak to Wilson for ten years – until more than a year after he resigned, when I made my peace with him through the good offices of our mutual friend Lord Weidenfeld. The first thing he said when we shook hands was, 'What a pity we fell out over the D-notice business. It was all my fault. It was a mistake and I am very sorry about it.'

It is also hard to resist a former Prime Minister who can say that.

George Brown had also been bitter about the way Radcliffe had exonerated me and the *Daily Express* and particularly by the report's virtual rejection of much of his evidence. I did not meet him again until one day early in 1974 when I walked to my old table at the Écu de France and I noticed him sitting with three other men at the next one. I did not know whether to nod or to cut him when he shouted 'Harry!' and we shook hands. My guest happened to be another Harry – Harry Hyams, the property magnate – and after Brown emerged from the cloakroom following his lunch I called him over to meet Hyams. He was affable but I noticed that he was standing rather awkwardly, though I saw no significance in this.

At our next meeting George explained what had happened. He had been lunching with his lawyers in the break between the court case in which he was eventually convicted of driving with an excess of alcohol in his blood. When he was in the cloakroom the zip on his flies had broken and he faced the prospect of going before a woman judge, who already appeared to be hostile to him, with his flies open, or risk further displeasure by being late if he went home to change. Eventually a fresh pair of trousers was rushed round to the court just in time and he had changed there. This was a further, if trivial, example of the luck which never seemed to flow for George.

As he left me on that occasion he said, in all sincerity, 'You know, we eccentrics should stick together. There aren't many of us left.'

*Chapter Twenty-four*

A Lady of Influence
in Number 10

WHEN Harold Wilson became Prime Minister in October 1964 he rightly considered that George Wigg, then sixty-three, had played a major role in putting him in that position both through his efforts to secure him the leadership of the party and through the Profumo affair. He therefore appointed him Paymaster-General, a non-executive post. Wigg telephoned me in advance of the official announcement to give me the news and ask this favour, 'If my head gets too big promise that you'll kick me up the arse.'

I did my best to oblige on a number of occasions but at that time we were close friends and Wigg explained to me there and then what his main function would be in addition to being a general trouble-shooter and confidential informant with an office inside Number 10. He was to hold a watching brief on the security set-up, do what he could to improve it, and, above all, keep Wilson informed of anything in that field that might cause trouble.

Wilson and Wigg knew that the Tories would be thirsting for revenge over Profumo and would strike the moment any Labour minister could be caught out in a sexual offence or security breach. The Denning report had insisted that there was no reason why Macmillan should have been told of Profumo's sexual activities any sooner than he had been, because it was not MI5's job to pry into private lives which did not impinge on security, but Wilson did not see it that way. He wanted to hear about the first whisper of any relevant impropriety and it was Wigg's job to tell him.

I published all this with Wigg's agreement on the day after his appointment but Tory MPs continued to claim that there was some great mystery about his job and Wilson mischievously declined to enlighten them officially, fear of 'Gestapo' accusations being a factor.

Wigg was well qualified for his assignment, having run such an excellent one-man Intelligence service as a back-bencher that MI5 had conducted its own inquiries to discover where he derived his information. Being specially interested in how he always appeared to know where every Army unit was located when he asked questions in Parliament, they were surprised to find that he accomplished this feat by taking all the local newspapers in the garrison towns and noting which units were playing which at football.

The new Paymaster-General was quickly nosing into the private lives of some of his colleagues and his interest in one, who had a regular mistress, aroused the animosity even of Tory MPs. Most of his concern, however, was quickly concentrated inside Number 10.

Lord Denning in his report had written, 'The admission of Mr Profumo that he had lied to the House of Commons so shook the confidence of the people of this country that they were ready to believe rumours which previously they would have rejected out of hand.'

They were indeed and the rumours were centred around Wilson's political secretary, Marcia Williams, now Lady Falkender, in such force that some of them still persist.

After the Profumo affair Quintin Hogg, now Lord Hailsham, had made a front-bench speech about adultery which was so pointed that Wilson went out of his way to assure a private meeting of the Parliamentary Labour Party that his secretary was 'white as the driven snow'. This speech (reported to me by the late George Caunt) may have touched off the rumours which crystallized into the widespread belief, just before the 1964 general election, that Marcia's husband, Edmund Williams, had been paid a large sum by wealthy supporters of Wilson to withdraw a divorce action which could have been embarrassing. Wigg, with Wilson's agreement, showed me documentary proof that there could not possibly be any truth in this story. It was a copy of the proceedings under which Williams had divorced Marcia in King County, Washington, USA back in 1960 before Wilson had ever become leader of the Labour Party.

The indisputable facts were that after Marcia had refused to follow her husband to Seattle, where the Boeing Corporation had

offered him a good job in 1959, because she wanted to continue her
career in Whitehall, she had reluctantly agreed to divorce him.
Further, when the rumours were at their height Williams was
already remarried with children.

I took this information into the *Express* editor, then Robert
Edwards, but he declined to print it on the grounds that it was unsafe
legally to print anything on that subject. I have resolved that problem by consulting Marcia who, during numerous discussions, has
provided first-hand details of those events in her private and professional life which have caused so much comment and suspicion,
together with full permission to publish them in the relevant chap-
ters of this book.

She has told me that her divorce from Edmund was at his request,
as he had met the girl he later married. It was on cruelty grounds,
but this was a legal device and they parted friends.

Such false rumours were by no means the first to be circulated
about Wilson and his secretary. I have a copy of an anonymous
circular given wide distribution to MPs, the Archbishop of Canter-
bury and other public figures making scurrilous suggestions about
Marcia's predecessor. Inquiries pointed to a pro-Rhodesian faction
as being the source.

Wigg's appointment involved close liaison with MI5 and I can
testify that, though this was ill received at first, the security service
was grateful for his attentions as nobody had taken much interest in
it before. He took the job very seriously, as could be expected of an
old soldier who was very much a patriot at heart and who had a
particular affection for the Army, being fond of describing himself as
a 'bloody good orderly room clerk'. (This use of barrack-room
language by ministers is by no means confined to old sweats. Though
many were surprised at Richard Nixon's liberal use of four-letter
words, when the Watergate tapes were released, there are those in
Westminster who out-curse him, particularly on the Labour side,
though no minister I have heard in action came near a certain
Defence chief who was in a league of his own.)

It was fascinating to see how Wigg's attitude to secrecy and
suppression changed when he became part of the Whitehall
machine. Previously he had been the arch-ferret demanding information from the government. Quickly he became the protector,
going to great lengths in his efforts to suppress the names of civil
servants who might be held to blame for security lapses. It was this

deep concern with security and a perhaps exaggerated approach to the need for secrecy which led him into conflict with Marcia.

Wigg gives the impression that it was battle stations with Marcia from the moment they entered Number 10 together. This was not so. I continued to lunch with Wigg while he was Paymaster-General and to talk to him on the telephone, ringing him, at his request, 'at reveille'. At first he spoke highly of Marcia, complained that she was much maligned and that they were only waiting for some newspaper to print the rumours as true to start a libel action which would set her up for life.

According to Wigg, with whom I have discussed the matter many times over the years, his fall-out with Marcia crystallized around her insistence on remaining in earshot while he wanted to discuss secret matters with the Prime Minister. Marcia denies this but Wigg has described several situations, the most memorable being the occasion when Marcia is supposed to have held her handbag under the Paymaster-General's nose and cried, 'Secrets! I've enough secrets in here to bring the government down.'

After he left Number 10 in November 1967 to become Chairman of the Horserace Betting Levy Board, racing being a consuming passion, and moved to the Lords, Wigg published an autobiography called *George Wigg by Lord Wigg*. It was excellently done but as I knew from our discussions before the book appeared it could have been much better. He wanted to give the precise reasons why he had left Number 10 but ran into legal difficulties which have not, I believe, been fully revealed before.

After he had completed the manuscript he sold it outright to the Thomson Organization which was to serialize it. After Lord Thomson had been approached by lawyers acting for Wilson and Marcia, Wigg was asked to make certain cuts on legal grounds. He refused and was then told that if he insisted on retaining the offending paragraphs he would have to indemnify the Thomson Organization for £50,000 to cover possible libel suits. In addition, legal fees would probably total £20,000.

Appalled by this demand, Wigg approached his old friend Lord Shinwell for advice. The old warrior immediately offered him a cheque for £5,000 plus any other help he might be able to afford later. Having sized up his own resources, Wigg had to give way and only mild criticisms of Marcia remained. 'It became all too clear that civil servants and ministerial colleagues had a formidable competitor for

the Prime Minister's ear in Mrs Williams. Unfortunately her growing influence was not in my view always exercised with wisdom or
discretion.'

Eventually almost all the incidents and points Wigg has originally
included were disclosed with greater force by Haines in his book and
there were no libel actions. Wigg had assured me, incidentally, that
there is no truth in a rumour that he intended to include photographs of the birth certificates of Marcia's children in the book. But
he believes that it was because he was suspected of having shown the
certificates around that he was leaned on by lawyers so heavily.

Wigg told me that immediately after Wilson moved into Number
10 the place became progressively filled with Marcia's relatives and
friends. 'I would go in to see the Prime Minister and find Marcia, her
brother, her sister, her boy-friend. The place was like a bloody
railway station.' (Regrettably it is not true that on this occasion
Wigg remarked, 'C'est magnifique mais ce n'est pas la gare.')

There was an explanation for this invasion by the Field family.
Marcia's father cooked Wilson's first dinner in Number 10, her
mother served him as a temporary housekeeper, her brother Tony, of
land deals fame, was Wilson's golfing partner and sometime manager of his Westminster office, while her tall and attractive sister,
Peggy, became secretary to Mary Wilson. Like Churchill, Wilson
surrounded himself with people he knew and trusted.

The departure of Wigg from Number 10, though mourned by few,
if any, of his colleagues, was a matter of political importance because
during the first two years he had wielded considerable influence on
the Prime Minister, being his closest confidant when other more
senior men, including Cabinet ministers, could not get near him. I
know, for example, from my dealings with him at the time, that he
exerted considerable influence over the first and most radical
defence cuts, being instrumental in saving the Territorial Army
almost from extinction and playing a surprising role in the destruction of the TSR2 bomber, an untold story which I will relate later.
He was also embroiled in ending the seamen's strike in a move
involving the security service (see Chapter Fourteen).

There is no doubt from my conversations with Wigg, Marcia and
Wilson on this matter that it was the strained relations with the
political secretary which made the Paymaster-General quit. Marcia
insists that she did all she could to encourage Wilson to make his old
friend stay but Wigg does not believe this.

There has been some public argument about whether or not Marcia had access to secret information and was properly positively vetted. Suffice it to say here that while Marcia denies that she saw secrets Wigg is adamant that she did. 'If anybody claims that Mrs William's did not see secrets he's a liar and you can quote me', he told me.

Marcia, who while being an ardent career girl was also a normal and personable woman, had several affairs which she hoped would end in marriage. They were of no public concern, though most of them have since been recorded in various books about her days in Number 10, but in 1967 she fell in love to a degree which could not fail to have political consequences so long as she remained in Downing Street, which she was determined to do. The way the facts have been previously recorded but has not done justice either to Marcia or to the man concerned, Walter Terry, a well known political journalist.

Believing that Terry intended to divorce his wife, which he almost certainly did, Marcia went to live with him, a not uncommon practice either in Fleet Street or Whitehall. She was already thirty-five and, wanting children, she thought it unwise to wait until the divorce process, which was going to be lengthy, had been completed. 'I had the children in quick succession,' she said. 'These days I needn't have gone through with it if I hadn't wanted to. I have a one-parent family and I'm thoroughly enjoying it.'

The divorce did not materialize and nobody who has seen her two fine red-haired sons, who look like twins, can but admire the way Marcia is bringing them up while continuing to earn her living. Her determination to continue as the Prime Minister's political secretary while producing two children in nineteen months and coping with them shows a most remarkable, forceful and, in some ways, admirable character. She now agrees that the energetic efforts to maintain secrecy about them were misguided: 'They gave rise to the false rumour that I was never positively vetted. I was in 1964. Naturally, I disliked inquiries into my private life when I came up for revetting in 1969, but had to put up with them'. I suspect the fears deriving from the Profumo case fell heavily on Number 10, where it was thought that the pro-Tory Press would angle the information in unpleasant ways.

Newspaper reporters heard about the births but none could substantiate them without copies of the birth certificates, which they failed to find despite rigorous searches in the Somerset House births registry.

Then the late George Caunt, Wilson's former campaign manager, whom Marcia prefers to call 'baggage master', discovered the birth certificates while working in Somerset House. Caunt, who was a likeable fellow, detested both Marcia and Wilson for reasons he never adequately explained. I believe Wilson to be a kind and generous man but for some reason he engenders hatred in people who have worked with him and Caunt was no exception. Marcia claims that it was because Caunt expected a life peerage and only got the OBE. In any event, he distributed copies of the birth certificates, which had been difficult to find because Marcia had given her maiden name as Williams-Terry on one and Williams-Field on the other instead of plain Field.

Marcia insists that this discrepancy was the fault of a rather vague registrar but the first certificate raised eyebrows because the father's name was not registered and the delivery had been supervised by Wilson's doctor, Joseph Stone (now Lord). On the second certificate, the name of the father was given as Walter Terry, who has fully admitted paternity of both children.

It was generally assumed that Marcia must have changed her name by deed poll, which she was perfectly entitled to do but, if so, she must have changed it back again. In 1974 when she was listed as a peeress in the *London Gazette*, where presumably the entry must be correct, her name was given as Marcia Williams. *Debrett* records that she changed her family name by deed poll to Falkender before becoming a peeress. Such a formality seems to be a requirement by the College of Heralds for those who take a title after the name of a person rather than a place. Thus her late friend Baron Plurenden, who took the title of a manor he had bought, gave his name in *Who's Who* as Rudy Sternberg. Marcia's entry gives her name as Marcia Matilda Falkender. She told me that this name, which gave rise to some newspaper interest, derives from family connections in the Whitby area.

I am in no doubt that had the public known the true facts about her infants, Marcia would have merited widespread sympathy. The truth might have made it more difficult for Wilson to award her a life peerage but, knowing him, I doubt that. Instead, the drive for secrecy predominated and it is this which had led to the numerous misinterpretations and innuendoes which have unnecessarily damaged both her and Sir Harold's reputations. Thus at the time of the Watergate scandal in Washington Tory back-benchers were promoting the idea that Wilson faced a 'Babygate'.

Wilson could have been understandably aggrieved that what, in those days, would have been seen as a considerable sexual scandal surrounding a previous Tory Cabinet minister had never even been hinted at by the Press, though the less sordid parts of it were known to many and involved interesting people, including a Tory peer then very much in the public eye. The full details, which could make a good novel full of high life, had been volunteered to Wilson by an informant with whom I have discussed them and who may recount them in forthcoming memoirs, but, so far as I am aware, Wilson refrained from mentioning them to anyone. I do not give them here because, as events turned out, they were of scant political consequence, though, had they proceeded to the divorce court they could have resulted in a resignation which might have changed the course of British political history.

Wilson's behaviour in standing by his political secretary when most men in his position would have insisted that she should quietly leave could also have won him approbation. There is, incidentally, no truth in the story that he has set up a trust fund of £60,000 for Marcia's children. What he did was to set up a trust fund of about one-third of that figure for Marcia on her retirement because, along with other Westminster political secretaries, she did not belong to any pension scheme. The only way her children could benefit from it would be in the event of her death.

The reader may ask what all these personal details have to do with the pursuit of power. In the first place they had a great deal to do with Marcia's determination to cling to her share of power, which was considerable. With two sons to bring up and educate she needed to remain in her prestigious post and do what she could to improve her position and reputation, the life peerage being the culmination.

The facts themselves affronted some of Wilson's close political colleagues, from whom they could not be hidden, and played some part in attempts to oust him from the premiership in 1969. As gossip pushed the facts around, they also affronted Labour Party workers and lowered Wilson's standing with them, as evidenced by anonymous letters, which I and others in Fleet Street received, urging us to expose the situation. Rumour engendered rumour and innocent events were interpreted as evidence of further scandal surrounding the Prime Minister. The mystery of the 'Mikoyan postcards' provides an excellent example.

In December 1961 Wilson received a New Year greetings card from Sergei Mikoyan, the son of Anastas Mikoyan, the Armenian who served so long as a member of the Politburo, surviving all the purges. Wilson had become friendly with the old man on his Moscow visits and the card from the son was to thank him for kindness shown during a visit to London. It also referred to Wilson's 'wonderful daughter' which, of course, he does not possess. A further card, showing the Moscow version of Noddy walking through the snow with a teddy-bear, was included for the 'daughter'.

Wilson took these cards with him to Number 10 in 1964 and round about 1968 they disappeared, this being attributed to an intruder. In fact they had been removed by a member of the Number 10 staff who later showed them around with the purpose of suggesting that Wilson might have a daughter hidden away somewhere. In 1974 they were shown to me and, after inquiries, I am in no doubt that Mikoyan was referring to Marcia, believing she was his daughter when they met briefly in London, and that the second card was for her. Nevertheless, Wilson's enemies searched the records of Somerset House looking for this fictitious girl and I even received letters assuring me where she was to be found – all of them anonymous and totally without foundation.

No other statesman has ever been subjected to such a stream of scurrilous rumour and much of it seems to have been invited by the unnecessary secrecy which, human nature being what it is, led to suspicions that there must be even more to hide.

Further, the secrecy over Marcia's children was a constant source of concern to Wilson. It intruded into his time and engendered bad publicity and suspicion, leading to his final alienation from the Press. Wilson's concern for Marcia's welfare has led to the suspicion that she must exercise some tremendous influence over him.

'Nobody has great influence over Harold except his wife', she insists. 'When he took my advice, it was because he valued it. I'm not used to mincing my words, and if I felt he was wrong, I would tell him. But he often rejected my views.'

She dismisses her reputation as a minister-maker. 'I sometimes acted as a go-between, but had I exerted influence, there are several ministers in high office who wouldn't be there, and others I would have liked to see promoted who got nothing.'

*Chapter Twenty-five*

## Politicians and Patronage

THE power of patronage which a Prime Minister finds in his hands as soon as he enters Downing Street is immense and, because of the honours system, possibly unparalleled in the world, even including the Soviet Union.

It is still commonly believed that it is the Queen who bestows the honours. Formally she does but there are few, if any, occasions when the monarch would turn down the recommendations of the Prime Minister. Even King George V, who objected to both the baronetcy and subsequent peerage bestowed on Beaverbrook, had to agree to them under pressure from Lloyd George. The Queen has a limited number of honours she can traditionally bestow but the bulk of the power of honours patronage lies with the Prime Minister.

So many men are avid to be called 'Sir' or 'Lord', and so many more of their wives are longing to be called 'Lady', that honours offer a cheap way of securing a man's loyalty or services. Titles also open doors to boardrooms and other appointments so their existence ensures that many will go out of their way to avoid offending a Prime Minister or government they may dislike.

The Prime Minister can also do a service for political colleagues and personal friends by organizing high honours not only for them but for people whom they recommend. This too can be put to advantage.

The withholding of honours which might reasonably be expected for services rendered also offers a Prime Minister a means of revenging himself on people who have offended or disappointed him. There are few Prime Ministers who have been able to resist exercising this aspect of their power. This can, of course, bring about the animosity of those who have been ignored and Marcia suspects that the behaviour of some of Wilson's former friends springs from just such resentments.

Most of the honours are put forward to the Prime Minister by Whitehall departmental heads and by various committees, set up and operating in considerable secrecy, on behalf of the worthies of the different sections of industry, commerce and society in general. By and large they tend to be accepted but there are occasions when the Prime Minister deletes some names and he may even insert others, whom he favours, in their stead. The extent to which executives and writers of the *Daily Mirror* were honoured by Wilson when the paper was pro-Labour did his reputation little good elsewhere though his automatic deletion of most names from *The Times* or *Express* group did him no harm, if only because so few knew about it.

While Prime Ministers may sometimes be rightly blamed for the repeated omission of obviously worthy candidates from the honours list, the fault usually lies with the system or with officials involved in it. The most unjust case in my experience is that of Professor R. V. Jones, now of Aberdeen University, whose contribution to victory in the Second World War through his genius for scientific Intelligence was so much greater than that of many who were loaded with honours. A knighthood was considered for him but, as he was only thirty-four at the end of the war, the mandarins argued that this automatically limited him to a CB, Commander of the Bath, which was the proper award for his rank. Once he had left Whitehall, though briefly recalled later, there was nobody with responsibility or willingness to recommend him as he grew older.

Some statistician has said that Wilson created more peerages than any other Prime Minister in this century – about 250. Lloyd George, who actively touted them, is in second place with 116.

Wilson's explanation is that he wanted to offset the huge Tory predominance in the House of Lords owing to inherited peerages – what one Labour friend of mine calls 'proper lords' – and was also determined to send 'unusual candidates' there. He certainly did so. 'Unusual' was hardly the word for some of them, but his choice was limited.

One of the Wilson honours which raised eyebrows was the knighthood conferred on Rudy Sternberg in 1970. When he was made a peer in 1975, taking the title Lord Plurenden, the eyebrows went even higher.

Sternberg, a German-born Jewish refugee, made himself a millionaire by trading with countries behind the Iron Curtain, particularly with East Germany, from which he secured a virtual monopoly on the import of potash to Britain. He admitted contributing £2,000 a year for four years to help pay for Wilson's private office while the Labour leader was in opposition, when the existence of a trust fund was uncovered in 1977, but he also threatened to sue a newspaper which reported that he was a close friend of Wilson's!

According to Marcia, Plurenden's account was true. He and Wilson were not friendly but he was a close friend of Lady Beattie Plummer, herself of Eastern European origin. Lady Plummer, whose influence seems to have been far-reaching, tried hard to interest Wilson in Sternberg, claiming that he was doing great things for British industry which should be recognized.

Wilson's reaction, Marcia claims, was that Sternberg was a spy and every time his name came up on the honours recommended from the Ministry of Agriculture he deleted it.

While Wilson was out of office and working at Meyer's, the timber firm, Sternberg repeatedly tried to get in touch with him and Wilson always declined. Eventually when Wilson was back in government the pressure from the Agriculture Ministry became so insistent that he asked for a formal security check on Sternberg. The result, Marcia says, was that, far from being a spy, Sternberg was using his Iron Curtain contacts in a way that was helpful to Western Intelligence. So the knighthood went through.

The peerage resulted for his export efforts, especially to Romania, though not all of these brought benefit. A senior Whitehall official told me that, in return for the Romanian purchase of British cropspraying equipment, Romanian blackcurrants had to be imported in such huge amounts that the deal ruined the British blackcurrant industry for years.

The high point of Sternberg's efforts in building good relations with Romania was to have been the visit of President Ceausescu to stay with the Queen in June 1978, but he died suddenly some months before.

The honour which caused most public concern and astonishment was the award of the peerage to Marcia on 24 May 1974. It was no great surprise to me because I had heard first-hand accounts of her

IS—17**

previous demands for a life peerage when she threatened to quit
Wilson's service after rows when both were under stress in Number
10. One such an occasion happened on an aeroplane flight in front of
several witnesses.

The possibility had also been forecast by the political correspondent of the *News of the World*, Noyes Thomas, who went slightly
further by speculating that Wilson intended not only to make her a
life peer but to give her a ministerial post, which he could do once she
was in the Lords. The vehemence with which both suggestions were
denied by Number 10 convinced me that something must be in the
wind.

Marcia already held the CBE and, if she was to be elevated
further, it would have to be at least with a damehood, as some
women civil servants had been. But Harold Macmillan's Press
secretary, Harold Evans, had been given a baronetcy, a hereditary
title, and at the level which Marcia functioned, she carried far
greater responsibility. So a life peerage was not an unreasonable
honour, especially when so many had been conferred on others who
had done far less for the Labour Party or for its leader.

It would have been normal practice for such an honour to be
conferred, as Harold Evans's was, on the final resignation of the
Prime Minister. But Marcia's peerage meant that she would continue in Wilson's service in Downing Street as a baroness. So, as with
Wilson's own resignation, it was the timing rather than the event
itself which remains intriguing.

Marcia has given me her own interpretation of this:

Harold knew there would have to be a general election in October
and could not be sure of winning it. He was thinking of quitting in
1975 anyway, and wanted to ensure that I could continue serving
the Labour Party as a peeress. He had to issue a list of fourteen
other Labour life-peers to reduce the imbalance of Tories in the
Lords, so he included me in it. He did not want me in a resignation
list but in a political list, which was also how I wanted it if I was to
be active in the Lords.

This sounds plausible but I suspect there were other factors, in
particular the fact that her two boys were shortly to enter a well
known public school as day pupils. Having a mother who was a
peeress in her own right to deliver and collect them every day could
be helpful, or at least I am sure that Marcia thought so.

I am quite convinced that Wilson's purpose in organizing the peerage was not simply to cock a snook at the Press over its response to the earlier possibility that his political secretary might be put in the Lords. I believe that he was doing a generous service for her and her children, though it remains something of a mystery why he should risk damaging his own political position for this purpose.

That it was a political risk there can be no doubt. I was immediately telephoned by Wigg, among others, who said they were affronted by the award. Wigg, who had been with Wilson on the previous evening and heard about it then, said that it could well lose Labour the election because so many staunch party workers would object to it. He was right to some extent. Marcia's life peerage was attacked in many areas including the *Political Quarterly* where it was said to 'show an insensitivity to public anxieties almost incredible for a leader of the Labour Party and a personal use of office of a kind more like monarchy than Cabinet government'. But Wilson did not lose the election.

Those who said that Marcia would be too embarrassed to take her seat in the Lords were also proved wrong when she was formally introduced there in July. To date, however, she has yet to make her maiden speech, though she assures me that she intends to do so when the time is more propitious. One of her problems seems to be deciding where to sit. She is so disenchanted with Labour's swing to the Left that she may well sit as an independent on the cross-benches.

I have also been advised that, whatever the Queen may have felt about Marcia's elevation in private, she raised no objection to it with Wilson. Indeed, it seems most unlikely that he would have recommended it had he thought it would cause Her Majesty any annoyance for, as Sir Martin Charteris, the Queen's secretary put it after Wilson resigned, 'He never did anything that would embarrass the shop.'

With good humour, the Queen asked Wilson if he was doing what she called 'a Harvey Smith' at the Press, referring to the occasion when that irascible show-jumper put two fingers up at a person he disliked and later claimed he was giving the V-sign. Wilson replied, 'To some extent, ma'am.'

In retrospect, Marcia certainly deserved the honour on grounds of loyalty. Almost alone of Wilson's former Kitchen Cabinet she has neither deserted nor turned against him.

Normally forthcoming honours are a very well kept secret, even if only because those who have been told they are being recommended fear that they might be disqualified if they talk. But on the occasion of Wilson's resignation honours list, which had to be prepared at short notice, concern that some of the awards might damage the entire system were so widespread in Whitehall that leaks were deliberately made to the Press in the hope that some might be forestalled.

An inquiry into the source of these leaks was said to have proved negative. I can only say that it must have been perfunctory in the extreme because I know the identities of two people who leaked and knew them at the time.

The most blatant of the leakages was the announcement on the front page of the *Daily Express* that James Goldsmith, the self-made businessman and outspoken Tory, who was known to have helped to finance Heath's office while the Tory leader was in opposition, was to become a peer. There was never any truth in this – he was never down for more than a knighthood – but the information was published in good faith because the editor felt that the source could not be questioned.

What had happened was that a close friend of Wilson who disapproved of the knighthood for Goldsmith wanted to stop it, also pressing at the same time for a peerage for one of his friends. When Wilson proved adamant he informed somebody in the *Express* organization of an impending peerage, hoping that the Labour reaction to publicity about it would cause even the knighthood to be withdrawn.

Wilson did not know Goldsmith well but was impressed with his intellectual powers and drive to the extent of suggesting that he should be invited to join the board of the Bank of England, which did not happen. Goldsmith did various services for Wilson, including promising not to take his Cavenham Foods empire out of Britain to France.

Because of Wilson's close friendship with the Jewish community there were many prominent Jews in the list – the two show-business brothers, Sir Lew Grade and Sir Bernard Delfont, Sir Joseph Kagan, the maker of Gannex raincoats, Sir Max Rayne, the property millionaire, Sir Eric Miller, Sir Joseph Stone, his doctor, Sigmund Sternberg and Sir George Weidenfeld. I too am close to leading figures in the Jewish community and I found that some of them were distressed by the list, feeling that it would do harm to them. They thought that Wilson had overdone it and did not agree with Lady

Falkender's eventual claim in *The Times* that the public objections raised against the list were anti-Semitic.

Some of the awards were strongly queried by the Political Honours Scrutiny Committee, resignation honours being traditionally regarded as political, though few in Wilson's list conformed with that description. Lady Summerskill, a member of the committee, later revealed that she and her colleagues had objected to half the names in the list but, when published, only one had been dropped.

Wilson, however, had already given his views on the restricted functions of the committee when answering a question aimed at Marcia's peerage in 1974. He said that with respect to each nomination the committee is furnished with a statement giving the reasons for the suggested award plus a certificate that no payment or expectation of payment to any party or political fund is directly or indirectly associated with the recommendation. The committee is also empowered to inquire about the past history or character of persons to be recommended for honours.

Later the awards were criticized at a meeting of the Parliamentary Labour Party, where more than a hundred MPs dissociated themselves from them, mainly on the grounds that some of the names were too closely associated with 'the less acceptable face of capitalism'.

In spite of these reactions Wilson stood his ground though he did give way to the pressure for the additional peerage I have mentioned, to which he had been opposed.

Much was made of the fact that Marcia had submitted a list of names on lavender notepaper, suggesting that they were all her personal choice. 'Many of the names were friends of both of us,' she explained. 'Harold was genuinely amazed at the fuss. The idea that Lord Weidenfeld, for instance, was my choice is ridiculous.' On the first occasion when I met Wilson and Weidenfeld together at the latter's flat Wilson took me aside and withdrew a slim volume from one of the bookshelves entitled *New Deal for Coal* by Harold Wilson published by Weidenfeld in 1945. It was Wilson's first book as an author and Weidenfeld's first as a publisher.

Eric Miller, the property man who later shot himself while being investigated by the Fraud Squad, was also said to have been given his knighthood after recommendation by Marcia. 'In fact, his name was put forward by Ron Hayward, the Labour Party secretary, who had served with him in the RAF,' Marcia told me.

The result of all the toing and froing was that one peer whom

Wilson had wanted and a knight were dropped from the list. The prospective peer can be named because he has since been sent to the Lords by Callaghan. He was Asa Briggs, the historian. The so-nearly-a-knight, who richly deserved the honour for his academic distinction, may have missed his only opportunity.

There was much discussion about a possible knighthood for Jarvis Astaire, a Jewish promoter of boxing and other entertainments. It is widely believed that he was dropped from the list as a result of the public outcry. I have been assured, however, that he was never on it though he may have been considered for inclusion.

It has been suggested, as in the case of Marcia's peerage, that Wilson was 'cocking a snook' at the Press by making these particular awards. I do not believe that. He seems to remain astonished that the public should react against awards for show-business people who, in his view, have done so much for public entertainment, charity and tourism. There is also the fact that, at that stage, he had some hopes of being recalled to power at a later date and would hardly have damaged his reputation deliberately.

I have little doubt that, being the obstinate man he is when challenged, his determination to have his way was strengthened by the outcry.

The reaction of those who received resignation honours them-selves is an interesting sidelight on human nature. All to whom I have spoken believed that they were, as Lord Vaizey, one of the recipients, put it to me 'in the cosmetic part' of the list – that part which made the rest tolerable.

Vaizey told me that he had only met Wilson about four times and that when he received the letter asking him if he would accept the peerage if the Prime Minister put his name forward to the Queen, he took the acceptance round by hand to Number 10 in case it might be delayed in the post.

Only in one instance have I had a hand in securing an honour for a friend. The circumstances were of some general interest in view of what happened to him later and because they arose out of a visit I paid to the Shah of Iran where I saw aspects of the pursuit of power in its most concentrated form.

Early in 1972 I was approached by a personal friend of the Shah to be asked if I would do both of them a service. It was explained that, while no announcement had yet been made, the Shah was to come to Britain in June to stay with the Queen at Windsor and attend the

Ascot races. While His Imperial Majesty was greatly looking forward to that social visit, his main objective was to pave the way for very large arms purchases, so it was rather important, from the export business viewpoint, that he should be well received. In the previous months the Shah felt he had been subjected to unfair criticism by the BBC, *The Times* and several other newspapers. So I was asked if I could afford him some good publicity shortly in advance of his arrival.

My reaction was that I would be delighted to go out to interview the Shah, but I could not guarantee him publicity of any kind unless he had something constructive, interesting and, above all, new, to say. I was assured that he would provide excellent material, so having secured the editor's approval for the cost of the visit – the *Daily Express* has always been opposed to accepting free travel or accommodation for such ventures – I was put in touch with a man who was to make the detailed arrangements.

He turned out to be a Mr Shapoor Reporter, whom I had met socially in London. He was a United Kingdom citizen but lived in Tehran and I knew that he had already been involved as an agent and consultant in several important Iranian arms purchases, including Chieftain tanks. Eventually after a briefing on protocol, he escorted me into the Shah's Niavaran Palace in the rather dull and untidy city of Tehran. He was well known to the armed uniformed guards and to the civilian bodyguards placed at every turn of every corridor and it was immediately obvious when we entered the Shah's study that the two were on close terms. In fact, as I later discovered, Reporter's father, who took that name because he was a journalist, had played some part in putting the Shah's late father on the throne of Persia, as Iran was then called.

Although the initiative had come from the Shah himself I was careful to respect the vanities of power, having been taught the journalistic value of this by my first ever news editor, Cyril Morton, who had taken clever advantage of it. This was on an occasion when the Channel Island of Sark had been invaded by journalists sent to secure an interview with the Dame of Sark, the autocratic ruler of that tiny community, who had done something rather feudal which had been made much of in the newspapers. She steadfastly refused to be interviewed and after sticking it out for a few days the several reporters who were staying at the same hotel all agreed to return to Fleet Street. Morton who had conceived a possible solution made some excuse to leave later than the rest, saying he wanted to look round the island, and telephoned the Dame's residence to ask for an *audience*. She immediately granted it and Morton achieved his scoop, which of course resulted in trouble for all his rivals who were accused by their editors of quitting too early. Morton told me that on reading what he had written the Dame regretted the audience.

The Shah turned out to be the easiest person to interview I have encountered. He seemed to have total recall for facts and figures and knew all the relevant details about every subject we discussed, from oil to the latest guided missiles.

Sipping milkless tea from a silver tumbler, he expressed dismay at the kid-glove way the British army was dealing with the terrorists in Northern Ireland and particularly about the existence of 'no-go' areas where the IRA ruled, even manning barricades.

'I would give them notice that in forty-eight hours my forces would be coming through with tanks to remove the barricades and deal with any terrorists remaining in the area. If the barricades were still there they would be bulldozed away and any houses from which anyone was firing would be shelled. A few innocent lives might be lost if they had ignored the warning but far more will be lost the way your people are tackling it.'

It was a unique experience to meet a man with such near-absolute power and the ability and determination to use it. He provided so much news that I knew there would be no difficulty in projecting a big article about his impending arrival in Britain, and what it could mean in the way of business for British firms.

When I briefed the British ambassador, Sir Peter Ramsbotham, on the outcome of the audience he was astonished that the Shah had said so much on the record, particularly concerning his attitude to oil prices. 'I shall have to warn London right away,' he said as we took tea in the splendid embassy garden, while parakeets flitted in and out from the Russian embassy across the road, equipped, so Ramsbotham joked, with eavesdropping bugs.

When I returned to London I went to see Lord Carrington, the Defence Secretary, whom the Shah had never met. In his room in the House of Lords I was able not only to give him advance information about defence issues the Shah would be raising but to warn him about certain secret requests, some of which would obviously have to be declined for political reasons.

I urged him to take due note of Reporter who would be accompanying the Shah, and of whom Carrington had not heard. I suggested that in the interests of further orders he should ensure that he was invited to accompany the Shah on the visits to weapons displays.

James Prior had breezed into the room as I was saying how much business Reporter had already brought to Britain and rather jokingly remarked, 'We'd better give him a gong.' In the ensuing New Year's honours Reporter received a knighthood, a KBE, because after my tip Carrington had made a check and found that he had already been responsible for Iranian arms orders for Britain worth about £800 million.

I had discovered that the knighthood was on the way because of a Whitehall disagreement about it. The Foreign Office objected, ostensibly on the grounds that it would offend some people in Tehran and make Reporter's life more difficult there by giving him prominence. I suspect however that the objections came from MI6. Reporter had for many years served as a useful source for British Intelligence, having once worked for US Intelligence while Mosaddeq was ruling Iran and the Shah was in exile. There were objections that Reporter could be more productive as a source if he retained a low profile.

Carrington confirmed to me that he had experienced difficulty in pushing the honour through.

*Chapter Twenty-six*

# Politicians and Health

THERE has been considerable discussion recently about the health hazards of being an MP because of the stress of the long hours and the responsibility, but those MPs who are really under stress, the senior ministers and particularly Prime Ministers, are not usually the ones who go down with the heart attacks or the nervous breakdowns. Perhaps those back-benchers who do so are suffering from the stress of frustration rather than the stress of physical or mental effort.

The theory that excessive pressure of work, physical or mental, causes heart attacks has been highly suspect for some years. I know this because Beaverbrook was so in love with life that he sent me to every conference where gerontology – the science of adding years to life and life to years – was under discussion, in the hope that I would bring back early news of some magic potion or treatment that would lengthen life span. He sent me to the USA, Belgium, Germany, Italy, Sweden and many other places but in spite of the welter of research papers to which I listened I always returned with the same story. There are only four proven ways of insuring against premature death – don't smoke, take regular exercise, don't become overweight and be a female.

The last did not appeal to Beaverbrook who was nothing if not intensely masculine. But the penultimate did. It may have been the unwitting result of my advice, but he suddenly took a great dislike to several of the fat men in the office and sacked some of them, even a few famous names. Seeing the signs, several of the others slimmed rather hurriedly.

It used to be said that Beaverbrook lived to a great age because his employees had his quota of diseases by proxy, due to the relentless pressure to which he subjected them. There might have been some truth in this but there were other reasons why some of them died young. He would never accept the theory that excessive work was a killer and was extremely angry when the *Daily Express* reprinted an American article entitled, 'Who wants to be the richest man in the cemetery?'

'It's rubbish,' he stormed. 'I've worked all my life and look at me. Look at Churchill. We'll all rest long enough in that little box.'

One Prime Minister who was averse to overwork, believing that it was counter-productive in the long term, was Harold Macmillan. He dispensed this wisdom in the form of little notices put up in his room for all who visited him to see. They proclaimed 'A day's work in a day', and 'Quiet, calm deliberation disentangles every knot'.

The recipe for health said to have been prescribed by Leslie Hore-Belisha, the former War Minister, whose lasting memorial is the Belisha beacon, was rather less practical because it could have brought Whitehall life to a standstill. Apparently he believed that being awakened by an alarm-clock or any other artificial means was a damaging shock to the system and that natural waking when brain and body decided it was time for consciousness was the Good Lord's intention. According to a former colleague, he often missed important meetings as a result.

Sir Carl Aarvold, the judge, told me how he had been playing golf on his honeymoon when Beaverbrook, then an active politician, wanted to play through. He was introduced to the self-made Canadian millionaire and newspaper owner and told him he was making a career at the bar.

'I'll give you three ingredients for success,' Beaverbrook volunteered. 'An unhappy marriage, poor health and being useless at games.'

Aarvold told me that with Beaverbrook's reputation with women, his asthma and poor performance on the golf course the advice must be sound.

I disagree with all of it. The emotional stresses of an unhappy marriage can do no good to an overburdened statesman and coping with them eats into his limited time. The time spent on games, provided it is not excessive, is a sound investment in health and there is plenty of evidence that poor health in statesmen can be disastrous for the nations they are elected to guide.

Beaverbrook was plagued by bad asthmatic attacks while overworking as Minister of Aircraft Production in readiness for the Battle of Britain and through it. Sir Winston Churchill recalled the story of how at a meeting with Stalin he thought he heard a cat mewing and then realized that the sound was coming from his colleague's chest. Beaverbrook gave his asthma as the excuse for his resignation from the government in 1942 though the appointments of Clement Attlee as Deputy Prime Minister and Sir Stafford Cripps as Leader of the Commons were more significant.

I have heard him wheezing a bit, but in his later years, when I spent much time in his company, his complaint was a minor nuisance, on which he played when it suited him. As an example, I cannot resist recording the occasion on one of his birthdays when Lady Dunn, the wealthy Canadian widow who later became his wife, faced the problem of what to give the man who had everything. She decided she would buy him a hurdy-gurdy and great efforts were made to secure an old one in a reasonable state of repair. This was achieved and, at great cost and effort on her part, a complete restoration job was accomplished, in which the glass panels, once painted with Italian scenes, were replaced by pictures of Beaver-brook's Canadian home.

Lady Dunn spirited the machine into the house without his Lord-ship's knowledge and she planned to be playing it in the hall when he walked slowly down the great staircase on his birthday morning. To complete the scene she hired an organ-grinder's monkey and, not content with this, a donkey to put in the shafts.

All was ready as Beaverbrook came down the stairs but the reception he gave to this extraordinary present was hardly what had been expected.

'Get rid of that donkey,' he barked. 'It'll do its business on my Bokhara carpet!'

Then after a few more steps he spied the monkey. 'And get that ape outta here. It'll give me asthma!'

A few days later Lady Dunn played the hurdy-gurdy for me as she told me the sad story. It must have been one of the few occasions in history where a woman worth every bit of thirty million dollars turned barrel-organist.

The charge that he selfishly clung to political office after his health demanded his resignation cannot be levelled at Beaverbrook, but history is littered with examples of leaders who were guilty of this social crime. There are few instances where the results were so far-reaching and so tragic as in the case of President Franklin Roosevelt.

Before the wartime summit talks at Yalta, where the Russians secured concessions disastrous for the West as a whole and catas-trophic for the millions who found themselves behind the Iron Curtain, Roosevelt, who insisted on giving Stalin so much, was near to death. He was emaciated, his lips were blue and he was so weak that he had to hold his head in his hands.

Neville Chamberlain was suffering from incurable cancer when he presided as Prime Minister over the disastrous Allied campaign against the Germans in Norway in 1940. He died only eight months after being forced out of office. Sir Stafford Cripps, Labour's post-war Chancellor, suffered from chronic ill-health and took the de-cision to devalue the pound after six weeks in a Swiss clinic. Ernest Bevin, the Foreign Secretary, had serious heart trouble and died within a month of a reluctant retirement.

Like everyone else in Beaverbrook's entourage I was forbidden to reveal Churchill's series of minor strokes during his last term as

Prime Minister, though his infirmity was such that my Whitehall friends were wondering how he would be able to reach his seat in the Commons. By the time Sir Anthony Eden, who had waited in the wings so long, managed to succeed to the premiership, he too was in the early debilitating stages of an illness from which he would never be free.

Eden's almost personal intervention in Suez, a disaster which showed what power a Prime Minister could wield, was made when he had serious liver trouble which may well have affected his judgement.

Later, while we both happened to be holidaying in Barbados, he gave me some account of his sufferings. His illness had been so severe that surgery on the bile duct had been essential but the operation was botched so badly that a repair operation for the insertion of what he called 'a tin tube' had to be undertaken in the USA. The time had come for a replacement because bile was again leaking into his bloodstream and he was concerned because he had just heard that his 'tin-tube specialist' had died.

In connection with Lord Avon, as Sir Anthony became, I can disclose a story which does credit to Margaret Thatcher. In 1976 I heard through a mutual friend that Lord Avon was terminally ill with cancer and, as he had never met Mrs Thatcher since she had become Tory leader, he wanted to discuss with her the future of the party he loved. This could not be done openly because it would seem like political interference on his part. So I was asked to approach Mrs Thatcher with an offer that the mutual friend would fly her down by helicopter to Lord Avon's Wiltshire home for lunch. When I told her of his condition she cancelled engagements to fly down the following day.

As regards the health of statesmen, things were little better on the other side of the Atlantic. While General Eisenhower was President he suffered three major episodes in three years – coronary thrombosis, intestinal obstruction and a slight stroke. Later when I discovered that President Kennedy was afflicted with Addison's Disease, a condition of the adrenal glands leading to anaemia, weakness and wasting, Beaverbrook forbade me to reveal it. He explained that he had already been told about it in great confidence and if it appeared in the *Daily Express* it would look as though he had leaked it.

This was a hazard which restricted me on many more frustrating occasions. I was sometimes able to talk him into agreeing that if I genuinely secured the information from another source – always easy once one knew it was true – I could use it. In Kennedy's case however, Beaverbrook sensed that I had been put on to the information by a cryptic memo from him sent from the USA asking, 'What is the normal dosage of cortisone for a case of Addison's disease?'

It can be argued that physical illness has no effect on mental capacity but there is strong evidence against this opinion. Anyone who has suffered toothache knows how pain can prevent deliberation and distort judgement. A painful, debilitating illness from which a senior statesman may be suffering without admitting it must have more insidious effects.

While statesmen's private fears that they may be seriously ill, or actual knowledge of it, must influence their performance, it is understandable why they remain reluctant to quit. They have usually struggled hard and long to reach the top and are touched with sufficient vanity genuinely to believe that it is in the nation's interests for them to stay. There is also the undoubted fact that because of circumstances which can always be imagined if they are not real, their quick departure would be damaging to the country or the party.

I have found that politicians are more sensitive about public references to their state of health than ordinary mortals. This was shown by the reaction of Edward Heath when I discovered in 1973, when he was Prime Minister, that he had been to the King Edward VII Hospital for a thorough medical check. Heath was furious when the *Express* printed the news though all his Press department had to do was to tell the truth to turn the news to his advantage.

Instead he ordered a full inquiry to discover how I had come by the news. Hospital staff were questioned but it was another distinguished patient who had kindly telephoned to tell me. The examination had given him a clean bill of health and more capital should have been made of the fact that he was setting an excellent example to other statesmen by having regular check-ups. Perhaps there should be compulsory medical checks for all holders of Cabinet office. It certainly seems ridiculous that when more and more firms are demanding a reasonable bill of health before employing an executive, men who may be physical wrecks are allowed to take on the running of the country.

A problem peculiar to the medical examination of important people is that doctors seem reluctant to accept a serious diagnosis – a kind of, 'it couldn't possibly happen to him' syndrome. This was exemplified with the complex illness of King George VI when leading specialists were unable to believe that he had lung cancer on top of his other arterial ailments. It seems to have been the local general practitioner at Balmoral who was first convinced of it.

During the war one of the most important admirals kept falling asleep at crucial defence meetings but, because he was so senior, nobody had the nerve to tell him that he might be ill as he was – mortally. Later while visiting the Burden Neurological Institute at Bristol I learned of another admiral who had been issuing crazy commands for months before he could be made to consult a doctor who diagnosed advanced brain disease. Happily this was in peacetime.

Though speech defects hardly qualify as an aspect of health, I have always found it extraordinary how so many MPs, for whom clear diction would appear to be essential, are afflicted by them. There are many who are incapable of pronouncing the letter r or the letter l yet they deliberately choose a profession dependent on powers of oratory to secure election and preferment.

Possibly it is the challenge of coping with a speech problem that helps to motivate some of them to take up politics. Such motives are well recorded in the psychological literature and I remember one Fleet Street character who had a major hand deformity and was also impotent yet drove himself to become an outstanding draughtsman specializing in drawing sexy girls!

There are, of course, examples where a politician can capitalize on a minor speech defect, as Churchill did with his difficulty over the letter s and as Enoch Powell does with the letter l. But with others it can be a handicap, as I believe it is with Roy Jenkins whose oratorical gifts are marred by his total inability to pronounce an r.

An interesting sidelight on human attitudes has been experienced by those cartoonists like Michael Cummings of the *Daily Express* who have occasionally made use of a speech defect in lampooning politicians like Jenkins. Readers write in complaining that it is a foul and in bad taste yet they raise no objections when Wigg's large ears, Heath's nose or Macmillan's eyebrows are exaggerated in cartoons.

The late Lord Horder, a doctor with a unique flair for diagnosis, was adamant that a person who was mortally ill should never be told because it was wrong to deprive anybody of hope. But should this humane approach be applied to statesmen responsible for a whole nation's affairs? The doctor in charge is in a difficult position because his first concern has to be the welfare of his patient. If he believes that telling the truth could devastate the patient it is his medical duty to withhold it, even in the case of a Prime Minister.

Because of the confidentiality of the doctor–patient relationship, especially at exalted levels, one rarely hears what really occurs but I was privy to the strange events surrounding Beaverbrook's last illness, which may be typical of what can happen when a famous man, on whom many others depend, is found to be mortally ill. In addition the details provide further insight into the character of this extraordinary man.

I was the first person outside the family to learn that Beaverbrook had incurable cancer and the way it happened was no credit to the medical profession. I was salmon fishing on the Dee near Aberdeen in 1962 and on returning to the hotel drifted into the bar for a drink before changing for dinner. There I was introduced to a famous radiologist who was also fishing. 'How is your boss?' he asked.

'Lord Beaverbrook? He seems fine. I dined with him a couple of nights ago and he was on great form.'

The radiologist grunted into his glass. 'He'll be dead in six months.'

'What do you mean?' I asked incredulously.

'He's got inoperable cancer of the prostate. I've seen the X-ray plates. There's no hope for him.'

I realized immediately that if this were true the news would have to be kept secret if possible because of the impact on the Beaverbrook shares and his other financial interests, apart from the personal implications. So on my return I managed to see Lady Dunn alone and told her what I knew. She was aghast and told me what had happened.

Lord Beaverbrook did indeed have a malignancy and because he had always insisted on being told the truth was given it. His confidence that he would face death with equanimity proved to be ill-founded. He was so much in love with life that he was devastated. The doctors had, however, reckoned without Lady Dunn. She called in Sir Daniel Davies who had given him the sad prognosis and ordered him to reverse it. At first he refused but under increasing pressure eventually agreed to call in a second opinion, who for mercy's sake would tell a lie. This was done and when Beaverbrook had been told there had been a mistake he appeared to become his old self again, though whether he really believed this second story or just pretended to do so may never be known.

On one occasion I was at Cherkley when he had been given cobalt bomb treatment for the secondary invasions in his bones. 'The cobalt bomb's a great thing for rheumatism, you know,' he assured me. 'It's used for cancer too, of course, but it's great for rheumatism.'

Personally I don't think he was really taken in though those much nearer to him believe he was. Not long before the end I was staying alone with him and Lady Beaverbrook, which Lady Dunn had become, at his villa at Cap d'Ail near Monte Carlo. It was a long way from the lounge to the dining-room and as he shuffled along between us he burst into a hymn, which was a common thing for him to do. As he reached the last line he stopped and his wife asked why.

'Ah, I don't like the last line. I'm not gonna sing it.'

'Please sing it, dear,' she insisted.

He obliged. 'Until I come to Thee.'

'Who the hell wants to go to Him,' he added. 'I don't. At least not yet.'

*Chapter Twenty-seven*

# Politicians and Sex

IT seems odd at first sight that the sex scandals which have proved damaging to the image of British politics have nearly all been associated with defence. First there was the Vassall case involving an Admiralty clerk recruited by the KGB through homosexuality, then the Profumo affair, followed by the sad case, in 1965, of Commander Courtney. In 1973 there was the call-girls scandal resulting in the resignations of Lord Lambton, Minister for the RAF, and Lord Jellicoe, a former First Lord of the Admiralty.

The exception is the most recent – the unprecedented experience of Jeremy Thorpe, whose resignation as Leader of the Liberal Party was brought about by the mere allegation of a homosexual relationship with a male model, many years in the past, an allegation which Thorpe has consistently denied.

The explanation almost certainly lies in the fact that as a rule neither the security authorites nor the police involve themselves in the private peccadilloes of ministers unless security might be involved and with the defence departments that is always considered possible and so must be investigated.

I first met Lord Lambton round Beaverbrook's table. He was then a regular contributor to the London *Evening Standard* and his articles, like his conversation, were of high quality. I was further impressed with his intelligence and his honesty when he served as Minister for the Royal Air Force. During that time – his first and last office – he consulted me in advance about some of his speeches to anticipate the Press reaction. I realized that he was not only a sound thinker but a dedicated House of Commons man and ambitious for further office, to which ends he declined the Earldom of Durham, his entitlement on his father's death.

Sadly, masculine nature is such that in many men the sex drive cuts clean across intelligence, honesty and ambition, leading them to take risks which in any other context they would reject as absurd. I learned that on the last occasion I saw him, when he came round to my flat in Mayfair to discuss a speech: his next assignment had been with a call-girl.

It had been common knowledge for long enough that women found Lord Lambton unusually attractive, with his height, thin features, the languid air behind his blue-tinted spectacles and other attributes, not least of which was his virtuoso performance in the shooting field. He eventually made it clear to me that he regarded prostitutes as part of the life of all manly men. 'I can't think what all the fuss is about,' he told me. 'Surely all men patronize whores.'

I had some difficulty assuring him that he was exaggerating the true position.

When the full circumstances of his bedroom activities were revealed it was obvious that he had been incredibly indiscreet. Nevertheless, it was just possible that he might have escaped public disgrace and even elimination from political life but for unfortunate circumstances, some of which have not, I believe, been told before.

The girl who brought about his downfall was called Norma Levy

POLITICIANS AND SEX 275

and her husband, who had a criminal record, had contrived to take photographs of his wife with Lambton and others in extremely compromising situations. The husband was proposing to make some money by selling the photographs to a newspaper and eventually did so. There was never at any time any attempt at blackmail and searching inquiries by MI5 produced no evidence of involvement with the KGB or any other foreign agency.

Lambton had, however, let his identity be known to the girl, even to the extent of paying her by cheques in his name. Knowing her husband's potentialities and her distinguished client's responsibilities, she was genuinely concerned.

As a sideline, Norma Levy sometimes worked as a hostess in a well known London night-club and she told her fears to the owner's wife, suggesting that the government should be warned in advance about the dangerous position Lambton was in. This lady was equally worried as she considered the possibilities and agreed that the government should be told, but only at top level. She told Norma that she thought she knew how this might be done.

She was aware that one of her regular customers moved in political circles and told him the story. After very careful consideration he decided to take action and contacted James Prior, then a close colleague of the Prime Minister, Edward Heath.

With memories of what the Profumo case had done to Macmillan, Heath was appalled at the news and it was agreed that Prior should see the night-club owner's wife, which he agreed to do but only in his Whitehall office and with a senior civil servant present. The lady duly agreed to impart her information – I have no doubt that it was taped – and the machinery which ended in Lambton's disgrace was set in motion.

MI5, which on being told the facts, claimed that it 'already had a whiff of the scandal', though not strong enough for them to initiate any action, was empowered to put the Minister for the RAF under surveillance to make sure that the KGB was not latching on to it. The similarities with the case of Commander Courtney were all too obvious.

Nobody believed that Lambton, then fifty, would have submitted to blackmail, even when it became known that he sometimes smoked cannabis while with the call-girls. Apart from reporting any attempt immediately he would surely have taken a 'publish and be damned' attitude. But the steamroller was again in motion and not only was he to be crushed by it but so was his political colleague Lord Jellicoe.

Lord Jellicoe was then Leader of the House of Lords, and as Lord Privy Seal, one of the highest State appointments, was responsible for the Civil Service Department, an important job which he was fulfilling admirably. The civil servants admired him and so did their unions. So there was little doubt that Jellicoe, who had previously served ably in the Admiralty, would have gone on to higher positions. Popular and brave, with a splendid war record, he was a man whom the Tory leadership could ill afford to lose.

By a complete coincidence the name Jellicoe had been mentioned. It had come to the notice of the police while they were investigating the Lambton situation and though he had never met Norma Levy, or had any illicit relations with anybody else involved in the Lambton affair, he was called to the presence of Mr Heath. Properly, he denied any connection with the case and that could have been the end of it. However, being the man he is, his integrity and loyalty to his leader were such that after brooding about it all night he went to see Heath again the following morning. He repeated that he had nothing whatever to do with Norma Levy but felt that he should admit that he had in the recent past patronized a Mayfair escort agency. These few occasions had been the result of spur-of-the-moment telephone calls on lonely evenings. As the girls had always been taken to his own flat there had been no risk of blackmail photographs.

All politicians with whom I have discussed this tragic case agree with me that Heath should have dismissed the information as irrelevant but it seems he took the view that if he were asked a question about Jellicoe in Parliament he would be unable to give a negative answer with complete honesty. So when Jellicoe offered his resignation Heath accepted it.

This act made nonsense of the former belief that Profumo had been disgraced not because he had consorted with a prostitute but because he lied to the House. Both Lambton and Jellicoe immediately told the truth – in Jellicoe's case he volunteered it – yet they suffered the same fate. The truth was – as it always has been and still is – that if people in public life behave as other mortals they will be judged by harsher standards if they are caught out.

Some of Jellicoe's ministerial colleagues were furious about this, seeing it as an example of the inflexibility of mind which would eventually destroy Heath politically and his government with him. Wilson behaved more maturely when a married senior colleague was confronted at Westminster by a discarded mistress, hysterically threatening to give a sheaf of passionate love-letters to the newspapers unless he returned to her. She was pacified and ushered from the precincts unobserved by the Press. The man, an unlikely Lothario, remains in the Cabinet.

When Lord Lambton resigned he disappeared to his country estate in Durham, and, because I had his ex-directory telephone number, I was able to talk with him exclusively. Though shattered by the end of his career not only as a minister but as an MP, he blamed nobody but himself saying that 'Any man who has access to secrets and goes to bed with a woman looks like a security risk' and admitting that he had behaved with 'credulous stupidity'. This was no exaggeration seeing that what he called 'the ruling passion' of his life – meaning politics – had been overruled by a passion of less significance but more immediately demanding.

In the evening after the announcement of Jellicoe's resignation I was a guest at a dinner attended by Lord Carrington, then Defence Secretary and Lambton's former chief, Robert Carr, then Home Secretary, and Edward Heath, who joined us later. Just as we were seated I was told that I was wanted on the telephone by Lord Lambton. The name electrified the table and with good reason. Lambton was alone in his large house and, as he was thought to be extremely distressed, his colleagues were concerned about him. They need not have been. What Lambton wanted to know was how Jellicoe had come to be involved.

I told him that there were other names on a 'black list' which had been shown to the Prime Minister. Heath had previously told Parliament that the list included no other minister but I gave Lambton the names of two of his former colleagues who might be named by newspapers. Lambton commented, 'The ways things are going it will soon be clear that Heath is the only member of the government who doesn't do it.'

I had barely begun the second course when Lambton telephoned again in search of further information. The ministers present knew what was going on because I was seated next to the charming wife of one of the Prime Minister's aides. Eventually I was able to put their minds at rest regarding their anxiety over Lambton's health.

To allay public and parliamentary concern Heath asked the Standing Security Commission, then headed by Lord Diplock, to investigate any possibility that a breach of security might have occurred because of the sensitive offices held by both Lambton and Jellicoe. The Commission satisfied itself that no breach had taken place and reported that had Jellicoe remained in office he should have been regarded as completely secure to see top-secret information. In Lambton's case, however, they would have felt bound to recommend that classified information should be withheld.

Some time later I told Enoch Powell the background to the Lambton affair and his reaction to the behaviour of the night-club owner's wife, whose patriotism had led her to inform the government, was illuminating: 'That woman's a good Tory!'

Lambton's reasonably safe seat was lost to the Liberals at the by-election created by his resignation. It is difficult to judge whether the scandals had any influence on the outcome of the next general election in 1974 when Heath was only narrowly defeated by Wilson. Obviously the miners' strike and the resulting three-day week were the overriding factors, but Heath did go to the country on a 'Who governs Britain?' ticket. So it is possible that a sufficient number of prudish voters thought that some of the Tory ministers had been unfit to do so.

So much publicity has been given to the case of Jeremy Thorpe and the allegations of a homosexual relationship by a male model called Norman Scott that there is no need for me to rake over it, but there are some aspects of the associated events which are of political significance.

I understand that at no time has MI5 ever suspected that there have been any security overtones to the issue, in spite of Thorpe's statement to Cyril Smith that he was 'bound to win because I have the three most important people in Britain on my side – Harold Wilson, Lord Goodman (Wilson and Thorpe's legal adviser) and MI5'. But I have evidence that the CIA wondered whether the KGB was behind the move to discredit the Liberal leader as part of a general drive to undermine confidence in the British parliamentary system and actually carried out investigations which proved to be completely negative.

I am in no doubt, however, that the unsubstantiated allegations of past homosexuality made by Scott were used by Liberal MPs and other supporters as a means of getting rid of Thorpe. Cyril Smith, the portly Liberal MP for Rochdale, told me that after the first public row over Scott's allegation there was a secret straw-vote among the twelve other Liberal MPs on whether Thorpe should remain leader or be required to resign. The result was ten to two against Thorpe but he managed to hold on to the leadership through his strong support in the country.

Later the political and publicity forces ranged against him became so strong that he did resign, an event I will discuss in connection with the resignation of Harold Wilson.

*Chapter Twenty-eight*

# Politicians and Money

IT is often said by Westminster apologists that a politician's private life is his own but, while this may be accepted by most voters as a reasonable principle, many of them take a harsher view in practice, particularly when a politician's private behaviour ill accords with his public sentiments.

There is no area which gives greater cause for comment in this respect than the attitude of many Labour MPs to money. While they preach for the fairer sharing of wealth, they seem to acquire more than their fair share for themselves. When they desert the cause to which they claim to be dedicated for better-paid employment they tend to attract public censure, not only from fellow Socialists, who have not been so fortunate, but from Tories who see them as hypocrites.

The difference between the attitudes to the two parties is well exemplified by the public reaction towards the considerable financial successes achieved by Heath and Wilson in writing books. Few seem to begrudge Heath his money but reports of the large sums acquired by Wilson from his memoirs attracted scathing criticism. By the same token it was almost regarded as an act of patriotism when Beaverbrook and the Duke of Westminster paid Churchill's accumulated debts, but when it was discovered that some pro-Labour millionaires had set up a trust fund to finance Wilson's office while he was in opposition there was an uproar.

This partisan attitude by the public and the Socialist reaction to it is illustrated by an extraordinary outburst, of which I have a taped record, when Wilson was being interviewed by David Dimbleby for the BBC.

Dimbleby suggested that Wilson had earned between £100,000 and £250,000 by writing his book on the Labour government. Wilson refused to discuss it, lost his temper and remarked, 'If you are interested in these things you'd better find out how people buy yachts. You have not put this question to Mr Heath. Did you ask him how he was able to pay for a yacht? When you've got an answer from him come and put the question to me.'

Wilson then insisted that the conversation should be eliminated from the recording which was being made. 'If the BBC put this question to me without putting it to Heath the interview is off. The whole programme is off . . . If this film is used or if this is leaked there's going to be a hell of a . . .' Much of the rest of the recording is indecipherable because of interruptions.

Wilson's anger was understandable but so is the public's partisan attitude. While Heath may have once remarked about the 'unacceptable face of capitalism' – to the eternal regret of most of his colleagues – Wilson and his colleagues have castigated large profits as obscene as a matter of party policy. Indeed Aneurin Bevan, who acquired a considerable fortune, referred to profit as 'private greed'.

Even some of those back-benchers much further to the Left have acquired considerable fortunes through the exercise of the capitalist activities they affect to despise.

There are other politicians, of course, with long and devoted service to their country who lack the facility or drive to accumulate money. One of these is Lord George-Brown, who recently told me of the rather embarrassing first meeting between his wife, Sophie, and Lady Dunn, the immensely wealthy Canadian widow who eventually married Beaverbrook. To make conversation Lady Dunn explained the dreadful problem of having to cope with the immense influx from the holdings she had inherited from her late husband. Sophie just sat and listened, but as George remarked later, 'To us at that time 500 quid would have been a godsend!'

Some of those Socialists who are most outspoken against private wealth take special delight in enjoying the fruits of it provided by others. Such a man was Aneurin Bevan who loved wining and dining at Beaverbrook's table at Cherkley. Indeed he considered himself such a connoisseur of champagne that he was known in the Beaver-brook circle as the 'Bollinger Bolshevik'.

Beaverbrook served some excellent wine and though he tended to prefer whisky at meals he liked to be complimented on his cellar. Usually he was but on one occasion he served some very old champagne which some people enjoy as a novelty. Not so Bevan, who gave him a truthful answer when asked to comment on it. 'I like champagne young, clear and sparkling. This is old, cloudy and flat.' In spite of this frankness or because of it Beaverbrook was so taken with Bevan as a table companion that he offered him a free country cottage on his Cherkley estate. Bevan declined on the grounds that it would be 'improper' for him and his wife Jennie Lee to live 'within the shadow of his castle walls'.

Michael Foot, who regarded himself as Bevan's natural successor, took a different view. He had what the Beaverbrook entourage called 'a tied cottage' on the Cherkley estate for many years. He was an intimate friend of Beaverbrook and though their political views were were wide apart, in Foot's eyes the Old Man could do no wrong.

Beaverbrook was rich before he entered politics and this was a great advantage because political life is very demanding on time and MPs are and always have been grossly underpaid. I have always believed that MPs have been mistaken in suspecting that the public at large would be incensed if they voted themselves pay increases which put them at a proper professional level. I know of several MPs, like Chris Chataway and Sir Anthony Royle, who could have served the country well but just could not afford to stay in full-time politics, which ministerial office demands. I know of several ministers who were relieved when they lost a general election because it meant that they could earn some money to replenish their depleted resources.

Others, of course, are so dedicated to political life that financial stringency does not seem to worry them. The shining example is Enoch Powell. Though he is far from well off he refuses to take any pay rise which MPs vote themselves until the following election when the voters can renew their contract with him on the new pay terms or reject it if they wish.

It is understandable that when Labour has been responsible for such penal levels of taxation for the promotion of Socialist policies, so many of which are patently wasteful, that there should be public resentment against Socialist ministers who, somehow, accumulate wealth. How many back-bench MPs acquire considerable fortunes while continuing in politics, where their modest incomes are public knowledge, is also a common cause of wonder.

In the past some of them, like Bevan, claimed to have made it through freelance journalism, but knowing what even big names are paid for this, it is not often an acceptable explanation.

The public itself tends to be ambivalent even to Socialist MPs. I once received the private bank statement of Harold Lever, then a financial adviser to the Labour government, showing that he was overdrawn at the bank. It had been sent to me by someone who may have recovered it from a dustbin with the argument, 'How can a man who is overdrawn in his private account get the country out of its financial mess?'

Of course, as Lever laughingly explained after I had returned his property to him, the way to make proper use of money is to borrow it at low rates and then use it creatively to make more. A Tory could not have put it more succinctly.

Lever is one of those anomalies – a Socialist millionaire in his own right who also has a very rich wife. He may do a great deal for charity but some of his colleagues deplore it when stories of his lush life appear in the gossip columns.

Another Socialist acquaintance who was not averse to acquiring great wealth and hanging on to it was the late Sir Leslie Plummer, Labour MP for Deptford. When he left the *Daily Express* to take charge of Labour's disastrous groundnuts scheme in Tanganyika, I was present at the farewell dinner which Beaverbrook gave for him. The Old Man handed him a going-away gift from the staff, then announced 'And this is my personal present', passing over a cheque. Rising to speak Plummer tried to avoid looking at the cheque and was astonished when he could no longer restrain his curiosity and he saw the value – £10,000, free of tax, a sizeable sum in those days. He summoned up a brilliant remark, 'All that I have I owe to Lord Beaverbrook. All that I owe he has now taken care of.'

In fact Plummer owed nothing. With his wife Beattie, who was a key and highly controversial figure in the career of Harold Wilson, as I mentioned in Chapter Twenty-five, he bought a notable country house and estate called Berwick Hall in Essex where she continued to live and entertain in some splendour long after his death in 1963.

When rich Socialists are questioned about their wealth they almost invariably take refuge in the transparent argument, 'It's the system we want to change. Meanwhile you can't abstract me from the system,' meaning, 'You can't blame me for taking personal advantage of it.' The Tory money-maker is on a much more honest wicket: 'We want everybody to make profits, which are good for the country, so there is no reason why I should not make my share.'

As recent cases have shown, it is essential that political money-makers should be more circumspect than ordinary members of the public, not only because they are in the public eye but because it is expected of them. John Cordle, the Tory MP for Bournemouth, who was forced out of Parliament for allegedly failing to declare an interest which had brought him a trivial sum, would not have been treated so viciously in any other walk of professional life.

While making general inquiries into the financial affairs of several politicians I discovered an astonishing tax concession which enables some of them to retain most of their earnings if they care to make use of it.

The concession arises out of the fact that in Britain senior ministers, especially Prime Ministers, are permitted to remove masses of documents they have accumulated when they are voted out of office or retire and to regard them as their personal property.

Take the case of a minister selling his memoirs outright to a publishing company for say £250,000. A professional writer, or an amateur who produced a highly successful first book, would be required to pay income tax, mostly at 83 per cent, on the whole of such a sum at the time of writing, barring the small amount deductible as expenses, which is why the Frederick Forsyths and Alistair Macleans quit the country for tax havens.

But a clever accountant acting for a politician can present a different case. He argues that the £250,000 really represents two payments – one for the expertise and effort in writing the script, the other for the value of the information in the documents used by the author in preparing it.

Only the part paid for the actual writing carries full income tax. The other part carries only capital gains of 30 per cent because the papers are 'assets' which the author has transferred to the purchaser.

With most politicians it can be argued that they cannot be expected to have special literary merit and that the saleability of their book depends mainly on the content, especially when the book has been produced in a short time.

Once this is conceded by the Inland Revenue, the accountant suggests that out of the £250,000 perhaps £25,000, or at the most

£50,000, represents the value of the writing. Income tax has to be paid on this but it can be spread over several years, as in the case of professional authors. On the £200,000 only 30 per cent is payable so the politician ends up with about £150,000 tax paid. If the contract with the publisher can first be arranged so that it states that £200,000 or more is for 'assets' the case is virtually cast iron.

The Inland Revenue may claim that this arrangement is not restricted to politicians but very few other people could qualify to use it because the inspectors insist that the documents must have a 'unique' value. However many papers an ordinary author may gather in years of research on an authoritative book, they are unlikely to be judged 'unique'.

My inquiries showed that this form of tax avoidance was first used by a former Tory Prime Minister. Marcia has confirmed to me that it was used by Wilson in connection with the memoirs he sold to the *Sunday Times*, a large number of documents being handed over, including the thick report on the incidents surrounding Profumo sent to Wilson by Stephen Ward, the osteopath.

It could not have been used by Heath because his highly success-ful books to date have not been based on documents with unique value. In theory, the option should be open to him if and when he comes to write his memoirs, as it will to Wilson with the record of his second term as Prime Minister, which he is now writing. But I have been told that under recent Labour legislation the 'unique papers' device may no longer be admissible.

In spite of Wilson's large, tax-paid lump sum from his first book he is not a rich man or certainly does not give any impression of being so. His flat in Ashley Gardens, which I have visited, is a modest abode for a former Prime Minister. His country home, Grange Farm at Great Missenden, cost about £17,000 and may now be worth double, while his bungalow in the Scillies is in no way impressive.

Still, as a fair-shares-for-all Socialist, he has not done badly and with his full-blown memoirs to follow the rather meatless books on the Labour government he has produced so far, his bank balance should remain at a healthy level.

It was because so many Labour politicians adopt a double stan-dard attitude to money, castigating others who acquire it while securing it themselves, that so much interest was aroused by what came to be known as the land deals affair in 1974.

As I was very much involved in this and, in fact, initiated the storm which broke over Wilson and members of his Kitchen Cabinet, I am in a position to say at the outset that he was in no way personally involved in the deals. Neither did he stand to gain anything from them in any way. But the way his name was introduced by others into the deals generated national interest and concern simply because those who were set to benefit were Socialist, the possible profits were huge and they centred on speculation in land, which Labour was supposed to abhor.

In his over-late statement to the Royal Commission on the Press, Wilson complained about Fleet Street's handling of the land deals affair, particularly by the *Daily Mail* and the *Daily Express*. The *Daily Mail* reports involving Ronald Milhench, a Wolverhampton entrepreneur who was eventually sent to prison, centred on a letter which proved to be a forgery and was suspected of being so by that newspaper. The *Daily Express* report under my name, which triggered off the controversy, was quite a different matter. It was based on three genuine letters and it was these which caused Wilson and his Kitchen Cabinet most concern.

Exactly how these letters came into my possession does nothing to support Wilson's contention about journalists scouring the country for damaging information, though I can understand why he believed this. Nor was there any justification for his belief that the *Daily Express* printed the report as part of a circulation war with the *Daily Mail*. This is what happened, according to documents, notes and a legal deposition which I made at the time.

In March 1974 a Birmingham reader, of whom I had never heard, telephoned with a claim that he had in his possession a letter which indicated that Wilson's name was involved in a proposed deal over 40 acres of building land at Solihull. The reader, who was an estate agent, felt this was wrong because the Labour government had been so hard on land and property speculators. Further the proposed deal involved a Birmingham man who was then an undischarged bankrupt, a Mr Victor Harper.

Through this reader I secured a copy of a letter which was from the Clerk of the Warwickshire County Council to Mr Harper. Dated 11 September 1972, when Wilson was leader of the opposition, it began, 'I have had passed to me by the Rt Hon. Harold Wilson MP, the enquiry you made of him for advice regarding possible future planning permission to develop in the Solihull area.' Harper was not a constituent of Wilson, who sat for Huyton, Lancs.

As it transpired, Wilson was emphatically not involved in the deal, nor did I ever suggest that he was, but the Clerk's letter showed why my informant had suspected otherwise.

My inquiries showed that the 40 acres of land, called Jerrings Hall Farm on the edge of the green belt, belonged to a seventy-year-old gentleman from whom Harper had secured a binding option to develop the land. Harper was a business associate of Anthony Field, Marcia's brother, who was not only a golfing friend of Wilson's but at the relevant time had been helping him in his office in the House of Commons. He had also been involved in previous land deals with Mr Harper.

In a letter to Field which began, 'My dear Tony,' and was addressed to Wilson's office at the House of Commons on 8 August 1972, Harper asked for assistance concerning the Jerrings Hall land. He wanted help in finding out when residential or any other planning application would be approved. His letters showed that his own efforts to secure the information direct from the local authorities had failed.

A fortnight later a letter was sent from Field's office on notepaper headed 'From the Rt Hon. Harold Wilson, MP' to the Clerk of the Warwickshire County Council requesting the information on Harper's behalf. It had been signed 'per pro H. A. Field' by a secretary but it was understandable why the Clerk should think that the request for information had been passed to him by Wilson. Indeed, Wilson himself was to tell Parliament later that it had been sent 'on his behalf'.

It seemed to me that the letter had been sent from Field's office in the belief that the use of Wilson's name and notepaper might induce the Council to part with the information to Harper more readily, which in fact it did not. This belief was confirmed a few days later when I secured a copy of the 'My dear Tony' letter which Harper had originally sent to Field.

Having decided that the facts merited a report in the *Daily Express* I consulted the library cuttings on Anthony Field and discovered that some three weeks previously the *Daily Mail* had written a detailed report about 30 acres of land at Ince-in-Makerfield, near Wigan, which Field and Harper had bought for £27,231 and sold to Milhench for £300,000. I had not read it previously and it had passed almost without comment because it had been tucked away inside the paper. Had it been on the front page it would have caused a political furore.

The *Mail* report showed that the Wigan deal involved a company registered in the Isle of Man where the tax situation is easier. Three mortgagees were named in the official records – Field and his two sisters, Marcia and Peggy. £103,000 provided to the company by the Field family was for the purpose of securing more development land at Ince-in-Makerfield, the site of what became known as the 'slag heaps' or the 'Wigan Alps'.

The situation looked invidious because earlier in the year Wilson had charged the Tories with setting free 'the speculators in land, property, commodities and finance to make the biggest and most provocative capital gains in British history'.

When my first report about the Jerrings Hall deal letters appeared on the front page of the *Express* on 3 April, the *Mail* immediately followed up in its next edition with a story based on the forged Milhench letter bearing the forged signature of Wilson.

As it was based on fraud the Milhench affair was a red herring but it took the spotlight off the Jerrings Hall deal, which set more difficult political problems for Wilson, who by then had become Prime Minister.

Tory politicians realized this and, with encouragement from me, did what they could in Parliament to pin the Prime Minister down. Wilson's position regarding his association with the Fields was not helped when it became known that the owner of Jerrings Hall Farm was disputing the validity of the option which Harper had already sold to a house-building company, for what the latter called a 'very substantial sum'.

Wilson's immediate reaction to the newspaper report was to issue writs for libel against the *Express* and the *Mail*. The writs followed the tabling of questions in Parliament referring to the way his private office was being run. There was even a Labour call for a parliamentary inquiry and the setting up of a select committee to 'inquire into the circumstances in which the House of Commons stationery and accommodation has been used to further private land deals'.

All Wilson needed to do when questioned in the Commons was to say that Field had taken this action without consulting him, if this was the case, as I suspected. On the morning of 5 April, when he was due to respond in Parliament, I was telephoned by Wigg who told me that Wilson had been advised to make a personal statement, explaining that in view of the concern expressed by MPs he would have an inquiry made into the matter and when that was completed would report to Parliament.

He could not be questioned on such a statement and by the time the inquiry had been completed much of the heat could be expected to have gone out of the issue, whatever the result of it. Wigg understood that Wilson had accepted this advice but, if that had been true, he had certainly changed his mind by the time he rose to speak.

He launched into a vigorous defence of Field and Marcia, claiming, to ribald laughter, that what they were involved in was not land speculation but land reclamation. By that time it was known that the 30 acres Field had bought near Wigan in 1967 had been a huge slag heap. Field had sold the slag and was understood to have made a turnover of more than £150,000 in his first year's trading. He then secured planning permission to turn the cleared site into an industrial estate and the Ince Council had spent £180,000 building an access road to it. It was for these reasons that he had been able to sell the site to Milhench for £300,000, though he was never paid following Milhench's eventual imprisonment.

Wilson's speech in which he said that the letter from Harper had been forwarded 'on his behalf' resulted in further questions in Parliament which were to continue for many months. Tory MPs were determined to harry him on various statements he had made in defence of the Fields in the hope of being able to accuse him of misleading the House, which could carry serious consequences. They also wanted an explanation of why he had defended the Fields so vigorously at what looked like personal political risk. They were wasting their time. The land deals affair was to prove to be an excellent example of how a politician can stave off trouble by stretching an embarrassing issue until Parliament, the public and the press gets bored with it – what I call the 'kick it about until you lose it' technique.

The long summer recess is of course the first objective because memories fade between August and November, which is a very long time indeed in politics. Later, I learned that the Tory leadership, headed by Edward Heath, were in no mood to continue harrying Wilson on the land deals or anything else. In what might be called 'the negative pursuit of power' the last thing they wanted was to precipitate a general election at that time or in the near future.

Eventually Wilson withdrew his libel actions against the *Express* and against me, received no damages and paid his own costs – amounting to some £4,000. In court his solicitors claimed that he had brought the action 'solely with a view to clearing his reputation'. In fact when he started both actions he was demanding 'exemplary damages'. All he secured by way of apology was an admission that the articles might have been capable of being misunderstood.

To date, Wilson has never satisfactorily explained what happened over the Jerrings Hall letter. An explanation could have been forced when he complained about it to the Royal Commission on the Press, but he avoided being questioned there. In his Press Commission statement Wilson also objected to publication by the *Daily Mail* of a photograph taken at a conference in Birmingham showing him with Milhench and Harper, suggesting that there was a huge crowd present on the occasion and that he just happened to be passing by. In fact the two men were friends of Tony Field who was also in the photograph and was a close friend of Wilson's.

Recently Marcia has told me that the land deals affair ruined her brother financially:

We lost all the money we put into the land deals. Milhench never paid up, and after the adverse publicity we could not sell the land. My brother went broke over it and now works mainly in Saudi Arabia. I am not well off myself. What little I made out of my book went mainly to the taxman. My London house does not belong to me, I rent it. My cottage in Bucks is quite small. I once had three houses on my hands because I was trying to sell one to pay for the cottage. I have since got rid of it.

There are some who admire a politician who can exercise obstructive devices. All Prime Ministers have been guilty of it to some extent. When Macmillan was to explain some embarrassing truth which had been leaked to the Press he would invariably try to dodge round it by pointing out, 'I am not responsible for what appears in the Press' or 'Honourable Members should not believe all that they read in the Press', hoping that the next parliamentary question would be called before dangerous probing could be taken further, as often happened.

I cannot say that, as either an occasional observer in the Press Gallery of the Commons or as a taxpayer, I found these evasions laudable on any score.

*Chapter Twenty-nine*

# Achievement of Arms

THE general effect of the political shift to the Left on Britain's defences can be illustrated by a true story which cost me a great deal of effort for no reward. After Labour achieved office in 1964, John Drew, a senior under-secretary at the Defence Ministry, who had been a contact of mine, decided to retire prematurely. Over a farewell lunch, John, who had been in charge of the Intelligence side of defence issues, especially that part involving cover-plans, suggested that we should cooperate in writing a novel. I had at that stage published two which had been modestly successful and John said, 'Look, nobody, not even C. P. Snow, has yet written a novel that really captures the atmosphere of Whitehall and how the machinery works. Why don't I provide the atmosphere, which I know intimately and between us we can work out a scenario which you can write?'

I thought it a good idea and we set about cobbling together a crude scenario which could later be refined. We decided that, as it had become clear that Kim Philby, the KGB spy, could almost certainly have become head of the British Secret Intelligence Service had his position not been prejudiced by the defections of Burgess and Maclean, it would have been even easier for a crypto-Communist MP to become Defence Minister or Prime Minister. That being so, we then had to decide what this man would do during his possibly brief term of office – say two or three years – to please his Russian masters. Obviously everything would have to be done so that it did not appear to be too obviously in the Kremlin's interest, so other excuses would have to be found and the changes would have to be as gradual as could be arranged. We decided that the man would make the following moves.

First he would seek means of cancelling all the future projects of danger to Russia, such as the TSR2 bomber, which was then well on its way towards production. Costs could be made the excuse for this and on economy grounds there could be a big reduction in defence spending all round.

Labour policy, which was anti-colonial, would enable all overseas bases to be closed. These were anathema to the Kremlin and once Aden, the Red Sea base, had been closed down the Russians could quickly move in.

The Forces reserves would be reduced again, with costs and alleged class privilege being the reason for cutting, or hopefully eliminating, the Territorial Army. The Navy, of course, would be a prime target with Russian expansion in sea-power being one of the Kremlin's prime objectives. So there would be an end to naval air-power with the cancellation of the new aircraft-carriers and the scrapping of the existing ships. The Navy could then be reduced to a coastal force.

There would be no air defence of the British homeland, which would be a prime target for Soviet airborne occupation in the event of a European war.

The nuclear deterrent, particularly hated by the Kremlin, would also be run down towards final elimination. There would be increasing pressure for the Americans to relinquish their bases in Britain, though it did not seem likely that any government could accomplish this without the real truth becoming apparent.

The Intelligence and security services would also be cut as part of the 'essential financial economies' to ease the task of the KGB.

Drew and I wrote some 30,000 words of this novel, inventing numerous characters, their wives, families and mistresses. We even had a tentative title, *Achievement of Arms*, but after about six months we had to abandon the project because as fast as we wrote a chapter the Labour government actually did what we predicted, with the exception of running down the deterrent, to which Labour's attitude is a story requiring separate treatment. Not only did the novel become old hat as we wrote it but libellous into the bargain.

This is not to suggest that either the real-life Prime Minister or Defence Minister had Communist leanings, much less that they were agents. What I believe happened was that they were required to take left-wing measures they would have preferred to avoid in order to pacify the demands of the Labour Left wing and its party executive.

I told this story at the time to a crowded Conservative meeting at Hatfield House, chaired by Lord Salisbury, and it became widely known in Whitehall. But it had no effect on the Labour government, which has continued to run down Britain's defences ever since.

Admittedly it has not done as much as the extreme Left would like. The real extremists would like to see Britain defenceless, and the Americans sent home, which would mean the end of NATO – the prime Soviet objective. That has so far not been possible though it is being demanded by Labour Party executives and moves towards ending the US Navy's nuclear base in Britain were promised in the last Labour election manifesto. I have no doubt that the erosion will continue at an increasing pace if Labour remains in power.

The far Left has continued to make outrageous demands for further defence cuts, which the National Executive of the party, loaded with Left-wingers, has sometimes been able to endorse. The technique is the same as that adopted by trade unions with wage demands – make a huge claim then settle for something lower but higher than you would have obtained by making a reasonable demand in the first place.

To what extent this defence gambit by the extreme Left is secretly encouraged by elements of the parliamentary leadership is not known. But there is little doubt that the report of the Labour Party Defence Study Group calling for further enormous cuts, rejected as totally unacceptable by the leadership, will be followed by actual cuts for which the leaders will claim credit on the grounds of being reasonable and having 'defeated' the Left. It was an ardent supporter of the Labour Party who said to me that this report, outrageous though it might seem, was worth millions of roubles to the Kremlin, through the doubt it must sow in the minds of our allies. The foreword was written by Ron Hayward, the Labour Party General Secretary, whose knowledge of defence problems is minimal while the introduction was by Ian Mikardo, whose links with Eastern Europe in trade are extremely close.

Though I have spent a large slice of my life investigating and trying to expose the machinations of the extreme Left against the interests of the country I love, there is one aspect of them which remains a mystery – the extremists' attitude towards the British nuclear deterrent.

When Wilson was striving to win the general election of 1964 he virtually committed himself to abandoning the four Polaris missile submarines which were being built to take over the H-bomb delivery task from the RAF. Now in 1978 – fourteen years later – the Labour government is investing hundreds of millions of pounds to ensure that the Polaris deterrent will continue to be effective against Russia throughout the 1980s. To this end it is carrying out underground nuclear tests. Yet the Labour Left-wingers in Parliament are almost silent about it. If they wanted to protest they would have a cast-iron case. Wilson promised to get rid of Polaris, built it up instead and now Callaghan is carrying on with it. Why don't the Left extremists complain?

The situation is rather like the Sherlock Holmes story of the dog that didn't bark. Why doesn't the dog bark? I have asked this question at all possible levels without adequate answer. The Whitehall view seems to reside in the belief that for some inexplicable reason the Russians do not want their Left-wing representatives in the British Parliament to make too much fuss.

This failure to give more than a muted yelp was particularly well demonstrated in June 1974 when I reported that the government was about to test a much-improved nuclear warhead for its Polaris missiles at an underground test site in the USA. If true, this was proof that the Wilson government had agreed to massive new investment to keep the deterrent in being, in total contradiction to the election manifesto statement.

There was some reaction by a few Left-wingers claiming in newspapers that 'all hell would break loose' if my report was confirmed. In fact when Wilson later admitted that the test had already taken place their objections were barely audible. Even when a further test explosion was carried out there was no outcry from the Left though it meant that production of 100 new Polaris warheads could be started.

Roy Mason, then the Defence Minister, told me that the decisions to stage the tests had been taken by the Cabinet Subcommittee on Defence with Wilson in the chair. Foot and Wedgwood Benn had not even been informed about it and they made little, if any, private protest afterwards.

Before looking closer at this mystery I must disabuse the reader of any suspicion that the British deterrent is so small that the Russians do not care about it anyway. That could not be further from the truth. On most days, the British Polaris missiles could destroy up to twenty Russian cities at a few minutes' notice, for because of their relatively small numbers they are aimed at cities rather than at military targets to achieve maximum deterrent effect.

The potency of between sixteen and sixty-four H-bombs delivered by Polaris, depending on the availability of the submarines, is illustrated by a story told to me by Harold Macmillan concerning a visit which he paid to Washington accompanied by Sir William Penney (now Lord) to discuss nuclear-weapons issues. Penney, a rather dry and deceptively ingenuous-looking man, was asked how many Russian H-bombs would be needed to knock out Britain in his opinion. He replied in his slow drawl, 'I think five would finish us or shall we say eight to be on the safe side.' Macmillan thought 'to be on the safe side' was hilarious.

There is a further reason why the Russians respect the British deterrent. Unlike the American submarine-launched missiles they are not under long-distance electronic control.

Ever since the days of President Kennedy, physical, apart from political, control of America's enormous nuclear strike force has resided in the homeland, however far away the submarines or planes may be. Until a radio signal, transmitted via satellites, is sent to the strategic force the nuclear bombs and warheads could do no more damage than dummies. This system has been set up and refined at enormous cost to increase control until the very last moment of fatal decision.

Britain's missiles and bombs are under no such control. The British Navy was offered such a 'permissive link' system but refused, partly to save the considerable expense of equipping every warhead with an electronic lock and a special signalling system to open it, but mainly because the Sea Lords were confident that any officers responsible enough to command a Polaris submarine could do without such a refinement.

The result has made the four British submarines and their missiles the joker in the deterrent pack. If British missiles were launched in anger against the Soviet Union, the Russians would quickly know that they had come from a submarine but would be unable to discern whether they were British or American. Being unwilling to take a chance, the Kremlin might then be driven to order instant retaliation against both countries before waiting for more warheads to arrive. So the British with their relatively tiny deterrent fleet have the physical capacity to embroil the United States in an all-out nuclear war against its wishes.

From time to time the Russians have urged the Americans to put pressure on the British to do something to eliminate this danger, but without result.

That this is still the case has been confirmed to me as recently as 1978 by a most senior British admiral who was involved in the earlier decision to turn down the American offer of arrangements for fitting 'permissive links'. He now regards this aspect of the British deterrent as being its most important attribute. 'If the Americans looked like backing down on using their strategic weapons for fear of retaliation against their own cities they know we could trigger things off on our own,' he told me. 'That would make them think again. More importantly, the Russians are aware of the situation and it strengthens the deterrent effect of both the British and the American systems.'

The British position is also stronger than the Left has been led to believe on another count. When the Polaris missiles became operational in the sixties, Parliament, the public and the Press were given to understand that the RAF V-bombers would cease to operate in a strategic role and their large stocks of H-bombs would be gradually eliminated. They would still have a nuclear role but it would be tactical – i.e., restricted to battlefield operations with smallish weapons. No such thing ever happened and I now have the authority of Air Chief Marshal Sir David Evans, the Commander-in-Chief of Strike Command for saying so.

The RAF's stockpile of thermonuclear (H-bomb) weapons has been steadily improved with new marks of more effective and more accurate bombs but it has in no way been reduced. The Vulcan bombers assigned to the NATO Supreme Commander are in the strategic role, i.e., for long-distance nuclear attack. The new Tornado strike bombers (formerly called MCRA), of which the RAF is scheduled to receive 220, will have a similar strategic capability so far as large areas behind the Iron Curtain are concerned.

Previously the nuclear bombs which would be carried by RAF planes in Germany were American and therefore under US control with a lock system. Even that was changed by a Labour government. They are now all-British and under the British government's control.

The only basic change that occurred in the late sixties was that the

RAF ceased to be responsible for the standby quick-reaction alert which was taken over by the Polaris vessels.

It is hard to believe that this information has not been available to left-wing members of the Cabinet like Michael Foot who, for years before achieving office, walked with the Aldermaston marchers and was vocal in other aspects of the Campaign for Nuclear Disarmament. Indeed, how Foot, with such an oversize conscience, has been able to go along with the pro-nuclear decisions made by Labour governments since he joined the front bench is a further mystery.

Of course, there is a major difference, so far as defence is concerned, between being in government and in opposition. Apart from the sudden accession of being responsible for defending the nation in an emergency – and that powerfully concentrates the mind – there is the undoubted fact that oppositions do not want to know the truth because it would hinder their opportunities for making allegations against the government which they would know to be untrue. So long as they only *suspect* that they are false or can even convince themselves that they may even be true they are not restricted in making what turn out to be irresponsible accusations in their speeches inside and outside Parliament.

What opposition politicians like is to be accurately informed on defence matters but not by any official source. This is why journalists like myself are used by them. They can ignore what I tell them when it suits.

I know of only one occasion when an opposition leader decided to be officially briefed on a highly secret defence matter and the result was disastrous. This is what happened.

In 1959 the chief scientist of the Defence Ministry, Sir Frederick Brundrett, a remarkable civil servant who was as straight as a gun barrel, approached me for help about the nuclear deterrent. At that time the RAF had more than a hundred nuclear weapons in its stockpile and was capable of doing enormous damage to Russia – as the Kremlin well knew.. In fact 80 per cent of the first nuclear retaliatory strike from the West would have been carried out by the RAF. Brundrett and the rest of the Defence Ministry planners were deeply concerned by the attitude being taken by George Brown and other Labour leaders to the deterrent. For political motives they were claiming that it was a useless waste of money and was too small and inefficient. This was having an effect on RAF morale but more importantly it was making inroads into American support for the

British deterrent. The Pentagon was fully aware of the true situation but Congress and the Senate were impressed when a person calling himself the Shadow Minister for Defence was making these allegations about the British position.

I explained to Brundrett that the fault did not lie with Brown who, though he could become the real Defence Minister at any time, was not given the true information about the nuclear deterrent because of the secrecy rules. Brundrett immediately offered to tell Brown what he called 'the nuclear facts of life' if I would arrange it.

Brown agreed to consider the proposition and I put on a lunch for the three of us at the Arts Theatre Club. Brundrett convinced Brown that he should know the secret facts and they arranged to meet for this purpose, which was duly done, Brown agreeing to pass for information on to his leader, Gaitskell. I already knew the information which was to be imparted but, for appearances' sake, Brundrett thought it better not to discuss any secret matters while I was present.

I assumed that, apart from settling the bill for the lunch, my contribution would end there, but it was not to be.

A few days later Macmillan was being questioned in the House about security leaks following an article of mine reporting that new atomic plants coming into commission would greatly increase the output of nuclear weapons. Brown knew this, having been briefed about it by Brundrett, but nevertheless to needle the Prime Minister had tabled a parliamentary question asking whether this disclosure had been made with Macmillan's authority.

Macmillan made his usual bland, stone-walling defence but Brown grew so angry that in the cut and thrust of the cross-questioning he demanded, 'Will you undertake an inquiry to establish which official adviser of the Ministry of Defence was responsible for claiming to have authority to disclose these figures on H- and A-bomb stocks?'

Immediately Gaitskell, Bevan and others of the Labour pack joined in the hunt with demands for an inquiry which could, of course, have led to Brundrett's disgrace.

When the agency tapes on this row were passed to me in the *Daily Express* office I was horrified and rushed down to the Commons to see Brown, who knew that Brundrett's purpose in giving this information to me, as it had been to him, had been to enhance the deterrent effect of Britain's H-bomb stocks both in Russian and

American eyes. While admitting that he had tried to get Brundrett named, he seemed astonished that I should be furious about it.

'But it would have involved him publicly in a major security scandal when all he has done is to try to help you and the country,' I protested.

'But that's exactly what we want – big headlines,' Brown responded. 'We're going into an election soon. We need big headlines!'

I seemed unable to convince George that he had done anything reprehensible. Once the scent of power was in the air – though distantly as it turned out – all moves were legitimate.

Even more strangely, Macmillan, who greatly admired Brundrett, thought it had all been fair game when I asked him about it much later. Least disturbed of all was Brundrett himself, who simply shrugged and said, 'Well you know what politicians are like,' when I saw him at his club that evening.

Since then defence has continued to be a political football to be kicked in different directions by Left and Right and, with annual costs running so high in spite of the run-down – about £7,000 million – this will continue to the detriment of morale and fighting efficiency.

Marshal of the RAF Sir Jack Slessor was not exaggerating when he said, 'The most important social service a government can do for its people is to keep them alive and free.' But the Left will continue to demand that defence be sacrificed to provide money for other social services.

*Chapter Thirty*

⌒⟶ℳℳ⟵⌒

# Missiles and Ministers

IN the piping days of Britain's power, politics were dominated by ideas generated and projected by statesmen. In the 1950s and 60s and to a considerable degree still, the international political scene has been dominated by nuclear missiles generated by scientists. Attitudes between East and West have changed as the Russians have caught up with the Americans in the capacity to produce and deliver weapons of mass destruction, then been surpassed by some further American 'breakthrough', like the multi-headed missile, only to catch up again and even overtake the USA in total destructive power.

It so happens that during that time nuclear missiles also exerted great influence on the careers of British politicians in events with which I was closely associated.

The first politician to become what might be called a victim of hardware was Duncan Sandys when he became Minister of Defence, as the office was then called, early in 1957. Sandys, who had been associated with countering both the German V1 flying bomb and the V2 rocket, was fascinated by the possibilities of the missile in future warfare, as were most of us who witnessed the astonishing extent to which German rocket scientists had progressed in so many directions in such a short time. In what became a watershed in British defence policy, with repercussions still being felt, particularly by the RAF, Sandys's 1957 defence White Paper announced that in future reliance would be placed on robot missiles instead of the manned bomber and the manned fighter.

The USA was producing a giant intercontinental missile called Atlas, capable of obliterating Russian cities from the US mainland, as a deterrent to war. Sandys and his colleagues secured enough information to make a scaled-down version, called Blue Streak, with range enough to threaten Soviet cities from Britain.

The missiles were to be buried deep in the ground in pits or 'silos' so that Russia would have difficulty in knocking them out in a surprise attack.

During this interlude while Blue Streak was under development some false Intelligence suggesting that the Russians were far more advanced in military rocketry than was true reached Washington. There was panic about a 'missile gap' which was resolved by a deal with Britain. The USA rushed through the production of a much smaller bombarding rocket called Thor to be sited on the east coast of England. Thors duly arrived in Britain to minimal local objections in 1958 and remained at immediate readiness, warheads and all, until they were phased out in 1963, when Atlases and other American-based missiles were available.

Blue Streak was a technical success but the costs of putting the missiles underground and the rapid development of Russian counter-missiles of such enormous destructive power that the few Blue Streaks Britain could afford might not survive them even deep down in rock, killed the entire project.

The end of Blue Streak as a weapon – it staggered on for several years as a satellite launcher – was expedited by the development of an even more remarkable American missile called Skybolt. This had the advantage of being launched from underneath an aeroplane which could stand off at a safe 1,000 miles from its target and did not have to be kept in a fixed vulnerable position like Blue Streak.

The advent of Skybolt meant that the RAF was back in the big-bomb business with manned aircraft, as the air marshals had always convinced themselves they would be ever since Duncan Sandys had infuriated them by remarking that he could see no point in spending millions just to enable pilots to drill holes in the sky. Skybolt would stretch the life of the V-bombers and keep their crews flying. (The RAF would have been responsible for operating Blue Streak but the air marshals hated the idea of having to pilot down holes when they could be in the sky.)

Because of my friendship with Sandys and several of his chief defence advisers, the *Daily Express*, with Beaverbrook's backing, had promoted the missile, so its demise supported Mountbatten's private jibe that whatever and whoever Beaverbrook supported would be bound to come unstuck.

Sandys had championed Blue Streak so strongly that he could no longer remain as Defence Minister when cancellation, with write-off losses of £100 million, became inevitable. He was moved sideways to the Aviation Ministry in 1959 and Harold Watkinson (now Lord) replaced him.

Watkinson soon disposed of Blue Streak but after he had been in the job a couple of years news began to leak from Washington that Kennedy was about to cancel Skybolt because of runaway costs and extreme technical problems. The only possible successor was the submarine-launched American missile Polaris, which Lockheed had been pushing hard at the British for some time. Watkinson, who favoured the RAF just as Sandys had almost dismembered it, was determined to secure Skybolt and hated the idea of Polaris so much that when one of his staff brought back a plastic model of Polaris from a visit to the USA he insisted that it should be removed from the ministry.

On my advice Beaverbrook had also supported Skybolt, so again Mountbatten's law seemed justified.

Watkinson, with whom I had also become friendly after an icy start, was replaced by Peter Thorneycroft (now Lord), who assured me that everything would be done to secure Skybolt and I and others were urged to go on clamouring for it in the newspapers. However, Britain could not afford to complete the development when Kennedy eventually offered all the development work to date gratis.

At a historic conference at Nassau in the Bahamas in December 1962 Macmillan agreed to take Polaris. The RAF was out of the big-bomb business and the Navy was in. No sensible punter would have backed the Navy to win the battle against the RAF but it had a powerful ally in the form of the 'Zuckbatten axis' – the joint action of Mountbatten, then Chief of the Defence Staff, and Zuckerman, the chief defence scientist, who had plugged away for Polaris.

Throughout these various changes, with the inevitable expenses always involved in cancellation, the Labour opposition had been making maximum capital out of the Tories' discomfiture. The reaction of the Labour leadership under Wilson is of considerable historic interest in view of subsequent events.

Ever since Gaitskell's day, left-wing extremists had been urging that Britain should make a unilateral gesture of goodwill towards the

world – and of course Russia in particular – by renouncing nuclear
weapons. With a general election not far away, Polaris became the
target and Wilson denigrated it to the maximum extent by referring
to it as 'the so-called nuclear, so-called independent, so-called deterrent.' He made promises indicating to his left-wing supporters that
he would abolish Polaris or at least renegotiate the Nassau agreement. He achieved office in 1964 and twelve years later when he
resigned, he had agreed to the spending of a further £400 million to
keep the Polaris deterrent in being throughout the 1980s!

There were several reasons why Wilson changed his mind as soon
as he was made privy to the facts of atomic life. From detailed
briefings, he was quickly convinced that the Navy's capability to
take out twenty Russian cities was a deterrent really to be feared. He
was also impressed by the degree of independence of the British
Polaris missiles, which I have already explained. Being master of
decision over the use of such power strengthens the position and
confidence of any political leader in international affairs, as witness
the attitude of the Russian leaders since they acquired nuclear
strength.

Wilson realised too, as Callaghan has, that with the French
determined to produce an effective nuclear deterrent of their own, as
they undoubtedly have, it was not in Britain's or Europe's interests
to allow them a European nuclear monopoly.

He learned that Polaris was an important contribution to NATO
and that its removal would be greatly resented there, that there were
stockpiles of nuclear bombs in Cyprus just as firmly committed to
the defence of Turkey, Iran and Pakistan, and that others in Singapore were committed to the South East Asia Treaty Organization.

Wilson also discovered, to his relief I believe, that the building of
the submarines under the direction of my old shooting companion,
the excellent Vice-Admiral Sir Hugh 'Rufus' Mackenzie, had been
pushed ahead so swiftly that cancellation costs would be astronomi-
cal. So he made the only sensible choice between the fantasy of
nuclear disarmament and the reality of nuclear might. His only
concession to the Left on his Polaris promise was to cancel arrangements to build and equip a fifth submarine, which the Tories would
almost certainly have done anyway.

I enjoyed myself over the years baiting Wilson and his left-wing
supporters for their continuation of Polaris, particularly as Labour
election manifestoes have continued the fiction that it will be elim-

inated. I was particularly delighted to be able to announce that Wilson had sanctioned further nuclear tests.

The way the continuation of substantial spending on Polaris and other nuclear weapons has been achieved in spite of the presence of anti-nuclear figures like Michael Foot, Anthony Greenwood (now Lord), Frank Cousins and others in the Cabinet is illuminating in itself. The decisions were taken by a standing Cabinet Committee from which such people have been carefully excluded. The same is true about other tough decisions which would not appeal to the Left, such as the use of Special Air Service troops against the IRA in Ulster. They too are taken by a small and carefully selected committee.

The Labour Cabinet ministers responsible for retaining and refurbishing Polaris have nevertheless felt constrained to avoid offending the Left by not being too brash about it.

The kind of behaviour this fear occasioned was demonstrated on the day when the first Polaris missile submarine, *Resolution*, was handed over to the Fleet, 2 October 1967. The Navy celebrated its accession to the responsibility for deterring a nuclear attack on the nation with a ceremony at the shipyard at Barrow-in-Furness, but not a single representative of the government attended it because on Wilson's orders they had boycotted the event. The official excuse was that the ceremony conflicted with the Labour Party conference opening at Scarborough on the same day, but the journey by helicopter for the Defence Secretary, Denis Healey, who could have been spared that day, was only half an hour.

The last thing the Labour leader wanted was for the Left wing sitting in the conference hall to be reminded of his promise to 'renegotiate' the Nassau agreement.

The boycott was particularly shameful because the Navy needed every possible boost to its morale after the damage inflicted by the decision to scrap the aircraft-carriers.

I did my best to expose it, as I did with the government's even more reprehensible snub to the RAF as a result of the Polaris take-over. For years a few dedicated aircrews worked almost intolerable hours to ensure that, in the event of a surprise Russian attack, a sufficient number of V-bombers would survive to deliver a devastating attack on Soviet cities. They, their planes and their bombs were kept in such a state of readiness that they could be airborne and out of danger of destruction on the ground within a couple of minutes, as

I frequently witnessed. The arrival of Polaris meant that they could at last stand down so far as the 'quick-reaction alert' was concerned and they could reasonably have expected some formal ministerial commendation for a job superbly done. None was forthcoming because that too would have involved a ceremony likely to attract publicity for Polaris. The government made it clear that any attempt by the RAF or Navy to promote publicity would meet with angry disapproval.

My reports on this situation resulted in a Tory motion of protest, which Labour MPs amended to a motion of congratulation to the RAF on 'being rid of a duty declared by the Labour Party to be incredible, unimpressive and non-deterrent'. Later, Healey sent a personal commendation to Bomber Command.

Power politics even intruded into the selection of the name *Resolution* for the first submarine, though this was in the life of the previous Tory government. The Sea Lords wanted to call it *Revenge*, after famous men-of-war which fought in the Armada battle, the Dutch Wars, Trafalgar and Jutland, and because the name was fitting for a vessel which would be used only in retaliation. The politicians decided that this was rather too inflammatory to the potential enemy so *Revenge* was held back for the name of the fourth submarine, by which time, it was thought, the Kremlin might not be so touchy.

There was a further occasion in which an event concerning Polaris was hushed up for political reasons but this escaped my intelligence net at the time. When *Resolution* went out to Cape Canaveral to carry out its first practice firing of a Polaris missile the British Press was invited to witness the event, which was scheduled for a Monday morning. On the previous Friday an American destroyer, pursuing the wrong course without advising *Resolution*, knocked off the submarine's mast with all the monitoring equipment, a much worse accident only being narrowly avoided.

To hide the Americans' shame, and its own, the Navy needed to get rid of the journalists before bringing in the 7,000 ton submarine with its mast hanging limp. This was achieved by the kind cooperation of the late Hubert Humphrey who happened to be in the area. He agreed to stage a Press conference on the Sunday to which all the British reporters were invited. *Resolution* came into port, a new mast with all parts was flown down and technicians worked all night to get it into position for the morning.

Another deception practised by the Labour leadership on its Left, which has only recently become apparent, centres on the V-bombers, formerly in Bomber Command, now incorporated into Strike Command.

Finding itself saddled with Polaris in 1964 the government was determined to reduce the bomber force of about 180 Victors, Vulcans and Valiants which, with in-flight refuelling, were once capable of delivering two hundred H-bombs on Iron Curtain targets, a formidable deterrent force indeed. Wigg, who, as an ardent supporter of the Army, had always opposed the nuclear deterrent, was in the forefront of this assault as the influential adviser to Wilson. One day in January 1965 he telephoned me with the joyous news, 'You will be surprised, my dear Harry, what the good Lord in his wisdom has done.' He would not explain what he meant but by delving I soon discovered that the RAF's entire fleet of Valiants – some fifty bombers costing £60 million – were about to be scrapped because they were unsafe to fly as a result of metal fatigue. With the resultant need to convert some Victors to in-flight refuelling tankers, the V-bomber force had been cut back to little more than a hundred front-line planes at a stroke.

Nobody in his right mind could accuse George Wigg of being unpatriotic. His delight was simply an expression of the oddball views about Britain's defences held by some Labour politicians. Wigg genuinely believed that the V-bombers were consuming valuable resources which would be better spent on the Army. Fortunately there were others in more powerful positions who disagreed with him.

As a sop to the Left 'disinformation' was gradually put about to the effect that the V-bombers were to be used by NATO tactically and in a conventional role – delivering ordinary weapons on the battlefield instead of carrying big-bang nuclear bombs behind the Iron Curtain. This subterfuge largely succeeded but it was entirely false. The NATO supremo, who is always an American, wanted to retain a strategic strike capability of his own and the V-bombers have continued to provide it to this day. Their H-bombs have been progressively improved as have those carried by the Buccaneer bombers, formerly with the Navy, now with the RAF.

Incidentally a situation, all too typical, was exposed by chance as a result of the scrapping of the Valiants. For five years, thirty of them equipped with nuclear bombs had been operating on behalf of the NATO supremo, then General Lemnitzer, from an airfield at

Marham in Norfolk. When they became unavailable it was found that the Iron Curtain targets to which they had been assigned and on which their crews had trained so laboriously had been fully covered all the time by American nuclear missiles.

What of the future? Labour continues to insist in Parliament that it has no intention of providing a successor to Polaris when the missiles and the submarines become unusable due to age, probably in the 1980s. I have sound reason for believing otherwise. Plans to keep an independent British deterrent going until the end of the century are far advanced inside the Defence Ministry and the planners are confident that, barring a Labour government really dominated by its Left wing, they will be put into effect.

It is hard to escape the conclusion that the Labour and Tory leaderships have had an understanding for several years that the deterrent should be treated as a non-party issue, though this is likely to be denied for party-political reasons. It is certain that at the time of writing a technical decision has been taken during the life of a Labour government to replace the four existing Polaris submarines with new submarines carrying much improved Polaris-type missiles. On cost grounds these are likely to be designed and manufactured in Britain, using much of the Polaris technology but with novel refinements both to the missile and its warhead.

The alternative possibility of buying American cruise missiles – subsonic robot planes which can be launched from aircraft – has been eliminated on two counts. First, because they are slow, they will be susceptible to destruction when the anti-aircraft laser beam becomes operational, perhaps within fifteen years. Secondly, there is a domestic political difficulty about them in a small island. Noisy objectors, like the Friends of the Earth and Campaigners for Nuclear Disarmament, could too easily indulge in demonstrations outside RAF airfields, where planes with large cruise missiles slung below would be only too visible. Demonstrations against submarine-borne missiles, discreetly locked away inside their launching-tubes and for much of their time submerged at sea, are rather more difficult to stage.

*Chapter Thirty-one*

# A Little Ship Goes Missing

FOR the past two years, anti-nuclear lobbyists have exploited the danger that nuclear explosives or even nuclear weapons themselves might fall into the hands of terrorists who could use them for political blackmail on an unparalleled scale. Had they known of a discovery I made in the early seventies they could have made immense political capital out of the terrorist threat years earlier and with far greater force.

A Naval contact in the Ministry of Defence told me how, a little while previously, there had been a terrific scare one dark and dirty night when a small Naval auxiliary was apparently missing in the Irish Sea. The auxiliary, which was unarmed, was carrying Polaris nuclear warheads from Portsmouth to the submarine base at Faslane in Scotland and had failed to report by radio. A destroyer was sent out to find the ship, did so and discovered that the trouble was simply a breakdown of radio equipment. The fear in the Admiralty was that if the ship, called the *Throsk*, really was missing it might have been captured by the IRA, nuclear warheads and all.

How this possibility ever arose staggered me when I learned more about it.

When the Navy took over responsibility for the quick-reaction nuclear deterrent with the entry of the first Polaris submarine into operational service in 1967, the Sea Lords decided that the warheads were just another form of munition and should be treated that way. It was standard practice for the Navy to use its Auxiliary Service for transporting munitions in harbours and around coasts. So the Admiralty decided to continue it, believing – with some truth – that because of the built-in safety devices, nuclear warheads in transit were safer than depth-charges or torpedoes. There was a further advantage in using a vessel classed more as a merchant ship than a warship. In the event of mechanical trouble or bad weather it could put into a civil port without causing a local uproar. No consideration seems to have been given at that stage to the possibility of a nuclear hijack even though, because of the missile firing range in Cardigan Bay, the 1,500-ton, coal-burning *Throsk* had to travel near the Irish coast, and had permission to seek shelter in Irish ports!

Such journeys became a regular ferry service because of a technical problem peculiar to nuclear weapons. The fuses and trigger mechanism need to be checked every few weeks because of the risk of corrosion and other factors which give them a short 'shelf-life'. The facilities for this exist only at the Royal Ordnance Factory at Burghfield, near Reading in Berkshire.

Further, because the internal structure of the Polaris warhead with its three separate bombs is so intricate, the arming mechanism cannot be removed at Faslane. So, winter and summer, for several years little unarmed auxiliaries brought nuclear warheads from Faslane to Portsmouth whence they were taken to Burghfield and then ferried the refurbished weapons back to Faslane.

To understand how this could ever have happened the immense prestige of the Royal Navy has to be appreciated. Over the centuries the Sea Lords had become autocrats, whose decisions were not to be questioned, and when they insisted that they would be responsible for their own transport of nuclear weapons nobody demurred. Even after the scare I have described the transport by sea continued until Sir William Cook, then chief scientist at the Defence Ministry, found out about it and insisted on a change for safety reasons.

By the time this change was made – the weapons are now transported by air or by road under heavy guard – the story was too old to tell in a newspaper so I used it as the basis for a nuclear hijack in a novel I published in 1976 called *The Eye of the Tornado*.

In a brief foreword I acknowledged my indebtedness to 'senior officials present and past, in the Defence Ministry, Royal Navy, the Secret Intelligence Service, and others'.

Inevitably the Prime Minister, James Callaghan, was asked in Parliament what assistance of this nature I had in fact been given. Also inevitably he replied, 'None that I know of.'

He could not have inquired very deeply. Not only was I given technical assistance as stated but the text was read and corrected by very senior government officials. The only concession I was asked to make was to omit reference to Burghfield and name the nearby Atomic Weapon Research Station at Aldermaston as the maintenance depot. This was not a security measure, for it was known that Soviet bloc Intelligence was well aware of Burghfield's function. It was to avoid anti-nuclear demonstrations outside the factory. Aldermaston was used to them.

All this information, given wide publicity in Parliament in questions about the novel, could have been expected to lead to an outcry from the Left, especially in view of my disclosure that the warheads had to be carried in such a state that an expert could make them live by bypassing the arming mechanism. But once again the dog did not bark. I wonder why not.

There was, however, a sequel of a different and more exciting kind which, by good fortune, in the form of a late-evening telephone call from a Foreign Office source, I was able to publicize.

Early in April 1976 the *Sunday Express* began to serialize *The Eye of the Tornado*. On 22 April two Hungarian diplomats, who were Soviet bloc Intelligence agents using their embassy as cover, were arrested after making an early-morning inspection of the Burghfield factory. They were held by police after a car chase and eventually released when they pleaded diplomatic immunity.

It is of interest that while Burghfield is outside the thirty-mile limit to which Russian diplomats are restricted no such restriction is placed on Hungarians, because they impose no limits in their country, where there is little of interest to British Intelligence.

There was some wonder about what these Hungarians could have hoped to obtain by just sitting outside the factory in their car and taking a few photographs. My information suggests that they had been engaged in this occupation on several occasions before and were interested in noting the arrival or departure of convoys of nuclear weapons and the routes they take.

What their precise purpose was in securing this information is never likely to be known. It may have been no more than the itch for knowing everything possible about Britain's nuclear endeavours. Or it may have been to secure information of use to terrorist organizations supported by Soviet bloc Intelligence such as the IRA and the Palestinians.

The government was greatly embarrassed by this incident – or rather by my disclosure of it – because, following Wilson's tradition, Callaghan had been trying to 'make amends' for Heath's courageous expulsion of 105 KGB agents posing as diplomats and trade officials.

For this reason the Foreign Office decided against expelling the two Hungarians, who hotly denied that they had been spying, explaining their presence in the Burghfield area as the result of visiting friends, whom they refused to identify. But within a few weeks they had left Britain – withdrawn back to Budapest.

I can reassure my readers, following a Defence Ministry briefing, that most rigorous safeguards are now in practice to protect nuclear weapons and explosives against hijack or destruction by terrorists. These were introduced after a secret Whitehall conference had agreed that the hijacking of nuclear weapons had become a serious threat and that the government – whatever its complexion – would probably give in to nuclear blackmail if there was only a 10 per cent chance that a terrorist claim to possess nuclear weapons or explosive could be true.

Guards at all the sensitive establishments are armed with machine-guns and any serious attempt to interfere with a convoy would result in a fight 'savage enough to attract the attention of the Army', as a senior Defence Ministry official put it to me.

No legislation was needed for arms to be used at Burghfield, Aldermaston, Faslane and other places under the control of the Defence Ministry but a special law had to be passed to enable guards to be armed at nuclear fuel plants.

Electronic alarms, television monitors and other devices to detect intruders have been fitted at the various establishments and dumps and are regularly tested in mock assaults by the SAS and Commando units. Even the possibility of an armed attack by a sizeable force of terrorists has been catered for and all these precautions are applied to the large numbers of American nuclear weapons stockpiled in Britain.

Recently – and sadly – serious attention is being paid to a new threat – the danger that a nuclear scientist who knows how to assemble a bomb might be kidnapped by terrorists. In case this might seem far-fetched in Britain, I put on record how recently I kept an appointment at the Defence Ministry to interview an old friend who is the number-one nuclear-weapons expert there. He had agreed to a personality profile but by the time I arrived other counsel had prevailed. In the light of Intelligence advice it had been decided that senior nuclear-weapons scientists should henceforth avoid publicity which could draw attention to their identities or their movements. Though a large number of nuclear scientists and technicians are involved in assembling bombs and warheads perhaps only about twenty in Britain have the complete know-how. My friend was one of these.

*Chapter Thirty-two*

# The Destruction of the TSR2

ONE of the most controversial events of the sixties was the scrapping of the TSR2 bomber by the Labour government. Much has been written about this but there are some rather extraordinary facets to the story which are not generally known.

First, I know from my close contacts with George Wigg, while Labour was still in opposition, that the leadership had made up its mind then to scrap the plane, which would have been so much in advance of other comparable machines that it could almost certainly have achieved large export sales. No doubt there were left-wing objections to spending large sums on a new supersonic atomic bomber that would enable Britain and NATO to defend themselves more effectively against the beloved Russians, but it soon became apparent that the real reason for the determination was the Labour view that the TSR2 was some kind of Tory toy and symbol of Tory extravagance.

While having no access to the secret performance estimates for the plane, Wigg had provided Wilson with what he believed were reliable technical details. Wigg's evidence had been derived from a freelance aerospace consultant called Richard Worcester, who published an Intelligence digest on aeronautical affairs, selling mainly in the USA.

Because of the unemployment problems which scrapping of the

TSR2 would cause at the British Aircraft Corporation, Rolls-Royce
and at many subcontractors, Labour made an election promise that
the plane would not be cancelled. But a few months after Labour's
victory Worcester indicated that the policy decision for scrapping
the TSR2, and other British planes, and to buy American instead
had been taken four months before the election.

In a document which he called *Labour's 100 Days* – referring to the
boast Wilson had made of '100 dynamic days' as soon as he achieved
power – he described 'sessions in Westminster with the Labour
leadership'. It implied that his master-plan for cancelling British
combat planes and integrating the aircraft industry with US firms
was accepted as official policy. Later, when I became friendly with
him, he confirmed the details to me personally.

At that time Wilson had given the TSR2 a reprieve following
anti-government protest marches by aircraft workers, but the intention to cancel was already firm.

There were those inside the Defence Ministry who wanted to be
rid of the TSR2 so that more money would be available for new
aircraft-carriers for the Navy. Prominent among these was Sir Solly
Zuckerman, the Chief Scientist, and Lord Mountbatten, Chief of the
Defence Staff.

They fought the battle cleverly and were greatly assisted by the
election of a Labour government already opposed to the TSR2. To
what extent Wilson had been advised by Zuckerman and Mountbatten before the election is not known but Sir Solly was certainly in
contact with him.

There was a chance at that early stage that the Australian
government would place an export order for the TSR2, which could
have enhanced its prospects of survival. But Mountbatten felt
duty-bound to warn the Australians that he believed the plane
would be cancelled. They ordered the American F111 bomber
instead – a decision which they have since regretted.

The new British government was quick to see that the F111, which
was originally to have been made in large numbers for the US
Forces, presented a convenient paper alternative to offer the RAF
and the British public. Healey was learning the American defence
jargon and a term he found especially expedient was 'cost-
effectiveness'. Since the development costs of the F111 were to be
paid by the American taxpayers, he was soon preaching that the
plane should be very cost-effective for Britain.

The extent to which cost-effectiveness, the principle that nothing should be attempted if there is a cheaper way of obtaining the same result, can be misleading was splendidly expressed by Sir Hermann Bondi, when he reached Whitehall. He pointed out that, by that argument, lavatories should never be installed in homes because they are occupied for only 2 per cent of the time. Public conveniences would satisfy the nation's needs more cost-effectively.

The final blow to the TSR2, which was already flying, was delivered in the most astonishing manner at a meeting of the Defence and Overseas Policy Committee, as described to me by a person who attended it.

Following the crash disasters of the Comet airliner, it had become standard practice to test the fuselage and wings of new aircraft in special devices built for the purpose at the Royal Aircraft Establishment at Farnborough, Hampshire. To determine the absolute strength of these parts pressure was progressively applied until they broke. In the case of the TSR2 the wings had withstood more pressure than any previous aircraft since the Valiant bomber, which had been exceptionally strong.

As the meeting opened Denis Healey, the Defence Secretary, remarked to Wilson who was chairing it, 'By the way, Prime Minister, we think you should know that the wing of the TSR2 broke under test at Farnborough yesterday.'

The effect of this news on the politicians who had little technical understanding can be imagined. Among these was Roy Jenkins, the Aviation Minister, who was furious that he had not been told about it because he was responsible for the Farnborough establishment and was there, supposedly, to defend the TSR2. When he returned to his office and the truth about the test was explained to him he was appalled. Nevertheless, any defence of the TSR2 or any other British aircraft he may ever have made was futile. As Aviation Minister he excelled only at defending the cancellations in debate.

The industrial objections to the cancellation of the TSR2 and two other advanced ventures mounted to the extent that TUC chiefs were complaining to Jenkins and there were mass marches and union-sponsored meetings of aircraft workers carrying banners proclaiming that Wilson must go. They were concerned not only about the loss of jobs but the loss of Britain's technological lead. Healey exacerbated the anger by scathing remarks about the air industry chiefs made to myself and other journalists like, 'It's not my job to wet-nurse overgrown and mentally retarded children in the domestic economy.'

The industrial unrest was bad enough but to cancel the TSR2 without a constitutional crisis Wilson felt he had to secure the support of the air marshals, then led by Chief of the Air Staff, Sir Charles 'Sam' Elworthy (now Lord). The only way to do this was to offer an alternative – the firm purchase of the F111 plane from America.

At this stage Wilson and his government were being subjected to American pressure to buy the F111, which incorporated the swing-wing principle designed to give it greater range. Wilson was dependent on the USA for financial aid and Healey had made a friend of Robert McNamara, his American counterpart. McNamara was in domestic political problems over the F111, which was in serious technical trouble. The announcement of an order from Britain for F111s would help him to rebut Congressional claims that the plane was a flop.

As the *Daily Express* was championing the British plane, I was close to the air chiefs who were determined to keep the TSR2, which represented the fruits of their long battle to reverse the Sandys edict that there would be no more manned bombers. Along with other correspondents I was invited in January 1965 to a cocktail party at the Defence Ministry where every air marshal of consequence in the battle was present. We were told, during off-the-record conversations, that the TSR2 was absolutely essential to the defence of the nation and that the F111 just would not do. I was urged to project this view in the newspaper as strongly as possible. With Sir Max Aitken, a former RAF air ace behind me, I had no difficulty in securing plenty of space.

Within a few days I received a telephone call from Group Captain James Wallis, then director of RAF public relations, complaining that I was knocking the F111 too hard, having previously been told by the air marshals that I could not possibly knock it hard enough. His argument was that the RAF might be forced to take it rather than nothing and if that happened they did not want their pilots to think they were getting an absolute dud.

Up to that moment the RAF had been battling against the government alongside the aircraft industry. Suddenly it seemed to be changing sides, a suspicion which was reinforced when I received a further complaint the next day suggesting that, though the TSR2 was a fine plane, it wasn't all that essential.

Soon afterwards I found out what had happened. I do not think it has been told before and it is an example of how history can be changed by secret events.

When it seemed that the RAF chiefs might possibly stand out for the TSR2 to the point of resignation Wilson handed the task of bringing them to heel to Wigg. The following day Wigg and Air Chief Marshal Elworthy met secretly at Northolt and flew to the RAF airfield at Abingdon where they spent most of the day. Exactly what happened there I do not know but by the time they returned to Northolt the fate of the TSR2 was sealed and it was immediately after that event that the RAF public relations began back-pedalling on the TSR2 and promoted the F111. I have little doubt that Elworthy was told bluntly that if the RAF did not accept the F111 it would get nothing.

I also suspect that it was suggested that since the government was going to give the RAF a different strategy involving more work East of Suez – Wilson had assured me privately that he had always been 'an East of Suez man' – the TSR2, which was essentially a nuclear bomber designed for use in Europe, was not the plane for that job.

The F111, which also had nuclear capability, was being projected as just the plane for the task, a quite sophisticated machine being needed in view of the Whitehall slogan, current then but forbidden now, 'Remember Wogs have MiGs.'

It must be said that the air marshals themselves were responsible for enabling the government to argue that the cost of the TSR2 – estimated at £750 million for 120 machines – was insupportable. They had insisted on incorporating more and more improvements – until the machine became known as the 'all-singing, all-dancing plane'.

When an Army artillery missile called Blue Water had been cancelled by the Tories to save money the air chiefs claimed that the TSR2 could be modifed to take over its battlefield bombardment role. Then when the Americans cancelled the long-range Skybolt H-bomb missile they jumped in with the suggestion that, with further changes, the TSR2 could take on that task too if converted to a strategic nuclear bomber. The politicians lapped up these suggestions because it helped them out of their immediate difficulties but it sent the costs soaring, though not as high as the £750 million claimed by the government. The manufacturers asked the Aviation Ministry to substantiate that huge figure, but without result, and an independent survey reported that the figure was exaggerated by £250 million. To bump up the estimate Healey's men had included the costs of general research at government establishments, which would have been done anyway, even down to work on flying-boots.

After securing the agreement of the air chiefs, Wilson still had the trade unions to pacify. He did this by announcing that the TSR2 would be reprieved for six months while further studies were made, even though to continue the work would cost £1 million a week. The plane was making such rapid progress, however, that he decided on a final cancellation only two months later and the way this was accomplished was typically Wilsonian. He arranged for the cancellation to be announced almost as an aside during Chancellor James Callaghan's budget speech in April. This meant that it could be presented as a measure to help to keep taxes down. And owing to a peculiar tradition of the House, Healey, the Defence Secretary, was allowed to explain the alleged reasons but could not be questioned about them.

In the ensuing days, when the politicians raved and counter-raved over the cancellation of the TSR2 bomber, the firms that suffered so grievously were strangely silent. The directors, who felt that the government's decision was the final act in the handover of aircraft leadership to the USA, were fuming in private and the workers were seething with resentment and anxiety about the future. But no critical statements were issued by the British Aircraft Corporation and Bristol Siddeley Engines, which had lost a joint order worth £450 million.

No moans were heard from Ferranti's or any of the other electronics firms, which had to sack hundreds because their splendid equipment was no longer needed.

The firms and their shareholders took their bitter medicine without a groan because they feared that if they attacked the government in public they would get no further orders.

On being summoned to the Aviation Ministry, Sir George Edwards, Lord Portal and the other directors were told that the TSR2 was scrapped. When they asked permission to telephone the news to their factories so that the workers could be informed courteously, Jenkins claimed that this was impossible. The Chancellor was to announce it in the budget, so it counted as a budget secret and could not be revealed.

As a result the workers heard the news over the radio.

The almost venomous antipathy of Labour to the TSR2 was demonstrated by a directive which went out to the British Aircraft Corporation ordering the destruction not only of the three existing TSR2s but of all the jigs and tools. Its purpose was to ensure that no subsequent Tory government could resurrect the plane. I suspected that this was one of the legends which tends to build up around controversial issues but Sir Ronald Ellis, now head of defence sales, confirmed to me that this was done.

The three TSR2s, or at least one of them, could have been used for supersonic research, as the Americans are using the existing models of the cancelled B1 bomber. Instead, the most advanced machine of its day ended up being used for target practice for machine-gunners on an army range.

The RAF had been expecting to get 120 TSR2s so the air marshals were offered 110 F111s as a replacement. Some of these were to operate from far-flung island bases which gave the deal added appeal.

In January 1966, however, I had dinner with Lord Shackleton, then Minister for the RAF, who told me that the F111 order was being cut to fifty. The new government thinking behind this was that the F111 was to be just a stop-gap while a more advanced plane was to be built in collaboration with the French – another paper aircraft which became known as the Anglo-French VG.

When I revealed that only fifty F111s were to be ordered, Wallis, the RAF public relations chief, telephoned me in a rage claiming that the RAF would never accept such a paltry number. But the air marshals did accept them, presumably on the promise of the new French plane which could not be ready for many years. Eventually the fifty F111s were cancelled in another round of Labour defence cuts.

I had always suspected that the F111 deal was nothing more than a device to induce the RAF to agree to the cancellation of the TSR2. Later I discovered that when the purchase was first mooted Aviation Ministry officials led by Sir Morien Morgan, the Controller of Aircraft, had submitted a memorandum to the Defence Ministry stating that they were convinced that the RAF would never get the F111 and that the government had never intended that it should.

It was at this time that Healey earned the reputation of being 'an inverted Micawber – always waiting for something to turn down'.

The dangerous degree of insecurity and uncertainty which he and his Labour colleagues created within the Forces was amusingly described to me by Air Chief Marshal Sir Peter Fletcher, then a chief RAF planner. After the rash of cancellations I asked Fletcher how he felt.

'We are all in a state of spanquillity,' he replied.

'What's that?' I asked.

'It's like the result of taking a mixture of Spanish fly and a tranquillizer. You want it but you don't mind any more if you don't get it.'

It was just as well, for with the total cancellation of the F111 the chain of island bases was abandoned too. Not long afterwards the great new Anglo-French VG plane also bit the dust before it left the drawing-board. Now, thirteen years after the cancellation of the TSR2, the RAF is about to get its replacement – the Tornado built in collaboration with Germany and Italy.

The farce of the Anglo-French VG provides another instance of how tortuous the thinking of ministers and their servants can be when it suits them.

After months of increasing disenchantment, the French decided to abandon the project. On 20 June 1967 I was privately informed that Pierre Messmer, the French Defence Minister, had given Healey advance warning that de Gaulle had turned against the plane for political reasons and that excessive costs would be given as the excuse for ending the partnership. I telephoned Healey's Press chief who confirmed my facts.

When I announced that 'the mainstay for the RAF through the seventies' had collapsed once again, Healey attempted to deny it in the Commons. An MP asked him about the letter he had received from Messmer and he simply denied receiving any letter. When I angrily sought an explanation from his Press chief I was blandly told that Healey had told the literal truth – Messmer's information had been given to him orally over the telephone!

What I find extraordinary about this kind of circumstance is that when the truth emerges – as it did only three weeks later when the Anglo-French project was formally scrapped – the minister who could be accused of misleading the House is hardly ever reminded of it. As Wilson said, a week is a long time in politics and in Parliament most ministers seem to be mainly concerned with getting round the problems of the moment – as, indeed, are most journalists.

I did my best to let the public know what had really happened and how, after a series of calamitous decisions, not only had the RAF been left without an advanced strike aircraft but irreparable damage had been done to the capability and prestige of the British aircraft industry. For once Healey, who normally treats censure with a hollow laugh, gave tongue to his resentment. A few days later, during which I happened to have published an article on salmon-fishing and he had told an interviewer that his main hobby was photography, he caught up with me as I was leaving the Defence Ministry.

'Why don't you stick to writing about fishing,' he asked scathingly.

I replied, 'I'll do a deal with you – in the national interest. I'll stick to angling if you'll stick to photography.'

He was not amused. In spite of the broad smiles on television I always found Healey humourless, as did his defence chiefs. This was in marked contract to his successor, Carrington, who gave pride of place in the waiting-room outside his office to the issues of the satirical magazine, *Private Eye*.

On one visit I made to him the new issue had just arrived as he was showing me out. It showed Heath wearing a Tank Regiment beret with his head sticking out of a Chieftain battle tank. Carrington picked it up and rocked with laughter as he saw the caption – 'Put a Grocer in your Tank'. On a later occasion when I visited the Defence Secretary, *Private Eye* was causing concern to his director of public relations, who had not dared to put the latest issue into the waiting-room because it was so crude. The cover featured a photograph of Lady Carrington, known affectionately to her family as 'Mother', dancing with Heath at a Conservative function with the caption, 'I love your Tory Balls'!

I suggested that it would be a good test of Carrington's humour if the issue was placed on top of the pile in the waiting-room while I was inside with him so that I could draw his attention to it when he showed me out. Carrington picked up the magazine, cried, 'Oh, look, it's Mother,' and subsided in mirth.

*Chapter Thirty-three*

# The Sad Saga of the Spanish Frigates

SOME of the saddest tragedies are the result of failure in communication between people who mean well but misunderstand or are misunderstood, and it is my experience that such failures are all too common both in Whitehall and Westminster.

It was such a failure of communication between people of goodwill which caused me to be the means of losing British industry export orders that could have totalled £100 million and of preventing a *rapprochement* between Britain and Spain which might have been of great political significance.

In June 1964, when the Tories were still in office, I gave lunch to a minister who had clearly come prepared to put me in the way of securing a major exclusive story for my newspaper. He told me that after all the years of animosity between successive British governments and General Franco, occasioned by his Fascism and the dispute over Gibraltar, a historic arms deal had just been concluded with the Spanish government.

Spain was to build several frigates of the British Leander class under licence from the Defence Ministry, paying royalties for the privilege and buying most of the equipment to be fitted in the ships from British firms. The initial order would be worth £14 million but as Franco moved ahead with his plan to modernize the Spanish fleet, follow-on orders worth £100 million or more seemed likely.

The minister pointed out that there was more than mere trade involved. 'Buying a warship from another country is like a marriage – you are stuck with it for years,' he explained. During that time relations between Britain and Spain would become closer through the technical contacts, and the rebuilding of the Spanish fleet would increase Spain's qualifications to join NATO, which would greatly strengthen the alliance against Communism.

He was particularly pleased because the government had managed to preserve total secrecy about the deal over many months knowing that if Labour supporters had heard about it they would have done everything to destroy it, so great was their hatred of the Franco regime. Some of them had fought against Franco in the Spanish Civil War and were very proud of it, though when the opportunity to put an end to Fascism occurred in 1939 some of them evaded their military duty since, at that stage, Stalin did not approve. The minister told me that the government was confident that once the contract was signed there would be nothing that Labour could do about it beyond making a noise. I was therefore urged to make sure that the deal had been signed before I wrote anything about it in the newspaper. We agreed that after a day or two I should check with the Defence Ministry Press office and that, once they could tell me that the contract was firm, I could go ahead and print.

I had no doubt that the minister's purpose – politicians nearly always have a purpose when they leak information – was to take the sting out of the row in Parliament which was inevitable. The uproar would be much greater if news of the deal first broke in Parliament itself as a result of some MP's question which would have to be answered.

I eventually telephoned the Navy press office and, using a device to conceal the true source, said I had heard through our Washington office that Britain had pulled off a big naval deal with Spain and that the Americans, who had been competing for the contract, were furious as a result. The Press officer in charge that day consulted the log-book which contains guidance on questions which journalists may ask. Sure enough the guidance was there to enable him to confirm officially that an order for frigates was firm together with some details about it.

Realizing the political implications of the news, I went down to the Defence Ministry to check with the Press officer on the spot and he repeated his confirmation that it was safe to go ahead. Regrettably, as it transpired, he had failed to see a warning in the log-book that nothing was to be said until confirmation of the signing had been received from Madrid, and this had not occurred. In fact the signing there had been delayed for bureaucratic reasons.

The following day the *Daily Express* splashed the news under the headline 'British ships deal. Frigates for Franco earn £14 million – and row looms.'

It was a fair prediction. Wilson, Michael Foot and others tabled a motion calculated to stop the contract and Labour's reaction in general was so violent and insulting to Spain that General Franco cancelled the deal, stating the reason as 'the attacks made on Spain by the leader of the British Labour Party, Harold Wilson'.

Madrid made it clear that judging by this outburst the Spanish government believed that Wilson would repudiate the contract if he won the next election. Such a thing had been unthinkable in the past and when a comparable situation arose later in regard to the supply of Buccaneer bombers to South Africa, Wilson, then Prime Minister, agreed to the completion of that contract but rejected a follow-on order.

As was made clear in the ensuing uproar over the frigates in Parliament, when tempers flared on both sides, the Press officer had made a genuine mistake. This may have been because, though I was unaware of it, he was ill and died soon afterwards.

Having mentioned an American source as a safety gambit during my opening inquiries, I was stuck with it and the government made use of it to deny Labour allegations that there had been a ministerial leak. I do not know if Thorneycroft, then Defence Secretary, knew the true source, but that wily old fox, George Wigg, sensed that the American origin was a cover.

In this regard, I might say that Whitehall officials are delighted if a leakage can be attributed to America. This is not because of any animosity in that direction but simply because it gets them out of security difficulties. Time and again when leaks of mine have led to witch-hunts in Whitehall, it has been suggested to me, often with great subtlety, that if only I could indicate that the source had been American all would be well. Even MI5 has been prepared to buy this excuse at times to call off the hounds when it suited them.

Spain has never renewed its order for British warships and until Franco died even the purchase of British Harrier jump-jets had to be negotiated as a sale by the USA, though the direct sale of the maritime version of the Harrier is now under discussion. Presumably Wilson would have no objections to arms sales to Spain now. He visited Spain recently and was received by King Juan Carlos.

Many of the Socialists who objected to the sale of arms to Spain were not merely concerned about increasing Franco's military strength or the sheer impropriety of dealing with a Fascist state. They objected to the sale of arms of any kind. These objectors are an interesting lot and they fall into two categories, genuine pacificists who believe that the manufacture of arms, particularly for export, is wrong, and crypto-Communists and Marxists who object to any strengthening of the West's defences against Russia.

Five members of the Labour government were among the left-wing group which induced Wilson to stop supplying arms to Chile, at considerable cost to employment in Britain. They were Michael Foot, Judith Hart, Joan Lestor, Wedgwood Benn and Eric Heffer.

Callaghan is under similar pressures. Under what would normally be regarded as a binding contract with the Central American state of El Salvador, an export consignment of scout cars and armoured cars was loaded ready for shipment in late 1977. After refusing to cancel the contract because of the damage it would do to Britain's commercial name, the Prime Minister gave way to left-wing pressure early in 1978, using the 'human rights' situation there as the reason.

A comparable circumstance arose in the early summer of 1966 when I discovered that the government had offered to manufacture bombs and naval rockets for the USA. Healey had promised to find the dollars to pay for his ill-fated purchase of American F111 bombers by selling British goods and the Americans wanted a million aircraft bombs. It must have been obvious from the start that such a deal would cause ructions from the Left because the weapons would be available for use in Vietnam. Nevertheless, before disclosing the situation, I had secured an official statement from a Ministry of Defence spokesman to the following effect: 'We are negotiating with the Americans so that the royal ordnance factories which badly need work can make the bombs and missiles and at the same time offset the costs of the F111s. We have suggested that we lay down a small production line and then expand it. I can't mention Vietnam in this context for obvious reasons but I can tell you that we are not imposing any restrictions on where these bombs can be used.'

When my report appeared Healey denied it but, under persistent questioning in the Commons, was driven to admit that the negotiations had been in progress but had been cancelled because of the publicity.

Labour's attitude to arms sales is often inconsistent in the extreme. The left-wingers are greatly opposed to the Shah of Iran, claiming that he is a tyrant ruler of a police state. Yet Iran, which in real terms means the Shah, has continued to be Britain's best arms customer simply because the trade he offers is so big that the government cannot refuse it. At the time of writing Wilson is with the Shah on a private goodwill visit.

Ironically it was a Labour government, under Wilson, which set up the Defence Sales Department in Whitehall and recruited the first government arms salesman, my good friend Ray Brown (now Sir) who negotiated the first big arms deals with Iran.

The left-wingers went through noisy motions complaining about his appointment, both in the Commons and the Lords, but their objections were brushed aside. Now, after a decade dominated by Labour, arms sales have become Britain's biggest growth industry. It could have been very much bigger but for objections to orders from South Africa, Spain, Greece and several other countries which offended Labour's conscience.

At the time of writing the government is even prepared to sell the Harrier jump-jet, one of the world's most sophisticated combat planes, to China, a deal to which Russia has the strongest objections. The government is also supporting negotiations being conducted by Rolls-Royce to re-engine vessels of the Chinese Navy with gas-turbines. There are doubts, however, about both of these deals, which could provide many jobs in Britain, because of the extreme hostility to them of the pro-Russian Labour Left.

Those who cry for unilateral nuclear disarmament but not for total disarmament, because they concede that some kind of defence is necessary, assume that a conventional war fought against Russia would somehow be tolerable. Information to which I have had access indicates that a further global war could be devastating to civilization whether fought with conventional weapons or with H-bombs.

In the first place, the pattern of big wars fought with automatic weapons, which were used for the first time in the American Civil War, shows them to be exhausting conflicts lasting at least four years. In addition to huge combat and civilian casualties, enormous numbers die from cruelty and malnutrition. Deaths inflicted in 'great' wars have risen exponentially and expert forecasts for another such conflict fought with non-atomic weapons put the killed at no less than 50 million!

Secondly, the destructive power of conventional weapons has increased to a degree which tends to be deliberately hidden from the public because they are so horrific. The fire-bomb, the flame-thrower and the high-explosive blockbuster, in their infancy in the Second World War, have been developed into weapons with a much higher kill-rate. Clouds of petroleum products can now be dispersed and exploded with terrifying results. Anti-personnel weapons have reached entirely new levels of lethality. On top of this there has been such progress in chemical warfare that, to quote no less an authority than Admiral of the Fleet Sir Peter Hill-Norton, the recently retired chairman of the NATO Military Committee, a quarter of all the shells deployed by the Soviet Union are designed to take poison gas.

Assuming that general disarmament is a pipe dream, which it is for the foreseeable future, the question which needs to be asked is: which is the greater deterrent to all-out war, nuclear arms or conventional arms? Because of their build-up as weapons of unprecedented horror, there can be little doubt that the nuclears carry far greater deterrent power, particularly in Russia, which has shown that it can not only weather a terrible conventional war, suffering millions of casualties, but can emerge relatively stronger than ever.

*Chapter Thirty-four*

# The Lurch to the Left

IT is difficult to study Harold Wilson's thirteen years of Labour Party leadership without concluding that he was basically a centre-moderate. He promoted East–West trade later but he preserved the Anglo-American alliance, retained and improved the nuclear deterrent, kept Britain in the Common Market and supported Israel, all moves which were disappointing for the Kremlin. A former director of Defence Intelligence told me that Wilson always

struck him as 'extremely secure' about whom he would have present
at secret briefings and did all he could to preserve the crucial joint
Intelligence arrangements with Washington.

Nevertheless, Wilson had to trim so much to retain Left-wing
support, so that he could remain in power, that his government
shifted far to the Left during his premiership. In his autobiography,
*Big Cyril*, Cyril Smith, the former Liberal whip, asks of Wilson's
reign, 'Was it coincidence that his period also saw the greatest
decline in the fortunes of Britain since the days of the Tudors? Was it
a historical inevitability or did Wilson accelerate the process? I know
my view; when the many crunches came and the interests of a united
Labour Party and the interests of the United Kingdom were at
variance, it was the Labour Party that won . . .'

Until the late 1950s, and particularly under Gaitskell's rule, the
Labour Party remained hostile to Communism but during the next
decade this attitude slowly changed as it did in the unions, where
powerful Labour figures who had been anti-Communist were
replaced by new men openly or covertly more sympathetic to
Soviet-style 'Socialism'. But it was not until 1972 that significant
contacts between the Labour Party and foreign Communist regimes
began to gather momentum.

It was in that year that the Labour Party sent a delegation to
Moscow headed by its General Secretary, Ron Hayward, who stated
on his return that, 'We believe this visit has built a firm foundation
for understanding and friendship between our two parties.' It was
also in that year that George Brown, who resigned from the party
four years later, deplored that 'extremists had captured control of
the Labour movement at every level'.

Since then the Labour Party has sent more delegations on visits to
Eastern Europe than it did in the previous twenty years. Eurocommunism has been welcomed by Labour Party Marxists, who domi-
nate the party's National Executive Committee and particularly
its International Committee which furthers the East–West contacts;
1977 saw the unprecedented attendance at the Labour Party Conference of leaders of the three main Eurocommunist parties, those of
Spain, Italy and France.

The most dangerous symptom in the eyes of the security
authorities was the Labour Party's decision in 1973 to lift its ban on
its members belonging to Communist and Communist-front organizations, which had been in force previously to avoid infiltration and

penetration of the genuine Labour movement. It meant that members of the Labour Party, including MPs, were free to join organizations such as the British-Soviet Friendship Society, the International Union of Students, the British Peace Committee and the World Peace Council, which has its headquarters in Moscow.

Labour MPs and even ministers are free to appear on Communist Party platforms and do so. They write in the Communist newspaper, the *Morning Star*, and, as the official record of monitored broadcasts from Moscow and other Communist capitals shows, their Communist sympathies are used for Soviet propaganda purposes. The most blatant of these recently was the broadcast made by Alex Kitson, a member of the Labour Party National Executive representing the party at the 1977 celebrations of sixty years of Communist dictatorship in Moscow. He told the Russians, 'You have managed to achieve so much that we are still far from achieving,' with other remarks so contrary to the truth that even some of his extremist friends felt he had gone too far, in view of the thousands suffering in Soviet labour camps and so-called mental institutions.

Until a short time previously Kitson had belonged to the 'Labour Research Department' which, in fact, has nothing to do with the Labour Party but was and is a Communist front organization. Until 1972 it was on the list of organizations proscribed by the Labour Party, yet several of its angled surveys have been reported unwittingly by journalists as though they had been carried out by Labour. The Communists like to latch on to the word 'Labour' just as they latched on to 'Peace', which always means 'Peace at Russia's price'.

Many of the executives of the Labour Research Department are Communist Party members or closely affiliated with the party. Its prime purpose is to disseminate Communist propaganda in the guise of the Labour Party. The Labour Party now does little or nothing to counter this.

By such fraudulent and surreptitious means, the Communist Party, with a diminishing membership of only about 25,000, is achieving great influence on British life though, as Wilson was keen to point out when trying to rebut claims of Communist infiltration, Communists are always derisively rejected if they stand for Parliament.

They are achieving success by adroitly blurring the differences between Socialism and Communism, though the foundation of the former is the commitment to parliamentary democracy, which the latter rejects. As Bert Ramelson, then the Communist Party's industrial organizer – meaning disorganizer – put it, 'We have only to float an idea one month to see it adopted as policy by the Labour Party the next.'

The Communists expect that membership of the Communist Party itself will eventually be open to members of the Labour Party. One of the most sensational of the overt signs was the appointment in 1977 of a Trotskyite member of the New Left revolutionaries, Andy Bevan, to be national youth officer of the Labour Party. While Prime Minister Callaghan objected, realizing that the choice could be damaging for Labour's image, Wedgwood Benn defended it and the Left prevailed.

Coincident with this infiltration, Marxist inroads have been made into the schools, universities, and the media. One of the essential conditions for a Communist-dominated regime is control of the Press, and by promoting a closed shop controlled by the National Union of Journalists, Michael Foot has paved the way for it.

Woodrow Wyatt, the former Labour MP, was so appalled with the sell-out to the Left that in 1977 he published a book, *What's Left of the Labour Party?*, urging Labour voters to support the Tories for at least two elections so that Labour should be forced into the wilderness to cleanse itself.

I have reason to believe that Harold Wilson now agrees with him. Since resignation made him independent of the Left, he has called for urgent action to save the Labour Party from a take-over by extremist infiltrators, whom he labelled 'political asset-strippers'. He has attacked the wrecking role of the Trotskyites and spoken out strongly against Eurocommunism, warning that while the Communist parties in some European countries claim to owe little or no loyalty to Moscow, that situation could quickly change once they achieved power.

Understandably, he has been taken to task for doing so little to prevent the slide while he was leader but his apparent conversion suggests that he was powerless to do so while in office. What is Callaghan doing about the legacy of left-wing infiltration? From the tone of the Labour Party conference, where 'comrades' has ousted 'brothers' and from the utterances of members of the Labour Party Executive, it seems that the tide of Communism will continue to rise.

## Chapter Thirty-five

CRAFF

# The Unions as a
# Power Base

DURING a recent lunch with Mr Arthur Scargill, leader of the
Yorkshire Miners' Union, who is politically motivated to a high
degree, he made it clear that he had no intention of entering party
politics because the real seat of power is in the unions.

'Parliament is just a talking-shop,' he said. 'It is with the unions
that the action lies and action is what interests me.'

There is much truth in that. The unions have greatly increased
their power over the past decade, and particularly since the Labour
Party dropped its plans to discipline them by legislation and since
the unions defeated Heath's attempt to do so.

The Labour government under Wilson and more so under
Callaghan has realized that securing continuing union support is
the best insurance against electoral defeat. As a result, legislation to
increase union power has been pushed through by Labour, which
expects union loyalty in return. The Trade Union and Labour
Relations Act and the Employment Protection Act have strengthened the rights of union members but the real increase in power has
been put into the hands of the trade union leaders and the TUC.
Even the Advisory Conciliation and Arbitration Service (ACAS) set
up to help resolve disputes, is so organized as to lean heavily in
favour of the unions, as a succession of industrial and commercial
organizations has discovered.

After meeting and speaking with trade union leaders over the
years I am convinced that far too many of them see union leadership

as a personal political power-base rather than as a means of improving the lot of their members, which is what their prime function is supposed to be. That they wield great personal power cannot be doubted and during the last few years of the reign of Jack Jones as General Secretary of the Transport and General Workers' Union many regarded him as the most influential man in Britain.

I remember hearing Len Murray, the TUC leader, stating at a private dinner shortly after Heath's defeat in 1974, '*We* are now dismantling the legislation of the previous Tory government,' making it quite clear that the unions were as much involved in this as the new Labour administration. Indeed, the TUC worked in the closest collaboration with Michael Foot's Employment Department in formulating the new pro-union laws.

Both parties have become scared of union power and its capacity to interfere with the policies they were elected to carry through, this of course being particularly true of the Tories. At the time of writing, some Tories seem so worried about what unions might do to a Conservative government, especially if elected with only a small majority, that they want the election deferred or even seem content for Labour to win!

'A Tory government might wreck the money market,' one high capitalist told me. Such people seem to ignore the probability that with further Labour governments moving ever more to the Left there might be no money market. Nevertheless there is sound reason for their concern. In August 1974 Hugh Scanlon, then General Secretary of the Amalgamated Union of Engineering Workers, threatened a winter of industrial chaos if Labour failed to win the next election.

In the motor-car industry, where strike action is orchestrated, trade unionists have shown repeatedly that they are prepared to damage the nation's economy for political motives and have largely succeeded in ruining British Leyland, even though it has been nationalized. The British Leyland factory at Speke, Liverpool, offered a typical example of how the revolutionary Left disrupts a factory to force a shut-down, then tries to prevent it by a sit-in, hopefully inducing police action. As soon as the decision to close the factory was made, the seventeen-week strike was called off and then attempts were made to spread the dispute to Coventry and elsewhere 'in sympathy'.

That there is some doubt about who governs Britain was shown plainly enough in the first election of 1974 when Heath went to the country on that question. Since then the unions have increased their control over the Labour government to such an extent that the answer should hardly be in doubt any more.

The National Executive Committee of the Labour Party which formulates party policy, though this is not always put into quick effect by a Labour government, is dominated by the trade unions because 60 per cent of its members are from unions or are among the 119 MPs sponsored by unions and expected to promote their union's line.

It is not surprising therefore that the British Communists, who hardly ever succeed in saving their deposit if they stand for Parliament, decided long ago that their surest road to political power was by infiltrating the unions. In this they have achieved remarkable success.

Out of a total work force of about 23 million, some 10 million are members of trade unions and of these only about 0·3 per cent are members of the Communist Party. Yet they are exerting pressure out of all proportion to their representation. An analysis by Geoffrey Stewart-Smith in 1974 showed that about 10 per cent of all officials of the major industrial trade unions were Communists or far-left revolutionary Marxists.

Since then there have been signs of a shift towards moderation in some quarters but the Communist representation is still dangerously high. Those who care about freedom should never forget that, at whatever level Communism has been established anywhere in the world, it has almost always been imposed by quite small minorities.

The Left extremists' prime purpose in infiltrating the unions is to influence Labour Party policy through the card vote which the trade unions wield at the conferences. It also gives them substantial control of industry, particularly with the move towards 'industrial democracy' – increased worker participation – which in the Communists' eyes is just a step towards total worker control. The Communist Party has cells in every major factory receiving instructions from party headquarters in King Street, London, on how to exacerbate each dispute and when to pull back if they are obviously defeated.

If unions dominated by Communists gain a substantial degree of industrial control then the complexion of the government is of minor concern to them, for a considerable degree of power will have been shifted from the floor of the Commons to the factory floor.

A further objective in which Communists have been joined by the so-called New Left – the International Socialists, Trotskyists and other revolutionary groups – is to cause dissension in industry by promoting or inventing grievances and to aggravate these by any means including violence, as the long drawn-out dispute at the Grunwick photographic processing factory demonstrated so often. When 115 people were charged with offences after clashing with the police outside the Grunwick factory, forty-five proved to be 'students', twenty-three were unemployed and most of the rest had nothing to do with the dispute at issue. Many of those chanting 'The workers united will never be defeated' outside factory gates have never done a full week's work.

The firemen who struck for better pay in the autumn of 1977 were exploited by Trotskyist and Marxist groups who cared little for their cause but saw the opportunity for creating chaos and the chance to brand the troops manfully doing the firemen's work as 'scabs'. Though there are some home-grown revolutionaries many of the more aggressive are of foreign origin. They are former aliens who wish to impose an alien political creed on the country which has permitted them to live here. Some of them have adopted English-sounding names.

MI5 and the CIA have grounds for believing that money to finance the use of flying pickets and other strong-arm groups comes into Britain from Iron Curtain countries. The influx of Russian money to help strikers was openly admitted by Les Dixon, a Communist member of the Amalgamated Union of Engineering Workers, during the miners' strike of 1974. In an interview recorded by Moscow Radio he was quoted as saying, 'In a recent dispute in Great Britain in which our mine-working industry was involved, the Soviet trade unions made a substantial contribution to their dispute fund in order to alleviate hardships of the workers.'

For the most part, the Communists have achieved their success by legitimate if rather reprehensible means, exploiting the apathy of most trade union members, which means that the majority do not vote on important issues. They hold sudden meetings which most would find difficulty in attending even if they wanted to and oppose postal ballot because they know they would lose it. Sometimes, however, they have acted illegally by rigging ballots to suit themselves, the most blatant example being that of the Electrical Trades Union, since deprived of its Communist leadership following court action and generally pursuing a policy of moderation under Frank Chapple. Where decisions have been taken by a show of hands at docks and factory gates, the counting has sometimes been so fraudulent as to be apparent even to those watching on television.

Communists or Communist sympathizers have progressively intensified the militancy of some unions and some Labour MPs and even ministers have shown their approval of it by appearing in picket lines.

It was Scargill who raised the militancy of the miners, normally intelligent and restrained, to a new level which eventually brought down the Heath government through his action in organizing thousands of pickets at the Saltley coke depot in Birmingham two years earlier. As he put it to me, 'Saltley, where the police gave in because they couldn't cope with so many pickets preventing lorries from taking coke to factories, was a historic day for the trade union movement and for me. It showed that the people could win against authority by sheer weight of numbers. When I saw those thousands of men with banners marching to join us . . .'

Some of the trade union leaders who once belonged to the Communist Party and later left it insist that they are no longer Communists. This, no doubt, is true of some of them but it is routine Communist practice that when a member succeeds in securing a position of influence he is often encouraged to go through the outward motions of breaking with the party on some pretext so that he can then weevil away in the party's interests without seeming to serve it. Even those who may have genuinely severed connection may still pursue the same aims. One such is Scargill, and when I told him that his belief that the workers should own and run all means of production was at the root of Communist policy, he replied, 'But it is also the original aim of the Labour Party and I will do all I can to further it as a good Socialist should.'

The line between Socialist and Communist becomes more and more blurred and, of course, the Communists want it that way.

The increasing influence of the Communists in industry has understandably caused concern to the security authorities, who are only too aware that while the Communist Party as a whole is being careful to behave strictly within the existing law, its aim is to overthrow democracy as the British people know it and then change the law to make a return to parliamentary democracy impossible. I was therefore not surprised when Maurice Macmillan told me that while he was Minister at the Department of Employment in 1973 two MI5 officers called to see him to complain of the inroads being made by Communists into the unions. They suggested that MI5 would welcome the introduction of legislation to curb Communist activities. Macmillan reported the visit to Heath, who said he would do what was necessary, but no legislation ensued and Communist penetration of the unions has intensified.

So long as the law continues to protect the activities of the extreme Left, and the present Labour government has strengthened it in that direction, it is difficult for ordinary citizens to do much that is practical to combat the menace, but I can claim one important instance in which I assisted in ridding one highly influential union of extreme left leadership. This was the Institution of Professional Civil Servants, the union which numbers the most senior civil servants, top administrators, government scientists and engineers among its members. My modest part may sound like treachery to a friend but I had reached the stage where a choice between loyalty to a friend or loyalty to the country had to be made.

In the postwar years until 1961 the General Secretary of the IPCS was an extremely affable, highly intelligent and able man called Stanley Mayne. Not only did he become a most excellent contact of mine, providing me with lead after lead, but also a personal friend, visiting my home. I was astonished at the range of his information, which covered all manner of secret areas. If there was anything Mayne did not know he could usually find it out because he had branch representatives in every station, including places like Harwell and the Aldermaston atomic weapons establishment. Though he was not allowed inside the most secret areas he had automatic entry to the administration departments to visit his members.

I knew Mayne for several years before I learned that his views were of the extreme Left and shortly before he retired in July 1961 I was told by a former member of the Communist Party that Mayne was not only a card-carrying member but took part in various meetings of party subcommittees.

I was not able to check the truth of this but I immediately raised the possibility of it with Sir Frederick Brundrett, then chief scientist in the Defence Ministry, who was also a prominent officer of the IPCS. He told me that he already had his suspicions and would look into the matter but I heard nothing more, though he may well have fed the information into the security machine.

In October 1961, when Mayne had retired, I gave evidence to a committee appointed by the Tory government to review 'security procedures and practices in the public service', which was chaired by Lord Radcliffe and included Field-Marshal Sir Gerald Templer, whom I knew and for whom I had enormous respect.

The terms of reference of the committee were to consider how to prevent secret information from getting into the hands of the Intelligence services of foreign powers and 'subversive organizations in this country, of which in current conditions the most formidable is the Communist Party with its fringe of associated bodies and sympathizers'.

I was questioned about D-notice matters but, having made my difficult personal decision, I volunteered the suggestion that it seemed rather pointless keeping Communists out of the secret departments when Communists or near-Communists in Civil Service unions were allowed access. When asked to give an example I cited the case of Mayne, stressing that I had no evidence whatever that he had ever betrayed any secrets and stating that I did not think it likely that he would ever do so. My main concern was with his successor. Mayne had made it plain to me that his successor would be a man of his choice. If Mayne was of the extreme Left the odds were that he would see to it that his choice was too.

Due note was taken and I was questioned further by Field-Marshal Templer.

When the committee's report emerged, a few months later, a whole section was devoted to Civil Service staff associations and trade unions, stating that the committee was disturbed at the number of Communists and Communist sympathizers holding positions either as full-time paid officials or unpaid officers – those in the secret departments. 'We regard this presumably deliberate massing of Communist effort in the Civil Service unions as most dangerous to security,' it stated.

The committee recommended that any department should have the right to refuse to negotiate with a named union official whom it had reason to believe was a Communist.

'We think that the dangers of the present situation are aggravated by the fact that very few people are aware that they exist,' the report added. This was virtually what I had told the committee.

No doubt other witnesses carrying greater weight had done the same but, knowing Radcliffe's reputation for fairness as well as his concern for security, the report confirmed that my decision had been the right one.

By that time Mayne's successor, Richard Nunn, had been appointed.

After he had been in office a little over a year, the defence departments made it clear that they would have no dealings with Nunn. He asked to be relieved of his post, denying that he was a member of the Communist Party or ever had been. William McCall, a young moderate, was appointed and has performed his union tasks to the satisfaction of Whitehall and his members ever since.

Though purged of Communist sympathizers in the early sixties the Civil Service unions are coming back under extreme left-wing influence and there has been an ominous growth of militancy throughout the Civil Service as a result.

Historically, the most important confrontation between the British government and unions was the 1973–4 impasse between the miners and the Heath administration which resulted in a premature general election and the return of a Labour government, which, at the time of writing, has lasted four years. The circumstances of what really happened are rather confused and I have devoted some time to trying to discover the truth.

Trade union leaders whom I have consulted claim that, apart from the maverick Mick McGahey, the most dedicated Communist official of the National Union of Mineworkers, the miners had no particular wish to bring the Tory government down and most of them thought it would be against their interests to do so, so long as they could get a reasonable settlement. That was certainly the view of Joe Gormley, the NUM president, and even Scargill assured me that he personally had no intention of helping to bring Heath down, arguing that such a move is outside the proper scope of any trade union.

Bill Keys, General Secretary of the Society of Graphical and Allied Trades, who was present at the crucial meeting of the TUC at which it was decided to offer Heath a way out, told me that the offer was completely genuine. It was to the effect that, if the government agreed to make a special case of the miners' claim, the TUC would guarantee that other unions would not take advantage of the situation to press their claims and there would be no more 'special cases'. Keys said that the only dissenting union was the National

Union of Journalists which, in his opinion, was the only one solidly determined to get rid of Heath.

When Len Murray, the TUC General Secretary, put the offer to Heath it was rejected after the Prime Minister had consulted with Whitelaw and other colleagues and a strike and the three-day week became inevitable.

There are many who believed that Heath made a cardinal blunder, especially since an independent inquiry later showed that the miners' claim was justified.

It is commonly argued that, even if Heath believed that the TUC guarantee was bound to break down, he should have accepted it and then called a general election, putting the blame squarely on the unions responsible. I have been assured, however, by one of Heath's colleagues involved in the discussions with the unions that acceptance was never possible because of an unknown factor.

This factor was a deal which had already been made with the electricians' union led by Frank Chapple. The electricians had only just received their settlement under the previous round of pay talks, 'Phase Two', and their union had agreed to a modest one on the firm understanding that no special cases would be made in 'Phase Three'. Chapple particularly insisted that no exception would be made for the miners and warned that, if the government went back on its word, he would bring out the power-station workers, who could force the country to a halt much more quickly than the miners could.

My informant insists that Chapple dealt directly with him on this issue and, when it seemed possible that the government might make a special case of the miners after all, he had to remind Heath of the warning.

Apparently, however, Heath had been fully aware of it and was already taking the view that the option offered by Murray was not really open.

My informant says that Whitelaw's activities also contributed to the catastrophe. Having returned from Northern Ireland to the Employment Ministry he took the view that there must be some way out if only reason could be allowed to prevail, and let this be known. Gormley, who up to that point seemed to be prepared to settle, suddenly saw that perhaps concessions were to be offered after all.

A further factor was supposed to be a failure of communication between Heath and Gormley. I have been told that Gormley had given the Prime Minister his home telephone number so that he could contact him privately. By some mischance, Gormley was telephoned at NUM headquarters from Downing Street and as this became widely known among his officials, it prejudiced any further man-to-man negotiations.

Another solution to Heath's problems was suggested by Lord Rothschild, then head of the Cabinet's 'Think-Tank'. As a result of the rapid rise in oil prices due to Arab action after the Yom Kippur war in 1973 it was obvious that the real value of coal and its importance to the nation must rise. Rothschild therefore suggested that the miners' wage claim could be justified on these grounds and that, to demonstrate the government's interest, Heath could announce the setting up of a royal commission on the mining industry to advise on how the industry could be developed and the position of the miners further improved.

This proposition was rejected also, perhaps because of the promise to the electricians.

The unions' potential power to interfere with Britain's defences was demonstrated very recently when Polaris submarines were blacked to influence the Government in a pay dispute, which involved other defence establishments and armaments factories.

Because of the increasing power of the unions, ministers who are ambitious for higher office understandably go out of their way to improve their standing with them and identify themselves with their aspirations. As I explain in Chapter Thirty-eight, in connection with Wilson's resignation, Callaghan owed much of his political clout to his carefully cultivated relations with individual unions and with the TUC. Wedgwood Benn is another politician who devotes much time to increasing his popularity with trade unionists, especially those of the far Left, particularly in the drive for 'industrial democracy'.

# Chapter Thirty-six

⟨∼∫∫∫∼⟩

# Politicians and Zionism

THE attitude of postwar British governments to the state of Israel
and to Zionism as a whole has been of particular interest to me
because of my close association with leading British Jews and,
through them, with Israeli politicians and officials.

I learned much at first hand from the late Lord Sieff, who as Israel
Sieff, one of the leading figures in the spectacular rise of the Marks
and Spencer organization, had played an important role with Chaim
Weizmann in establishing Israel as a homeland for the Jews.

I have been able to see, at close quarters, the enormous effort and
personal sacrifice made by British Jews to assist Israel with private
money, commercial enterprise and through the exercise of political
influence.

On visits to Israel as a guest of Lord Sieff and of Lord Rothschild I
have been afforded special facilities to see the astonishing development in that basically arid and stony country in agriculture, industry
and defence. Though not Jewish myself, I have been able to achieve
some understanding of the remarkable attachment of the Zionists to
their hard-won land, where many have a life of dignity for the first
time and which they will defend to the death – in the last resort
because they have nowhere to run.

The natural inclination of the Foreign Office, even before oil
became so important, has been to favour the Arab countries. When
Sir Michael Hadow was ambassador to Israel he described to me
how, when he was recalled to London for talks about the Middle
East, he would find himself a lone figure with a dozen or more
ambassadors to Arab countries ranged against his interests. There is

a pro-Arab mystique in the Foreign Office where the 'Arabists' – those with knowledge of the Arabic language and culture and
a feeling for the Bedouin way of life – have long regarded themselves
as a select and rather envied band. Since the Arabs made oil into a
political weapon and grew so rich, their champions in Whitehall
have found themselves with even more diplomatic clout.

Richard Crossman was the first minister I met with unequivocal
pro-Israeli sympathies, but he was not then in any government
position where he could express them, apart from occasional
speeches.

Eden was not pro-Jewish but was so anti-Nasser that he approved
the secret collusion with Israel, as well as with France, for the Suez
invasion, which, when the operation was suddenly abandoned,
ended in a fiasco which embarrassed no one more than the MI6 men
who had been specially attached to the Israelis.

Macmillan seemed neutral, while Douglas-Home tended to be
pro-Arab, while doing his best to look neutral, but with the accession
of Harold Wilson in 1964 the Israelis had a British Prime Minister
firmly biased in their favour, a personal stand from which he
has never deviated, though his political expression of it has often
been limited by events, by his colleagues and by the Whitehall
machine.

The intensity of Wilson's Zionism, in which he was joined whole-
heartedly by Marcia, was such that her home became something of
an unofficial Foreign Office where visiting Israeli politicians, like
Yigal Allon, could meet Wilson and others so that Anglo-Israeli ties
could be strengthened at an unofficial level, which must have
incensed the Whitehall Arabists as well as the various Foreign
Secretaries. When Marcia and her chief are accused of extremist
left-wing bias and even of pro-Soviet intentions they cite this work
for Israel as proof against. Comfort and assistance for Israel were the
last things the Russians wanted, though since his retirement as
Prime Minister Wilson has pointed out that support for Israel and
friendship with Russia need not be mutually exclusive.

The Israelis have recently recognized their debt to him by presenting him with the Golden Book of the Jewish National Fund to 'mark
his outstanding record both in and out of office, as a friend of Israel
and the Jewish people', by awarding him an honorary degree at the
Weizmann Institute, and making him a patron of the Heroes of Israel
Forest being planted by the Jewish National Fund 'to salute the

heroism of the Israel defence forces, particularly in connection with the rescue at Entebbe'.

My main journalistic interest has been with the supply of weapons and equipment to the Israelis and their brilliant use of it in two wars. Britain's record in assisting Israel to become the only assured bastion of Western influence in the Middle East is viewed there with little better than disgust.

The pre-1964 Tory governments had refused to supply Rolls-Royce engines to the Israeli air force, with the result that they had bought French machines. They showed these with pride during a visit I paid to one of the major airfields with ambassador Hadow, but I well remember the wistful expression on the face of the commandant, who was soon to make a name for himself in the Six-Day War, as he said, 'We'd so much rather have Rolls-Royce engines but your government won't supply them.'

In spite of the technical ban on advanced machinery a long, continuing contract had been signed to equip the Israeli Army with reconditioned Centurion tanks, surplus to Britain's requirements. All went well with this until the Six-Day War in June 1967 when Britain suddenly had to appear to be neutral. The Foreign Secretary at that time was George Brown, who was on record as saying that he was 'an Arab at heart' and, though his wife was from a well known Jewish family, he had deep differences with the Israeli government culminating in a most unpleasant personal row with their leaders while on a visit to Israel.

Nevertheless, when the Six-Day War started with a pre-emptive strike by Israel against Nasser's menacing forces, Brown behaved in a way which won my applause. He was alerted to the fact that a large consignment of spares for Centurion tanks and special tank ammunition was due for delivery to Israel. On his personal instructions, and against the pressures from the Arabists, the Israelis were immediately notified that the crates could not be delivered because of the need to preserve the appearance of neutrality but they were offered special secret facilities to collect them themselves if they could manage to complete it within twenty-four hours. The crates were transported to remote RAF airfields where the Israelis duly picked them up by flying-in planes late at night, and the contents were available for the battle.

Brown told me later that I had almost been the cause of an international incident, which could have prejudiced his position with his pro-Arab colleagues, by unwittingly revealing what was happening. A local correspondent had telephoned a short item to the effect that planes with Israeli markings had been seen landing at night at an RAF airfield, and after checking with the Defence Ministry, which disclaimed all knowledge, I wrote a brief report about the 'mystery'. Fortunately nobody appreciated its significance.

Brown later held up the resumption of Centurion sales several times in the hope of using it to persuade the Israelis to return former Jordanian territory to Hussein, who was in need of some political achievement. 'What can I do for the little King?' he frequently exclaimed. He has since told me that he believes it was his anti-Zionism and pro-Arab stand which cost him the premiership when he failed to win the Labour leadership in contest with Wilson. I was with him on the night before the ballot, when he was convincing himself he was going to win. His intense disappointment and distress at what has happened since to the Labour Party, which he has left in disgust, may help to account for those past emotional outbursts when dealing with the Israelis.

Shortly after the Six-Day War the Israelis had shown great interest in the British Chieftain tank, which seemed ideal for their conditions. The Defence Ministry desperately wanted a foreign customer for the Chieftain to help offset its great cost to the Army and so there was general delight in the possibility that the Israelis might buy it.

With the agreement of the Labour government, Chieftains were sent out for trials under desert conditions. They were something of a disaster because the engine, which had been designed for use in Europe, could not cope with extreme quantities of sand and dust. The Israelis were so keen, however, that they set about solving the problems and by 1969 were all set to place a £60 million order with cash-on-the-nail payment. At that stage, though no conflict was in prospect, Whitehall gave way to the Arabists despite the fact that the Foreign Secretary, then Michael Stewart, opposed them and the sale was banned on the grounds that the tank would upset the balance of power in the Middle East and prejudice trade with Arab states.

The Israelis were furious, especially when the government decided to sell the Chieftain to the Libyans instead. Though the Libyan ruler, then King Idris, was pro-British I did what I could to scupper that deal, which also included self-propelled Abbot field-guns, by announcing it prematurely and with considerable prominence, pointing out that the tank would be useless in Libya were it not for the anti-sand modifications for which the Israelis had been responsible. The Jewish MPs and others in Parliament sprang to the attack and forced an emergency debate based on my disclosure, which the government could not deny. However, under pressure from the Arabists, and in spite of Wilson's preference, Stewart insisted that the sale should go through as Libya was far from Israel and the tanks were needed purely for defence.

The Libyan deal had to be hurriedly cancelled after King Idris was overthrown in September 1969 by the fanatically Muslim Gadhafi, who was only too keen to make any Chieftains available for an attack on Israel. The Israelis credited Wilson for this reversal.

In the end it was Iran which became the big customer for the Chieftain but the sale was possible only because of the work the Israelis has done on it. (The Arabists even successfully interfered with orders from the Iranians, who pride themselves on not being Arabs. The Shah was keen to have warships which he was buying from Britain equipped with an Israeli anti-ship missile, called Gabriel, because it was the most effective, and the Foreign Office refused to allow it because 'it might upset the Arabs'.)

Though the Chieftain was banned, Centurions continued to be supplied to Israel after the Six-Day War by both the Wilson and Heath governments as discreetly as possible, and the Israelis greatly improved them by fitting different engines and guns. When the Egyptians and Syrians launched their surprise attack in October 1973, the Centurion played a major role in what resulted in near defeat for the Arabs on all fronts. Once again there was a rush requirement for spares and armour-piercing ammunition, which Britain was supposed to supply according to the contract terms. And once again the Foreign Office, then under Douglas-Home, insisted on banning all arms supplies to both sides, a move which favoured the Arabs because their spares and ammunition were of Russian origin.

Crates of spares and ammunition were on the docks and Israeli ships were ready to load them but the British authorities refused to release them in spite of Israel's precarious position during the early days of the ferocious tank battles. Jewish MPs and their supporters attacked the Tory government for the breach of contract and on television Wilson opposed the embargo because it operated unfairly against Israel, but without result.

On the first evening of the Centurion row George Brown happened to meet Sir Alec at a party and asked, 'Did you cheat like we did?' Sir Alec did not reply.

As the biggest tank battles in history raged on the Syrian and Egyptian fronts nobody regretted the absence of Chieftains from the fray more than the British Army Staff. The battle experience against the Russian tanks, which the Israelis would have shared, would have been invaluable to Rhine Army.

Perhaps the most intriguing defence deal with Israel and the one which successive governments tried hardest to keep secret was the Tory decision in 1972 to allow the Vickers shipyard at Barrow-in-Furness to build three submarines for the Israeli Navy. The boats were copies of a German design and the Israelis would have preferred the Germans to build them but the West German government declined. So the compromise was arranged.

I was not popular with my Israeli friends for revealing this, though it was an Israeli defence attaché who told me about it.

Meanwhile big defence deals with the Arabs, and particularly with Saudi Arabia, were under way, so in February 1974 the Foreign Office announced the ending of the Middle East arms embargo, to caustic comment from Moshe Dayan. Lord Carrington, however, then the Defence Secretary, played more than fairly with the Israelis. Saudi Arabia wanted to buy British Jaguar strike planes and export orders for this excellent machine were badly needed. The Saudis refused to sign an undertaking that they would not pass the planes on to any other country, meaning Egypt in particular. So Carrington withdrew the export offer and the Saudis bought Mirage jets from France instead.

That is the result of most of such political arms embargoes. Somebody else supplies the demand and all that Britain receives is balm to the consciences of the politicians and Foreign Office men.

My own relationship with Israeli Intelligence built up over the years has paid off professionally many times but never more handsomely than in December 1967 when I was able to announce with authority that the Suez Canal, which had been closed since the Six-Day War, would remain shut indefinitely, probably for years – a prospect which was not generally appreciated, least of all by the many nations which urgently wanted it opened for trade purposes. George Brown, then Foreign Secretary, ridiculed my prediction, but though I did not reveal it at the time, my information was better than his.

I had made a friend of Brigadier Zwi Zamir, the Israeli defence attaché who was returning to Israel to become the chief of Mossad, the Israeli Intelligence service, of which I knew he was a member. As a parting gesture he telephoned me to ask if I would like an exclusive interview with General Yitzhak Rabin, the victor of the Six-Day War, who was passing through London on his way to become ambassador in Washington (he later became Prime Minister). It was clear that Rabin wanted to talk.

In a brief but meaty interview in the Hyde Park Hotel, Rabin assured me that not only did the Israelis want the Canal kept shut but the Americans were backing them in that resolve and the US government was the only one capable of exerting effective pressure on Israel to reopen it.

Rabin first explained why the Israelis wanted the Canal closed. So long as they sat on the bank, Nasser had to keep his Russian MiGs on airfields out of Israeli artillery range and they then did not have enough range to bomb Tel Aviv. The Israeli defence line against a tank attack could be much shorter and there were other tactical advantages. The US interests in keeping the Canal shut were strategic. The Russians could not use it to ship arms to Vietnam as they had done before, and it also blocked their easy route to the Red Sea and the Indian Ocean.

The Canal remained shut for eight years.

Because of his pro-Arab policy, which was greatly strengthened after the Arab oil embargo and price increases, Heath's relations with Israel and with Golda Meir, then the Israeli Premier, were not good. Wilson's, perhaps, were too good and when he was photographed hugging her in public in late 1974, when he was back in office, Arab ambassadors complained to the Foreign Office about this 'over-friendly attitude'.

Wilson further emphasized his attachment to Israel during a dinner in Mrs Meir's honour by telling a story of how during a Palestinian hijack, a little while previously, the terrorists had demanded that he should 'express grovelling regret' for Britain's part in establishing the state of Israel. He delighted his audience by claiming, 'There could only be one answer even though twenty British lives were at stake. I refused without calling the Cabinet!'

Later, however, Arab diplomats, including the Tunisians who had negotiated with the hijackers, denied that any such demand had ever been made.

Even my Israeli Intelligence friends could provide no support for Wilson's contention but they had solved an intriguing mystery for me concerning the blowing up of a Japanese jumbo-jet by terrorists at Benghazi in Libya the previous year. The hijack had been a shambles from the start, with the terrorists securing nothing and making only muddled demands, and the explanation was fascinating.

The operation, involving three Arabs and a Japanese, was being led by a Christian Iraqi woman with the unlikely name of Katie Thomas. She had replaced Leila Khaled, the Palestinian terrorist set free by the Heath government, as chief operator in Europe for the Popular Front for the Liberation of Palestine. She apparently intended to demand several million pounds ransom from Japan for the release of the plane and its passengers but, for security reasons, had given no details of the plan to her co-terrorists. As she was sitting in the jumbo's cocktail bar having a glass of champagne, a grenade concealed in her clothes exploded, killing her instantly. The three remaining hijackers then took over the plane but had no idea what to do next. They flew around, staying for days in the blistering heat of the airfield at Dubai, waiting for orders that never came. Finally, at Benghazi, having told all the passengers and crew to get out, they set fire to the plane, creating a £10 million funeral pyre for Katie, whose identity they wished to preserve.

Understandably, this was one terrorist incident for which the PFLP did not admit responsibility.

In the spring of 1975 Wilson spurned a Libyan offer to recycle £1,000 million of its oil money by placing arms orders in Britain. Though my disclosure of this was angled to show what the deals could have meant to British firms, I knew, as did my informant, that the details would kill it forever. The order included Jaguar strike planes and six submarines. Apart from other considerations it was the submarines which enabled Wilson to reject the package in spite of all the employment the orders would have created. Two years previously Gadhafi, the Libyan dictator, had planned to use a submarine to sink the British liner *QE2* when she was carrying Jews to Israel.

My disclosure of the refusal of the Libyan order brought denials from Number 10, but on the following day we were able to print the letter which Sir Lester Suffield, then the chief Whitehall arms sales-man, had sent to the Libyan purchasing office on behalf of the Prime Minister.

Wilson was awarded great credit by the Israelis for this rejection of orders that would have pleased several of his back-benchers with seats in areas which would have benefited, but no other Prime Minister would have accepted them.

The origins of Wilson's Zionism and his close connections with rich and influential Jews in Britain is of considerable interest because of the effects it had on his long tenure of office and on his political reputation. According to Marcia the origin was Biblical and rooted in his Yorkshire upbringing. She told me that he had always been imbued with the mystique of the Holy Land, which exists for most people brought up in the Christian tradition, and had visited Israel before she met him. Apparently he used to bring back bottles of Jordan water and on presenting one of them to a priest in Liverpool was surprised to be told, 'Our Holy Water usually comes from the tap.'

His interest in Jewry was undoubtedly stimulated during his time at the Board of Trade, first as Secretary for Overseas Trade then as President from October 1947 until April 1951. From the start he was keen to promote East–West trade, no doubt believing that it would break down the barriers between Britain and the Soviet Union, which were hardening after the end of the war, and through that he met a group of East European Jewish refugees who had retained and developed contacts behind the Iron Curtain. Most of them have gone on to make remarkable financial successes of their businesses and have been honoured and, in several cases, ennobled by Wilson.

While collecting honours, wealth and in some cases, like Lord Schon, appointments, these immigrants have managed to keep an astonishingly low profile, though in the case of Joseph Kagan (now Lord), who was born in Lithuania, Wilson himself provided continuing publicity by wearing his Gannex coats.

Some of these men have helped him financially in his political life. When he was in opposition between 1970 and 1974 about a dozen wealthy Socialists, many of them Jewish, supported a secret trust fund of some £25,000 a year to help meet the costs of running his office. Of the five trustees, four were Jewish, including Lord Goodman, the solicitor, and Sir Rudy Sternberg (later Lord Plurenden). Contributors included Cyril Stein of Ladbroke's, an ardent Zionist, and Arieh Handler, a City financial consultant. The trust was kept secret from the Labour Party and even from the chief whip, its first chairman, Lord Brown (no relation to George) explaining that they did not want the party 'to get their fingers into it'. In 1973 another trust fund to provide about £40,000 a year to recruit special advisers for the Labour shadow Cabinet was set up by Sigmund Sternberg (now Sir), a Hungarian-born immigrant who was no relation to Plurenden but was also involved in trade with Eastern Europe.

A key figure in effecting these friendships with recent Jewish immigrants specializing in East–West trade was Beattie Plummer.

Lady Plummer – Beattie to her numerous Labour friends – was born Beatrice Lapsker and married Leslie 'Dick' Plummer, who was also Jewish. Plummer was a managerial executive on Express News-papers when I joined the company and I came to know him quite well. He was always of the Left but gave no indication of being of the extreme Left, as his wife seems always to have been.

Because of her connections, Plummer was appointed to take charge of the Labour government's ill-fated groundnuts scheme in East Africa and I attended his farewell dinner, suffering the fate of being called upon by Beaverbrook to make a short speech there after he had presented the guest with a £10,000 personal present. When Plummer returned from the groundnuts disaster, he presumably received another golden handshake from the Government and became Labour MP for Deptford in 1951.

After he died suddenly in 1963 Beattie continued to play an important political role, cultivating Wilson to such a degree that when she died in 1971 he wrote her obituary in *The Times*, recalling how she had been 'passionately devoted to improving East–West relations'. She was present with the Wilson entourage at the Adelphi Hotel in Liverpool when he won the election in 1964 and was a regular visitor to Downing Street and to Chequers. In return Wilson, Marcia and others of the Labour hierarchy were frequent guests at Beattie's country house, Berwick Hall.

She was instrumental in introducing Wilson to many of the Jewish businessmen to whom he later awarded honours. Her contacts with the East Germans were such that she was regarded by the security authorities as a Communist agent of sympathy and she was a fre-quent and welcome visitor to the Soviet embassy.

Shortly before Plummer died he and his wife stayed at a Soviet resort on the Black Sea where they met Kruschev at his private beach-house. When they returned to England, they revealed that their relationship was sufficiently intimate for the Russian Premier to tell them that he was shortly to resume nuclear tests, though this meant breaking the previous nuclear test-ban agreement. Even some of Lady Plummer's closest friends, whom I have questioned, including Marcia, now have doubts about where her loyalties lay.

In 1977, following reports of MI5's interests in Labour ministers, George Caunt, a former member of Wilson's Kitchen Cabinet, named Lady Plummer as a major cause of security concern in his day. She managed to avoid publicity and attention from newspapers but, as Marcia now admits, there was more to her political activities than met the eye.

When Wilson resigned from the Board of Trade in 1951, it was ostensibly to go with Aneurin Bevan as a protest against heavy defence spending, though some of his less charitable colleagues, such as Woodrow Wyatt, believe that he went because he expected an adverse trade situation for which he might be blamed. Whatever the reason, Wilson found additional employment as a back-bencher by becoming a consultant to Montague Meyer, the Jewish firm of timber-importing merchants, where he remained for nine years and where he was joined in October 1956 by Marcia who worked with him as his secretary in the Meyer office in the Strand, which could hardly have been more convenient for Westminster.

There is an aspect of Wilson's term at the Board of Trade which generated considerable interest when it was raised in 1974 by a letter written to *The Times* by Lord Shawcross, the former Labour minister and Attorney-General. As a result of conversations with Shawcross I can dispose of certain rumours which at the time were damaging to Wilson and have never been publicly rebutted.

Following the parliamentary criticism over £500 said to have been paid to Edward Short by T. Dan Smith, a corrupt businessman, Shawcross wrote the letter to record an event which happened after he had succeeded Wilson at the Board of Trade in 1951. He disclosed that 'one individual highly placed in public life had corruptly received large sums of money', and stated that though he felt it was his duty to expose this man, and possibly others associated with him, he had been unable to do so for professional ethical reasons. 'So the evil doers continue to flourish,' he added.

Many people assumed that the individual was a politician and some inferred that it might be Wilson himself but Shawcross told me that he was, in fact, a very senior civil servant who is now dead. He had been paid large bribes to provide export credit guarantees to firms and people trading behind the Iron Curtain.

Shawcross discovered this only when one firm, which had paid the money -but not received the guarantee, attempted to expose the official. He felt that it was his duty to inform the Prime Minister, then Attlee, but when he took advice from the Bar Council he was told that it would be a breach of professional privilege to do so. His only recourse, Shawcross told me, was to urge the disgruntled firm to go to the police, but it declined because any action would have involved it in a corruption charge.

There was no evidence that Wilson knew anything about the matter but Shawcross hinted at one politician who had 'sailed near the wind' in connection with it.

I can appreciate Shawcross's difficulty because of my own experiences in trying to expose corruption by Whitehall officials. The late Geoffrey Edwards, a close friend of mine who made a fortune from commissions when selling British aircraft, missiles and other military equipment to Saudi Arabia, frequently complained to me that he had been required to pay out bribes in various forms to British government officials but could never expose them because he had committed an offence himself in doing so. I am not suggesting that corruption in Whitehall is rife. The British Civil Service is probably the least corrupt of any in the world but there have been several other occasions when angry businessmen have sought my assistance because they were being pressured for money and services without which trading difficulties could not be overcome. The laws of libel as well as other considerations have invariably allowed officials, who have been named to me, to 'continue to flourish'.

Wilson's work for Meyer's took him to Moscow on several occasions and Marcia accompanied him, recalling in her memoirs how his Board of Trade experience of East–West trade, especially in the timber business, proved to be extremely valuable to the company.

Wilson's governments have contained a substantial proportion of Jews including Harold Lever, John Silkin, Sam Silkin, Reg Freeson, Gerald Kaufman, Lady Birk, Stanley Clinton Davis and Joel Barnett.

There are also influential Jewish back-benchers like Ian Mikardo, the ultra Left-winger who has served as Chairman of the Labour Party, and Jewish peers, created by Wilson and promoting Labour's cause in the Lords.

Wilson has also been subjected to pro-Jewish influence from the Jews in his Kitchen Cabinet and his official entourage. Marcia records how Gerald Kaufman, then on the Downing Street staff and now Minister of State for Industry, pressed Wilson hard in Israel's interest during the Six-Day War.

Zuckerman, however, Wilson's 'court scientist', though Jewish, has identified himself so little with Zionism that when I met his brother, who lives in Israel, he was extremely scathing about him in this respect. Lord Rothschild, head of the Cabinet 'Think-Tank' during part of Wilson's premiership, is the British head of a family not only committed to Israel but deeply involved in its origin, but, knowing him as I do, he would never allow any interest of that nature to intrude into his precise, scientific advice. On the contrary he would studiously avoid doing so.

Among Wilson's personal Jewish friends, Lord Goodman has probably had the greatest influence, advising him on all manner of issues, apart from legal matters, and being one of his private emissaries in attempts to solve the Rhodesian problem.

Outside his family and staff, Wilson's closest personal friend is probably Lord Weidenfeld, his Austrian-born publisher who is such a staunch Zionist that he served for a year as Political Adviser and Chief of Cabinet to Israel's President Weizmann. Wilson is much more gregarious and convivial than is generally thought and is a frequent guest at the dinners which Weidenfeld holds at his elegant Chelsea home, for literary, political and social personalities. It was Weidenfeld, for example, who provided the late supper on the night of Wilson's resignation.

In addition, Wilson had the reputation of always being approachable by other Jewish leaders wishing to talk about Zionist affairs or anti-terrorism, in contrast to Heath, though the Tory Prime Minister had a few close Jewish friends.

The possibility that Wilson's attachment to Israel affected the whole of the government's foreign policy has led to considerable comment by pro-Arab writers. The Jews with whom he associated are almost all outstanding people, both in native ability and aptitude for applying it, and no doubt he benefited from their advice and support, but I find it difficult to see what, in real terms, he accomplished for Israel. Perhaps the Israelis were just grateful to see one committed statesman holding out a friendly hand from a hostile multitude. Or Wilson may have been more active in their interests behind the scenes than is yet known.

By supporting the Israeli cause as openly as he did, Wilson put his life in some risk from the attention of Palestinian terrorists. He always had an armed detective – one of them so quick on the draw that the Prime Minister delighted in making him demonstrate his prowess to his guests – but the risk was real enough, as the experience of Edward Sieff, now senior member of the Marks and Spencer family, showed. He escaped assassination in his home at the hands of a terrorist intruder, believed to be the infamous 'Carlos', only because the bullet which was fired into his mouth happened to miss vital tissues.

Sadly, another dear friend, Bruce McKenzie, who admittedly was connected with the Israelis in rather more dangerous circumstances, did not escape death, though it is not certain that Palestinians or their supporters were responsible, as Israeli Intelligence suspects.

*Chapter Thirty-seven*

# Operation Jonathan

THE use of murder, terror and hostages in the pursuit of political power stretches back far into history but now, because of rapid transport by road and by air, it has assumed a degree of internationalism which was not possible before. In crowded cities the motor car offers an all too easy means of sudden attack or seizure and escape, across borders if necessary, while the airliner presents hostages neatly packaged for the taking, with consequent world publicity guaranteed.

While professionally I have been involved in several hijacks as an interpretative journalist with useful Intelligence contacts in the Middle East, I have been connected with only one of them in what might loosely be called an operational function. This happened, however, to be the most memorable incident of all, the Palestinian hijack centred on Entebbe Airport in Uganda and the subsequent raid by Israeli commandos to kill the terrorists and release the hostages. My modest part, conducted from the safety of my study in the Surrey countryside, was very much concerned with international power politics.

On 27 June 1976 a mixed force of six Arab and German terrorists, including one woman, seized an Air France airliner which they had boarded at Athens. They directed it at gunpoint to Benghazi in Libya and then to Entebbe.

By Friday 2 July the Palestinians, who were demanding the release of more than fifty of their comrades held mainly by the Israelis, had agreed to free the non-Jewish hostages – some 165 people who were flown back to Paris. On their arrival there they had all been instructed to say nothing that might inflame the situation for the 110 remaining hostages and to their great credit they remained silent, though offers from the media to talk must have been tempting. All that was known was that Amin was taking a personal interest in the situation at the airport, acting as a negotiator and making political capital out of it. In Mauritius, to which he had flown for a meeting of the Organization for African Unity, he claimed that if he had refused to act as negotiator the hijackers might have killed all 275 hostages.

Early on that Friday morning I was telephoned from Paris by a friend in Mossad, the Israeli Intelligence service, who provided me with an exclusive story on what had been learned from the released hostages during their interrogation in Paris. I was urged to give it maximum publicity.

I could detect from the tone of my Israeli informant that publication of the information without delay was regarded as being of great importance. At that stage I assumed that it was part of a general Israeli psychological warfare exercise against the hijack and all associated with it. I was completely confident about the accuracy of the statements because, over a period of years of contact with Mossad, I had never been given any information which proved incorrect.

Having written the report I dropped in that evening to see Bruce McKenzie, who commuted between Nairobi and Cranleigh, Surrey, and told him what I had done. I learned that he had hardly been off the telephone all day and was in a very mysterious mood, refusing to say much about the Entebbe situation beyond remarking that he hoped the *Daily Express* would make the fullest use of the information I had been given, which he knew to be true.

Happily there was no great conflicting news that night and my report appeared as the front-page splash on Saturday morning under the headline 'Amin's deadly hijack game'. It stated that Amin, who as a Muslim supported the Palestinian cause, had been assisting the terrorists. The hostages had revealed that Amin had given the terrorists extra weapons, including sub machine-guns. He had allowed two more Arabs to join them and provided Ugandan troops to help guard the hostages, with orders to shoot any who tried to escape, so that the hijackers could sleep. This made it impossible for the Israelis to adopt the standard tactic of prolonging negotiations to exhaust the hijackers and break their resolve. Amin was even said to have embraced the terrorists on their arrival and it was his troops which had separated the Jews and non-Jews.

Amin's purpose, apart from eventually saving the lives of the hostages, was to secure the release of the Palestinian prisoners from Israel, which would bring him much needed prestige in black Africa and in several Muslim quarters.

Early on the Saturday morning I received another telephone call from my Israeli contact in Paris. The effusiveness of his gratitude made me suspect that there was more to the story than I had suspected but I was given no clues. Later that evening I again saw McKenzie who was more mysterious than ever and somewhat exhausted after another day of hectic international telephone calls. I asked him if he thought it possible that the Israelis might somehow attempt a rescue and he pointedly did not reply.

On the way home my wife, who had been with me at Entebbe and seen the Russian MiG fighters parked there, suddenly said, 'I know what the Israelis are going to do. They will stage a surprise attack by plane, blow up the MiGs to cause a diversion and then free the hostages.' I told her I thought it was a great idea but regrettably, Entebbe was out of range for such a venture unless it was mounted from Nairobi and that this was unthinkable even with Kenya's close links with Israel and McKenzie's undoubted influence on President Kenyatta and some of his senior aides.

When we awoke early on Sunday morning it was to the news of the brilliant Israeli rescue and complete justification of my wife's prediction.

The disclosure of Kenya's involvement in the raid, to the extent that the Israeli planes were permitted to refuel at Nairobi on the way home and deal with their wounded, explained the Mossad move and why my front-page Saturday morning report, which had been picked up by the wire-services and transmitted world-wide, was regarded as having such significance. To free the hostages the Israelis had to infringe sovereign Ugandan territory, probably kill Ugandan nationals and give the appearance of having to infringe Kenyan territory by arriving at Nairobi uninvited. It had therefore been essential for the world to know in advance that there had been deep Ugandan involvement in the terrorist situation at Entebbe to give the Israelis justification for their action and reduce the impact of the outcry certain to be raised by Uganda's friends. This could not be done by an official release of the information from Tel Aviv because then it would not necessarily have been believed and might well have indicated that some operation was in the wind. Done through me it just looked like a bad leak from Paris.

In the result, the Mossad move was well conceived. Reaction to the infringement of Ugandan sovereignty was minimal and quickly lost in the admiration for Operation Jonathan, as the raid was code-named.

I was able to enlarge on Amin's treachery in the next issue of the *Daily Express* with exclusive details of a sensational story which I had been nursing for five months. This did not please the Israelis and still less did it please my Kenyan friends but, given the opportunity, it was news which had to be told.

When the terrorists were making their demands at Entebbe they insisted on the release of five of their comrades held by Kenya. The newspapers were intrigued by this demand because only a handful of people, of whom I was one, knew what the Palestinians were talking about. The Kenyans denied having any terrorists, which was true then but only because of an extraordinary series of events, which are still having international repercussions.

While I had been with McKenzie in Kenya and in Uganda earlier that year I learned of an appalling attempt by Palestinian terrorists to shoot down an Israeli El Al airliner packed with passengers at Nairobi Airport. On Sunday 18 January 1976, three Palestinian Arabs equipped with Russian SAM-7 hand-launched anti-aircraft missiles had arrived by car at the perimeter of the airport shortly before the expected arrival of an El Al Boeing jet touching down on its way from Johannesburg to Tel Aviv.

Their objective had been to shoot down the plane as it came in to land, causing maximum casualties, which could have included Kenyans because there are many homes near the airport.

Fortunately, security men of the Kenyan General Service Unit, an organization set up on the lines of the British SAS, had been alerted by Israeli Intelligence and pounced on the men before they could assemble the missiles. The car contained sub machine-guns, grenades, and pistols which, together with the SAM missiles, had almost certainly been smuggled into Kenya from Uganda.

It was quickly established that two of the Arabs had staged the abortive attack by bazooka rocket on an El Al airliner at Orly Airport, Paris, in the previous year. They had all entered Kenya unarmed, and with visitors' visas.

On the following Tuesday two further terrorists, a man and a woman using South African passports but really West German citizens, flew in to find out why the attack had failed. Security men were waiting for them and when the woman was examined she was found to have further instructions for the Palestinians written across her abdomen in invisible ink. These told them to try the operation again on the next El Al plane, or failing that on an American, French, German or British plane in that order of priority.

Having prevented the attack, the Kenyan authorities were then presented with the problem of what to do with the five terrorists, who, of course, were those whose release was eventually demanded by the hijackers at Entebbe. Under Kenyan law, unlike the situation in Uganda, they could not be quietly executed. To try them and imprison them would raise very difficult security problems for Kenya. So the Israelis offered to take them off Kenya's hands and it was because I spotted the senior Israeli Intelligence official who had negotiated the take-over that I learned of the facts. I had been immediately sworn to silence and being a guest and not on duty I had no option but to oblige.

After the Entebbe raid, however, the story assumed such significance that I secured permission to tell it. Uganda's complicity in the attempted attack on the airliner helped to explain why the Kenyan authorities, whom I have since been assured did not include Kenyatta, agreed to allow the Israelis to land at Nairobi after the operation.

The Israelis promptly denied any knowledge of the Nairobi incident but eventually acknowledged its truth by putting all five on secret trial, which has been in progress for many months at the time of writing. The Kenyan authorities not only denied it but let me know through friends that I would not be welcome in their country again. In spite of this, however, I was making arrangements to go there in the spring of 1978 when what looked like the last revenge for Entebbe took place in circumstances more like something out of a novel than real life.

Though the bare facts of McKenzie's part in helping to organize the Israeli use of Nairobi Airport had been made public through an American paperback book about the Entebbe raid, and though it was known that he had been awarded a medal for his part in Operation Jonathan, he was such a remarkable and courageous man that he had managed to repair his old personal relationship with Amin. In spite of all the past problems centred on the reputation of Amin and his henchmen as brutal killers, the restoration of trade and political relations between Kenya and Uganda had become increasingly necessary. McKenzie, who had once served as the only white minister in Kenyatta's Cabinet, and had continued as confidant to the Kenyan President, agreed to act as go-between to accomplish it.

While I was lunching with him in April 1978 at his home in Surrey, he told me he had already been to see Amin and was convinced that he wanted to repair his reputation with the West. He suggested that I should assist by flying out with him to interview Amin and secure evidence of his good intentions at first hand. After discussing the project with my editor I agreed to go and McKenzie promised to try to make the arrangements.

On 24 May McKenzie flew from Nairobi to Entebbe accompanied by Keith Savage, his white Kenyan business partner, and Gavin Whitelaw, then managing director of Lonrho Export, who was leaving that company to join McKenzie in various trading enterprises. All three were personal friends of mine and the purpose of seeing Amin was to promote trade details with Kenyan enterprises in which they were personally interested.

While they were seeing Amin in Kampala their small twin-engined Piper plane was parked unattended at Entebbe. In the evening they set off for Nairobi and as they were flying over the Ngong Hills the plane blew up, killing all three passengers and the pilot. Forensic examination of the bodies and the wreckage proved that the explosion was due to a bomb, probably handed in as a parcel for kind delivery in Nairobi. Examination of fragments in Britain showed that it had been professionally made, being actuated by a military time-fuse, not a wrist-watch.

I am in no doubt that the target was McKenzie. The time-bomb may have been handed in by some pro-Palestinian or by one of Amin's henchmen in revenge for Entebbe. Or, as the Kenyan authorities suspect, it might have been planted by someone with political objections to any renewal of relations between Uganda and Kenya or between Amin and McKenzie in particular. Whoever committed this appalling crime would certainly seem to have had some political motive.

Apart from my *Daily Express* tribute to McKenzie, an international figure friendly with the political leaders of many countries, including Britain, little publicity was given to the outrage by the Western press, radio or television. The murder of Steve Biko, a black African agitator with no British connections, was exploited for weeks.

On his own initiative Sir Harold Wilson wrote an obituary notice on McKenzie for *The Times*, expressing his gratitude for the wise counsel the white Kenyan had given Kenyatta over the years and for his other activities as ambassador extraordinary. Regrettably, the notice was so tough about Amin, urging his own people to get rid of this 'thug' so the he could no longer 'pollute Commonwealth soil', that *The Times* declined it.

*Chapter Thirty-eight*

# The Resignation of Harold Wilson

FOR the past two years I have been making intensive inquiries into what many people regard as the biggest mystery of postwar politics – why Harold Wilson resigned the premiership to make way for an older man.

During that time I have investigated many popular theories and rumours – some of them fantastic, a few scurrilous – but the facts which I have been able to establish accord with only one solution, which I now propose to present. It is the only solution which accounts not only for Wilson's departure when he might have been expected to continue through jubilee year, but also for several other associated mysteries. These include his spirited effort to save Jeremy Thorpe from losing the Liberal leadership, and his astonishing assertions about a South African connection. The theme which underlies every aspect of it is the pursuit of political power.

Shortly before Wilson announced his resignation honours list one of the peers he was about to create was called to Number 10 to be given the offer. He responded by saying, 'Of course, Prime Minister, I accept, but I am only sorry that when I sit in the Upper House I shall not be serving you.'

According to this peer, Wilson replied, 'You may still be able to do so. In a few months time I could well be back.'

He then explained that he anticipated the early defeat of the Callaghan government and a Tory fiasco under Margaret Thatcher because the unions would create industrial unrest. He believed that if the Queen then had to look round for someone to summon to lead a government of national unity he could well be the only possible candidate.

Wilson had some justification for such a view at that time. Callaghan would have been defeated in an election because everything was running against him. But a Thatcher government might well have been short-lived, with the Ulster Unionists under Enoch Powell's influence being anti-Tory and the Scottish Nationalists then on the increase. In the ensuing crisis neither of those defeated leaders would be likely choices. Edward Heath could hardly be a starter, having lost the support of his own party, and others with prime ministerial experience were too old.

Shortly after Wilson resigned, Marcia had lunch with Lord Chalfont in the Lords and told him a similar story. She has also told me that, while Wilson is fundamentally opposed to coalition, in such a circumstance he might well feel that he had to accept and that, in any case, he could not refuse the Queen anything, being so devoted to her that he carries a photograph of her in his wallet at all times.

On the day in December 1976 that Reg Prentice resigned from the Labour government because of his general disillusion with its policies, Lord Kagan, the Gannex coat manufacturer who had been ennobled by Wilson, saw Mrs Marjorie Halls, an official in the Lord Chancellor's office, who has figured elsewhere in the book, in a corridor of the House of Lords. After giving Mrs Halls an autographed copy of his maiden speech he told her that Wilson was furious with Prentice for 'jumping the gun'.

'In this affair, timing is everything,' he said.

When Mrs Halls asked what he meant, Kagan explained that Wilson had resigned because he foresaw that Callaghan would be defeated and a subsequent Thatcher government would collapse. In those circumstances Wilson could be recalled by the Queen. According to Mrs Halls, who gave me this information before I had heard similar stories from others, it was even suggested that the quick award to Wilson of the Garter was to give him additional dignity to ease a possible recall. (With Mrs Halls's permission I reported this occasion in the *Daily Express* on 8 February 1977 with no ensuing comment from Kagan.)

I questioned Marcia about this myself early in 1978. At that stage she thought it unlikely that Wilson might be recalled, and that it had been something of a pipe dream, but believed that in the event of a hung election he could still be the only man experienced enough to lead a government of national unity.

Both Marcia and Wilson, who see conspiracies everywhere, view the continuing attacks on his reputation, as in *The Politics of Power*, the recollections of Joe Haines, *Sir Harold Wilson, Yorkshire Walter Mitty* by Andrew Roth, *The Pencourt File* and the memoirs of the political correspondent James Margach, *The Abuse of Power*, as denigrating the former Prime Minister's reputation to improve the image of his successor and prevent any return to office.

I do not believe that Wilson resigned just to be called back later, having made some more money by writing lucrative books, which he is doing at an astonishing pace. The situation was much more complicated than that. But the facts indicate that he did not regard his career as a statesman as finished, and the idea of recall was possibly a factor in reaching his decision to resign.

It will be wondered why, if he seriously entertained the idea of a glorious return, he inflicted so much damage to his reputation by his controversial honours list and his sterile pursuit of the 'South African connection'. As I said in Chapter Twenty-five he did not regard the honours list as extraordinary, was astonished by the reaction to it and still defends it.

As for the South African connection I am satisfied that it was much more than a suddenly concocted gimmick. It was, I believe, a deliberate, perhaps desperate, bid to prevent a development which has delayed the flow of British political history and may have diverted it. I refer to the Lib-Lab pact.

The pact between the Labour Party and the Liberals, which kept a broken-backed government in office long after it would otherwise have been swept away, appeared to arise suddenly in March 1977. It is my contention that it was in gestation for many months before that and was largely responsible for Wilson's resignation and for putting Callaghan in Number 10.

The chain of events that culminated in that leadership change reached right back to 1968 when Wilson's popularity with the unions suffered a tremendous decline with his decision to introduce legislation against unofficial strikers. The proposal, introduced in a White Paper called *In Place of Strife*, included a compulsory twenty-eight-day conciliation pause for unofficial strikers, who could be prosecuted if they refused to return to work during that period.

Labour's extreme Left, with solid union support, was determined to defeat the Bill and as more and more Cabinet ministers defected, Wilson and his Employment and Productivity Secretary, Mrs Castle, were soon left as its only supporters. Wilson was allowed to escape from his position by claiming that the legislation was no longer necessary because the unions had given a 'solemn and binding undertaking' to intervene in unofficial stoppages. As expected, this turned out to be no more than a device to enable the Bill to be dropped.

It was that moment, I believe, which eventually led to Wilson's resignation and to Callaghan's accession. During the battle over *In Place of Strife*, Callaghan let it be known that he was absolutely opposed to trade union reform through legislation and had fought to defeat it. This assured him of future trade union support and there are those very close to Wilson who claim that, ever afterwards, Wilson had to rely on Callaghan to deliver union support when it became necessary.

Callaghan's behaviour fully accorded with the recipe for political success he had given to George Wigg way back in the forties: 'Wait until the trade unions decide their line and follow them.'

In the previous year Callaghan had made several half-hearted attempts to oust Wilson as leader. One of his Cabinet colleagues has described to me how he used to go round from time to time counting heads to find out how many would support him, but could never find enough.

During the conflict over *In Place of Strife* he made one further attempt to gain enough support while Wilson was out of the country on a visit to Nigeria and Ethiopia. One of the RAF officers on the Prime Minister's flight has told me how he had to hand Wilson a radio message warning him what was happening back home. The officer was lost in admiration for the way Wilson dealt with the situation while airborne thousands of miles away.

Callaghan was also unable to move against Mrs Castle but as soon as he became Prime Minister the unions got their revenge when he ostentatiously fired her from the government.

Wilson remained convinced that the country's economic situation would have become much sounder if the trade union legislation had been passed, so his relations with Callaghan were cool. They improved, however, after Callaghan supported him inside the party over entry into the Common Market.

A further factor in this improvement, according to an informant close to the action, was the operation for removal of the prostate gland which Callaghan underwent successfully in January 1972, while he was shadow Employment Secretary during the interval in opposition. He appeared to lose much of his aggressive drive after that event and took on a rather bland avuncular personality, showing no pretensions to the leadership. He even told Wilson that he considered himself out of the running.

Whether that was just a temporary effect of the medical operation or not, it brought Wilson and Callaghan closer and over the next three years Wilson decided that he preferred his former rival as a successor rather than either Jenkins or Healey. He regarded Healey as too abrasive and brash even to make him Foreign Secretary, the post he always wanted.

Early in 1975 Wilson had definitely decided that he would not continue as Prime Minister long after his sixtieth birthday, which was in the following year. He was certainly disenchanted with being Prime Minister, having to face a minority situation and an increasingly hostile Left wing, but his decision may have been partly prompted by medical fears.

In January 1975, while approaching Washington airport, Wilson and other ministers were subjected to a very bumpy and dangerous

landing in an RAF VC10 which had been given the wrong instructions from the control tower. He experienced some unpleasant heart
flutters as a result and though a medical examination showed that
there were no signs of heart defect, he was advised to take things
more gently.

This frightening experience naturally increased the pressure to
retire which his wife had been exerting on him for many months.
Wilson had been a young Oxford University don when she had
married him and a quiet, backwater life was what she had expected
and wanted. She greatly disliked cut-and-thrust politics with all its
personality problems, disappointments, publicity and, above all, the
lack of privacy which her introspective nature needed. Marcia told
me that she once found Mary Wilson in tears in Number 10 because
some male official had blundered into her room while she was still in
her night-dress. George Wigg has also recalled a different occasion
when he found Mary weeping in the flat at Number 10 after an
altercation with another official.

It was experiences like these which made her refuse to live there
after her husband was restored to the premiership in 1974. According to close friends, her exasperation with being a Prime Minister's
wife had become so intense in 1975 that she issued something of an
ultimatum – she was prepared to move out of London if Wilson
insisted on remaining in power.

Wilson is very fond of his wife and there can be little doubt that her
views were an important factor in his general decision not to continue indefinitely.

(Later when Callaghan was Premier-elect but not in command he
was asked if he still feared that Wilson might yet change his mind.
His reply was, 'No. Mary wouldn't let him.')

A Buckingham Palace contact has told me that Wilson mentioned
the medical advice he had been given to the Queen during 1975. The
contact said that it seems she may have misinterpreted this as a
suggestion that his doctors had recommended that Wilson should
retire. This belief, that the Prime Minister might be seriously ill, may
have been reinforced when he told the Queen in December that he
wanted to go soon after his sixtieth birthday and may account for her
quick award of his knighthood. Further medical checks, however,
have shown that the fears were groundless.

George Thomas, the Speaker of the House of Commons, has
confirmed that Wilson told him of his impending departure 'many

months previously' though without giving a specific date. During the Labour Party conference in the autumn of 1975 Wilson asked his principal private secretary to draw up a 'scenario' for announcing his resignation and this was completed by November of that year.

Marcia and several other members of the Kitchen Cabinet knew of the 'scenario' and one or more of them leaked the news to James Callaghan, the obvious successor, at an early date.

It is therefore inescapable that, whether for medical, domestic, political or some other reasons, Wilson had decided some time in 1975 that he would not continue as Prime Minister for much longer. There was still, however, no certainty that he would name a date as early as 16 March 1976, the day he eventually chose. Many older men in positions of great responsibility tell their friends, during times of excessive strain and weariness, that they intend to retire 'soon' but somehow find the energy and the justification for continuing.

My inquiries show that he was jollied along into staying at Number 10 through 1975 mainly by Marcia: 'Some of us convinced him he would be making a mistake by leaving early. I'm sure we were right. I wish in the country's interests he had stayed longer.'

This could conceivably have continued right through into 1977 because that was to be jubilee year. It would seem reasonable to suppose that such an admirer of the Queen would have preferred to soldier on through the celebrations and announce his retirement at the end of them. I have it on good authority that in January 1976 Callaghan remarked that Wilson was saying he would retire 'shortly' but he did not expect him to do so before the end of jubilee year.

Wilson takes pride in pointing out that he was the longest-serving peacetime Prime Minister of this century, only Churchill and Asquith having served longer because of wars. Had he continued for a while longer he might have been able to claim the outright distinction, of which he would have been even prouder.

What then was the event which brought about his sudden decision to name the day? That it was sudden there can be little doubt because Marcia, his closest political confidante, has repeatedly assured me that she was not told the actual date until the Sunday before the Tuesday on which the announcement was made. 'I knew something was in the wind but I had to ask him to tell me the date.'

It is my conclusion that early in 1976 a new political factor suddenly gave Callaghan an unassailable advantage over Wilson as Prime Minister. This was the absolute necessity for some deal with the Liberals or some other Parliamentary group if the government was going to survive until a much more favourable time for a general election. Wilson was irrevocably opposed to such a deal but Callaghan was not.

This situation, which crystallized in near disaster for the government early in March, was appreciated by Callaghan and his close supporters. Callaghan's old ambition to replace Wilson, revived over the past year through his knowledge that the Prime Minister was half-wanting to go, was intensified. He was able to push Wilson into a political corner and, though resisted for a while, this extra pressure proved too much on top of the medical fear, the supplications of Mary, the wear and tear of the years and the problems of running a minority government containing a restless group of Left extremists making insistent demands.

Let us examine the facts. At the start of 1976 the difficulties for the minority Labour government were increasing, with the Left becoming more and more vocal over unemployment and the impending government efforts to stem inflation by cutting public spending. It seemed clear from opinion polls and by-election results that if a general election were to be held the Conservatives would be returned with a large majority, so it was imperative to prevent one. Only one realistic solution was to hand – a solution vainly attempted by Heath after the first 1974 election – to come to some arrangement ensuring Liberal support on occasions when the government might otherwise be defeated.

This move, common enough in Europe, was not open to Wilson in spite of his reputation as a political trimmer. As far back as the Labour Party conference in October 1973 Wilson had told the delegates that, so long as he was leader, he would not enter into any coalition with any other party, Liberal or Conservative. 'There will be no electoral treaty, no political alliance, no understanding, no deal, no arrangement, no fix.' He promised that if a Labour government was returned with only a small majority it would go forward with its policies and if the Liberals made that impossible the issue would be taken back to the people for a decision.

He stood by this firmly and it remained his view as the political and economic difficulties became worse. I have established to my satisfaction that if Wilson had remained in office he would have called an election in 1976, knowing that he was virtually bound to lose it, rather than come to any deal with the Liberals that would have been certain to influence Labour's policies and legislative programme.

Marcia, who sees Wilson daily because she continues to be his political secretary, has assured me that though the Lib-Lab pact has kept Labour in office for more than a year, he still deplores it. Wilson thinks it is fraudulent to go to the country on a policy which then has to be altered to suit another party which the voters have rejected, in most constituencies, with contempt.

Callaghan, who was Foreign Secretary, was in no such inflexible position and, through his dealings with West Germany, had seen how a minority Socialist government could remain in office almost indefinitely through a firm deal with another small party.

Like most of his Cabinet colleagues he was totally opposed to an election that would put the Tories back in office for at least four years, meaning that he would then be sixty-eight and out of the running for the premiership. He believed – rightly as it transpired – that, if the government could hang on for a further eighteen months, conditions could change radically, particularly as North Sea oil was beginning to flow.

Even the Cabinet's left-wingers, who opposed a pact with the Liberals in principle, were prepared to go along with it to avoid an election. If Wilson remained in command an early election was almost inevitable. Either he had to be induced to change his view, which seemed unchangeable, or he had to make way for someone else. The latter was the choice with greatest appeal for the left-wingers who by no means regarded Callaghan as a certainty for successor. They had a dark horse in the shape of Michael Foot.

At this stage, at the start of 1976, even the Kitchen Cabinet, with the sole exception of Marcia, was in favour of Wilson's departure and the accession of Callaghan, with whom some of them were making their dispositions. Marcia still had hopes of inducing him to stay on through jubilee year but a crisis point was reached on 10 March when Wilson and his government were defeated on a major issue by twenty-eight votes. This was during the debate on the cuts in government expenditure which were essential to secure the support of the International Monetary Fund, without which the economy could collapse, but which the left-wingers strenuously opposed. Enough left-wingers revolted to cause a constitutional crisis.

Wilson's disenchantment with his Left wing was now complete and pressures from the Right for him to make way for Callaghan were increasing. He knew that if he remained he would be sure to lose the election he felt he would soon be driven to call. Industrial production was not rising and the sterling reserves were about to suffer a catastrophic fall due to massive withdrawals by oil states, of which he had been warned. For a man who regarded himself as a statesman of stature the most sensible course was to retire voluntarily and let his successor face the eventual verdict of the people.

Still reserving the right to tender the whole government's resignation to the Queen – and letting this be known to the rebels – he remained for the immediate vote of confidence which had become essential following the defeat in the House on 10 March. This was held next day and, though the rebels continued their attacks on their own side, enough of them were sufficiently fearful of forcing an election to vote for the government, which survived by seventeen votes.

Without Liberal support – given because the Liberals dared not face an election either – the majority would have been derisory and this rubbed home the need for guaranteed Liberal votes in future confidence situations.

There is no doubt that Wilson had decided on a date to go shortly or immediately before the confidence debate. I am also as certain as I can be that there was collusion with Callaghan before the debate to ensure that Denis Healey, the Chancellor, could not possibly succeed in the contest for the party leadership that Wilson's resignation would entail.

Healey had behaved so arrogantly in his dealings with foreign powers while Defence Secretary – objecting to being 'a sort of white slaver for the Arab states' – that Wilson was convinced he would make a dangerous Prime Minister on that score, apart from his in-built defects in dealing with Parliament and his own party. Naturally, this was also Callaghan's view.

Healey was given no warning of Wilson's imminent resignation and during the censure debate was encouraged to respond to the left-wing onslaught with a loyal fighting speech so strongly worded that one Labour MP walked out of the chamber in disgust, giving his own Chancellor the V-sign. His performance alienated possible left-wing supporters so severely that he had no chance whatever when he eventually insisted on competing for the vacant leadership and it is reasonable to suppose that, had he known what was about to happen, he would have been less forceful.

Possibly to placate Healey, Wilson later claimed that nobody else in the Cabinet knew that he was about to resign.

It is true that most of the Cabinet did not know and some were deeply shocked when Wilson broke the news to them, Short being in tears, but Callaghan definitely did know, through Kitchen-Cabinet leaks if through no other source, and Wilson was aware of this.

Michael Foot put up a surprisingly effective performance as champion of the Left in the leadership struggle, demonstrating how far the Parliamentary Labour Party had moved in that direction. But Callaghan was Wilson's choice. The Prime Minister might have been pushed into going earlier than he had intended but once he knew that he had to go, he preferred the moderate Callaghan to the firebrand Foot or the abrasive Healey.

Marcia later told me that, in return, Callaghan had asked Wilson to stay on as Foreign Secretary, as Alec Douglas-Home had done after resigning the Tory leadership. Since Callaghan, the former Foreign Secretary, wanted to keep a tight control on that department, Wilson could be relieved of most of the responsibility and travel the world as a Labour ambassador extraordinary. Wilson refused.

In his resignation statement Wilson went out of his way to insist that there were no hidden scandals or problems of any kind, political or personal, behind his resignation.

While I have met scores of people, including senior politicians of both main parties, former Chiefs of Staff and top civil servants, who are all convinced that there must be a secret and, so they suspect, scandalous reason why Wilson quit the premiership in 1976 rather than in 1977, I have encountered only one who claimed to know exactly what it was. He declined to enlighten me for what he called 'international reasons' and if he really did know some secret he died with it.

I have drawn Sir Harold's attention to the fact that journalists and others are still trying to discover the secret reason for his departure. He could not have been more relaxed. Removing his large-bowled pipe he remarked, 'Well, they've had two years to search and they haven't discovered anything yet have they?'

## Chapter Thirty-nine

⸙⸙⸙

# The South African Connection and the Lib-Lab Pact

JEREMY THORPE must have been a key figure in any early Labour deliberations about the feasibility of a Lib-Lab pact for he retained the leadership of the Liberal Party for two months after Wilson retired. He was not particularly keen on the general idea of any deal with Labour, believing that Liberal MPs were sent to Parliament to pursue Liberal aspirations independently. This was proved after the hung election in March 1974 when Heath offered him either a full-blown coalition with a Cabinet post for him or, failing that, some arrangement which would guarantee enough Liberal support to enable the Tories to continue in office. After taking soundings inside his party he declined.

This attitude, which seems to have continued, offers a plausible explanation for the South African connection affair.

At the turn of 1976 it was clear to Fleet Street journalists, and I suspect to many MPs, including Labour ministers, that Thorpe's days as leader were numbered. The allegations of a past homosexual relationship with Norman Scott, a male model, persisted and there was an impending court case which would be certain to put the matter back into public discussion.

This was the trial of a former airline pilot called Andrew Newton, who was later to be convicted of threatening Scott's life and of shooting his dog on a lonely moor in October 1975.

There is evidence that Thorpe knew that Scott would raise the homosexuality charge again at this trial because he warned Cyril Smith, then Liberal chief whip, about this in January, though the trial was not scheduled to take place until 16 March, the day on which Wilson eventually resigned. Smith told me that the way Thorpe was able to do this has continued to mystify him. 'How did Thorpe know what Scott was going to say two months in advance of the trial?' he asked me. The answer may be that the information came to Thorpe simply as a result of normal exchanges between lawyers involved in the preparations of the case.

Whatever Thorpe may or may not have known, he told a meeting of the Young Liberal Council on 31 January that he intended to remain leader 'for years to come'.

That Wilson was thoroughly aware of Thorpe's predicament was demonstrated on 3 February when the Liberal leader left his seat in the Commons to keep a 4 p.m. appointment with the then Prime Minister behind the Speaker's Chair. When he returned he had what Cyril Smith called 'an enigmatic expression'.

Reluctant at first to tell his chief whip what had happened, Thorpe eventually answered Smith's insistent question, 'Come on – is it good or bad?'

'It's good. It will all be pushed on to South Africa.'

'What the hell does that mean?' Smith demanded.

'The PM believes that there are South African influences at work,' Thorpe snapped.

The eventual result was a statement by Wilson in the Commons on 9 March – a week before the announcement of his resignation and about two days, I believe, before he firmed up that decision – that he had no doubts at all that 'there is strong South African participation in the recent activities relating to the leader of the Liberal Party'.

He then went on to claim that these activities were 'based on massive reserves of business money and private agents of various kinds and qualities'.

This was a considered statement made, I suspect, in response to a supplementary question, which he knew was going to be raised, and I have since discussed it privately with Wilson.

He told me that his evidence for the South African interference was first based on information given to him via the Cabinet Office from MI5. 'There had been suspicions that people used by BOSS [the South African Intelligence organization] had been paying attention to certain black Commonwealth diplomats in London,' he said. 'As regards Thorpe, MI5 could not say that the South Africans were guilty but they could not say they were innocent either. There had also been one or two suggestive articles in the South African papers, so I felt justified in going ahead.'

This allegation about BOSS was likely to be true because all countries have a few Intelligence men attached to their embassies under diplomatic cover and it would be the South Africans' duty to report on the intentions of any black Commonwealth diplomats believed to be operating against South Africa's interests – which means most of them. But in my view it was a thin basis for the very serious parliamentary accusation.

What, then, was Wilson's purpose in making it? Again I have a first-hand answer.

'My intervention was purely for the purpose of coming to the aid of a parliamentary colleague,' Wilson said during a formal interview.

He insisted that he had no knowledge then of any alleged murder attempt or plot against Scott. And he admitted that he might have been wrong about his South African connection allegations and might be prepared to withdraw them. He would not say whether he or Thorpe had first thought of the South African 'scenario'.

It therefore seems that Wilson had been looking for a life-raft to throw to Thorpe and simply seized on the South African idea, flimsy though it was. He was reasonably friendly with the Liberal leader but not, I believe, to the extent of feeling that for reasons of personal relationship it was his duty to try to save him. What other reason could there have been for this rash act, which, in the result, has not added to the former Prime Minister's reputation for sound judgement? The only answer which makes sense to me is that he wanted to keep Thorpe in control of the Liberal Party for his own political reasons.

I suggest that one of them, perhaps the dominant one, was to prevent a pact with the Liberals to which he was totally opposed. So long as Thorpe was in command such a pact seemed unlikely. With Thorpe's obvious successor, David Steel, the position would be very different. As far back as February 1974 Steel, then Liberal chief whip, had been spelling out policies which Liberals should demand in return for supporting a minority government. Steel has since told me that he remained increasingly in favour of it as a means of imposing some Liberal influence on Labour policies.

What could be Wilson's purpose in wanting to prevent a Lib-Lab pact if he was giving up the leadership anyway? First, there is the probability that at the time he attempted to save Thorpe he had not firmed up his departure date and still intended to continue in office for a while. So long as Thorpe remained leader he could counter pressures from his Cabinet and party colleagues for a Lib-Lab pact by pointing out that the whole idea was a non-starter because Thorpe would not have it anyway. With Steel in command he would stand no chance.

Secondly, he was convinced that a pact with the Liberals was thoroughly bad for the long-term image of the Labour Party, whoever was in charge of it. The thought of the party to which he had devoted his life being manipulated in any way by a handful of Liberals revolted him.

A further explanation resides in the possibility that he knew that a Lib-Lab pact could delay a general election and that he was not averse to an early election which Labour might lose, so long as he did not have to fight it. After talks with him, with Marcia and other close friends I consider it possible that he had become so concerned about the infiltration of left-wing extremists into the Labour Party that, privately, he believed that a sojourn in opposition would enable the genuine Social Democrats, of whom he is undoubtedly one, to dissociate themselves from the far Left and regenerate Labour into a truly democratic alternative.

The sound reasons why genuine Social Democrats feel that sloughing off the far Left is imperative have been convincingly presented by Woodrow Wyatt, the former Labour MP, in his book *What's Left of the Labour Party?* and I have reason to believe that Wilson basically agrees with them in spite of Wyatt's attacks on his past leadership. At the time of writing, Marcia believes that Margaret Thatcher will win the next election and says that Wilson agrees with her. I sense that Marcia wants her to win, though she has not specifically said so.

It is by no means unknown, nor need it be disloyal, for a staunch supporter of a political party – even a former leader – to believe sincerely that it would benefit by a sojourn out of office. Since his retirement Wilson had consistently warned against the left-wing infiltration of the Labour Party and its machinery and has come out strongly against Eurocommunism, which is a long-term aspect of the infiltration process in democratic disguise.

The suggestion that Wilson's purpose in coming to Thorpe's aid was to keep him in command of the Liberal Party and so prevent a Lib-Lab pact is supported by the strange fact that Wilson continued to assist him by promoting the South African connection on 4 April, after he had given up the premiership.

On Saturday, 8 May, more than a month after he had finally stepped down, Wilson went to Halifax to make what he described to me as a 'speech on Eurocommunism' but he used it to expand his allegations about South Africa, hinting that Labour as well as Liberal politicians could be involved in a smear campaign.

In the next day's *Sunday Times*, Thorpe issued a six-point denial of Norman Scott's allegations, which meant that the copy had been in the hands of the newspaper on the previous day or possibly sooner. In support, certain letters from Thorpe to Scott, which had been with Scotland Yard for years, were also published. As this move was likely to induce Scott to issue a writ for libel – which he did, though eventually he withdrew it – it could only have been a last-ditch effort by Thorpe to avoid resigning the Liberal leadership. And because of the timing of Wilson's speech, which was given publicity in that Sunday's newspapers, it is difficult to avoid the conclusion that Wilson knew of Thorpe's rather desperate move and was trying to help him.

Thorpe resigned as leader the following day, 10 May, giving a 'sustained Press witch-hunt' as his reason in his letter to David Steel.

As he is such a survivor by nature and had withstood the Press assault with admirable calm, it is hard to believe that this was the real reason. Some other pressures may have proved irresistible on that weekend

Wilson continued to pursue his South African connection theory even after Thorpe's departure. He collaborated with a BBC team who originally intended to produce a television and radio series proving it to be true. This led to suspicions that Wilson must be grinding some axe of his own, the popular theory being that the South Africans had some embarrassing information and that he wanted to discredit them in advance in case they revealed it.

Caryl de Wet, the South African ambassador in London at the time, was a personal friend of mine and he assured me after inquiries in Pretoria that no such embarrassing information existed and that the South African government and its Intelligence agency were totally at a loss to explain Wilson's behaviour. This has later been confirmed to me personally by de Wet's successor.

Another possibility is that Wilson continued to help Thorpe in view of Scott's libel writ. Letters from Wilson to Tory MP Peter Blaker and from Sir Charles Curran, the former BBC Director-General, to me, show that Wilson began his BBC collaboration on the South African connection while the writ, which Scott withdrew on 14 May, was still in force.

It is also possible, of course, that Wilson pursued the issue simply to show that he had been correct, as, like most politicians, he has always had an aversion to being proved wrong. Or it may even have been an expression of what I call the 'show-biz syndrome' – an insatiable desire to keep on hitting the headlines, with even bad publicity being better than no publicity at all.

In the result the BBC inquiries were ended because it soon became apparent that no South African connection existed. Wilson's collaborative effort ended sadly for both himself and for Thorpe with the publication of *The Pencourt File* by BBC investigators who went freelance.

The names of various other politicians were dragged into the South African saga, which generated some of the wildest fantasies in my thirty years of covering Whitehall. One of the most hilarious was told to me by Cyril Smith who received a visit from the police following a mad allegation that he had held a horse while another MP had masturbated it. When the person making the allegation was induced to name the other MP it turned out he had only one arm! Even the sponsor then had to admit that his story must be false.

The terminal event which suddenly caused Wilson to fix 16 March for the irrevocable announcement of his resignation has been the subject of rather sensational speculation.

It has been suggested that Wilson selected it to oblige the Queen. The separation of Princess Margaret and Lord Snowdon was about to be announced officially and there has been some publicity for a theory that Wilson agreed to time his resignation announcement to coincide with it in the hope that this would help to blanket Press coverage of the break-up of the royal marriage.

Wilson has assured me that there is no truth in this. 'Never at any time did I discuss the Queen's family with her except when state occasions, like Prince Charles's investiture, were involved,' he asserted. 'She would never have raised a family issue with me.'

I am in no doubt that this is correct, especially as the idea made little sense to anybody knowledgeable about Fleet Street. Given a choice of a lead story on the end of a royal marriage or a Prime Minister's career, the mass-circulation papers would go for the royal interest every time. (A comparable situation had arisen when the news of Queen Mary's death looked like coinciding with Stalin's. The *Daily Express* editor much preferred to lead on the former.)

In the result the problem did not arise for most papers because the official announcement of the break-up was not made until 19 March, but the point I have just made was proved. My colleague John Warden, the political correspondent, secured a 'scoop' leak on the royal separation and it was published at the same time as the news of Wilson's resignation. It took almost the whole of the front page while the resignation was relegated to the inside of the paper.

I established that Warden had not been told by any source in Buckingham Palace. In fact the public relations department there knew nothing about the impending announcement, to their great annoyance.

There is just one further possibility that the timing of Wilson's resignation could have been connected with a matter of royal concern. During the interrogation of Norman Scott by journalists, the model had claimed that on the night he stayed in Thorpe's home, which Thorpe does not deny, they stopped on the way to visit Lord Snowdon. The journalists sensed that Scott might mention Snowdon, if pressed, during the opening of the court case which, as it happened, did coincide exactly with the resignation date – 16 March. It is therefore not impossible that, spontaneously, Wilson might have done the Palace a good turn by hoping to blanket any publicity on that score. Wilson completely denies it, however, and my inquiries with Buckingham Palace sources suggest that if anybody there had heard of this minor connection with the Thorpe–Scott affair they were completely relaxed about it as being of no consequence.

However, if there was just a chance that a member of the royal family might be dragged into the story, however peripherally, MI5, which has the protection of royalty as a major function, might have made it its business to take an interest. This could explain why Thorpe had mentioned the counter-subversion organization in his conversation with Cyril Smith.

At the time of writing, nobody I have questioned among Wilson's closest friends and colleagues appears to know exactly why he chose 16 March. Marcia insists that he has still not told her. An

Intelligence source has assured me that Callaghan does not know, which may explain the message I received from a very senior member of MI6 that I would not be wasting my time trying to find out why Wilson resigned because there was 'something of a mystery there'.

Whether Wilson regrets having left is hard to say. I have been closely in his company on several occasions and all he wants to talk about is politics and his political career. I suspect that he does regret it.

A year elapsed between the accession of James Callaghan and the announcement of a Lib-Lab pact, which enabled him to survive a no-confidence motion proposed by Mrs Thatcher in March 1977. Some political commentators argued then that the pact was unlikely to survive because it had been rushed into too hurriedly. I believe that the reason it survived so long was because it was very carefully planned well in advance.

Nothing much could be done before Thorpe departed, and a new leader as young and inexperienced as Steel, who was thirty-eight, had to play himself in. Further, Steel could not move openly before the Liberal Party conference in the autumn when the idea of the pact would have to be sold to the party, where there had been strong opposition to any deal with Labour or Tories, especially from the Young Liberals.

On 31 August, during the long parliamentary recess, which also delayed any overt moves, *The Times* reported that Steel was prepared to form a coalition and intended to make the idea an important issue at the conference, which he did, battling his way to the conference hall through Young Liberals waving banners which spelled out 'No to Coalition!'

Steel has told me that until that time he had received no approach from Callaghan, who had been enjoying the quiet 'honeymoon' period which a British opposition traditionally awards to a new Prime Minister. When Callaghan did move it was in most peculiar circumstances.

While Steel was attending a meeting of European Liberals in November 1976 he met Hans-Dietrich Genscher, the West German Vice-Chancellor and Foreign Secretary. He was the leader of the small German Liberal party, called the Free Democrats, and was in the government by virtue of a coalition with Helmut Schmidt, leader of the Social Democrats, who could not govern without Genscher's support.

Genscher, who was a friend of Callaghan's from the recent days when both had been Foreign Secretaries, suggested to Steel that he should form a similar pact with the Labour government.

'I told him I had been pressing my party to agree to Liberal participation in a coalition or agreement,' Steel told me. He then added, 'The following month, Genscher telephoned me from Germany to say that he had discussed the matter with Jim Callaghan, who had given him a message for me: Jim would be delighted if I went to see him to discuss the possibility of a pact or some other form of cooperation.'

Genscher's original overture to Steel was something of an intrusion into British politics, suggesting, perhaps, that Schmidt, his leader, preferred a Socialist administration in London. I find it hard to believe it was done without first consulting Callaghan. Indeed it is not impossible that Callaghan organized such an indirect approach because he wanted to tell his Left-wing government colleagues and back-benchers, who were still opposed to a pact in principle, that the initiative had come from Steel.

This is exactly what Cyril Smith suspected when Steel discussed it with him.

'I told him he would be mad to volunteer to approach Callaghan,' Smith told me. 'He would be putting his head in a noose if he took the initiative. "Let him come to us", I said, "if he wants us." '

Meanwhile, according to information given to me by Enoch Powell, Callaghan was negotiating a potential pact with the Ulster Unionists, which could have been a major political coup because, until the recent past, the Unionists had been solid with the Tories and automatically counted as part of a Conservative majority. This was admitted in rather vague terms by the Prime Minister in his speech about the government's future on 23 March 1977 to shouts of 'Bribery' from the opposition. Powell and James Molyneaux, the leader of the Ulster Unionists, had been to see Callaghan about an increased number of parliamentary seats for Ulster, which was to be the government's part of the bargain. Michael Foot, the Leader of the House, had been present at the discussions and also referred to them. They came to nothing because, according to Powell, the Ulster Unionists 'could not deliver', presumably meaning that not enough of them would agree to a binding pact simply in return for a promise that a Speaker's conference would look at the electoral representation in Northern Ireland.

Callaghan therefore seized on the Liberal offer for keeping Labour in office, which Steel announced on 12 March 1977. The terms were something of an ultimatum, and though Steel insists that Callaghan, at that point, had not approached him directly – he was still negotiating with the Ulster Unionists – I find it hard to believe that he had not been assured in advance that some means of accepting his offer would be found. For a new Liberal leader to have suffered a public rebuff from the Labour Prime Minister would have been disastrous.

When Callaghan did accept, it was to prevent certain defeat in the Commons, so he knew that he would be able to carry his left-wing objectors with him.

Once he had secured the pact, Callaghan was not only assured of many more months in Number 10 but was able to control his left-wingers by claiming that he was unable to carry out measures they were demanding because the Liberals had to be appeased.

No objective observer of the Whitehall–Westminster scene can doubt that the Liberals' main motive was to prevent a general election which could have cut their Parliamentary membership back to half a dozen or less. This has been apparent to a sufficient number of their former supporters to cost them many future votes. As Jo Grimond put it, 'To some people we seem to have become the poodles of Labour, fearful of an election and uncertain of the future.'

Steel found an excuse to keep the pact going even when 116 Labour MPs voted against the Liberal requirement of proportional representation for the election of MPs to the European Parliament as a prelude to the adoption of the same system for Westminster.

The Liberal pretence of influencing Labour fiscal policy continued even after the April 1977 Budget, which must have been a profound disappointment to Steel. In the previous January, Cyril Smith, who opposed the pact, had disclosed to me that Steel had assured him that, in return for continuing support, Chancellor Denis Healey had promised that personal income tax would be reduced from its current basic rate, to a figure less than that which Labour had inherited from the Tories. This meant a reduction from 34 per cent to less than 30 per cent and nothing like that happened.

Steel's position in holding the pact, with more and more Liberal supporters deserting the party, became even more untenable after the 1978 budget and what amounted to a mini-budget a few weeks later. In June he announced that the pact would formally end in July, taking it to the end of the parliamentary session. This was long enough for Callaghan to make further use of it to survive a censure motion which would probably have brought his government down.

CRIII

*Chapter Forty*

CIIII

# My Friend Enoch Powell

NO consideration of the pursuit of political power in Britain should ignore Enoch Powell, who for years has been driven by the desire to become leader of the Tory Party and Prime Minister. Whether he has the necessary array of talents for either post is arguable. He is perhaps the nation's most intelligent politician, probably the most honest, and certainly the most eloquent. He is a brilliant debater, has an immense capacity for work, an impeccable private life and unchallengeable integrity. But there are those among his former colleagues who believe that he lacks political judgement and the capacity to compromise, which many regard as an essential qualification for ministerial office in a democracy.

There are very few, however, who doubt that Powell's estrangement from the Conservative Party has weakened not only that party but British politics as a whole by confining such a rare talent to membership, not even leadership, of a tiny group, the Ulster Unionists.

'I was born a Tory and I will die a Tory,' I have heard him say. Yet, even though Heath, his old enemy, is on the sidelines himself, he looks like remaining outside the Tory Party as MP for Down (South) in Northern Ireland.

I was in close touch with him at the time of the crucial event which marked the beginning of his alienation – the occasion when Heath removed him from his front-bench position of shadow Minister of Defence. This happened immediately after he had made his famous – some would say infamous – speech against the dangers of uncontrolled immigration, claiming, as he still does, that it will lead to racial bloodshed. Most people believe that this speech was the reason why Heath sacked him. In fact it was only the excuse for a move which the Tory leaders had been wanting to make for many months.

There is no doubt that Heath felt uncomfortable with Powell, who so obviously had his eyes on the leadership. Enoch had also irritated his colleagues by speaking out against the stated defence policy of the party which required that British Forces must remain in their bases East of Suez to continue Britain's influence there. As shadow Foreign Secretary, Sir Alec Douglas-Home promoted this policy in his public speeches and anybody else giving tongue on that subject, especially the shadow Minister for Defence himself, was required to do the same.

Powell, with his customary political longsightedness, saw that Britain would not be able to sustain the costs of continuing the air and naval base at Aden, the facilities in the Persian Gulf, the large base at Singapore and other smaller overseas establishments. Further, he did not subscribe to the Tory view that if Britain moved out of these bases the Russians or local Communists backed by the Kremlin would one day move into them or that it would matter if they did so. He believes the Tories have an unjustified fixation about the Russians, the Americans and the Europeans being Britain's most dangerous opponents in the political and economic field. He therefore urged publicly that the Forces should be withdrawn from East of Suez to the NATO theatre as soon as convenient.

He appeared to be splitting the party on defence, a position which opponents can always exploit, and he was warned about it by his colleagues. Being unable to trim on any issue in which he believes, he pressed ahead with airing his views.

A lesser man could have resolved the difficulty by resigning the defence post – he had, after all, once resigned from office in the Treasury – or by waiting quietly for a reshuffle.

To this day Powell insists that the speech he made on immigration in his own constituency of Wolverhampton, where there was already a large coloured population, was fully in support of Tory Party policy. The party had decided to oppose the Race Relations Act and

Enoch expected no adverse reaction from his colleagues. He might have proved right about this, but on the Sunday after he made the speech, which was given great prominence in the newspapers, Heath was telephoned by *The Times* to be asked what he was going to do about it. Heath saw the opportunity and sacked Powell.

Naturally, this made Powell bitter against Heath, whom he did not regard as an effective leader, and his resentment was reinforced when events proved that his defence policy had been correct. The Tories loudly opposed the East of Suez withdrawals carried through by Labour, but when they came to power in 1970 they continued them. The new government had the option of reversing the Labour decisions to quit the Persian gulf but decided that, in spite of the importance of the oil there, Britain could not afford to remain. Enoch's predictions had, in fact, been dead right.

While those who constitute what Enoch calls 'the race relations industry' – those who make a good living out of promoting good race relations – were horrified by his stand against coloured immigration, it had wide appeal throughout the country. As he put it to me at the time, 'Things will never be the same again.' Nor have they been. As I can testify, people, especially the elderly, still stop Powell in the street to shake his hand and urge him to continue with his campaign, which he does from time to time in spite of a warning from Labour's Attorney-General that he risks prosecution under the amended Race Relations Act.

Irritatingly perhaps for some, he has been proved right again and again on his claims that the Home Office estimates of the number of coloured immigrants and their birth rates were pitched too low and I can put an interesting little gloss on that.

One evening I was late for a small private dinner at a friend's house because some official immigration figures showing that Powell had been right had finally been issued by the Home Office and I had to write about them. Harold Lever, then a member of the Labour front bench, was present at the table when I explained to my host why I was late.

'But we always knew Enoch was right,' Lever remarked.

'In that case why did your side always say he was wrong?' I asked.

'Because he's a racist,' came the honest reply.

After many talks with Powell on the immigration issue I do not believe that he is a racist in the sense that he is prejudiced against any breed or creed.

Powell spent much of the war in India and has no feelings of dislike for coloured people or feelings of superiority over them. He simply objects to the way whole areas of major cities have been taken over by Asians and West Indians who have no real ties with Britain.

What motivates him is a profound feeling for nationhood, which he believes to be one of the mainsprings of a country's energy, and which in Britain's case is being diluted by an influx of aliens which he believes can never now be stemmed. As he put it in Parliament, when he warned about the numbers of Asians entering Britain – and it is the numbers which concern him – 'We are trying to bail out an ocean.'

I have heard him argue that just as a feeling of kinship helps to bind a nation together, the lack of it in a multiracial society can be divisive, as the colour prejudice problems experienced in the United States have demonstrated over the years.

The kind of love which Powell feels for his native soil used to be extolled in poetry and prose but is now derided by those who believe, or affect to believe, that there is something particularly splendid about a multiracial community. He expresses it in almost everything he says and does, sometimes in rather startling ways.

Usually when I go to visit Enoch in his home near Sloane Square we talk in the upstairs sitting-room, but on one occasion I was taken into his study, a small room lined with books and with the papers for the current book he was writing neatly arranged on his desk.

As I entered I noticed a glass frame on the wall behind the desk containing his wartime epaulettes with the crown and pips insignia of his rank of brigadier. His regimental buttons were mounted below them.

'Ah, you've kept your epaulettes,' I remarked, knowing that reaching brigadier from the ranks so quickly was a feat of which he was justifiably proud.

'I've kept my whole uniform,' he replied. 'I'm going to be buried. in it.'

'With your hat on?' I asked incredulously, imagining that unforgettable face motionless and at rest wearing the red-banded hat.

'Yes, with my hat on!'

I could see that he meant it.

No doubt this story will be grist for those of his opponents who say, 'Enoch is mad, haven't you seen his eyes?' In my experience anybody more logically sane would be hard to find. The eyes stare because the brain behind them is computing the consequences of everything he is asked or utters.

No race legislation curtailing freedom of speech is going to silence Powell, who has an inbuilt streak of stubbornness which is expressed in his private as well as his political life. One of his quirks on which he is not to be moved is his belief that the way to combat extreme heat is to wear a great deal of clothing to keep it out. In theory, insulation when the outside temperature is higher than the body temperature makes sense but he had personal proof that it does not work during a visit to Spain. On a very hot day in Andalusia he insisted on wearing a tweed suit and waistcoat, his only concession being a panama hat. After sweltering at the bullfight in Cadiz he and two other politicians, more suitably dressed, decided to visit the village of Medina Sidonia, home of the Spanish commander defeated by Drake in the Armada battle. Enoch suddenly felt ill with a temperature of 104 degrees. The Spanish doctor summoned to the scene could find no infection and when told what the patient had been wearing diagnosed heat-stroke. Nevertheless, if I ever see Enoch on a hot day it is odds on that he will still be wearing a waistcoat.

In spite of Powell's antipathy towards Heath he did all he could to secure the return of the Tory Party to office and of Heath to Downing Street in 1970 and is convinced that he was instrumental in achieving that. 'I am bitter about the complete reversal of all the grounds for which I put Edward Heath into office in 1970,' he said to me some years later.

That may sound grandiose but there is much evidence to support his view that it was his late intervention on immigration and other issues culminating in a 'Vote Tory' call by him which converted an opinion-poll swing against the Conservatives to a thirty-one-seat majority. In those days Powell had a massive following because of his stand against immigration, especially in the Midlands where concentrations of coloured people were high.

Though this may sound even more grandiose, I believe that I had a hand in that victory – with the assistance of Maurice Macmillan, Harold Macmillan's son and a former Minister in the Treasury – through the 'cooking the books' episode I described in Chapter Twenty-one.

Enoch's final break with his party came in the 1974 election when he urged his followers to vote Labour, a seemingly renegade move which may well have swung the five Midland seats which put Wilson back into Number 10.

His reason for this was his total opposition to British membership of the Common Market and his belief, which proved to be unfounded, that Labour would withdraw from it. Enoch was in a very small minority in believing that Wilson had any intention of taking Britain out of the Common Market and Labour's eventual 'renegotiations' of the treaty bordered on farce, but the Tories offered no prospect of withdrawal.

Powell's Tory friends, of whom many remain, think that he should at least have kept his opinions to himself during the election out of party loyalty but his burning need to abide by the rule, 'To thine own self be true', made this unthinkable.

'After I had voted against my party on the Common Market time after time in Parliament, how could I support them on an election platform?' he asked me.

Such a resolute stand made it impossible for him to fight as a Tory MP for Wolverhampton which he had represented for twenty-three years. It was a tremendous break and Enoch told the truth when some heckler called him 'Judas' while he was speaking for Labour.

'Judas was paid,' he responded. 'I have made a sacrifice.'

Only those who know how much Enoch enjoyed and valued being the member for Wolverhampton can appreciate the extent of that sacrifice.

Had the full facts of Powell's links with Labour over the Common Market been known at the time he would have experienced a much rougher ride. He has since told me that he was in direct contact with Wilson during the run-up to the election on the timing of anti-Common Market speeches and during the election was in contact through intermediaries. These included Wigg, who has confirmed this to me and Haines, Wilson's Press adviser. Wigg, who remains opposed to Common Market membership as does Powell, is proud of his collaboration with his most unlikely bedfellow. He too believes that their joint effort gave Wilson the five crucial seats in the Midlands.

As with all people who are regarded as turncoats, Powell did not derive much long-term respect from Wilson, not that it will bother him.

I suspect that Enoch even believes he was at least partly responsible for the defeat of Heath by Mrs Thatcher in the election for the Tory leadership after the second 1974 election defeat. When I telephoned him on the morning after her victory his reaction was, 'I've shot my fox, haven't I?'

Some of Powell's supporters think and hope that he will still emerge as leader of a coalition. He himself believes that his own actions have made this impossible and maintains that, though people are disinclined to believe it, he is no longer pursuing personal power but working in the interests of Northern Ireland. 'In political history men who become detached from their own party are more likely to go further than to do a U-turn,' he observed. However, I have reason to know that the possibility of power, remote though it may be, still appeals and he came near to achieving a degree of it in collaboration with Callaghan, as I related in Chapter Thirty-nine.

I do not think he will join the Labour Party, though that is not impossible, so at sixty-six I doubt that he has any ministerial future. Nevertheless he will continue to command attention and respect. As he puts it himself, 'If I have committed political suicide I am an uncommonly lively corpse.'

CRENED

*Chapter Forty-one*

CRENED

# The Power Syndrome

THE essence of power lies in the capacity for controlling the lives of others. Most people enjoy wielding it to some degree – the foreman, the shop steward, the manager, the landed lord, the strict father, the commander-in-chief, the editor. But it is in the field of politics where power offers its greatest potential for such control.

From Westminster and Whitehall a few politicians exert remote control over more than fifty million people to an extent which has become incredibly pervasive with the relentless increase of government intrusion into private life. In Britain now, politicians confiscate wealth, sieze land and property, control working hours, food prices, housing, education and transport, and can, through their agents, invade the privacy of the home.

These various agents partake of the power by delegation and it is my experience that many of them, from the senior civil servant to the Inland Revenue collector, enjoy exercising it.

The closer they are to the pinnacle of power the greater their influence and air of authority, a situation epitomized by the Downing Street joke about the visiting VIP who was told, 'Lady Falkender is busy but the Prime Minister could see you.'

The enormous increase in the number of officials over the last twenty years has not only strengthened the government's control over people but substantially improved a Labour administration's chances of remaining in power. With the nationalized industries, the government now employs about 30 per cent of the total labour force. This 'payroll vote' is unlikely to be attracted to a party which, in the interest of the national economy, proposes to reduce the over-manning either in the Civil Service or the nationalized industries.

Many of the unions also represent a major extension of the power of a Labour government with the determination of their officials to keep Labour in office, or secure its quick return, to continue controlling the lives of the population in the ways they desire.

Those with inordinate ambition to get to the top are usually easily discernible, though some are clever at concealing it, and in both Westminster and Whitehall they tend to be known these days as 'fliers'. Being a flier seems to be admired but not long ago, when such thrusters were called 'careerists', they were frowned upon.

It has been fascinating to watch over the years how some fliers succeed up to a point then seem to give up the struggle. A few find the strain intolerable as did John Biffen, who seemed destined for high office in a Tory administration. A few are sidetracked by financial offers like Brian Walden, who moved into television. Others just seem to lose heart, Geoffrey Rippon being a good example. He used to explain to me how he must eventually succeed to the Tory leadership or something very near it because he was the right age and nobody else had so much experience so young, which then was true. But having become Secretary of State for the Environment, a post he seemed to dislike, he faded from the running.

Duncan Sandys was another friend who seemed groomed for one of the highest offices but achieved nothing higher than Secretary of State for Commonwealth Relations. I sensed the drive was departing when he alerted me to an interesting situation while he was in opposition. I readily agreed to write about it but, he then explained that he could not be present in Parliament to follow it up in debate because he had been invited to the Guyana independence celebrations and wanted to go there.

This change in attitude surprised me because I knew that Sandys enjoyed power more than most, having seen him in action when dealing, rather cavalierly, with Chiefs of Staff as tough as Field-Marshal Sir Gerald Templer, while pushing through his radical – now much regretted – defence changes. I also recall the relish with which he told me – long after the event – how he had been suddenly diverted, during a trip abroad, to see the Shah of Iran, who was about to sign a treaty with Russia. Ordered from Downing Street to 'Stop the Shah signing at all costs', Sandys did so with great skill, to the fury of Kruschev. The Kremlin complained bitterly that Sandys had interfered in its affairs, which was music to his ears.

An essential attribute for success in the political power game is a following of MPs in the parliamentary party. Without it, securing the leadership, which leads to the premiership, is almost impossible.

A following is achieved not only through respect for political or oratorical skill but through personal popularity, and cultivating it requires frequent visits to the House of Commons Smoking Room to keep in touch with back-benchers, who may be bores. Duncan Sandys was one of several fliers who were not prepared to go through these motions and so never acquired a following.

Of course, a following, however faithful, is not enough. R. A. Butler (now Lord), had one but, on his own recent admission, lacked what it took to push himself when the Tory leadership became available. The same might be said of Reginald Maudling.

Wartime not only increases the control which politicians can exert over people through the assumption of emergency powers but provides it in the ultimate degree to the military Chiefs of Staff who have the authority to send people to their death. When a war is over, such power is largely taken away from the military men but the politicians invariably retain some of the extra authority they acquired, usually without much complaint from the public, which has become used to controls.

Formerly in peacetime the British Chiefs of Staff had such prestige and authority that the resignation of a First Sea Lord, for instance, over a dispute with a government would have been of high political significance. In my time in Whitehall, the Staff Chiefs have been so shorn of power that if they rightly warn the public that forces' morale is being dangerously sapped by poor pay and conditions, as they did recently, they are publicly rebuked by the Prime Minister for attempting to influence political matters. The threat is the same as that embodied in Churchill's alleged wartime treatment of General de Gaulle when, in his famous fractured French, he warned, 'Si vous m'opposerez je vous get-ridderez.'

The civil servants have not been deprived of power by the politicians. It is much more difficult to get rid of a permanent secretary whom a minister dislikes, or who may even be drinking too much, than to retire a Staff Chief prematurely. Treasury and Foreign Office officials in particular still exert a dominating influence, often banefully, through the advice they give to their political chiefs, who are often frankly lost without it.

This situation must continue in all positions demanding a high degree of professionalism so long as ministers are shuffled from one ministry to another every two years or so. Enoch Powell once explained to me why, in his experience, two years is enough. 'For the first six months you are learning the job and implementing decisions agreed by your predecessor. Over the next year you may gradually get your own ideas across if you are forceful. After that you become part of the machine and it's time you were on your way.'

Following the Second World War a new breed of civil servant with great potential power has appeared in Whitehall – the scientist, to whom non-technical people feel they must defer if only because they cannot grasp the technological problems at issue. Britain's scientists had made such a contribution to victory that, for some years, they were held in awe by the politicians and the results were not always beneficial, as the following example demonstrates.

Shortly after the war, Sir Ben Lockspeiser, the Supply Ministry's chief scientist, announced that Britain's attempts to solve the problems of supersonic flight would be made by small robot planes because he and his colleagues, 'hadn't the heart to ask pilots to risk their lives in such a dangerous enterprise'. Test pilots, both civilian and RAF, disagreed and wanted to try flights through the so-called sound-barrier with a Miles aircraft designed for that purpose and nearing completion.

While the scientists were still experimenting with their robots, rather unsuccessfully, American pilots showed that the supersonic problems had been vastly exaggerated and breached the sound-barrier with ease. From then on the United States dominated the development and production of supersonic fighters.

Later I learned that Lockspeiser, who meant well, had been influenced by my revered friend, Sir Barnes Wallis, the inventor of the bouncing bombs of the famous 'dam-buster' raids on Germany. Wallis was so distressed by the casualties in that operation that he vowed he would never be responsible for risking pilots' lives again. He proposed the robot solution and Lockspeiser accepted it. The politicians played virtually no part in that decision, which they regarded as being outside their competence, though it had great economic consequences. This error of judgement was followed by another science-based project to make Australia the 'arsenal of the Empire'. It was argued that Britain was too small to accommodate the development of supersonic planes and missiles, so many millions of pounds were spent on building a 2,000-mile rocket range at Woomera in the Australian desert with other ancillary facilities. British aircraft and electronics firms were to move substantial parts of their operations to the other side of the world. The entire project, to which ministers had readily agreed, was a costly failure and there are many Australians who have not forgiven Britain for inducing their government to share the costs of it.

With weapons as secret and difficult to understand as nuclear bombs, even the Chiefs of Staff have had to rely on scientific advice and there have been times when they have been excluded from the decision-making process on which they were really the experts. At one Anglo-American naval meeting in Washington, to decide on the size of aircraft-carriers which each ally should build, not a single member of either the Royal or US Navy was present. The power of recommendation, which, in such technical cases, has so often been virtually the power of decision, was entirely in the hands of scientists and civil servants.

As can be imagined, the established civil servants did not relish the sharing of their power by scientists and still don't. The Whitehall cry was, 'Scientists should be on tap but not on top,' and there are still echoes of it. The outstanding talents of some scientists like Professor R. V. Jones, so valuable in helping to win the war against Germany, were largely wasted after it because of Civil Service jealousy.

The Civil Service response to the prospect of power-sharing when a Defence Minister decided to bring in a personal adviser from outside was brisk to the point of brutality. The minister was Duncan Sandys and the adviser, Colonel Kenneth Post. As Churchill, Sandys's father-in-law, had used Lord Cherwell as a tame professor, Sandys wanted Post, who was highly intelligent, at hand to protect him against being blinded by the scientists and bamboozled by the Service Chiefs. Their friendship dated back to undergraduate days at Oxford when they had staged what became a historic raid on the Proctors' quarters.

With great difficulty Sandys had Post, who received no payment, cleared for sitting in on secret policy meetings. Within days I was told by one top civil servant, 'We're not having it. There are we advising the minister in the afternoon about some vitally important matter and there is Post in the evening sitting on the edge of the minister's bath advising against us. We're not having it.'

They were as good as their word. They made every kind of difficulty for Post, particularly about the fact that he had an office with his name on it, and he was soon ousted.

To some extent power resembles money in that there are people who quickly learn how to use it while others are destroyed by it. The danger is enhanced by the fact that in politics, accession to enormous power can be sudden, rather like winning the pools.

As people who acquire money are fearful of losing it so it is with power. This is especially true at the top political levels where it can lead to suspicion of conspiracies which usually do not exist. Combating these 'plots' can be time-wasting and Wilson expended an inordinate amount of his energies in that direction. The commonest comment about power is that it corrupts. What do people mean by this? Some think that it means that power makes men corruptible for money but I have seen little evidence of that. Some politicians may be corrupted in that sense on the way up to power but what power really does is to corrupt the capacity for sound judgement. When a man acquires great power and begins to enjoy exercising it, human frailty is such that he becomes increasingly averse to any disagreement with his actions and may end up believing that he cannot be wrong. This can lead to decisions which to others are obviously imprudent, or even wild, while he remains blind to his follies.

This corruption of judgement expresses itself most commonly as arrogance, leading politicians to treat their parliamentary colleagues and the public with some degree of contempt. Of those in office at the time of writing, Healey has this arrogance in fullest measure. George Brown was touched with it while he held office. He has been described to me by a Foreign Office man of great discernment as having 'the finest untutored mind' in his experience. Yet when he gave evidence to the Radcliffe committee on the D-notice affair his attitude was that they just had to accept his interpretation of events because he was the Foreign Secretary. It was not accepted, but lesser men than those on the committee could have been overborne. Even the urbane Macmillan gave his D-notice chairman, Sir Richard Way, a rough time because he could not see why the Press could not be told what not to print.

A further demonstration of the way power corrupts judgement is through the use of it to grant favours to friends to a degree which, to the perceptive public, looks like blatant misuse even if it is not. Wilson's resignation honours and his inability to foresee the public reaction provide a memorable example. One more recent was the appointment of Callaghan's son-in-law, Peter Jay, a young man with no diplomatic experience, to the most important diplomatic post there is – the ambassadorship in Washington.

Public reaction to such events, though sharp at the time, is so short-lived that one can hardly blame the politicians for being unconcerned about it.

If the increasing power of the politicians and of their machinery for enforcing it are a matter for public disquiet, what about the power of the Press? That, I am sure, is on the decline and has been greatly exaggerated anyway during the thirty-two years in which I have attempted to wield it.

In the long-term sense that people must be influenced by what they read, there is still some substance in the Press's power, though steady inroads are being made by television. But, in my experience, journalists exert little effect on specific issues if their views happen to be contrary to what the government of the day is determined to do.

On many occasions I and others have exposed situations which almost certainly incensed the majority of those who read our reports, but I cannot recall any major instance where this caused the government to change its programme or even to modify it. An exposure may be nothing short of damning and may cause an uproar in Parliament but if a government has a majority, or can secure one through a deal with another party, it can steamroller its wishes through and usually does. The Press has an essential function in alerting the public about what is really going on but, unless a general election is imminent, the public's attitude carries little weight with a government determined on a course of action. The frequently spurious assertion, 'We have a mandate. . . ,' is sufficient self-justification for most politicians.

Nevertheless I can record one remarkable occasion when I really did exert power through one of my Press reports – the revelation that the Committee on Drug Safety was about to make an important announcement about birth-control pills. This, I forecast, would warn that there were medical doubts about the use over a long time of one of the main ingredients in some of the pills taken by about 500,000 women.

The Committee had intended to stage a Press conference to present its findings in such a way that the fears of women users would be somewhat assuaged, but my premature disclosure forestalled that.

About a year later Sir George Godber, then Chief Medical Officer, took me to lunch at his club to inform me that so many women had taken fright at my report that there had been a sudden rise in the birthrate and that I had, in fact, been responsible for the siring of some 20,000 children.

That was power indeed!

Through excessive zeal it is also possible for a journalist to encompass somebody's death and I was very nearly responsible for such a tragedy at a rather important level.

In July 1973 Maurice Oldfield, a highly professional Intelligence officer, was appointed Director-General of the Secret Intelligence Sevice (MI6) by Heath, who was then Prime Minister. This delighted me and others who felt that he should have been given the job two years previously, when a diplomat had been preferred, and one of his admirers suggested that the occasion called for some publicity.

As Wilson had assured Parliament, the identity of the MI6 chief was not a matter of national security but there was a D-notice convention to cover it because, being publicly pointed out as 'M', was hardly conducive to secret operations.

While taking advice from a mutual friend, it was indicated to me that Oldfield shared several characteristics with Heath. Both were fifty-seven-year-old bachelors who had reached the pinnacle of their profession from humble origins. They had been scholarship boys who pursued similar interests at university, then served in the Army through the Second World War, reaching the rank of lieutenant-colonel. Both had been awarded the MBE. Though they were of different build they were inclined to overweight and both were organists.

I made use of this subterfuge to write about Oldfield without naming him, but within a few days his name was deduced and given in an American magazine. It was then picked up by the British papers which also printed a photograph of him after this had appeared in the West German Press.

Oldfield's cover was well and truly blown, but this did not seem important until a new dimension entered the lives of certain people, of whom he was one.

In October 1975 a large holdall containing a 30-pound bomb was planted by an IRA terrorist on the window sill of Locket's restaurant not far from the House of Commons. After an alert porter had spotted it and the bomb had been defused, within three minutes of exploding, it was generally assumed that it had been intended for MPs who occasionally dine there.

It was far more likely that it was intended for Oldfield who, before he retired in 1978, had a flat above the restaurant and was in it at the time. Some months later, when an IRA hideout was raided, the police found newspaper cuttings, including mine, about Oldfield.

I have to admit that, with respect to that incident, which could so easily have deprived the nation of its Director-General of Secret Intelligence, my modicum of power had corrupted my judgement.

# INDEX